320.609
AF743703
7000263148

OLLAND

12192/2
LL

Justice and Home Affairs in the EU

Liberty and Security Issues after Enlargement

Edited by

Joanna Apap

Head of Unit and Research Fellow on Justice and Home Affairs, Centre for European Policy Studies, Brussels

CE
PS

U.W.E.
23 APR 2004
LAW
Library Services

UWE BRISTOL
WITHDRAWN
LIBRARY SERVICES

Edward Elgar
Cheltenham, UK • Northampton, MA, USA

© Joanna Apap 2004

All rights reserved. No part of this publication may be reproduced, stored in a retrieval system or transmitted in any form or by any means, electronic, mechanical or photocopying, recording, or otherwise without the prior permission of the publisher.

Published by
Edward Elgar Publishing Limited
Glensanda House
Montpellier Parade
Cheltenham
Glos GL50 1UA
UK

Edward Elgar Publishing, Inc.
136 West Street
Suite 202
Northampton
Massachusetts 01060
USA

A catalogue record for this book
is available from the British Library

ISBN 1 84376 787 2

Printed and bound in Great Britain by MPG Books Ltd, Bodmin, Cornwall

Contents

Tables

Contributors

Colonel Marek Adamczyk is Head of the Polish Border Guard

Prof. Dr Malcolm Anderson is Senior Fellow, the Centre for European Policy Studies, CEPS, in Brussels, Belgium

Dr Joanna Apap is Head of Unit and Research Fellow on Justice and Home Affairs, the Centre for European Policy Studies, CEPS, in Brussels, Belgium

Dr Willy Bruggeman is Senior Deputy Director Europol, The Hague, The Netherlands

Mr Sergio Carrera is Research Assistant on Justice and Home Affairs, Centre for European Policy Studies, CEPS, in Brussels, Belgium

Prof. Dr Ryszard Cholewinski is Professor at the University of Leicester, Centre for European Law and Integration, United Kingdom

Mr Jorge Costa is Procurateur Général, Lisbon, Portugal

Dr Monica den Boer is Managing Director EULEC (European Institute for Law Enforcement Co-operation), Brussels, Belgium

Prof. Dr Paul de Hert is Associated Professor, Faculty of Law, University of Leiden, The Netherlands

Prof. Dr Elspeth Guild is Professor of European Immigration Law, University of Nijmegen, The Netherlands

Dr Bernard Hemingway is Expert in the Office of the Special Coordinator of the Stability Pact, Brussels, Belgium

Baroness Sarah Ludford is a British Member of the European Liberal Democrat and Reform Group (ELDR), European Parliament. She also sits on the Committee on Citizens' Freedoms and Rights, Justice and Home Affairs

Prof. Dr Jörg Monar is Co-director of the Sussex European Institute

Dr Ferruccio Pastore is Deputy Director of the Centro Studi di Politica Internazionale, CeSPI, Roma, Italy

Dr Jörg Polakiewicz is Head ad interim of the Legal Advice Department and Treaty Office, Directorate General 1 – Legal Affairs, Council of Europe

Dr Olga Potemkina is Head of Regional Studies, Institute of Europe, Russian Academy of Sciences, Moscow, Russia

Mr Luc Schaerlaekens is the Advisor for General Coordination and Enlargement of the European Anti-fraud Office, OLAF

Dr Doris Schmidt is Assistant to Mrs D. Theato who is a German MEP in the group of the European People's Party (Christian Democrats)

Prof. Dr Giuseppe Sciortino is Professor at the Università di Trento, Italy

Dr Jacob Söderman is the former European Ombudsman, 1995–2003

Prof. Dr Constança Urbano de Sousa is Professor at Universidade Autónoma, Portugal

Mr Johannes van der Klaauw is Senior European Affairs Officer, UNCHR, Brussels

Preface

This book analyses the main difficulties facing the European Union (EU) and the candidate countries of Central and Eastern Europe in the area of Justice and Home Affairs on the eve of enlargement. It represents a detailed compendium of constructive policy recommendations in the principal areas of policy, which we hope will be of interest to a very wide audience – policy-makers, scholars and the practitioners of Justice and Home Affairs cooperation in the Member States and in the EU Institutions. The policy recommendations have been framed on the basis of 21 chapters which reflect both the richness and depth of the debate on sensitive issues of security, liberty and justice. The book's over-arching theme is to raise the question whether a desirable balance has been struck between security, liberty and justice in the EU.

The different chapters contain contributions by leading analysts and practitioners who represent the views of both insiders and outsiders in the policy process. Their contributions have been grouped under three main headings, which are preceded by an overview of the progress and obstacles in the area of Justice and Home Affairs: The first focuses on what should be the fundamentals of Justice and Home Affairs policies in a post-enlargement EU. The second, 'Scenarios for crime, law and justice in an enlarged European Union', and the third, 'Towards an immigration and asylum policy for Europe', explores in great depth how policy-makers in the twin fields of criminal justice cooperation and the creation of a common immigration and asylum policy have gone about trying to meet the Tampere targets (as modified somewhat by subsequent European summits).

Close attention is given throughout the book to the difficulties faced by the EU in developing legislative and institutional systems that can be regarded as both effective in security terms while at the same time guaranteeing adequate protection of civil liberties and fundamental rights. At a minimum, we hope that the tensions between the goals of freedom, security and justice have been highlighted. The book tries to be innovative in analysing these elements holistically.

In the concluding chapter a practical set of recommendations in each of the following five areas is presented: Consequences of enlargement on Justice and Home Affairs; Fundamentals of EU Justice and Home Affairs

Policy post-enlargement; Scenarios of crime, law and justice in an enlarged EU; Towards an immigration and asylum policy for Europe; and future of Justice and Home Affairs policies and processes. These were the five key themes of the conference run jointly by the Academy of European Law in Trier and the Centre for European Policy Studies (CEPS) in Brussels from 4–6 July in Trier, which provided the inspiration for this book.

Joanna Apap
Head of Unit and Research Fellow on JHA,
Centre for European Policy Studies
CEPS

September 2003

Acknowledgements

The editor would like to express her gratitude to all the authors for their excellent contributions. Very special and warm thanks go to Sergio Carrera and Robert Cooper for their assistance with proof reading and formatting of the chapters.

Gratitude is also expressed to the Academy of European Law (ERA) and Transcrime of the University of Trento which co-organised and co-sponsored with CEPS the conference of 4–6 July held in Trier on the same theme as this book. The conference enabled the editor to put together a set of excellent papers which eventually became the chapters of this collective volume.

1. Progress and Obstacles in the Area of Justice and Home Affairs in an Enlarging Europe: An Overview

Joanna Apap and Sergio Carrera

1.1 INTRODUCTION

Justice and Home Affairs (JHA) has been the most dynamic policy domain in the European Union (EU) since the Treaty of Amsterdam came into force on 1 May 1999. The policies grouped under the heading of JHA are numerous, as well as diverse. They are also characterised as being the most difficult and 'sensitive' areas for the EU because of the great divide between elites in Member States, European Institutions and large populations throughout the EU. In the Amsterdam Treaty, these areas were grouped together under the new Heading IV of the European Community Treaties (TEC) and enshrined under three dimensions: Freedom, Security and Justice (FSJ) and judicial cooperation in penal matters – the vestiges of the old third pillar which is found under Heading VI of the Treaty on European Union (TEU). The EU adopted an ambitious work programme at the Tampere European Council of 15–16 October 1999, which aimed at crystallising a proper balance between freedom, security and justice. It also outlined a timetable – the Tampere scoreboard – which set objectives as well as deadlines and gave structure to the agenda in this area.

This introductory chapter assesses the achievements made so far in the objectives set by the Amsterdam Treaty and the Tampere European Council. Some policy areas have experienced a greater degree of development or convergence than others. We will also evaluate the reasons why certain policies have not achieved the expected outcome, as well as the practical consequences of existing frictions and strains between Member States.

1.2 TO WHAT EXTENT HAS CONVERGENCE BEEN ACHIEVED IN THE JHA AREA?

This section analyses the key measures for achievements in the Area of Freedom, Security and Justice (AFSJ), and their development so far based on the Commission's biannual update of the scoreboard to review progress on the creation of an AFSJ in the EU, during the first half of 2003.

1.2.1 Immigration

Based on the Amsterdam Treaty, the policy orientations established in the Tampere European Council of 15–16 October 1999 and the Seville Conclusions of 21–22 June 2002, the Commission has formulated the main elements needed to create a 'common policy on migration'. In the Laeken European Council in December 2001, the objective to establish a common EU policy in this area was reaffirmed. Thus, since that time the Commission has increased its authority and is becoming a prominent actor. The activity of the Commission to date has been positive and forward-looking. It merits more recognition and greater support than it has so far received. Yet these areas of policy remain governed by the unanimity rule until 1st May 2004 (Art. 67, EC Treaty) and agreement is not easy on many measures, with Member States seeking to preserve as much of their authority as possible. Consensus on the general strategy for dealing with illegal immigrants has not been easy, as was demonstrated by the weak compromise reached at the June 2002 Seville Council. Thus, even though the European Commission has already made proposals in a wide number of areas that provide the first elements for a common legislative framework, the Council has not followed up with sufficient support. This is exemplified by two Commission Communications, on a community immigration policy and on an open method of coordination for the policy. There has not been a concrete response by the Council in relation to either communication, even though their adoption would represent a key step towards the achievement of a 'common immigration policy' at EU level. This raises questions of whether or not national governments are genuinely committed to cooperate in this field.

The June 2002 meeting of the European Council in Seville highlighted the need to speed up the implementation of all aspects of the programme presented at Tampere and to develop a 'common policy on immigration'. It welcomed the comprehensive plan to combat illegal immigration and trafficking of human beings in the EU that was adopted by the Council on 28 February 2002. The plan aimed at defining a common and integrated approach to these issues and identified seven areas where action was considered necessary.[1] Consequently, a high priority was given to the fight against illegal immigration and the trafficking/smuggling of human beings. Regarding relations with countries of origin, the idea of placing sanctions on them for failing to control illegal immigration was presented as a real option. Thankfully, this proposal to sanction poor countries was not considered practical, because it was recognised as virtually impossible for any non-totalitarian regime to effectively control exit from its territory. It was agreed instead that migration diplomacy (to reach agreements on legal immigration to the EU) and co-development programmes (to reduce migratory pressures) should be actively pursued. The Seville European Council asked for the conclusion of these agreements to be speeded up and for new negotiating mandates to be approved. This has been developed in the Communication from the Commission to the Council and the European Parliament, integrating migration issues in the European Union's relations with third countries, COM(2002)703 final, of 3 December 2002. The Commission is in the process of negotiating several readmission agreements between the European Community and third countries, in which both parties agree to accept the return of illegal migrants into their territory.[2]

Indeed, an area of increasing concern for the Member States is the prevention and fight against illegal immigration, which is essential to a common asylum policy of the EU. This is a point where the first and third EU pillars come together. A major trend towards convergence at EU level can be seen in this area since the Seville Conclusions were presented in June. Among others, the following legal instruments need special consideration:

- Proposal for a Council Directive on the short-term residence permit issued to those victims of illegal immigration or trafficking in human beings who cooperate with the competent authorities COM(2002)0071 final - CNS(2002)0043, 11 February 2002;
- Council Directive on the mutual recognition of decisions about the expulsion of third-country nationals. The Directive was adopted by the Council on the initiative of the French presidency on 28 May 2001.

[1] These seven areas include: visa policy, the exchange of information, readmission and repatriation policies, the monitoring of borders and measures to take when borders are crossed, Europol and penalties, and the adoption of measures aimed at combating immigration and trafficking in human beings more effectively.

[2] The first EC Readmission Agreement to enter into force was signed with Hong Kong on 27 November 2002. Agreements with Macao and Sri Lanka were initiated on 30 May 2002 and 18 October 2002 respectively, and are in the process of being ratified. Moreover, the Council has adopted decisions authorising the Commission to negotiate readmission agreements between the EC and Russia, Pakistan, Morocco and Ukraine. Negotiations started in November with Ukraine and informal discussions are continuing with Morocco. Further proposals to negotiate such agreements with Albania, Algeria, China and Turkey were submitted to the Council in October 2002.

The main purpose of the Directive is to ensure that once an individual is expelled by one Member State, s/he becomes a *persona non grata* in the whole Schengen area. Trust in the national administration of other Member States for enforcing a restrictive measure does not seem to pose a problem in this field;

- Communication from the Commission to the Council and the European Parliament on a common policy on illegal immigration COM(2001)0672 final, 15 November 2001;
- Council Decision adopting an action programme for administrative cooperation in the fields of external borders, visas, asylum and immigration (ARGO programme), 2002/463/EC, OJ L 161, 19 June 2003;
- Framework Decision of 19 July 2002 on combating trafficking in human beings, 2002/629/JHA;
- Framework Decision on the strengthening of the penal framework to prevent the facilitation of unauthorised entry, transit and residence, 2002/946, 28 November 2002; and
- Council Directive defining the facilitation of unauthorised entry, transit and residence, 2002/90, 28 November 2002.[3]

1.2.2 Third-country nationals

Regarding non-EU citizens or so-called third-country nationals, the Treaty of Amsterdam neither framed a coherent strategy nor a comprehensive approach to them in Articles 61, 62 and 63 TEC. After the first few years of applying these provisions, the European Commission forwarded proposals to the Council for various Directives to integrate these policy issues further. Yet once again, the response by the Council has been insufficient.

Among the legislative agenda, the following legal instruments that pertain to third-country nationals should be highlighted:

- One of the first post-Amsterdam initiatives proposed by the Commission in the area of immigration is the draft Directive on the right to family reunification, submitted to the Council on 1 December 1999. The Commission presented an amended proposal, COM(2002)225 to the Council of Ministers on 2 May 2002, that has been finally adopted by the Council of Ministers of the European Union on 22 September 2003, 2003/86/EC (OJ L 251/12). Although

[3] These three last measures have been adopted by the Council on the initiative of France.

this represents an important step, the promise of equal treatment for third-country nationals is still far from achieved;[4]

- In March 2001, the Commission proposed a Directive to the Council concerning the status of resident third-country nationals who are long-term residents to extend their free movement rights, on the basis of Art. 63(4), COM(2001)127 final. The proposed Directive has now been politically agreed upon by the JHA Council on 24 July 2003;
- Council Regulation to extend the provisions of Regulation EEC No. 1408/71 to nationals of third countries who are not already covered by these provisions solely on the grounds of their nationality COM(2003)859, 14 May 2003;
- The Commission proposed a Council Directive on the conditions of entry and residence of third-country nationals for the purpose of studies, vocational training or voluntary service COM(2002)548, 7 October 2002; and
- The Commission's Proposal for a Council Directive, COM(2001)0386 final, of 11 July 2001, on conditions of entry and residence of third-country nationals for the purposes of paid employment and self-employed economic activity is another move forward in the same direction.

The adoption by the Council of some of the Commission's proposals, such as the Proposal for a Council Directive COM(2002)0071 final, of 11 February 2002 (on the short-term residence permit issued to those victims of illegal immigration or trafficking who cooperate with the authorities) and the Proposal for a Council Framework Decision (on combating racism and xenophobia), COM(2001)0664 final, as well as the others mentioned above, would represent a positive step towards the goal of harmonisation.

1.2.3 Asylum

The European Commission proposed a Council Decision for a European Refugee Fund on 14 December 1999. The objective was a framework for 'structural measures' to facilitate the reception and voluntary repatriation of asylum seekers. Emergency aid was also included to help Member States face the financial burden in the event of an unexpected arrival of large numbers of refugees or displaced persons – the first attempt at burden-sharing and common responsibility for refugees by the EU Member States. The proposal

[4] While the Commission's Explanatory Memorandum for the proposal explains that several provisions in the proposal are based on Community law, it is important to recall that none of these instruments is expressly mentioned in the legal measure itself, with the exception of Regulation 1612/68/EEC (which concerns the abolition of reverse discrimination between member state nationals and EU citizens who are using their freedom of movement).

establishing the European Refugee Fund was adopted as Council Decision 2000/596/EC on 28 September 2000.
The provision of minimum temporary protection for displaced persons, including residence permits, access to employment, accommodation and housing, means of subsistence, access to medical treatment, the right to education of minors, and so on, was proposed by the Commission in May 2000. The initiative aimed at harmonising the temporary protection measures across national borders in the EU, while preventing 'asylum-shopping' and simplifying decision-making mechanisms. The European Parliament approved the proposal on 13 March 2001. The Directive (2001/55/EC) was formally adopted by the Council on 20 July 2001, and became the first serious achievement towards European regulation of asylum.

Other initiatives to develop a common European asylum policy include:

- Council Regulation 2725/2000 of 11 December 2000, to establish Eurodac for fingerprints of asylum seekers. The Eurodac system is meant to aid the application of the 'first safe haven' principle of the Dublin Convention. As agreed in Copenhagen 2002, Eurodac became operational for the 15 Member States in January 2003; and
- Council Directive 2001/55/EC, of 20 July 2001, on minimum standards for giving temporary protection in the event of a mass influx of displaced persons and on measures promoting a balance of efforts between Member States in receiving such persons and bearing the consequences thereof.

The European Commission persistently seeks to devise a comprehensive European asylum regime. In September 2000, it tabled a proposal for a Council Directive on minimum standards for procedures in Member States to grant and withdraw refugee status. The approach respects national regulatory systems and avoids the introduction of uniform procedures. The Member States have wide discretion to apply their national procedures as long as they ensure certain minimum standards with respect to granting and withdrawing refugee status. This proposal was amended on 18 June 2002 by the Commission proposal COM(2002)326, in accordance with the conclusions of the Laeken European Council.

The following recent developments should also be emphasised:

- The Commission presented a draft Directive outlining minimum standards for the reception of asylum seekers COM(2001)181. This Directive has been recently adopted by the Council of Ministers of the European Union on 27 January 2003. The Member States will have to implement its provisions by 6 February 2005, following its Art. 26. Despite its general nature and the wide room for exceptions or adaptation that it allows, it represents significant progress in overcoming the difficulties caused by different standards across the Member States;

- Regarding the so-called Dublin II Regulation, the Council agreed on 18 December 2002 on the basis of the Danish Presidency compromise. On the eve of the JHA Council of 19 December 2002, it agreed on the Commission's proposal for a Dublin II Regulation. The Council Regulation (EC) No. 343/2003 was adopted on 18 February 2003, establishing the criteria and mechanisms of determining the Member State responsible for examining an asylum application lodged in one of the Member States by a third-country national. This Convention will replace the one that determines the state responsible for examining asylum applications lodged in one of the Member States of the European Community, signed in Dublin on 15 June 1990 (Dublin Convention). It has maintained the structure of the Dublin Convention, while improving several aspects of it that proved to be unsatisfactory.

The Commission is planning a progress report on work on the common asylum procedure and the uniform status, and on the implementation of the first-stage instruments in 2003. In addition, two communications are planned to be presented at the end of 2003 that concern the examination of asylum applications outside the EU and the establishment of a single procedure for examining applications for protection within the Member States.

Again, as far as asylum matters are concerned, the main Commission proposals have not yet been adopted by the European Council, such as the Communication from the Commission to the Council and the European Parliament, towards a common asylum procedure and a uniform status, valid throughout the Union, for persons granted asylum, Brussels, 22 November 2000, COM(2000)755 final. The Communication from the Commission to the Council and the European Parliament on the common asylum policy, introducing an open-coordination method – the first report by the Commission on the application of Communication COM(2000)755 final of 22 November 2000 – is still pending. Also awaiting adoption by the Council is the Proposal for a Council Directive on minimum standards for the qualification and status of third-country nationals and stateless persons as refugees or as persons who otherwise need international protection, COM(2001)0510 final. Furthermore, the practical implementation by the Member States of existing EU and national legislative regimes may not fully safeguard the human rights of victims, nor offer them the necessary protection that our humanitarian traditions require (in particular the protection set out in the Geneva Convention). This has been clearly shown in the report on the situation of fundamental rights in the European Union and Member States, in which the current practices of the different member states have been studied and criticised.

1.2.4 Judicial cooperation in criminal matters

After the events of 11 September 2001, the EU third pillar made internal security affairs a matter of intergovernmental cooperation between the member states for the first time. It provided the means to develop an integrated and coherent anti-terrorist policy.

The subject of 'terrorism' is primarily dealt with by the third pillar of the TEU – Title VI, Articles 29–42. After the Amsterdam Treaty, police and judicial cooperation in criminal matters remained uncovered by the Community, and continue to be of an intergovernmental nature. The stated objective of the Union in this area, according to Article 29 TEU, is to provide a 'high level of safety' by adopting common actions among the Member States in police and judicial cooperation and by preventing racism and xenophobia.

This has been the main legal framework used by the Council of Ministers to adopt the legislative measures after the events of 11 September 2001. At its extraordinary meeting on 21 September 2001, the European Council stated that 'terrorism is a real challenge to the world and to Europe and that the fight against terrorism will be a priority objective of the European Union'. Indeed, within ten days, the JHA Council decided on a package of anti-terrorist measures in the areas of judicial and police cooperation, the prevention of financing of terrorism, improved border controls and cooperation with the United States. All of these radical measures were subject to less controversy and agreed more quickly than could have conceivably been the case without the events of 11 September 2001.

The core legislative developments in this field are:

- Framework Decision of 13 June 2002 on the European arrest warrant, 2002/584/JHA;
- Framework Decision on combating terrorism, 2002/475/JHA, of 13 June 2002;
- Regulation (EC) No. 2199/2001 amending Council Regulation (EC) No. 467/2001, and prohibiting the export of certain goods and services to Afghanistan, strengthening the flight ban and extending the freezing of funds and other financial resources relating to the Taliban of Afghanistan;
- Regulation (EC) No. 342/2003, amending for the twelfth time the Council Regulation (EC) No. 881/2002, and imposing certain specific restrictive measures directed against certain persons and entities

associated with Usama bin Laden, the Al-Qaida network and the Taliban, 21 February 2003;

- Council Regulation (EC) No. 561/2003 amending, (as regards exceptions to the freezing of funds and economic resources) Regulation (EC) No. 881/2002, and imposing specific restrictive measures directed against certain persons and entities associated with Usama bin Laden, the Al-Qaida network and the Taliban, 27 March 2003;
- Council Decision 2003/48/JHA, on the implementation of specific measures for police and judicial cooperation to combat terrorism, 19 December 2002;
- 2001/500/JHA, the Council Framework Decision of 26 June 2001 on money laundering, the identification, tracing, freezing, seizing and confiscation of instrumentalities and the proceeds of crime; and
- Council Regulation (EC) No. 2580/2001 of 27 December 2001 on specific restrictive measures directed against certain persons and entities with a view to combating terrorism.[5]

In addition, in the aftermath of the events of 11 September, the EU was able to make progress on a number of other policy issues that are of importance in terrorist action, such as the amendment of the Directive on money laundering and the setting up of the Eurojust cross-border prosecution unit. Nevertheless, these measures clearly have a general impact that extends far beyond combating terrorism. Decisions were also taken on improved cooperation between police and intelligence services. These included charging the Police Chiefs Task Force with cooperation with third countries; guaranteeing a high level of security, particularly in air safety; and, considering the missions given to a team of counter-terrorist specialists within Europol. A further strengthening of controls at the external borders was also agreed, for which the Police Chiefs Task Force was also made responsible. The strengthening of surveillance measures under Article 2.3, Schengen 1990, was agreed as well.

1.3 MAIN REASONS FOR THE PERSISTENCE OF FRICTIONS AND STRAINS IN THE JHA ARENA

In this section the potential frictions and strains that exist on the eve of enlargement are analysed. The implementation of policy related to

[5] See the Order of the President of the Court of First Instance in Case T-47/03 *R. José Maria Sison v Council and Commission.*

establishing an Area of Freedom, Security and Justice has been fundamentally affected by the rise of frictions and strains among Member States, as well as their relations with the candidate countries and the neighbouring states. These frictions can be identified as the main obstacles and/or tensions that have either prevented or negatively affected a further convergence of policies between the Member States in the JHA arena.

The reasons why some JHA policy areas have not achieved the expected level of development can be summarised as follows:

1. *Weakness of political resolve in European cooperation.* The EU suffers from weak legitimacy in this area, making the cooperation of governments and citizens less than reliable. The political decision-making processes are inefficient. Member States are ambivalent, pushing for measures and then failing to implement them. As a matter of fact, very few of the Commission's ideas have so far been translated into legislation by the Member States, raising questions of whether national governments are genuinely committed to cooperate in this field. The sorry record of third pillar Conventions – with only one ratified and implemented out of the 25 negotiated – is a graphic illustration of this point. When the solution to a problem is entirely in their hands (such as the supply of criminal intelligence to Europol) the Member States tend not to live up to their commitments. Furthermore, wide variations in perceptions of problems, priorities and unresolved contradictions among the policy objectives also represent a major problem. The excessive complexity of programmes and cooperative arrangements creates additional strains.

2. *Operation of national legal systems.* Different approaches to legal issues among the Member States represent potential points of conflict and can cause tensions between them in certain areas, for example: the use of pre-trial detention in some countries; varying standards of due process and fair trial; the existence of excessive delays; the lack of common definitions of crime (particularly of fraud); the so-called forum- or jurisdiction-shopping; the variations in sentencing practice in the different states; and, the lack of response to new European systems of coordination such as Eurojust. In the vertical information exchange (local–national–European), there is quite often a failure to communicate with Europol – which a good response to the creation of Eurojust would help to address. Each state varies in its reception of international law conventions and in non-recognition of European soft law by national courts, (which is not legally binding). Double penalisation of foreigners and the existence of collective expulsions, which are contrary to the guidelines set up by the UNHCR, are also points of contention.

3. *Police practices.* The practices and malpractices of police represent another area of friction, and may provoke hostile reactions and incomprehension between partner states, e.g. the unjustified use of firearms, illegitimate violence (particularly against suspects, and legal and illegal immigrants), or the use of riot control measures against transnational demonstrators, football fans and holiday-makers. Furthermore, the existence of police corruption in the different Member States (especially in the new applicant states) is of major importance, as is the interface of security services and police, with the former seeking or being accorded new policing roles. The marginalisation of official European channels of communication and cooperation is a problem as well. There is an absence of information-sharing. Also, the lack of adequate training for police in handling immigrants at the borders of different Member States is another common concern.

4. *Difficulties of arriving at European policies on immigration and asylum.* The reactions in favour of a 'half-open door' immigration policy, given high structural unemployment in some Member States, put a real strain on further policy developments. In addition, the slow and inefficient asylum procedures, giving rise to a high number of persons remaining in a legal limbo for several years and the eventual need for amnesties, generates even more tension. The persistence of clandestine immigration, allegations of laxity in border controls and surveillance, and the perceived connections between the transitional period for free movement of nationals of new members and immigration of third-country nationals are also major sources of strains. Additional sources of friction are the different interpretations of a well-founded claim for asylum and the existence of the safe third-country classification, which could prevent genuine asylum seekers from presenting their claims. Finally, the lack of structure in the system of work/residence permits for workers causes some to alternate between legality and illegality.

5. *Corruption.* There is a perception that closer European integration brings the risk that corrupt practices from some other Member States will become even more widespread. Attempts to impose higher anti-corruption standards in the new Member States than those practised by some old member states are a major cause of tension. Corrupt connections are prevalent among foreign, security and trade policies in the arms trade among others. A lack of respect for agreed European standards in foreign trade is another example. Finally, the illegitimate interference of political and economic interests in trade and competition policy, along with the failure to implement European Directives can be qualified as one more source of friction.

6. *The lack of consistency owing to the practice of rotating the EU presidency.* The priorities change greatly with each presidency, and there is a

real risk each time of substantial policy shifts. Furthermore, some countries holding the EU Council presidency still promote their own particular interests exclusively.

7. *Unsatisfactory and unclear character of the EU pillar structure.* The variety of legal instruments in each of the pillars, which are not always the most suitable instruments for JHA, contributes to the confusion. Ambiguity in the division of powers between the pillars as well as within the pillars also characterises the system, which should be replaced in the proposals for the next intergovernmental conference by a simple division of powers. This should entail transferring maximum competence to the first pillar (which is at the Community level), while retaining a minimum of the most sensitive areas under the exclusive responsibility of the Member States, along with some powers to be exercised solely by the European institutions. In addition, the introduction of a qualified majority voting is necessary for all JHA policies, allowing for unanimity voting only for those issues that remain the exclusive competence of the Member States. The introduction of such a system will be particularly necessary after enlargement, to avoid blockages in decision-making that could result in complete stalemate on some issues.

1.4 CONCLUSION

The road to establish a genuine Area of Freedom, Security and Justice is still a long one. The widely held view that these issues are matters of national sovereignty continues to create obstacles to progress in this area. The legislative progress attained so far shows the difficulties of arriving at European policies on immigration and asylum, as well as the rights of third-country nationals. A low level of convergence towards 'freedom' concerns in these three areas can be appreciated by looking at the Tampere scoreboard. Higher levels of trust, flexibility, coordination and efficiency, in terms of cost and rapidity of response, are required to overcome the mentioned tensions and strains (see Anderson and Apap 2002). The right balance between Freedom, Security and Justice needs to be ensured. Security and law enforcement policies need to be developed with 'freedom' as the point of departure. A danger of the aftermath of the 11 September 2001 terrorist attacks and the current preoccupation with undocumented/illegal immigration is that a pattern may be established that leads to overly zealous security policies for European society, with adverse effects on the internal cohesion of Europe. In particular, certain minority groups may feel, as they already do in some cases that they are subject to excessive attention by security forces. In addition, it is also perceived that the terrorist attacks in the USA have radically changed perceptions of security in the EU. Undoubtedly, these attacks have provided a new impetus for the development of the AFSJ. The Member States' governments, security agencies and public opinion have been made dramatically aware of the extent to which international forms of crime threaten traditional internal security. The AFSJ provides the perfect framework for positive action to be taken. They have had, and continue to have, a powerful influence over the Justice and Home Affairs agenda. Consequently, the problem of balance between security and freedom has become more acute and needs to be carefully studied, along with the policy developments and concrete legislative instruments adopted so far by the Council of Ministers of the European Union.

Progress in these areas will need constant attention, particularly as the inevitable attempts to shore up national sovereignty result in the perverse effects of undermining accountability and the rule of law. Active citizen participation, increased transparency of decision-making and a constant effort by authorities at all levels to inform and explain their actions to the public are needed. Nevertheless, these conditions are extremely difficult to fulfil.

REFERENCES

Anderson, M. (2000), 'Counterterrorism as an Objective of European Police Cooperation', in F. Reinares (ed.) (2000), *European Democracies against Terrorism: Governmental Policies and Intergovernmental Cooperation*, The Oñati International Institute of the Sociology of Law, London: Ashgate.

Anderson, M. and J. Apap (2002), *Police and Justice Cooperation and the New European Borders*, The Hague: Kluwer Law International.

Anderson, M. and J. Apap (2002), *Striking a Balance between Freedom, Security and Justice in an Enlarged European Union*, Centre for European Policy Studies, CEPS, Brussels.

Apap, J. (2001), *Freedom of Movement of Persons in the EU: A Practitioner's Guide*, The Hague: Kluwer Law International.

Arendt, H. (1963), *On Revolution*, USA: Viking Press.

Battjes, H. (2002), 'A Balance between Fairness and Efficiency? The Directive on International Protection and the Dublin Regulation', *European Journal of Migration and Law*, **4**, Kluwer Law International, 159–92.

Bieber, R. and J. Monar (eds) (1997), *Justice and Home Affairs in the European Union: The Development of the Third Pillar*, Brussels: European University Press.

Bigo, D. (1994), 'The European Internal Security Field: Stakes and Rivalries in a Newly Developing Area of Police Intervention', in M. Anderson and M. den Boer (eds), *Policing Across National Boundaries*, London: Pinter.

Bonnefoi, S. (1998), *Europe et sécurité intérieure: Trevi, Union Européenne, Schengen*, Paris: Delmas.

Bruggeman, W. (2000), 'Europol – A European FBI in the Making?', lecture in the Cicero Foundation Great Debate as part of the seminar on Justice and Home Affairs: How to implement the Amsterdam Treaty, Paris, 13–14 April.

Cha, V.D. (2000), 'Globalisation and the Study of International Security', *Journal of Peace Research*, **37** (3), 391 ff.

Cholewinski, R. (2002), 'Family Reunification and Conditions Placed on Family Members: Dismantling a Fundamental Human Right', *European Journal of Migration and Law*, **4**, Kluwer Law International, 271–90.

Christodoulidis, E. and T. Scott Veitch (1994), 'Terrorism and Systems Terror', *Economy and Society*, Routledge, **23** (2).

Davis, P. and L. Finch (1993), *Defence Planning in the Post-Cold War Era: Going to Flexibility, Adaptiveness and Robustness of Capability*, Santa Monica, CA: Rand Corporation.

Den Boer, M. (1996), 'Police Cooperation', in J. Monar, N. Neuwahl, D. O'Keefe and W. Robinson (eds), *Butterworths' Guide to the EU 1996*, London: Butterworths, pp. 247–49.

Den Boer, M. (1998), *Taming the Third Pillar: Improving the Management of Justice and Home Affairs Cooperation in the EU*, European Institute of Public Administration, EIPA, Maastricht.

De Ruyver, B., G. Vermeulen and T. Vander Beken (2002), *Strategies of the EU and the US in Combating Transnational Organised Crime*, Institute for International Research on Criminal Policy (IRCP), Ghent University, Maklu (Antwerp/Apeldoorn).

Guild, E. and C. Harlow (eds) (2001), *Implementing Amsterdam: Immigration and Asylum Rights in EC Law*, Oxford: Hart Publishing.

Hailbronner, K. (1998), 'European Immigration and Asylum Law under the Amsterdam Treaty', *Common Market Law Review*, **35**, 1047–67.

Hermant, D. and D. Bigo (2000), 'Les politiques de Lutte contre le Terrorisme: Enjeux français', in F. Reinares (ed.), *European Democracies against Terrorism: Governmental Policies and Intergovernmental Cooperation*, the Oñati International Institute of the Sociology of Law, London: Ashgate.

Huysmans, J. (2000), 'The European Union and the Securitisation of Migration', *Journal of Common Market Studies*, **38**(5), pp. 751–778.

Monar, J. and W. Wessels (eds) (2001), *The Treaty of Amsterdam: Challenges and Opportunities for the European Union*, London: Pinter.

Palidda, S. (1999), 'La criminalisation des migrants', *Actes de la Recherche en Sciences Sociales*, **129**, 39–49.

Pastore, F. (2001), 'Reconciling the Prince's Two 'Arms'. Internal–External Security Policy Coordination in the EU', Occasional Paper No. 30, Institute for Security Studies, Western European Union (ISS/WEU), Paris.

Reinares, F. (ed.) (2000), *European Democracies against Terrorism: Governmental Policies and Intergovernmental Cooperation*, The Oñati International Institute of the Sociology of Law, London: Ashgate.

Smith, S. (1999), 'The Increasing Insecurity of Security Studies: Conceptualising Security and Change', *Special issue of Contemporary Security Policy*, **20** (3), 72 ff.

Terrif, T., S. Croft, L. James and P.M. Morgan (1999), *Security Studies Today*, Cambridge: Polity Press.

Tilly, C. (ed.) (1975), *The Formation of National States in Europe*, Princeton, N.J: Princeton University Press.
Vercher, A. (1992), *Terrorism in Europe. An International Comparative Legal Analysis*, Oxford: Clarendon Press.

APPENDIX I

This appendix presents a review of the Commission Communication, the Bi-annual update of the Tampere scoreboard to review progress on the creation of an AFSJ in the European Union, first half of 2003, Brussels, 22.5.2003, COM(2003)291 final. The main legislative instruments proposed to date, as far as immigration, asylum, third-country nationals and third pillar matters are concerned, are shown in Tables 1A.1-1A.3.[6]

Table 1A.1 EU legislation governing immigration policy and the rights of third-country nationals

MEASURES	PROPOSALS	STATUS
Directive	Commission Proposal for a Council Directive on the implementation of the principle of equal treatment of all persons without distinction as to race or ethnic origin, COM(1999)566, 25.11.1999	Adopted by the Council OJ L 180, 19 June 2000, p. 22
Directive	Proposal for a Council Directive establishing a general framework for equal treatment in employment and occupation COM(1999)565, 25.11.1999 / Amended in October 2000, COM(2000)652, 12.10.2000	The Council adopted in November 2000, OJ L 303, 2.12.2000, the Amended Commission Proposal for a Council Directive establishing a general framework for equal treatment in employment and occupation.

[6] This is not an exhaustive list of legislation, but cites some of the most important legal measures introduced to date. This version has been updated through September 2003.

Commission Communication	Commission Communication to the Council and the European Parliament on a Community Immigration Policy, COM(2000) 757, 22.11.2000.	
Commission Communication	Commission Communication on an open method of coordination for the Community Immigration Policy, COM(2001)387, 11.7.2001.	
Directive	Proposal for a Council Directive concerning the status of third-country nationals who are long-term residents COM(2001)127, 13.3.2001	Politically agreed upon by the Council on 24 July 2003
Directive	Council Directive on the mutual recognition of decisions on the expulsion of third-country nationals, 2001/40/EC	Adopted by the Council on 28 May 2001
Directive	Proposal for a Council Directive on the conditions of entry and residence of third-country nationals for the purpose of paid employment and self-employed economic activities COM(2001)386, 11.7.2001	
Directive	Proposal for a Council Directive on the conditions of entry and residence of third-country nationals for the purpose of studies, vocational training or voluntary service COM(2002)548, 7.10.2002	

Commission Communication	Commission Communication on a common policy on illegal immigration, COM(2001) 0672 final, 15.11.2001	
Regulation	Proposal for a Council Regulation extending the provisions of Regulation (EEC) No. 1408/71 to nationals of third countries who are not already covered by these provisions solely on the grounds of their nationality, COM(2002)59, 6.2.2002	Adopted by the Council in 14 May 2003, Council Regulation 859/2003 extending the provisions of Regulation (EEC) No. 1408/71 and Regulation (EEC) No. 574/72 to nationals of third countries.
Directive	Proposal for a Council Directive on the short-term residence permit issued to victims of action to facilitate illegal immigration or trafficking in human being who cooperate with the competent authorities, COM(2002)71 final, 11.02.2002	
Green Paper	In April 2002, the Commission presented a Green Paper and a Communication on a Community return policy on illegal residents COM(2002)175, 10.4.2002	In November 2002, the Council adopted a repatriation programme on the basis of the Commission Green Paper and a programme for the return of refugees to Afghanistan
Directive	Proposal for Council Directive on the right to family reunification, COM(1999)638, 1.12.1999 / Amended Proposal COM(2002)225, 2.5.2002	Adopted by the Council on 22 September 2003, 2003/86/EC, OJ L 251/12.

Council Decision	Proposal for a Council Decision adopting an action programme for administrative cooperation in the fields of external borders, visas, asylum and immigration (ARGO), COM (2001)0567, 29.01.2002	Adopted by the Council in Decision 2002/463/EC, in OJ L 161 of 19 June 2003.
Comprehensive Plan	Proposal for a Comprehensive Plan to combat illegal immigration and trafficking of human beings in the European Union, 2002/C 142/02	Adopted by the Council on 28 February 2002
Framework Decision	Framework Decision on combating trafficking in human beings, 2002/629/JHA	Adopted by the Council on 19 July 2002
Green Paper	In April 2002, the Commission presented a Green Paper on a common policy on repatriation of persons residing unlawfully in the EU, COM(2002)0175 final	
Framework Decision	Council Framework Decision on the strengthening of the penal framework to prevent the facilitation of unauthorised entry, transit and residence, 2002/946/JHA	Adopted by the Council on 28 November 2002
Directive	Council Directive defining the facilitation of unauthorised entry, transit and residence, 2002/90	Adopted by the Council on 28 November 2002

Regulation	Commission Proposal for a Council Regulation amending Regulation No. 539/2001, listing the third countries whose nationals must be in possession of visas when crossing external borders and those whose nationals are exempt from that requirement, COM(2002)679, 28.11.2002	Adopted by the Council on 6 March 2003. Council Regulation 453/2003 amending Regulation No. 539/2001 listing the countries whose nationals must be in possession of visas when crossing external borders and those whose nationals are exempt from that requirement.
Commission Communication	Commission Communication on a Community return policy on illegal residents COM(2002)564, 14.10.2002	
Commission Communication	Commission Communication to the Council and the European Parliament, integrating migration issues in the European Union's relations with third countries, COM(2002)703 final, 3.12.2002	
Commission Communication	Commission Communication to the Council and the European Parliament to present an action plan for the collection and analysis of Community statistics in the field of immigration, COM(2003)179, 15.4.2003	
Commission Communication	Commission Communication on immigration, integration and employment, Brussels, 3.6.2003 COM(2003) 336 final.	

Commission Communication	Communication from the Commission to the Council and the European Parliament, in view of the European Council of Thessaloniki on the development of a common policy on illegal immigration, smuggling and trafficking of human beings, external borders and the return of illegal residents, COM(2003) 323 final, 3.6.2003.	

Table 1A.2 EU legislation governing asylum policy

MEASURES	PROPOSALS	STATUS
Decision	Commission Proposal for a Council Decision on the European Refugee Fund COM(1999)686, 14.12.1999	Council Decision 2000/596/EC on 28 September 2000 adopting a proposal establishing the European Refugee Fund
Directive	Commission Proposal for a Council Directive on minimum standards for giving temporary protection in the event of mass influx of displaced persons and on measures promoting a balance of efforts between Member States in receiving such persons and bearing the consequences thereof COM(2000)303, 24.5.2000.	Council Directive (2001/55/EC) of 20 July 2001, about minimum temporary protection for displaced persons. Adopted by the Council on July 2001.

Regulation	Commission Proposal for a Council Regulation concerning the establishment of Eurodac COM(1999)260, 26.5.1999 / Amended proposal for a Council Regulation concerning the establishment of Eurodac to facilitate the implementation of the Dublin Convention COM(2000)100, 15.3.2000	Council Regulation laying down certain detailed rules for the application of the Regulation 2725/2000 of 11 December 2000 concerning the setting up of the Eurodac system, OJ L 62, 5.3.2002
Commission Communication	Commission Communication on a common asylum system based on a common procedure and a uniform status, 22.11.2000, COM(2000) 755	
Working Document	Commission Working Document on the relationship between safeguarding internal security and complying with international protection obligations and instruments, COM(2001)743, 05.12.2001	
Directive	Commission Proposal for a Council Directive on minimum standards for the reception of applicants for asylum in Member States COM(2001)181, 3.4.2001	Adopted by the Council on 27 January 2003
Regulation	Commission Proposal for a Regulation laying down the criteria and mechanisms for determining the Member States responsible for examining an asylum application lodged in one of the Member States by a third-country national COM(2001)447, 26.7.2001	Council Regulation (EC) No. 343/2003, 18.2.2003, establishing the criteria and mechanisms for determining the Member State responsible for examining an asylum application lodged by a third-country national

Commission Communication	Commission Communication on the Common Asylum Policy, Introducing an Open Coordination Method, COM(2001) 170, 28.11.2001.	
Directive	Proposal for Council Directive on minimum standards for the qualification and status of third-country nationals and stateless persons as refugees or as persons who otherwise need international protection, COM(2001) 510 final, 12.9.2001.	
Directive	Proposal for a Council Directive on minimum standards on procedures in member states for granting and withdrawing refugee status, COM(2001) 510, 12.9.2001.	
Commission Communication	Commission Communication on the common asylum policy and the Agenda for protection (Second Commission report on the implementation of Communication COM(2000)755 final of 22 November 2000), Brussels, 26.03.2003, COM(2003)152 final	
Commission Communication	Commission Communication to the Council and the European Parliament, Towards more accessible, equitable and managed asylum systems, 3.6.2003, COM(2003)315 final.	

Decision	In the latter half of 2003, the Commission plans to present a proposal for a Decision on the implementation of the European Refugee Fund for 2005–2009	

Table 1A.3 EU legislation governing third pillar matters

MEASURES	PROPOSALS	STATUS
Council Regulation	Council Regulation (EC) No. 337/2000, concerning a flight ban and a freeze of funds and other financial resources in respect of the Taliban of Afghanistan	Adopted by the Council on 14 February 2000
Council Regulation	Council Regulation (EC) No. 467/2001, prohibiting the export of certain goods and services to Afghanistan, strengthening the flight ban and extending the freeze of funds and other financial resources in respect of the Taliban of Afghanistan, and repealing Regulation (EC) No. 337/2000	Adopted by the Council on 6 March 2001
Commission Regulation	Commission Regulation (EC) No. 2199/2001 amending, for the fourth time, Council Regulation (EC) No. 467/2001 prohibiting the export of certain goods and services to Afghanistan, strengthening the flight ban and extending the freeze on funds and other financial resources in respect of the Taliban of Afghanistan and repealing Regulation (EC) No. 337/2000	Adopted by the Council on 12 November 2001

Commission Regulation	Commission Regulation (EC) No. 342/2003, amending for the twelfth time Council Regulation (EC) No. 881/2002 imposing certain specific restrictive measures directed against certain persons and entities associated with Usama bin Laden, the Al-Qaida network and the Taliban, and repealing Council Regulation (EC) No. 467/2001; followed by Commission Regulation No. 414/2003 15.03.2003	Adopted by the Council on 21 February 2003
Council Regulation	Council Regulation (EC) No. 561/2003 amending, as regards exceptions to the freezing of funds and economic resources, Regulation (EC) No 881/2002, imposing certain specific restrictive measures directed against certain persons and entities associated with Usama bin Laden, the Al-Qaida network and the Taliban	Adopted by the Council on 27 March 2003
Framework Decision	Council Framework Decision on the European Arrest Warrant, 2002/584/JHA	Adopted by the Council on 18 July 2002
Framework Decision	Council Framework Decision on combating terrorism, 2002/475/JHA	Adopted by the Council on 13 June 2002
Council Decision	Council Decision 2003/48/JHA, on the implementation of specific measures for police and judicial cooperation to combat terrorism	Adopted by the Council on 19 December 2002

PART I

FUNDAMENTALS OF EU JUSTICE AND HOME AFFAIRS POLICY POST ENLARGEMENT

2. An EU JHA Policy: What should it Comprise?

Sarah Ludford

2.1 INTRODUCTION

This chapter evaluates the directions in which Justice and Home Affairs (JHA) policy ought to go in the future leading up to and after enlargement. I will start by assessing the relative achievements and failings to date, taking account of the 1997 pledge to create an Area of Freedom, Security and Justice (AFSJ). In this chapter, processes and mechanisms will be discussed as much as content, also taking into account the European Liberal Democrat and Reform (ELDR) group's position on those matters. In an 'integrating Europe' a common immigration and asylum policy is essential. On the other hand, if we are developing common powers and policing at EU level, then we must also develop the 'European safeguards' necessary for the defence of civil liberties. The harmonisation of asylum and migration must not be based on 'lowest common denominator' standards or create fear and suspicion towards ethnic minorities. The remarks presented in this chapter will highlight the need for three particular developments:

- for EU Justice and Home Affairs policy to be decided and managed along with democracy and openness;
- for a better-balanced content through a different conception of what is trying to be achieved; and
- for a more assertive 'peer review'.

A discussion regarding the future of Justice and Home Affairs policy represents a timely debate following the Seville European Council. The questions of asylum and immigration made it to the top of the EU's political agenda there, just as fighting crime and terrorism did at Laeken, although some severe political reservations exist as to the substance and tone of the debates.

The development of EU JHA policy is an ambitious and complex project that is currently being built on delicate foundations, where cross-border vision is necessary without stepping too much on the sensitive sovereign toes of Member States.

In a world in which criminal activity and terrorism respect no frontiers, law enforcement must also become cross-border. In a Europe where we expect free movement of people internally to be a reality, common immigration and asylum policies in a context of responsibility sharing, and interacting justice systems, are also highly necessary. However, as I have already mentioned, if we are developing common powers and policing at EU level, then we must also develop the 'European safeguards' necessary for defence of civil liberties. The harmonisation of asylum and migration must not be based on 'lowest common denominator' standards or create fear and suspicion towards ethnic minorities.

The Liberal Democrat Group does not imply that everything in JHA should be made uniform. There will be some proposals we may believe to be unnecessary or which could be dealt with more appropriately on a national level, not least so that public support is not undermined by a 'more Europe' or moving too far without democratic or protective safeguards. But we do so on pragmatic and principled grounds rather than through an obsessively ideological agenda about sovereignty or subsidiarity.

2.2 DEMOCRACY AND COHERENCE

Justice and Home Affairs policy is a relatively new area as compared to much of the Community acquis, and its coherent development is hampered by various elements. The policy remains as yet cumbersome, including time-consuming procedures or ineffective structures, as well as decision-making procedures that lack both transparency and democracy.

In an enlarged union the legislative process needs to be clear, workable and able to service efficiently a Union and its citizens of potentially almost 30 States and over 500 million citizens. However, this is not the case at present. Even if the first pillar measures in asylum, immigration, non-discrimination and civil law, are under Community competence, however the legislative procedure still remains not to be fully co-decision (with Parliament or the qualified majority voting), which is now the norm for single market, social or environmental matters. For initiatives at EU level under the third pillar of police and judicial cooperation, the situation is even worse since these are negotiated through intergovernmental procedures in the same way as international treaties. The directly elected European Parliament has a marginal influence, as far as it is limited to a 'consultative' role with no real power in the decision-making procedure. Most national parliaments get even less of a look; in the UK, the government intends to legislate most third pillar instruments into national law through secondary rather than primary legislation (government order with no automatic or thorough parliamentary debate). It only backed down from doing this for the European Arrest Warrant as there was such an outcry, but this is intended to be an exception from the general rule. This 'democratic deficit' on laws that may have a serious impact on the fundamental rights and civil liberties of individuals – such as laws on terrorism, the European Arrest Warrant, and alignment of criminal offences and penalties – needs to be addressed. Similarly, the very partial scope of review by the European Court of Justice (ECJ) of third pillar matters may be considered as unacceptable given the sensitivity of the matters covered. It also seems difficult, five years on, to justify Article 35(5) TEU inserted by the Treaty of Amsterdam:

> The Court of Justice shall have no jurisdiction to review the validity or proportionality of operations carried out by the police or other law enforcement agencies of a Member State or the exercise of the responsibilities incumbent upon Member States with regard to the maintenance of law and order and the safeguarding of internal security.

In addition to the lack of scrutiny and accountability, we are also cursed with incoherence in this area. On all JHA matters, Member States have a right of initiative co-existing with that of the Commission. JHA Commissioner Antonio Vitorino recently did the sums and calculated that national governments have made more proposals (51) that the Commission (38) in the last three years. Most of these initiatives are designed as press stunts, at the beginning of a Presidency, and have very little value. Otherwise they could be achieved administratively without legislation. This is exemplified by the recent Spanish proposals for a 'Network of contact points for private security officials', which was among several recently rejected by the Parliament.

It is particularly galling for the Parliament to have to waste its time delivering an opinion on each of these gimmicky proposals, instead of spending more time on calling to account the Presidency and Council of Ministers at least politically, if not with legislative power. The Parliament usually has a left-Liberal majority on JHA Policy compared to a right-Liberal one on economic policy, though faith in the Socialists' civil liberties reliability was threatened by their collusion with the Right recently on breaches of data privacy. Thus the more involvement there is, the more it is possible, usually, to stop objectives of control being the dominant driver of policy. The Committee on Citizens' Rights and Freedoms, Justice and Home Affairs ought to examine its own working methods to see if there are ways to have more persuasive influence and a higher profile.

Also welcome is the work of the Convention on the Future of Europe in this area, and it is hoped that the European Parliament's calls for bringing JHA law-making fully into the scope of a 'conventional' open legislature will be successful.

An EU JHA policy should consist of Commission-proposed workable legal instruments, transparent decision-making procedures and full democratic scrutiny by the European and national Parliaments as well as full judicial supervision by the ECJ. 'Democratic oversight' and 'judicial review' of a new generation of European policy in the field of Justice and Home Affairs is vital to ensure both the protection of the rights of EU citizens and the openness essential to maintaining public confidence in supranational competence.

2.3 BALANCE BETWEEN THE ELEMENTS FREEDOM, SECURITY AND JUSTICE

One of the key components in an EU JHA policy is the commitment, in developing legislation and policy, to give equal regard to freedom and justice as to security.

It is striking that when ministers meet to discuss asylum issues, two-thirds of them are Interior Ministers. Therefore their focus is understandably very much on public order and their perspective is one of control and deterrence, rather than human rights, race equality or integration. They are also the ones responsible for the programme on harmonisation of criminal law. While freedom from crime is one important aspect of freedom, however security is the 'dominant impulse'. Thus when European-level law enforcement instruments such as the anti-terrorism measures or European arrest warrant are developed, the commitment to upholding the rights of the individual and safeguards for the defendant may be weaker than the determination to fight wrongdoing. While law enforcement agencies such as Europol and Eurojust must be able to ensure that they are effective in tackling cross-border obstructions to investigations of crime, collecting evidence and bringing to justice, those powers – such as surveillance – must be deployed within a context of accountability.

The fact that these programmes are being decided and managed principally by national ministers, civil servants and police or security officers, who operate comfortably within a culture of repression and secrecy rather than liberation and openness, makes it all the more important both that judicial and democratic scrutiny should be comprehensive and that rights should be strengthened. Also, these powers affect fundamental rights, making this gap all the more astonishing. Public pressure is lacking only because the

EU powers are not well understood; and because the European Parliament has no legislative 'clout', our reasonable concerns are not well reported – only the occasional hysterical outburst from a (usually British) Eurosceptic opposed to all pooling of sovereignty.

The Liberal group sees the agreement on supranational criminal justice powers such as in the European Arrest Warrant as a catalyst for complementary agreement on a programme of safeguards for defendants, without which the former is open to criticism. While it is indefensible to leave only the criminals and not the law-enforcers benefiting from cross-border cooperation, there must be balanced completion of a common legal area. The Commission's current work on harmonisation and raising of standards in defendants' and victims' rights is a positive development. Ensuring that the mechanisms employed in the development of 'Euro-justice' do not impinge on those rights and civil liberties is one of the key challenges facing JHA policy to date.

Upholding fundamental rights as defined in article 6 TEU must be a key tenet of EU JHA policy. Moreover it must be ensured that the Charter of Fundamental Rights is not mere rhetoric, but offers real legal guarantees of true protection to our citizens. For this reason the work undertaken within the Convention on the Future of Europe is welcome mainly in assessing whether the charter should be incorporated into the treaties. In my opinion it should be included. In addition, the personal view of the President of the ECJ should be followed, expressed recently at a meeting in the Parliament that the EU should accede to the European Convention on Human Rights.

As mentioned before, by providing a society that is safe and secure from crime, people can be helped to enjoy freedom and justice. But there are other definitions of security, such as security from prejudice and oppression. That is why the anti-discrimination laws passed both before (gender) and since 1997 (race, religion, sexual orientation, age, disability) are so important, and why we need the rights in the charter to be legally binding. It is an interesting reflection of what the treaty drafters – i.e. the national governments up to now – have defined as freedom, security and justice that neither the provisions (Articles 13 and 141) outlawing discrimination nor the provisions on citizenship including free movement of people are normally classified as within 'AFSJ', and the charter sometimes gets left out too.

The Tampere programme was itself not complete as a definition of an Area of Freedom, Security and Justice. This was perhaps understandable, given the concentration on the novel new powers in asylum and immigration and cross-border policing. But even before 11 September – though even more since – ministers have given in to the temptation to implement even the Tampere agenda only partially.

It is worrying that in the present political climate national governments are focusing even more just on 'interior minister' notions of security. They have a pretext to neglect and weaken civil rights, such as rights to protest peacefully, or by defining as 'terrorists' groups fighting oppression. They pander to, rather than resist against, the pan-European renaissance of the extremist Right by giving in to a climate of fear and suspicion. The impact on racial harmony and respect for diversity could be very damaging; in particular this fear may be encouraging the growth of 'Islamophobia'. There is an urgent need to balance our objectives in the measures being developed to ensure security and free movement within an enlarged EU through the policing of our external borders. It is encouraging that there is a strong sense of solidarity and commitment being shown by the Member States and the Commission in ensuring that our Union is safe. We have an interest in the development of the necessary mutual trust so that arguments against the UK's participation in the free movement provisions of Schengen can be refuted.

But plans for integrated management of the Union's external borders, and the possibility of a European Border Guard to offer assistance to countries more challenged than others, must not become a tool for building a so-called 'Fortress Europe'. The scourge of trafficking in human beings must be tackled. But we must be as tough on the causes of people-smuggling and illegal immigration – poverty, human rights abuses, environmental degradation, arms sales – as we are on those phenomena. If those who have taken flight are penalised because they are in need of protection and neglect our international obligations to offer asylum, the reputation of the EU will be unforgivably impoverished.

In addition, a managed policy of legal migration need to be developed, to allow a reasonable number of those looking for economic self-improvement and prosperity to enter our territory. The dynamic contribution and cultural richness given by migrants as well as refugees to our societies and our economies should be welcomed. Of course migration levels must be set within Member States' demographic and labour market capacities, but along with encouraging the integration and fair treatment of third-country nationals, as stated at Tampere.

2.4 A MECHANISM FOR PEER REVIEW

Commitments of EU solidarity and the development of cooperation on justice matters must be reconciled with each Member State's own culture of rights, constitutional and legal history and civic organisation.

Objections to EU-level developments on the basis of these arguments should not be invoked routinely because of bureaucratic inertia, protection of empires or resistance to true reform, but only if grounded in valid socio-cultural differences.

An example of the latter is the question of identity cards, where any imposition of harmonization would be unacceptable. Another example is the differing national attitudes in European countries to what the UK, in shorthand, knows as 'ethnic monitoring'. This is the counting of employees and users of public services, as well as the population in the census, by racial or ethnic characteristics. It is now regarded after initial unease as perfectly acceptable, as long as it is done sensitively, and is seen as a useful tool to track whether anti-discrimination laws are working and whether services like housing and health are offering equal access. Indeed, the Sikh community, recognised 20 years ago in case law as having not only a religious but also an ethnic identity but whom government bodies refuse to count in this way, converged on Parliament earlier this year to lobby for such official recognition.

However, attitudes among different countries differ in that concern. The very term 'ethnic monitoring' sends a shudder of distaste down the spines of, for example, French, Swedish and German colleagues.

Cultural assumptions must not become a barrier to the robust assertion of the universality, not only in the world, but also within Europe, of civil rights standards. And we must find a way to make each European the co-guardian of the enjoyment of those rights by every other.

Europe is taking significant but piecemeal steps to becoming a human rights community. The very essence of the EU is non-discrimination on the grounds of nationality and free movement. The EC Treaty had from the beginning provisions on gender equality – however much inspired by fears of cheap labour competition rather than altruism. Then provisions on citizenship and respect for fundamental rights were progressively inserted and strengthened in the last decade, not least through the elaboration of the Charter of Fundamental Rights.

However, the nervous and awkward application of the provisions of Articles 6 and 7 of the Treaty of European Union in 1999, in response to Jorg Haider's entry into government in Austria, showed how much development they need in practice. In particular, the application of sanctions by other EU countries was denounced by some as 'unacceptable interference', especially as bullying by big countries of a small one.

But the prospect of enlargement offers a challenge and a great opportunity. The candidate countries cannot accede to the EU without satisfying the Copenhagen criteria on democracy, stability of institutions, rule of law, human rights and respect for and protection of minorities. But the fact is that the regular Commission reports have shown continuing weaknesses particularly in judicial independence and minority rights. No candidate state has yet developed comprehensive anti-discrimination legislation. In 2001 around 20 000 asylum applications were submitted to EU countries by nationals of candidate states – perhaps in itself a figure that needs to be treated with caution – but, more significantly, almost 300 were accepted. It is likely that a high proportion of those were Roma population.

However, the EU's ability to insist on the adoption of prescriptive standards in the Justice and Home Affairs domain has been handicapped by the lack of clear unambiguous and stable standards for the EU itself. Even in the area of women's and minority rights, the acquis is constantly being updated. For justice matters, there are norms from the Council of Europe, the OSCE, and even the UN, but little that is specific to the EU. This means a lack of clarity and confused messages for accession countries, even if there was the real political commitment from both them and the EU to enforcement of consistent higher standards.

It is not possible to affirm that everything is rosy in the EU garden. There are currently five UK citizens detained in Guatanamo Bay, for eight months without charge, whose fundamental right to a fair trial the UK government has done nothing to advance. There is similarly a foreign national detained without charge in a British prison under domestic anti-terrorism legislation, whose mental health has reportedly deteriorated to a life-threatening extent. Another example is the recent Amnesty International's report on Spain, about ill-treatment, even torture, of ethnic minority immigrants. Fourteen innocent, British and Dutch 'plane-spotters' on holidays were convicted in April 2002 of espionage in Greece, in a gross miscarriage of justice, a case happily resolved though in November 2002 by the admirable acquittal decision by an Appeal Court.

What all this points to is the need for an EU Human Rights policy, under which all EU countries, new and old, open themselves to scrutiny. Two years ago Amnesty proposed guidelines against torture, which EU ministers in the Council adopted for external policy, i.e for foreigners to observe, but balked at applying to themselves. It is a helpful development that the European Parliament's annual human rights reports use a new methodology, taking the articles of the Charter as a benchmark for noting progress and deficiencies.

Developing a consistent mechanism of peer review means a change of habit and mindset. A paradox can be found dealing with the UK government over the case of the 'plane-spotters'. The Home Office is busy agreeing in Brussels to a programme of harmonisation in law enforcement and mutual recognition of decisions. This does mean to a considerable extent that we involve ourselves in the systems in other countries. But the Foreign Office, responsible for consular matters, maintains loftily that it cannot possibly interfere in the conduct of criminal justice in another state.

In my opinion care needs to be taken, not only about how our fellow national citizens are treated in another Member State and theirs in ours, but also about how our fellow EU citizens and residents are treated in their own country. We must care intrusively, and not be put off by false claims of invasion of sovereignty. Constructing such a policy will require a difficult balance between, on the one hand, harmonising standards and quality of decisions but on the other hand not being overly prescriptive about justice structures and methods. But it is necessary to seek that goal.

2.5 CONCLUSION

An EU JHA policy in an enlarged European Union should be more comprehensive and balanced, not through expansive new policy criteria and proposals but through the implementation and logical elaboration of the Tampere mandate.

It is time that the Council and the Member States committed themselves to this – from the lowest level working group to the European Council itself. In an enlarged Union will be able even less than now to accept ambitious biannual political rhetoric on this subject and little practical accord. We have bitten off a truly ambitious goal – an Area of Freedom, Security and Justice – and it must be carried through wholeheartedly.

3. Maintaining the Justice and Home Affairs Acquis in an Enlarged Europe

Jörg Monar

3.1 INTRODUCTION

This chapter will assess the key post-enlargement challenges in the Justice and Home Affairs (JHA) domain, as well as the potentials and limits of major post-enlargement diversity management instruments, and the various possibilities to maintain and/or enhance decision-making and implementation capabilities, finishing with a consideration of the importance of trust and confidence for developing the JHA acquis after enlargement.

Starting with a brief comment on the title, the term 'maintaining' suggests a relatively stable, if not even largely completed acquis of the European Union in the area of Justice and Home Affairs (JHA) at the time of enlargement. Yet this is a rather unlikely scenario: over the last three years the Council has adopted between 80 and 100 texts – most of which are legally binding – per year, and still only a small part of the Treaty objectives of Titles IV TEC and Title VI TEU, and of the ambitious Tampere 'milestones', have been implemented so far. Although some major legislative proposals – especially in the areas of asylum and immigration policy – have been seriously delayed because of disagreements in the Council, the pace of progress is still impressive, especially if compared to the 1990s. Much remains to be done to implement the Amsterdam and Tampere objectives, and a lot of this is likely to be on the agenda when the first 'new members' will just have joined.

One also has to take into account that there have been some important initial breakthroughs in certain areas, which are likely to fully realise their effects only in 2004 and beyond. A major example has been the introduction of the European Arrest Warrant – formally adopted in June 2002[1] but due to be fully implemented only in 2004 – which has been a breakthrough for the

[1] OJ L 190 of 17.06.2002.

principle of mutual recognition in the JHA domain, and could represent the starting point of more legislative measures on mutual recognition in criminal matters (see Barbe 2002). One therefore has to start from the assumption that the JHA acquis will continue to evolve and, mostly in certain areas, with a considerable dynamic.

Therefore, the task for the EU after enlargement regarding the JHA acquis is a double one:

- 'maintaining' the acquis in the sense of preserving what has been achieved already and ensuring that it is effectively implemented; and
- 'developing' the acquis in the sense of ensuring that the momentum is not lost.

3.2 KEY POST-ENLARGEMENT CHALLENGES

3.2.1 Increased diversity in political, structural and implementation capability terms

Each enlargement imports new diversity into the EU; not all of this diversity is negative, as there are also different experiences, know-how and priorities which come into the Union which can add to the variety and effectiveness of its action. Yet increased diversity is clearly also a 'challenge', a challenge whose risks the EU's insistence on full adoption of the acquis and the various efforts made during the pre-accession process try to minimise.

In the JHA domain the challenge of diversity is a fairly specific one – different in nature from those in other EU policy-making areas and more sensitive – because the AFSJ is in essence a developing common zone of internal security. Internal security is an essential public good, and a highly sensitive one of immediate concern to citizens and voters. Yet what is true for any security system – be it a bank, a protected data-base or a car – is also true for the AFSJ – the system is only as strong as its weakest link, with one weakness in one part of it having potentially serious implications for all other parts. It is worthwhile to stress this very simple – even banal – logic because it is one that is understood not only by practitioners but also by the public and the media. If the diversity which is coming into the EU with the next enlargement brings weaknesses into the system then this is not simply a question of further adjustment to the economic and administrative functioning of the single market – which might at the worst lead to some temporary economic distortions – but a question of the efficiency and the credibility of the system as a whole as regards the delivery of internal security to the citizens of the EU.

All the candidate countries have made substantial progress towards adopting the legal acquis in the JHA area, and there is every reason to assume that the process of formal adaptation of national legislation to the EU JHA acquis will be largely completed by the time of accession. Yet the same cannot be said with confidence about other forms of diversity, these being:

Political diversity

Fundamental differences between national political approaches to certain JHA issues – such as over internal border controls and responses to drug addiction – continue to hamper progress towards common policy-making among the current 15 Member States. The future new Member States will inevitably add their own specific political interests and approaches to the existing diversity. Two areas may be taken as an example:

The first one is that of external border management. During the 1990s the EU has moved more and more towards a tightening of external border controls. For some Member States (especially current frontline Schengen countries like Austria, Germany and Italy) ensuring a high degree of border security through sophisticated and extensive checks is clearly a central objective in the JHA area. The Union's new Eastern European Member States are not likely to share this approach fully. For those of them who will be *nolens volens* in charge of part of the EU's new Eastern borders, implementing the EU/Schengen external border regime entails major costs in form of a disruption of relations with ethnic minorities on the other side of the border, political relations with neighbouring countries and well-established cross-border trade. These countries may at the moment still give a high political priority to the upgrading of their Eastern border controls because this is part of the conditions they have to fulfil for EU membership. Yet after enlargement the full implementation or even further development of the EU/Schengen external border acquis could well become much less of a priority for some of the new Member States, perhaps even an area where they would seek a revision of the current acquis.

The second example is that of the fight against money laundering. Measures against money laundering have become a core area of EU policy in the fight against organised crime and rank high on the current Member States' agenda as this was again confirmed by the Conclusions of the Tampere European Council and action taken after 11 September 2001. Yet the political perspective of the future new Member States may not fully coincide with this priority. A very strict application (or even tightening) of the rules against money laundering could have (or be perceived to have) a dampening effect on the inflow of capital, and new Member States could well take the view that they can less afford this sort of restriction than the more developed economies of the current Member States. Another reason is that the full implementation of the EU's acquis and objectives in this area requires quite considerable financial and administrative efforts (for the setting up of a special agency to monitor financial operations, for instance) which the applicant countries with their huge needs in other areas might prefer to reduce or postpone as far as possible. Both of these reasons provide ample grounds for a different political approach, and it is certainly not by chance, for instance, that the Commission's 2002 progress report on Poland noted that there has been little progress in aligning Polish legislation with the EU money laundering acquis.

These and other instances of potential additional political diversity could clearly have an impact on both decision-making and policy implementation.

Structural diversity

Efficient EU JHA cooperation requires a certain degree of compatibility of law enforcement and administrative structures. This continues to be a major challenge among the current Member States with their diversity, for instance, in the areas of police and court structures. The new Member States will inevitably add to this diversity, with some more specific problems regarding an uncompleted 'catch-up' of the new Member States with organisational standards required by the EU acquis. One example is migration management. While most candidate countries have gone through extensive structural changes in the management of migration, including the introduction of computerised data-bases on aliens, unclear competence demarcation lines and inadequate cooperation between administrative and security authorities at the central and local level could not only reduce the effectiveness of legislation adapted to the EU acquis but also make cooperation with counterparts in the old Member States more difficult. It is also not yet clear, to take another example, whether all of the candidates which – like Slovakia – currently have not yet fully demilitarised their border guards and still use conscripts, will have completed the process of creating independent specialised civilian border police forces on the day of accession.

Implementation capability diversity

This is likely to be the area with the highest degree of post-enlargement diversity. Most of the candidate countries have substantial staffing, training and equipment deficits, which will still need several years to be overcome. It does not help that, because of financial constraints and bureaucratic obstacles, the build-up of some crucial implementation capabilities is postponed until the 'last minute' before accession. One example among many is the problem of understaffing because of recruitment problems and/or financial difficulties. In both Hungary and Poland, for instance, actual staff numbers of border guards in 2001 fell around 30% short of the official target numbers, and the

Commission's recent progress report on Slovenia, one of the frontrunners in adaptation to the JHA acquis, noted with concern that in August 2002 the Slovenian government had only approved the appointment of 392 border police staff in 2002 and 200 in 2003 instead of the 700 in 2002 and 540 in 2003 originally foreseen in its Schengen Action Plan. Another problem is that in a number of cases the likely future new Member States are tending to postpone necessary adaptation to almost the 'last minute' before accession. The later these changes are introduced, however, the more likely they are to lead to a significant degree of implementation capability diversity in the enlarged EU. Examples are the late full alignment of national rules to EU visa requirements, such as in the case of Poland and Slovakia, for instance, and the slow progress with the organisation of data-protection authorities, which are of central importance for the participation in Europol and other computerised EU cooperation networks.

A rather specific implementation capability problem is corruption. It can have serious implications for implementation of JHA measures as police officers and prosecutors in old Member States could be very reluctant to cooperate and share information with counterparts in new Member States that are perceived to be highly vulnerable to corruption. Not all of the candidate countries have so far been equally successful in tackling the problem, leaving considerable differences in the risks of corruption. The Commission's recent progress report on the Czech Republic, for instance, noted that the number of corruption-related criminal offences was increasing, that latent corruption is widespread, including in administrative police departments. Much higher levels of corruption in some Member States could obviously have negative implications on the willingness of all to further develop intense cooperation on particularly sensitive internal security issues.

3.2.2 The impact of post-enlargement diversity on decision making: Implementation capability and trust

All three of the above dimensions of diversity will remain after enlargement, and they will make the decision-making in the JHA area more difficult. The obvious response to this challenge would be the need for a more strongly developed EU decision-making capacity. Yet this is – at least under the current treaty provisions and institutional arrangements – clearly not on offer. The main reason for that is the persistence of the unanimity rule which even in the Tampere progress evaluation report drawn up by the Belgian Presidency in December 2001 was explicitly identified, especially in the areas of asylum and immigration, as clearly a serious hindrance to progress. Yet there is also the problem of the continuing lack of mutual confidence of Member States in their respective standards and procedures – unlikely to be increased with the coming in of up to 10 largely 'untested' new Member

States adding to the variety of standards and procedures – and the persisting reluctance to change existing national laws which in the Council are in many cases still defended by national delegations as if each of them had obviously the best legislation on the respective JHA issues in place. As a result the problems of the blockage of initiatives, delays and of the watering down of texts under deliberation could well significantly increase in a Union of up to 25 Member States.

The post-enlargement EU will face increased implementation problems in the JHA domain. One major factor will be the aforementioned deficits in capabilities, which, at least in the case of some of the new Member States, will last well beyond the day of accession. Stating this does not mean that the current candidates are blamed for everything. It most cases their implementation capability problems are not due to a lack of political will but to lack of resources and sufficient time to adapt their national systems to an EU acquis which has grown enormously since the 1990s and still continues to grow at a pace which makes the 'catching-up' an ever evolving challenge.

Yet the particular difficulties of the new Member States will not be the only strain on the EU implementation capability. There are also likely to be new security challenges linked to enlargement, such as longer and more exposed borders and a potentially increased attractiveness of the enlarged internal market for organised crime and traffickers and facilitators involved in the huge business that illegal immigration has become. All this means that rather than aiming only at 'maintaining' implementation capabilities the Union will actually need more effective instruments and procedures for implementing its JHA measures than those it currently has.

A functioning Area of Freedom, Security and Justice depends to a very large extent on trust. This involves trust between law enforcement and judicial authorities across the boundaries of the different legal systems, law enforcement structures and traditions, but also trust of politicians and their voters in that EU action in the JHA domain provides 'value added' in terms of enhanced internal security and does not, on the contrary, create new risks, for instance, through porous external borders or the leaking of confidential data to crime (see Walker 2002).[2] This trust is still not yet fully developed among the current Member States. This is shown, for instance, by the fact that some national police forces continue to be very reluctant to systematically provide Europol with relevant data, which is a constant problem for the work of Europol. It will be even more difficult, at least initially, to build sufficient trust vis-à-vis partners in the new Member States, in part simply because they are new, yet partly also because of negative perceptions about insufficient training, potential lower standards and corruption. Trust in the capacity of the

[2] On the interrelationship between trust and security in the context of the enlargement in the JHA domain see Walker, 2002, pp. 19–34.

EU to deliver 'value added' in the domain of internal security has gradually increased over the last few years. Yet it still remains limited and fragile. Any evidence, however 'thin' it actually may be, that some internal security problems might actually be increasing after enlargement could easily destroy much of that trust and make Member States less inclined to maintain the momentum of the construction of the AFSJ. Because of this reason, but also in view of an effective integration of the 'newcomers' in the existing EU structures and networks, building up trust in the Member States should be regarded as one of the most essential tasks in the JHA domain in the first few years after enlargement.

3.3 POTENTIALS AND LIMITS OF MAJOR DIVERSITY MANAGEMENT INSTRUMENTS

3.3.1 The Community method

The Community method with its emphasis on binding legal instruments, majority voting, the Commission's exclusive right of initiative and comprehensive control by the Court of Justice, has the great advantage of producing common approaches codified in Community law on the basis of a well defined decision-making process within a single legal and institutional ('constitutional') framework. Yet it also has its clear disadvantages because in some areas – such as legal immigration, police legislation and penal laws – Member States are extremely reluctant to go down the road of common legal norms and resist any attempt to surrender national powers to the Community system. As a result many tend to prefer the absence of common action – or at least very long delays before such action is taken – to a full use of the Community method. It is quite characteristic that when the areas now under Title IV TEC were 'communitarised' by the Treaty of Amsterdam the Member States actually agreed to this step only on the basis of maintaining unanimity and making the Commission's right of initiative non-exclusive. There can be little doubt that some current Member States have, and some future Member States may have in principle objections against the use of the Community in some areas such as police cooperation.

A further problem with the Community method is that it operates on the basis of rather cumbersome decision-making procedures, which – if combined with unanimity – can lead to long delays and least common denominator agreements. Also in other respects it cannot always be taken for granted that the classic Community approach would be the most effective way forward. The last few years have shown, for instance, that it can sometimes be quite useful, or even more effective, to have a shared right of initiative of the

Member States rather than an exclusive one of the Commission. This is because initiatives from the Member States may have the advantage of more expertise on certain issues and may – especially if Member States bring in joint initiatives – build up a critical mass for decision-making in the Council rather than a Commission initiative. An example for that was the so-called 'Four Presidencies' initiative on the establishment of Eurojust in July 2000 (see Monar 2001).

In the enlarged EU the Community method should therefore be maintained or even extended wherever possible, but it seems most unlikely that it will or can be used across all JHA areas, and it may not even be always the best option for ensuring effective decision-making capacity. Some flexibility should therefore be applied: There should still be a bias in favour of the Community method because of the high degree of integration and legal certainty it produces, but not necessarily for all issues and with all of its traditional components.

3.3.2 Enhanced cooperation[3]

The advantages and disadvantages of 'enhanced cooperation', as an instrument of flexibility in EU integration, have attracted much debate (and literature) since the Treaty of Amsterdam, and do not need to be discussed in this contribution. The main issue is the trade-off involved between the desirability of common policy-making – with all Member States participating and moving forward at the same time – because of the legal and political coherence this ensures, and the need to avoid a complete standstill in certain areas if some Member States keep blocking further progress which others want.

If unanimity is to a large extent maintained in the JHA domain it seems more and more likely that enhanced cooperation could actually be used as a diversity management instrument after enlargement. The fact that the Belgian Presidency – with the backing of most of the other Member States – threatened the Italian Berlusconi government with a potential use of that instrument when Italy was preventing unanimity on the European Arrest Warrant in December 2001, can be taken as an indication that it is no longer considered as a purely abstract possibility. With unanimity in an EU of 25 being obviously much more difficult to achieve, groups of eight or more Member States – according to the new rules introduced by the Treaty of Nice – might prefer this instrument to months or years of delays and blockage.

Saying that enhanced cooperation could well be used does not necessarily mean saying that it will only be used to exclude unwilling or unable new Member States. It seems perfectly well feasible, for instance, that some new

[3] We use the Nice Treaty term instead of 'closer cooperation'.

Member States might be willing to go ahead with some of the old Member States in areas where other old Member States are not willing to follow. In the run-up to the Seville European Council in June 2002 it seemed, for instance, that some of the current Member States, especially the United Kingdom, did not favour the idea, backed *inter alia* by Italy and Germany to gradually move towards a common European Corps of Border Guards, whereas some of the current candidate countries gave some support to the idea.

It should be emphasised, however, that a proliferation of enhanced cooperation frameworks would come at a price in terms of political and legal fragmentation within the AFSJ, drastically increasing the complexity and difficulty of common policy-making and reducing transparency. It should therefore be regarded as it has been defined in Article 43(1)(c), as a measure of 'last resort'.

3.3.3 The open method of coordination

The open method of coordination – much invoked and discussed as a new EU governance instrument – has already found its way on to the EU agenda in the JHA domain. Before the background of the difficulties of implementing the Tampere agenda through common legislative measures, the Commission suggested in two communications of July and November 2001 that the open method of coordination be used for both immigration and asylum policy, proposing the adoption of multi-annual guidelines to be implemented through national action plans and monitored by the Commission which would also make new legislative proposals wherever needed.[4] The Commission made clear that the use of the open method would come on top of some common legislation – part of which it had already proposed – and not replace it, but it was fairly clear that the Commission saw this as a temporary alternative to avoid protracted deadlocks in certain areas of the development of a common approach to migration, especially in areas of primary Member State responsibility, such as admission of economic migrants and integration policy.

Could the open method of coordination, then, also be used as a post-enlargement diversity management instrument? Essentially, the open method could allow for some progress to be made in areas where:

1. the Community method is likely to produce deadlocks because of the Member States' unwillingness to accept tightly binding policy outcomes; and
2. closer/enhanced cooperation is undesirable because of its break-up effects on a common approach.

[4] See COM (2001) 387 and 710.

With regard to the new Member States' implementation capability problems, the open method could have the advantage of making it easier for them to accept certain common targets and guidelines as those would be combined with a longer time horizon and a certain margin of national flexibility for the implementation of these targets and guidelines.

Yet the open method of coordination also carries some risks precisely because of its nature as an essentially intergovernmental coordination instrument. The guidelines would be likely to be open to different interpretations, their non-adherence not subject to any legal sanction and the 'peer pressure' might not be sufficient to ensure respect of deadlines set. There are already plenty of examples in the JHA domain of legally non-binding deadlines – such as those in the 1998 Vienna Action Plan – being missed and rather silently put aside.

In all cases where significant degrees of approximation or even harmonisation of laws and practices are needed to ensure the effectiveness of EU policies in a relatively short period of time, the open method is clearly not an appropriate instrument. There would have been little point, for instance, in applying the open method to most of the measures taken by the EU in response to the terrorist attacks of 11 September 2001. There will always be some areas – such as harmonisation of penalties for serious forms of cross-border crime – where the open method cannot be applied effectively.

3.3.4 EU aid programmes

Financial transfers through specific EU programmes are also substantial diversity-reducing instruments in that 'weaker partners' can be helped with bringing their implementation capabilities up to the required standards. From 1997 to 2001 a total of 541 million Euros under the PHARE programme were allocated to various programmes in the JHA domain (see de Lobkowicz 2002). As quite substantial implementation capability deficits – especially in the areas of training and equipment – are likely to persist after enlargement it seems crucial that specific aid instruments are designed in time which can replace the existing pre-accession instruments which are currently scheduled to end at the latest with the day of accession.

It should not be too difficult to politically justify the introduction of specific post-enlargement EU JHA aid programmes; if the idea of a common 'area of security' with its corollary of the 'weakest link' is taken seriously then it should be possible to make parliaments, the media and citizens understand that every Euro spent, for instance on the control of the EU's external borders, is also a Euro spent on their own security. Apart from specific programmes for training and equipment, upgrading new instruments of financial solidarity for the costs of the intended 'high level of safety' within the AFSJ should be developed.[5] Community funding for the gradual build-up of common border guard structures for the Union's external land borders could be one such programme.

3.4 MAINTAINING / IMPROVING THE DECISION-MAKING CAPACITY

3.4.1 The crucial issue of majority voting

The importance of majority voting for maintenance and development of the acquis after enlargement does not need further lengthy explanations. The EU cannot afford risking years of delays or complete deadlock in the JHA domain because of the unanimity requirement. EU experience has shown that in areas of majority voting Member States often behave right from the beginning much more flexibly and are more willing to engage in compromise building than in areas of unanimity. The mere possibility of a qualified majority vote makes its actual use often superfluous as consensus is in most cases reached well before Member States take the risk of being formally outvoted.

By virtue of Article 67 TEC the Council can decide in 2004 to introduce the co-decision procedure for part or all of the communitarised areas falling under Title IV TEC. To take this step – which requires unanimity – is the very least which the Union has to do to preserve its decision-making capacity in an enlarged EU. The third pillar should also not be regarded as immune to the introduction of majority voting, although certain areas of police cooperation – such as potential operational powers for Europol – and approximation or harmonisation of penal laws may still be for quite a few years too sensitive to subject Member States to the common discipline of majority votes.

3.4.2 Streamlining the decision-making system's structures and procedures

The current working structure in the Council – very much based on the approach of having 'a box', i.e. a committee or working party, for any problem area or issue – may satisfy the desire of senior officials in the ministries to be fully involved in Brussels, but has become increasingly complex and overextended. A reduction of the number of working parties and the transformation of some of them into multidisciplinary groups with a broader remit could not only reduce the necessary coordination effort and

[5] According to Article 29 TEU.

speed up certain procedures, but also facilitate the insertion of the new Member States into the decision-making system.

The 'Haga process', initiated under the Swedish Presidency in 2001, has also highlighted certain problems in decision-making procedures such as Member States submitting overlapping or badly timed national initiatives. In an EU of 25, such problems could proliferate if the Council's rules of procedure are not adapted accordingly.

3.4.3 Increased use of deadlines

Only a part of the current JHA objectives in the treaties is linked to legally binding deadlines. Where this has been done, however, the pressure on Council and Commission to act has been greater than in the non-deadline linked areas. The Commission's half-yearly scoreboard also derives a considerable part of its usefulness as a peer pressure instrument from the deadlines set in the treaties, the Vienna Action Plan and Tampere. There can be no doubt that deadlines introduce an additional dimension of urgency into the decision-making process. For the EU after enlargement, therefore, any JHA objective defined in the Treaties should also be linked to a deadline for adopting the respective measures.

3.4.4 Increased use of 'stand-still' and 'sunset' clauses

The EU's decision-making capacity in the JHA domain has repeatedly been impaired by Member States continuing to prepare and adopt diverging legislation in relevant JHA areas, which complicates or even obstructs the adoption of common measures. A recent example is the new German immigration law (*Zuwanderungsgesetz*) which last year made the German delegation in the Council repeatedly argue that it could not commit itself to EU legislation in this area before the new legislation at the national level was completed. Some parts of this legislation, such as those on family reunification, clearly do not make the adoption of common EU measures easier. Within a larger EU this sort of problem could increase. A useful remedy could be the increased use of 'stand-still' clauses obliging Member States not to adopt any new legislation that might provide an obstacle to common legal instruments in the respective area. They should be applied whenever and as soon as a legislative text has been formally proposed to the Council.

It is all too often a fairly painless option for Member States to struggle endlessly for a better deal in the Council on new EU legislation or to accept long delays with the introduction of national implementing legislation as long as the existing arrangements still provide an acceptable fall-back position. The use of 'sunset clauses' – for instance in the context of legislative acts requiring implementing legislation – can increase the pressure to act as they provide that existing bi- or multilateral arrangements will become invalid on a certain date if they have not been changed or replaced by a common legal instrument or followed by appropriate national implementing legislation.

3.5 MAINTAINING / IMPROVING THE IMPLEMENTATION CAPACITY

3.5.1 Strengthening monitoring procedures (including benchmarking)

The EU has already acquired quite substantial experience with collective evaluation mechanisms, the Standing Committee on the Evaluation and Implementation of Schengen being the most notable example. Such monitoring mechanisms will be even more important in an enlarged Union in which some of the new Member States might have special difficulties with meeting standards set by the old and where it will be important to increase transparency between all Member States to avoid false suspicion and distrust. These evaluation mechanisms should obviously apply to all Member States (not only the newcomers). The Schengen Standing Committee could serve as a model. Yet there should be separate evaluation mechanisms for all parts of the acquis, not only for the Schengen acquis, which remains heavily focused on border controls and compensatory measures.

Such monitoring mechanisms should be combined with a system of benchmarking, with Member States then being given some sort of 'marks' for their respective performance, which should increase pressure on those with 'low scores'. The monitoring could also be linked to a system of 'incentives', with penalties imposed on authorities failing the standards and financial rewards to those performing above average. Developing a sensible penalty system could be difficult, however, as imposing a fine or withdrawing EU support could be both highly controversial and counterproductive if funding shortages are part of the problem in the first place.

3.5.2 Improved 'best practice' identification and transfer

The Member States are a huge reservoir of different experiences and practices. By analysing and evaluating those and identifying practices which are producing the best results Member States can be given an incentive to learn from each other, and common EU measures can be based on best practices rather than on a compromise between good and less good ones. Best practice identification and transfer already plays a substantial part in the work of some of the special EU agencies in the JHA area – such as the European

Police College (CEPOL), the European Monitoring Centre for Racism and Xenophobia in Vienna and the GROTIUS training programme. In the enlarged EU best practice identification should be elevated to a major objective of the AFSJ, generalised across all areas and made a central element of all training programmes. The major advantage of best practice identification and transfer as a diversity management instrument is that it is both a relatively painless process – as there are no formal sanctions – and a cost-effective way of improving implementation capabilities.

3.5.3 Increased use of common institutional structures and 'joint teams'

Both the creation of common institutional structures – such as Europol and Eurojust currently, and in the future perhaps a common European Corps of Border Guards – and the formation of 'joint teams' have the triple advantage of increasing the operational expertise available to officers on law enforcement or control missions, generating learning effects and increasing trust. In the enlarged EU such common institutional structures should be appreciated and also used as agents for the continuous exchange of expertise and experience. The formation of joint operational teams, such as the 'investigation teams' provided for by the Framework Decision of 13 June 2002 bringing together officials from old and new Member States, could be particularly valuable in the first years after enlargement. [6]

3.5.4 Introduction of rapidly adaptable support programmes for 'weak spots'

Both external events – such as the sudden increase of migration or refugee pressure on certain parts of the EU's external borders – and weaknesses identified in monitoring exercises could justify the use of EU aid instruments for strengthening 'weak spots' of the AFSJ in the interest of the whole. Some instruments – such as the European Refugee Fund – have already been put into place, but overall there are very few of these 'emergency aid' instruments and they tend to be under-funded and cumbersome to use. In an enlarged EU – where more 'weak spots' are likely to appear – a more extended and flexible system of rapidly adaptable support instruments should be put into place. Financial reserves, which could be called up at short notice, should be provided for by the EU budget in the context of broadly defined JHA programmes. A further possibility would be the EU supported lending of personnel by Member States to other Member States experiencing temporary problems at external borders or over particular law enforcement issues, such

[6] OJ L 162 of 20.6.2002.

as the fight against organised crime, traffickers in human beings or terrorism. The possibility envisaged in the June 2002 external border management plan of Member States, being able to request the intervention of a rapid response unit consisting of officers from other Member States for problems at border crossing points, goes in that direction.

3.6 TRUST AND CONFIDENCE BUILDING

3.6.1 The importance of common structures and training for trust generation

The proliferation of special common structures in the JHA domain – ranging from institutions such as Europol over monitoring centres to networks such as the European Judicial Network – has recently attracted some criticism, and there is, of course, a problem with creating structures – such as the Police Chiefs Task Force – whose role and position have been ill defined. Yet such common structures can play a very useful role after enlargement because they constitute points of regular contact and cooperation between practitioners of old and new Member States. These can help spread knowledge about their respective law enforcement and judiciary systems, increase transparency and create trust through the routine of cooperation. An early and full integration of officials from the new Member States into the work of common JHA structures – which in the case of Europol is now already well under way – should therefore be regarded as a priority for both the remaining time before accession and the first months after accession.

3.6.2 The potential crucial role of a common management of external borders

In this context the action plan for the integrated management of the external borders adopted by the Seville European Council in June 2002 with – as its final objective – the potential creation of a European Corps of Border Guards could play a crucial role in building trust. External border security is clearly one of the primary enlargement-related concerns among the current Member States. Elements such as common operational coordination, exchange of personnel, formation of joint operational teams and the introduction of burden-sharing mechanisms as part of a gradual move towards a European Corps would give the old Member States a feeling of having an insight into and influence on the way the new external borders are managed. This would also provide ample opportunities for sharing experiences between officials from old and new Member States and facilitate the transfer of expertise. All this would make a substantial contribution to trust building.

3.6.3 More extensive use of liaison agents and exchange of experts

Liaison agents placed in ministries and police headquarters or border control posts have played a very useful role in increasing trust and operational efficiency in cooperation between current Member States. The same applies to the exchange and temporary posting of experts. This system should be expanded in the enlarged EU, especially as the current programmes of pre-accession advisers will have come to an end by then. Staff shortages in ministries and law enforcement agencies certainly impose serious constraints in this area, but the benefits on the trust building side would be very considerable.

3.6.4 Generating support and confidence among citizens through transparency and a better balance between Freedom, Security and Justice

The AFSJ needs as a basis not only trust between the practitioners involved in implementing it, but also the support of the citizens. This support should not be taken for granted. There is some degree of suspicion amongst civil liberties groups in the current Member States as regards the structures and policies currently developed by the EU. These have been accused of being essentially repressive in nature and following the logic of a sort of EU fortress watched over by a central 'big brother' with huge data-bases at his disposal and decisions being taken behind closed doors and outside effective parliamentary control. Citizens in the new Member States – having still vivid memories of their own 'big brothers' with their omnipresent instruments of control and repression – could well be even more sceptical about the build-up of central EU structures and policies in the internal security area. In several of the new Member States the negative impact of the Schengen acquis on the traditionally rather open borders to Eastern neighbours is unlikely to fuel enthusiasm about the AFSJ.

It will therefore be of considerable importance to increase the transparency of the AFSJ through a better communication of its objectives and progress to parliaments, the media and citizens and more effective parliamentary control. It is no less important to ensure that beside the internal security dimension the Freedom and Justice objectives of the AFSJ are not neglected, which means that the institutions should aim at a better balance between the three essential public goods that the title of the AFSJ promises to citizens. Making the Charter of Fundamental Rights a legally binding part of AFSJ and further increasing European citizens' access to justice across borders would be important elements in such a re-balancing effort. It would give to the citizens of the new Member States a signal that EU Justice and Home Affairs are not only about law enforcement but also about guaranteeing their freedoms and – as the Vienna Action Plan said – generating a 'common sense of justice' across the EU.

REFERENCES

Action plan for the integrated management of the external borders adopted by the Seville European Council in June 2002, Council documents no. SN 200/1/02 REV 1 and 10019/02.

Barbe, E. (2002), 'Le mandat d'arrêt européen: en tirera-t-on toutes les conséquences?', in G. De Kerchove and A. Weyembergh (eds), *L'espace pénal européen: enjeux et perspectives*, Brussels: Editions de l'Université de Bruxelles, pp. 113–7.

De Lobkowicz W. (2002), 'L'Europe et la securité intérieure', Paris: *La documentation Française*, pp. 91–3.

European Commission: 2002 *Regular report on Poland's progress towards accession*, SEC(2002)1408, p. 117.

European Commission: 2002 *Regular report on Slovenia's progress towards accession*, SEC (2002) 1411, p. 100.

European Commission: 2002 *Regular report on Czech Republic's progress towards accession*, SEC (2002)1402, p. 114.

Evaluation of the conclusions of the Tampere European Council submitted to the General Affairs Council and the European Council on 6 December and formally adopted by the Laeken European Council on 14/15 December (Council document no. 14926/01).

Monar, J. (2001), 'Justice and Home Affairs', in G. Edwards and G. Wiessala (eds), *The European Union. Annual Review of the EU 2000/2001*, Blackwell, published in association with *Journal of Common Market Studies*, pp. 131–2.

Walker, N. (2002), 'The Problem of Trust in an Enlarged Area of Freedom, Security and Justice', in M. Anderson and J. Apap (eds), *Police and Justice Cooperation and the New European Borders*, The Hague: Kluwer Law International, pp. 19–34.

4. Division of Competencies between National and European Levels with regard to Justice and Home Affairs

Paul de Hert

4.1 INTRODUCTION

This chapter discusses the division of competencies between national and European levels in the area of Justice and Home Affairs. Two divisions merit our attention: firstly, the division between the national and the European legal order (when does an issue become European?), and secondly, the division between the first and third pillar (when does a European issue become a Community one?).

To my initial surprise these two divisions are not identical and have different logics and division keys. My aim will be to discuss them in a critical perspective taking fully into account the very sensitive nature of Justice and Home Affairs with regard to fundamental rights and freedoms. Awareness of this highly sensitive nature is needed especially in the field of criminal law issues.

With regard to criminal matters, we depart from the traditional liberal view on criminal law (echoed by all European institutions) as a last resort. This view implies that the use non-penal and non-custodial sanctions and measures should be stimulated as much as possible.[1] It also explains why

[1] Traditional principles of criminal justice – in the liberal tradition – such as the principle of subsidiarity and proportionality are applied to keep an important amount of conflict cases out of the criminal process. The most important is the famous subsidiarity principle which means not only that primary criminalization (penalization) should not be used when other social systems will be able to deal effectively with problematic behaviours (*ultimum remedium/ultima ratio*), but also that, when a certain behaviour is criminalized one should still strive for the minimal intervention and the minimal sanction in concrete cases. The criminal procedure is a chain of decision-levels – starting with decisions on the level of police, followed by decisions by the public prosecutors, the courts and the agencies responsible for executing the punishment – and

making criminal law a European issue is far from evident. National authorities can be seen as best placed to decide through legislation which sanctions should be possible for which offences. Keeping criminal law within State borders may well be a very legitimate policy. This idea will be developed in our first section and picked up in our final sections discussing some legal pathologies built in the Union structure. These defects explain to a great extent our thesis that under the current regime the division between the national and European sphere should be arranged in the advantage of the former. Learning to live with them is best avoided. Until legal morality is restored through amendments of the Treaty provisions, no single issue pertaining to Justice and Home Affairs should be entrusted to the third pillar.

4.2 KEEPING CRIMINAL LAW WITHIN STATE BORDERS

4.2.1 Three border functions

Country borders are not arbitrary creations. They play a part at three levels (see Van Der Net 2000). In the first place, country borders have meaning for the state itself. By applying the criminal law to the land within the borders, the internal sovereignty of a state is most clearly expressed. A state has a right to determine what is and what is not criminally punishable in its territory and what actions are threatening public order. The powers of the investigating and policing authorities extend in principle to the entire territory. Hence, the possibility to enforce effectively the current criminal norms and public order values within borders. The voters who live in the territory and who are under the states' authority legitimize the choice of criminal norms and public order values.

Borders also play a role in the international legal relations between states. They have an international authority allocation function. This function has been recognized by international public law. States may not interfere in another State's internal affairs. There must be a meaningful relationship between the events that occurred and the state that claims jurisdiction over these events. States must act with reserve in claiming criminal jurisdiction over events that take place wholly or partly outside the country borders.

In the third place, borders play an important informative role in the relationship between the state claiming criminal jurisdiction and the person subjected to that jurisdiction. On the basis of the principle of recognizability,

on each level questions should be answered with regard to what constitutes an optimal sanction. In the classical, liberal tradition the subsidiarity principle indicates that a minimal sanction is at the same time optimal.

the application of a specific criminal law must always be actually knowable or foreseeable by the person subjected to it. This principle seldom leads to problems when a system of borders remains in place. Country borders normally provide a sufficient signal that one legal order is being left and another is being entered.

The third function of borders, viz. reconcilability, closely resembles the principle of legality elaborated by the European Court of Human Rights. This Court has held that interference contravenes Article 8 – protecting privacy, correspondence, family life and the inviolability of houses – unless it is 'in accordance with the law'. This expression requires firstly that the impugned measure should have some basis in domestic law; it also refers to the quality of the law in question, requiring that it should be accessible to the person concerned, who must moreover be able to foresee its consequences for him, and compatible with the rule of law.[2] Thus, accessibility and foreseeability of the law are important requirements that emerge from the phrase 'in accordance with the law'. Both can be endangered when borders are taken away.

The last requirement, the law's foreseeability as to the meaning and nature of the applicable measures, refers back to the quality of the law, requiring it to be compatible with the rule of law. The law must be sufficiently clear in its terms to give citizens an adequate indication as to the circumstances in which and the conditions on which public authorities are empowered to resort to interference with the right to respect for private life and correspondence. 'Consequently, the law must indicate the scope of any such discretion conferred on the competent authorities and the manner of its exercise with sufficient clarity to give the individual adequate protection against arbitrary interference'.[3]

It is not easy to preserve the values behind borders in a supranational context. Take the first, political function. Early modern thinkers have rightly insisted on the need for public consensus underlying law enforcement. For Rousseau sovereignty cannot be delegated to any group of people (or elected representatives), because this alienates people (citizens) from political participation.[4]

A system by which every citizen is entitled to vote on every issue is to be preferred. Clearly such a system could only work in a very small state and with relatively simple issues to decide; otherwise the logistics of getting the whole citizenship together and getting through the business of government would thwart all other activity. Criminal law, Beccaria writes, is a necessary ingredient of the contract to punish those contractors 'seeking to extract from

[2] ECHR, *Huvig v. France*, 27 March 1990, par. 25–6, http://www.dhcour.coe.fr/eng/.

[3] ECHR, *Huvig v. France*, 27 March 1990, par. 29.

[4] This also explains why there is one contract, the social contract to be distinguished from the act whereby the sovereign (the people) set up (institute) the government.

the repository not only his own due but also the portions which are owing to others' (see Beccaria 1995). Hence, criminal law is not God-given,[5] but should be regarded as the sword of the social contract. Beccaria attaches many legal principles to this principle of consent. For instance the principle of legality in criminal law, the principle that laws may only be framed in general terms, the principle of strict legal interpretation by criminal judges, the principle that laws should be clear and written (Beccaria 1995), the prohibition of the death penalty, and the principle that criminal laws should only apply within state borders. International cooperation in criminal matters is far from evident for Beccaria who stresses the value of borders in terms of liberty. A way of preserving this political function of borders in a supranational context is to guarantee democratic transparency and a high level of involvement by legislative bodies. Another solution is the adoption of the principle of subsidiarity.

The third principle calls for prudence when action is taken at a supranational level. Is there an intelligible reason to undertake international action? Is the instrument drafted in explicit terms? Are the consequences of the instrument clear?

The second principle can also be transposed to a supranational level: states may not interfere in another state's internal affairs by putting domestic issues on supranational agendas. There must be a meaningful relationship between these issues and the goals pursued by the supranational institution. Illegitimate 'jumping of scale' should be prevented.

4.2.2 The politics of scale

Contemporary political scientists pay much attention to the phenomenon of 'jumping of scales or bypassing levels of competences' (see Swyngedouw 1997b and Denayer 2001). This mechanism, i.e. choosing a certain institutional level of action to achieve political goals, is at work behind many ongoing processes of change.

Many studies have illustrated recent conservative preferences for downsizing national problems to the local level, obliging local entities, especially cities, to become mutual competitors (the birth of the entrepreneurial city) and to respond to problems such as unemployment with

[5] 'And by "justice" I mean nothing other than the restraint necessary to hold particular interests together, without which they would collapse into the old state of unsociability. Any punishment that goes beyond the need to preserve this bond is unjust by its very nature. We must be careful not to attach any notion of something real to this word justice, such as a physical force or an actual entity. It is simply a way whereby humans conceive of things, a way which influences beyond measure the happiness of all. Nor do I speak here of that justice which flows from God and whose direct bearing is on the punishments and rewards of the after-life', Beccaria, 1995, Ch. 2, p. 10.

inadequate resources. Very often this strategy favours a type of local governance in which a form of privatism is favoured. Political power is redistributed onto a variety of new agents, some politically unelected (Swyngedouw 1997b).[6]

'Scales' is not only a mechanism for downsizing problems. It is to be found at all levels, including the supranational level. On the European scale also, bypassing competences to other levels makes strong players stronger. Democratic procedures are replaced by undemocratic and unaccountable networks serving highly particularistic or dominant interest.

> The nation state may have been eroded from above and from below, but the nature of this erosion has been different in each case. Below the nation state, local regulatory systems (...) have been conferred responsibility without power: regulatory responsibilities have been handed down from the nation state level, but localities can wield little in the way of political-economic power in the context of globalizing accumulation and global deregulation. Above the nation state, supranational regulatory systems haven inherited power without responsibility (Peck and Tickell 1994, pp. 280–315).

Often, political scientists focus on the economic and democratic consequences of this conservative strategy. Part of the analysis, however, can be relevant for our purposes. We can ask ourselves whether a transfer of criminal law issues to the European level leads to more autocratic and undemocratic apparatuses serving dominant interests. Is there an advantage for certain actors to jump to the European scale and put an issue on the supranational agenda? On the other hand, is there within the European framework a guarantee against such use or abuse of the European structure? Can the principle of subsidiarity be considered to be such a guarantee?

4.3 WHEN DOES A JUSTICE AND HOME AFFAIRS ISSUE BECOME EUROPEAN?

4.3.1 Article 5 to the Treaty of the European Community

Article 5 (ex Article 3a-c) of the Treaty of the European Community (TEC) forms a key provision to answer the question 'when does an issue become European?'. It states that:

[6] This can take the form of an increased representation of business in social and economic state institutions, such as regional development societies. Swyngedouw stresses that these evolutions empower some, but exclude many.

> The Community shall act within the limits of the powers conferred upon it by its Treaty and of the objectives assigned to it therein. In areas which do not fall within its exclusive competence, the Community shall take action, in accordance with the principle of subsidiarity, only if and insofar as the objectives of the proposed action cannot be sufficiently achieved by the Member States and can therefore, by reason of the scale or effects of the proposed action, be better achieved by the Community. Any action by the Community shall not go beyond what is necessary to achieve the objectives of this Treaty.

The first paragraph of Article 5 TEC contains 'the principle of attribution of powers' for Community institutions. No issue is European by its nature. The European institutions can undertake action with legal effect only if they are empowered to do so by a provision of the Treaty and of the objectives assigned to it therein. The last words suggest that the principle is not absolute, since issues that are not explicitly mentioned in the Treaties can become European if they fall within the objectives of the Community.[7]

This possibility of including issues in the Community sphere may lead the Community institutions a long way. The second paragraph, principle of subsidiarity, and third paragraph, principle of proportionality, aim to control this wider range of action. In exercising the powers conferred on it, each institution must ensure that the principle of subsidiarity is complied with. Europe must not be used if the Member States can do the job better. The European institutions must also ensure compliance with the principle of proportionality, according to which any action by the Community must not go beyond what is necessary to achieve the objectives of the Treaty.[8]

These two limiting principles are also the object of certain limitations. In Protocol 30, published in 1997, and annexed to the Treaty of the European Community, it is stated that the application of the principles of subsidiarity and proportionality must respect the general provisions and objectives of the Treaty, particularly as regards the maintaining in full of the acquis of the Community and the institutional balance. It should not affect the principles developed by the Court of Justice regarding the relationship between national and Community law, and it should take into account Article F(4) of the Treaty

[7] Hence the idea of mixed competence and the existence of areas shared between the Community and the Member States, next to areas which fall within the exclusive competence of the Community or those which fall within exclusively national competence.

[8] The principle of proportionality, contained in the third paragraph of Article 5 applies to all actions of the Community institutions. The scope of the principle of subsidiarity is more limited. The criteria referred to in the second paragraph of Article 5 of the Treaty only relate to areas for which the Community does not have exclusive competence. The principle of subsidiarity does not call into question the powers conferred on the European Community by the Treaty, as interpreted by the Court of Justice. The principle of proportionality will not be discussed here, but its importance needs emphasizing: every time Community institutions consider recourse to criminal law they should keep in mind the last resort characteristic of criminal law.

on European Union, according to which the Union shall provide itself with the means necessary to attain its objectives and carry through its policies.

4.3.2 The principle of subsidiarity

The principle of subsidiarity is contained in Article 5, second paragraph TEC. Interesting is the lack of a precise definition. The principle is named and then followed immediately by a set of criteria that give a flavour of what the principle can mean in this context. Protocol 30 equally refrains from defining the principle. According to this protocol the principle provides a guide as to how those powers are to be exercised at the Community level. 'Subsidiarity is a dynamic concept and should be applied in the light of the objectives set out in the Treaty. It allows Community action within the limits of its powers to be expanded where circumstances so require, and conversely, to be restricted or discontinued where it is no longer justified'. We do not learn very much from this characterization.

Fortunately, a European Parliament fact sheet on the matter is more elaborate. It rightly considers the principle of subsidiarity from the perspective of the Member States. This is the only right perspective. In public law the principle forms the institutional basis for federal states. Its general aim is to guarantee a degree of independence for a lower authority in relation to a higher body or for a local authority in respect of a central authority. It therefore involves the sharing of powers between several levels of authority. When applied in a Community context, the principle means that the Member States remain responsible for areas which they are capable of managing more effectively themselves, while the Community is given those powers which the Member States cannot discharge satisfactorily.[9]

As said before, the principle has no impact when the Community has exclusive powers. In areas in which the Treaty gives responsibility to the Community – shared with the Member States – the principle is a yardstick for measuring that responsibility (limiting the exercise of powers). In areas in which the Treaty does not give the Community responsibility, the principle does not create additional competence (no allocation of powers).[10]

This last aspect of the principle is pivotal in a supranational context, but often neglected. It is not because the Community is best placed to do something, as the Protocol seems to suggest, that the Community may do something. No issue is European by nature: there has to be a legal ground for action in the Treaty (principle of attribution of powers).

However, as seen above, the principle of attribution of powers for Community institutions is not absolute. The dividing line between areas that

[9] See 'Subsidiarity' fact sheet 1.2.1, 16 November 2000, p. 1, www.europarl.eu.int.
[10] 'Subsidiarity' *loc. cit.*, p. 2.

fall within the exclusive competence of the Community and those that fall within exclusively national competence is blurred. Next to Article F(4) of the Treaty on European Union,[11] reference should be made to Article 308 (ex Article 235) TEC. On the basis of this provision the Community's areas of competence can be extended, if, for instance, action by the Community proves necessary to attain Treaty objectives.

The demarcation of the areas of exclusive Community competence and of exclusive national competence continues to be a problem, particularly because it is laid down in the Treaties not by reference to specific fields but by means of a functional description.

To solve this problem, Article 5, second paragraph, TEC contains three preconditions for Community action in accordance with the principle of subsidiarity:

- the area concerned must not fall within the Community's exclusive competence;
- the objectives of the proposed action cannot be sufficiently achieved by the Member States; and
- the Community can, by reason of its scale or effects, implement the action more successfully.

Protocol 30 furnishes three additional guidelines that should be used to examine whether the above-mentioned conditions are fulfilled.[12] According to these guidelines:

- the issue under consideration must have transnational aspects that cannot be satisfactorily regulated by action by Member States;
- actions by Member States alone or lack of Community action would conflict with the requirements of the Treaty (such as the need to correct distortion of competition or avoid disguised restrictions on trade or strengthen economic and social cohesion) or would otherwise significantly damage Member States' interests; and
- action at Community level would produce clear benefits by reason of its scale or effects compared with action at the level of the Member States.

[11] According to this provision 'the Union shall provide itself with the means necessary to attain its objectives and carry through its policies'.
[12] Cf. Protocol 30, sub (5).

4.3.3 Justice and Home Affairs and the subsidiarity principle

Protocol 30 does not refer in any way to Justice and Home Affairs. If examples are used in the protocol they refer to economic issues. All seems to suggest that the principle only applies within the areas covered by the first pillar.[13] However, a rather complex reading operation of the Treaties shows that the principle also comes into play in the area of Justice and Home Affairs.

Indeed, Article 5, second paragraph TEC should be read in conjunction with the 12 recital in the preamble to the Treaty on the European Union (TEU)[14] and with Article 2 (ex Article B), last paragraph TEU.[15] As a practical consequence, the principle of subsidiarity applies to all the Community institutions.

A discussion with third pillar officials shows, however, that the principle is rarely taken into account within this structure.[16] Almost all subjects that are put on the working agenda are accepted without discussion. The story goes that only once, with regard to a German initiative on the ownership of dangerous dogs, was opposition made to an inclusion of this issue in the agenda. It is to review all the measures and initiatives taken so far in the area of Justice and Home Affairs.

In particular, the first guideline set out in Protocol 30 with regard to the transnational nature of events seems to create problems with certain third pillar initiatives taken in the past. What is, for instance, so transnational about the Belgian Dutroux case, a child sexual abuse case involving accusations of satanic ritual abuse, and why can it not be satisfactorily regulated by action of Member States? The question becomes all the more pressing since all accusations involving networks of child molesters were dropped (see Klip 1997).[17]

What is, to give a second example, so transnational about traffic security and why do we need Community intervention with regard to safety belts and aid to victims of traffic incidents?

[13] On the first pillar, see below.

[14] 'Resolved to continue the process of creating an ever closer union among the peoples of Europe, in which decisions are taken as closely as possible to the citizen in accordance with the principle of subsidiarity'.

[15] 'The objectives of the Union shall be achieved as provided in this Treaty and in accordance with the conditions and the timetable set out therein while respecting the principle of subsidiarity as defined in Article 5 of the Treaty establishing the European Community'.

[16] On the third pillar, see below.

[17] Comparing, this author heavily criticizes the Joint Action of the European Union on Human Trade and Sexual Abuse (adopted 24 February, 1997, *Official Journal* (*O.J.*) (1997), L63/2)). The document falsely suggests that lack of explicit and updated legislation and international coordination, and not the lack of good management and professionalism as was the case in the Dutroux case, causes sexual child abuse scandals.

The European Parliament regards as priorities the respect of fundamental rights and the opposition to discrimination of any kind. Vietnamese people in Poland are reported to experience many kinds of inconveniences and setbacks. The problem is serious, but is it a European problem? Ethically all kinds of injustice are a problem of mankind, but this is not how a federally inspired principle such as the principle of subsidiarity works.

Why, to give a last example, have a European policy against (the use of) drugs? What legal ground can Europe invoke to defend its decision to monitor the use of drugs in the Member States?[18] In December 1999 the Helsinki European Council adopted an EU action plan on combating drugs (2000–2004).[19] This issue, considered to be a top issue of the internal and external policy of the Union, was met with scepticism by the European Parliament, arguing that the problem is not as much a lack of means or instruments, but absence of political will and far reaching engagement. With regard to the growing acceptance of drug use in certain Member States it is unclear whether all aspects of the action plan would pass a strict application of the principle of subsidiarity.

4.3.4 Strict scrutiny of the principle of subsidiarity?

The principle of subsidiarity is explicitly referred to in Article 5, second paragraph TEC as well as in Article 2 (B) last paragraph TEU and is therefore subject to judicial testing.[20] This has not always been so,[21] and one can hardly say that there exists a tradition of strict scrutiny of the application of the principle. The testing carried out by the Court remains rather theoretical. Where its application is concerned the EU's bodies have wide discretion regarding the form that this takes, which the Court is bound to respect. In

[18] Combating drug addiction became one of the nine areas of 'common interest' in the field of Justice and Home Affairs under the Treaty of Maastricht (*infra*).

[19] The Council approved the plan on 13 September 2000.

[20] In its judgments of 12 November 1996 in Case C-84/94 (*ECR* I-5755) and 13 May 1997 in Case C-233/94 (*ECR* I-2405), the Court found that compliance with the principle of subsidiarity was one of the conditions covered by the requirement to state the reasons for Community acts, under Article 253 (190) TEC. This requirement is met even if the principle is not expressly mentioned in the act's recitals but it is clear from reading the recitals as a whole that the principle has been complied with.

[21] The principle of subsidiarity has not just applied since its incorporation in Article 5 TEC. As long ago as 1951, Article 5 of the ECSC Treaty stipulated that the Community should exert direct influence on production only when circumstances so required. And although it was not expressly so defined, a subsidiarity criterion was included in Article 130r TEEC, on the environment, by the Single European Act in 1987. However, the Court of First Instance of the EC ruled in its judgment of 21 February 1995 that the subsidiarity principle was not a general principle of law, against which the legality of Community action should be tested, before the EU Treaty entered into force. Cf. 'Subsidiarity', *loc. cit.*, 1 with ref. to Court of First Instance, Judgment of 21 February 1995, *ECR*, II-289 at 331.

general terms, it can be said that the extent of the Court's jurisdiction is in inverse proportion to the extent to which the Member States are effectively involved in a decision on the substance that includes: the scale of measures under consideration; whether the consideration of the question of necessity has been thorough and has done justice to the interests involved; and which institutions and legal entities concerned (including those below national level) have been fully consulted.[22]

The foregoing shows that the principle of subsidiarity in its current formulation is not capable of safeguarding a strict division between the national and European sphere. The power of judicial review is limited and much is left to political interplay. This is especially true in the third pillar where almost no action is taken without involvement of the Member States. Whereas in Community matters Member States are considered to be the prime actors in protecting the division (to the benefit of the national sphere that could be endangered), in the third pillar they actually could form a threat to the principle. In its current formulation the principle does not protect against activist states jumping scales for non-legitimate (this is non-treaty based) objectives. Pending proposals to improve the 'reviewability' of the principle are, in this connection, insufficient.[23]

Citizens of the Union cannot derive any rights directly from Article 5, second paragraph, ECT or Article 2, last paragraph TEU. Since Justice and Home Affairs are intimately connected to liberty interest, they should be given a right to have judicial testing done by the Court. Moreover, the principle should be more explicitly reaffirmed in the Treaty chapters on the Third Pillar. The duty to respect the principle should be laid more firmly on the shoulders of the Member States.

Another option is to rewrite Protocol 30. This text obliges the Commission to consult widely before proposing legislation and, wherever appropriate, publish consultation documents and to justify the relevance of its proposals with regard to the principle of subsidiarity; whenever necessary, the explanatory memorandum accompanying a proposal will give details in this respect.[24] This and other obligations that demand a true engagement to the

[22] 'Subsidiarity', *loc. cit.*, 3.

[23] As long ago as 1990 Parliament suggested the introduction of an Article 172 (a) into the TEC to give the Court of Justice the right to determine whether a proposal breaches the limits of Community competence (referral to the Court would take place after a legal act was adopted but before it was implemented, and would be open both to the Member States and the Institutions).

[24] Protocol 30 obliges the Commission to consult widely before proposing legislation and, wherever appropriate, publish consultation documents (except in cases of particular urgency or confidentiality); justify the relevance of its proposals with regard to the principle of subsidiarity; whenever necessary, the explanatory memorandum accompanying a proposal will give details in this respect. The financing of Community action in whole or in part from the Community budget should require an explanation; take duly into account the need for any burden, whether financial or administrative, falling upon the Community, national governments, local authorities,

principles are useful instruments that qualify for being applied to the Member States.

4.4 WHAT MAKES A EUROPEAN JHA ISSUE A FIRST OR THIRD PILLAR ONE?

4.4.1 The Treaties of Maastricht, Amsterdam and Nice

The 1957 treaties establishing the European Communities, the European Coal and Steel Community (ECSC) and the European Atomic Energy Community (EAEC) established the European structure. These treaties have been amended and revised over the years, including by the Single European Act (1987), the Treaty on European Union, 'Maastricht Treaty' (1992), the Treaty of Amsterdam (1997), and lately by the Treaty of Nice (2001) (see Schutte 2000; Cloos et al. 1993).

The Treaty on European Union, known as the Maastricht Treaty, was signed in Maastricht on 7 February 1992 and came into force on 1 November 1993. Supplementing the Community by a more ambitious construct, the European Union, the Maastricht Treaty marked a new step in the process of creating an ever-closer union among the peoples of Europe. The European Union has three pillars. The first pillar is not actually saying anything really new. It consists of the European Communities, providing a framework within which the Member States, through the Community Institutions, can jointly exercise their sovereignty in the areas covered by the Treaties. The second pillar is new. It is a structure meant to elaborate a common foreign and security policy laid down in Title V of the Treaty on European Union. The third pillar is also new and makes possible cooperation in the fields of Justice and Home Affairs laid down in Title VI of the Treaty on European Union.[25]

Maastricht represented only a starting point for further reform. Partisans of a stronger Europe called for reform (see Apap 2002).[26] It triggered a process of reflection on the soundness and effectiveness of the legal framework and of the democratic nature of its procedures (see Ludlow 2001,

economic operators and citizens, to be minimized and proportionate to the objective to be achieved; submit an annual report to the European Council, the European Parliament and the Council on the application of the principle of subsidiarity. This annual report must also be sent to the Committee of the Regions and to the Economic and Social Committee.

[25] Titles V and VI provide for intergovernmental cooperation using the common institutions, with certain supranational features such as associating the Commission and consulting Parliament.

[26] The idea behind three pillars, i.e. three approaches towards Europe, should be viewed as a compromise between the partisans of the intergovernmental method and the partisans of the more communitarian or supranational approach, the former carrying more weight.

p. 23).[27] The Treaty of Amsterdam, signed in Amsterdam on 2 October 1997, was the first outcome of this process. It amends the Treaty on European Union, the treaties establishing the European Communities and certain related acts. This Treaty, which came into force on 1 May 1999, amplifies the content of the Maastricht treaty in five main areas: freedom, security and justice; citizenship of the Union; external policy; EU Institutions and closer cooperation. It also contains provisions aiming to simplify and codify the treaties, in particular by renumbering the Articles and removing from the European Treaties all provisions that the passage of time has rendered void or obsolete.[28]

Again the Treaty of Amsterdam was not considered to be an ending-point. It represented substantial progress on the 'constitutional' bases of EU and Community policies and the process of democratization, but did not include all the institutional reforms (extension of qualified majority voting, re-weighting of votes in the Council and composition of the Commission), desired by institutions such as the European Parliament or partisans of the supranational method.[29] Amsterdam also did not respond to the structural need of cross-pillar coordination that was felt after Maastricht (see Pastore 2002).[30] Provision was made for further institutional adjustment. An intergovernmental conference, convened in February 2000, concentrated on points that had not been resolved in Amsterdam. The result of this conference and the political debates gave way to the Treaty of Nice (see Best 2002).

Once ratified this treaty will make considerable progress towards qualified majority voting and abandon the unanimity requirement for most first pillar issues.[31] The rule of unanimity has a bad press (see Monar 2002).[32] Qualified-majority voting is said to be a more effective system in cases where an

[27] This author uses the term 'Monnet method'.

[28] For legal and political reasons the treaty was signed and submitted for ratification in the form of amendments to the existing treaties. In order to make it more comprehensible and facilitate practical work, a consolidated version of the EU Treaty and the treaty establishing the European Community was published, incorporating all the changes made by the Amsterdam Treaty.

[29] See 'The Maastricht and Amsterdam Treaties: Prospects for the European Union', Fact sheet 1.1.3, published on 16 November, 2000, www.europarl.eu.int.

[30] Some even hold that the integration progresses in both the second and the third pillar (with its splitting and partial communitarization) which followed Amsterdam have made fragmentation risks all the more concrete and, correspondingly, the need for cross-pillar coordination all the more urgent.

[31] For an historical overview and a description of the Nice implications: 'Qualified Majority Voting: General Overview', Fact sheet via http://europa.eu.int/comm/archives/igc2000/geninfo, consulted in December 2002, p. 4.

[32] It is considered to be one of the reasons behind the Union's inability to live up to expectations in areas such as asylum, immigration, judicial cooperation and the fight against international crime.

operational policy needs to be developed (Monar 2002).[33] Since the Amsterdam Treaty (1996), the Council has adopted most legislative instruments by qualified majority and in conjunction with the European Parliament under the co-decision procedure.[34] Most Justice and Home Affairs are however still firmly in the grip of the unanimity rule. The events of 11 September 2001 have stimulated the debate about an extension of qualified majority voting to most areas of Justice and Home Affairs (Monar 2002), but the preliminary post-Nice agenda does not provide for any further reform of the institutions.[35]

4.4.2 The first pillar

At the heart of the EC is the single market with its four basic freedoms (free movement of goods, free movement of workers, freedom to provide services and free movement of capital and payments) and its rules on competition. Policy areas for which the Community is responsible include: economic and monetary affairs (centred around the single European currency, the euro), agriculture, visa requirements, asylum and immigration, transport, taxation, employment, trade, social welfare, education and youth welfare; culture, consumer protection and health, trans-European networks, industry, economic and social cohesion, research and technology, the environment, and development aid.

The first pillar is a contemporary label used for those powers or competencies explicitly conferred to the Community in the treaties establishing the European Communities.[36] Within this framework the

[33] Under the unanimity rule, each Member State has a right of veto. As the number of Member States increases, the danger that one of them may exercise that right increases accordingly. The veto can be used to block the decision-making process.

[34] The policy areas in the first pillar, which remain subject to unanimity, include taxation, industry, culture, regional and social funds and the framework programme for research and technology development.

[35] This ending of institutional reform was backed up with the argument that all the big projects required to construct a political union, with most if not all the attributes of a European state – EMU, the Single Market, the Area of Freedom, Security and Justice, the Common Foreign, Security and Defence Policy – are underway. Critical of this view, arguing that many issues and questions are still unresolved is Ludlow, 2001, p. 2. Note however, that in 2004 a new intergovernmental conference is to be convened to consider a more precise delimitation of competencies between the European Union and the Member States, the status of the Charter of Fundamental Rights, simplification of the treaties and the role of the national parliaments, Best, 2002, p. 8.

[36] The first pillar is made up of the three European Communities (EEC, Euratom, ECSC), which have been deepened and enlarged by economic and monetary union. When the EU was established, the European Economic Community was renamed the European Community. The EEC Treaty became the EC Treaty. This change was intended to give expression to the transition from a purely economic community to a political union. However, this change of name did not affect the three existing Communities (ECSC, Euratom, EC) since it did not entail any formal

Community institutions may draw up legislation in their respective areas of responsibility. This EC law applies directly in the Member States and may claim precedence over national law.

Until 1993 there was only this one pillar, and there was definitely no such thing as a third pillar creating a European forum to discuss matters relating to public order. Justice and Home Affairs did not exist as a policy-making area within the scope of the Treaties (Monar 2002). Law enforcement or operational policies are national prerogatives. The Member States are also responsible for the enforcement of Community law. Matters relating to public order remained the sole playing ground of the Member States and in particular their Ministries of Justice and of the Interior, a situation which gave birth to the term 'Justice and Home Affairs'. Community law had simply nothing to say on such matters.

Hence, Europe remained a merely economical instrument until the late 1990s and important initiatives in the field of Justice and Home Affairs, such as Trevi and Schengen,[37] were set up outside the European structure. This was a deliberate choice due to sensitivities about sovereignty and problems of a practical and ideological nature. Unlike the single market, cooperation and policy-making in this area involves continuing and increasingly intensive cooperation between government agencies in the Member States. Moreover, creating a European judicial area involves policy convergence and approximation of laws. It also involves ideological concepts – e.g. 'a high level of security' as well as argument on basic values. All these may be conceived differently in different national settings.

unification of them. In the course of the establishment of the EU, some institutions of the EC changed their names. The Council of the European Communities has since 8 November 1993 been referred to as the Council of the European Union. The Commission of the European Communities has become the European Commission. On 17 January 1994, the Court of Auditors was renamed the European Court of Auditors. However, the legal acts of the respective bodies still constitute legal acts of the Community at any given time.

[37] Formal police cooperation between the Member States' representatives began in 1976 with the creation of working parties known as 'Trevi groups'. Its main subjects were terrorism and the organization and training problems of police departments. By 1989 there were four working parties, on terrorism, police cooperation, organized crime and the free movement of persons, headed by a group of senior civil servants responsible for preparing decisions for the Council of Ministers. This system prefigured the intergovernmental structure set up by the Schengen agreements and the Treaty of Maastricht. In the early 1990s a majority of 13 EU Member States had jointly paved the way for reinforced cooperation in multiple areas, such as external borders control, asylum policy, and police and justice cooperation in criminal matters, through the Schengen Agreements. From the outset, Schengen was launched as a temporary initiative in order to test a common framework of internal security control and to gradually expand this framework to the whole European Community. This integration was meant to bring an end to the undesirable external institutional, political and legal existence outside the European Union. The incorporation of the Schengen acquis into the framework of the European Union became a fact when the Treaty on European Union (TEU) entered into force on 1 May 1999.

As a consequence, the Community has never adopted any directives or regulations aimed at the harmonization of rules of procedural, civil administrative or criminal law in the Member States.[38] However, the water runs wherever there is a hole. Communitarian initiatives with a Justice and Home Affairs stamp did see the light within the European structure. As early as 1962 a working group dealing with the criminal aspects of Community law was set up by the European Commission (see Thomas 1993, Bleeker 1993 and Stessens 1994). Before Maastricht, and with no clear authorization, the Community was accommodating the request to elaborate legislation at EC level covering new forms of offences with an international character (see Demanet 1985). The EC Community was pushing Member States to adopt criminal sanctions with regard to money laundering, drugs and weapon trafficking (Buruma 1995).

One important initiative was the creation in 1989 of the Anti-Fraud Unit of the European Commission (UCLAF) with a view to protecting the financial interests of the European Communities (see De Hert 1995). UCLAF (since 1999 OLAF) plays a coordinating role in the complex investigations in the Member States concerning the prosecution of this form of serious crime. Furthermore, the 1991 EC Money Laundering Directive obliged the Member States to create financial intelligence structures that collect and analyse information from financial institutions on irregular and/or suspicious transactions. The foregoing examples show that some Justice and Home Affairs issues were dealt with within the Community structure (first pillar) without explicit mandate. We will see in the following sections that after the creation of a specific structure ('pillar') next to this first pillar, more issues will be transferred to the Community institutions.

4.4.3 The third pillar

We have seen how the Treaty on European Union added further dimensions to the construction of Europe. It integrated an existing economical construct into a political union under construction. At once Justice and Home Affairs stopped being purely national issues. Cooperation in this area became one of the objectives of the new political construct. According to Article B of the TEU in the Maastricht version 'The Union shall set itself the following objectives: (....) to develop close cooperation on Justice and Home Affairs (...)'.

The way this objective should be developed is worked out in Title VI of the TEU, 'Provisions on cooperation in the fields of justice and home affairs'.

[38] 'Under the terms of the Community treaties (...) the harmonisation or approximation of the provisions of procedural law of the Member States was not considered a Community objective, even if it could be argued that such harmonisation is not necessarily excluded by the terms of Article 100, 100a and 235 TEC (in the Treaty of Maastricht versions)', in Schutte, 2000, p. 45.

This title contains a list of areas of 'common interest', drawn up by the Member States that negotiated the Treaty on European Union. This ambitious list included matters relating to asylum, immigration, controls at the Union's external frontiers, drugs, international fraud, civil and criminal justice, customs cooperation and police cooperation, particularly against international crime and terrorism.[39] Through the third pillar European cooperation in this field of Justice and Home Affairs is made possible.[40] The widening of the scope of the European institutions was deemed necessary to maintain and develop the Union as an Area of Freedom, Security and Justice (AFSJ), in which the free movement of persons is assured (cf. Article 2 TEU). Europeanization of Justice and Home Affairs was seen as part of a series of flanking measures intended to compensate for the security deficit arguably arising from the abolition of internal border control. This explanation, rooted in the idea of subsidiarity,[41] may account for issues such as asylum,

[39] The first Article of this Title (Article K.1.) states that: 'For the purpose of achieving the objectives of the Union, in particular the free movement of persons, and without prejudice to the powers of the European Community, Member States shall regard the following areas as matters of common interest: 1. asylum policy; 2. rules governing the crossing by persons of the external borders of the Member States and the exercise of controls thereon; 3. immigration policy and policy regarding nationals of third countries:

(a) conditions of entry and movement by nationals of third countries on the territory of Member States;
(b) conditions of residence by nationals of third countries on the territory of Member States, including family reunion and access to employment;
(c) combating unauthorised immigration, residence and work by nationals of third countries on the territory of Member States;

4. combating drug addiction in so far as this is not covered by 7 to 9; 5. combating fraud on an international scale in so far as this is not covered by 7 to 9; 6. judicial cooperation in civil matters; 7. judicial cooperation in criminal matters; 8. customs cooperation; 9. police cooperation for the purpose of preventing and combating terrorism, unlawful drug-trafficking and other serious forms of international crime, including if necessary certain aspects of customs cooperation, in connection with the organisation of a Union-wide system for exchanging information within a European Police Office (Europol)'.

[40] The third pillar brings together the Ministries of Justice and of the Interior, and their departments, of the Member States of the European Union. The Community institutions (Council, Parliament, Commission and court) are also involved. The third pillar permits dialogue, mutual assistance, joint effort and cooperation between the police, customs, immigration services and justice departments of the Member States. See Council of the EU (2002), European fact sheet on Cooperation in the Field of Justice and Home Affairs, Office of European Publications, Luxembourg.

[41] By doing away with the frontiers between Member States, the latter were deprived of an important national instrument for controlling and filtering the entry and identity of persons and ensuring internal security within their territory. A person present in one state can cross the frontiers of another state without hindrance, whether land, air or sea frontiers. To ensure the same level of security without that tool, controls at the external frontiers, i.e. between a Member State of the Union and a third state, need to be strengthened and solidarity between the states of the Union should be guaranteed: any state responsible for controls at frontiers with a third

immigration and control of frontiers, but does it account for the inclusion of issues such as drugs and organized crime? On one of the European fact sheets the question is answered positively, but a closer look reveals a quick step from 'problems of great concern to all the Member States' to 'problems that should be dealt with on a European level'.[42]

It is closer to the truth behind the third pillar list, to consider a part of this list as an attempt to rationalize various ongoing initiatives regarding police, customs and judicial cooperation which were launched by the Member States in the 1970s (judicial cooperation, for example, originated in the framework of the Council of Europe and dates back to the 1950s). Groups of experts in various areas used to meet and they multiplied on an intergovernmental basis, with no direct link with the European Communities.

The Treaty on European Union, and in particular Title VI of the treaty, provided a framework for that cooperation. It provided a new structure with a permanent secretariat, combined efforts and named the actors and joint instruments for dealing with sensitive issues.[43] Another way of understanding Maastricht and of viewing the third pillar is to look at it as a settlement between two opposing views on the future of Europe: supranational or intergovernmental. Through the third pillar idea the partisans of the intergovernmental method are given comfort in areas related to Justice and Home Affairs (see Apap 2002). In light of this discussion between supranationalism and intergovernmentalism, it is important to read through the legal provisions with care. All the terms used have their meaning. The policy

country is automatically the guarantor not only of its own security, but also of the security of the other states of the Union. The strengthening of the Union's external frontiers, a measure to compensate for the disappearance of internal frontiers, requires increased cooperation between the interior and justice ministries and, more particularly, the police forces, customs and immigration services. Therefore, the Tampere European Council of October 1999 adopted an ambitious work programme clearly stating the need to manage these policies at Community level. In a large area where there are no internal borders, the Member States will no longer be able to manage the movement of third-country nationals at national level alone. (Qualified-Majority Voting: Visas, Asylum and Immigration, http://europa.eu.int/comm/archives/igc2000).

[42] 'The Member States of the European Union can no longer tackle certain problems in dispersed order, but must combine their efforts. Drugs, organised crime, international fraud, trafficking in human beings and the sexual exploitation of children are all problems of great concern to all the Member States of the European Union. These disorders know no frontiers. The aim of the European Union is to become an area of freedom, security and justice, and not an area for all manner of trafficking. The Union's citizens want to be able to benefit fully from the freedom of movement being brought about by the development of the Union, and at the same time to be protected from threats to their personal security. That security must remain an important objective in the context of enlargement of the Union', Chapter II 'Is there a need for cooperation in the fields of Justice and Home Affairs?' in Council of the EU (2002), European fact sheet on *Cooperation in the Field of Justice and Home Affairs*, Office of European Publications, Luxembourg.

[43] Cf. Chapter IV. 'Is cooperation in the field of Justice and Home Affairs effective?' in fact sheet on *Cooperation in the Field of Justice and Home Affairs*, *loc. cit.*, pp. 7–8.

sectors covered by Title VI in the Maastricht version of the TEU are not 'powers', but 'matters of common interest' (Apap 2002).[44] Moreover the policy sectors are only picked up on a European level 'for the purpose of achieving the objectives of the Union', and 'without prejudice to the powers of the European Community'. Also it is not said that these matters of common interest fall completely under the third pillar construction. The language used for areas such as 'immigration policy'; 'conditions of residence by nationals of third countries' and the fight against 'drug addiction' is much less restrictive than that for 'fraud', 'civil matters' and 'criminal matters'. Only transnational aspects of these second groups or domains are considered.

It is not easy to describe what the third pillar really involved in the period between the entry into force of the Treaty of Maastricht and the entry into force of the Treaty of Amsterdam. A closer look reveals that the focus is merely on facilitating international cooperation, not on harmonization of criminal laws or rules of procedure or on operational policies.[45] Without doubt this prudent use of the third pillar is due to legal impediments,[46] legal vagueness,[47] and self-imposed intergovernmental caution.[48] Everything that came close to the hearth of law enforcement was dealt with in conventions, all the rest was dealt with in soft-law instruments such as resolutions and joint actions.[49]

[44] This author considers these terms as a 'weak statement of intent'.

[45] Under the heading 'cooperation in civil matters', the third pillar actors dealt with problems connected with the mutual recognition of judgments in divorce or child custody cases or commercial questions (bankruptcy) where two or more Member States are involved. Cooperation in criminal matters concerned questions relating to extradition or mutual legal assistance.

[46] Article K.5. TEU (Maastricht version) is very clear with regard to operational policies: 'This Title shall not affect the exercise of the responsibilities incumbent upon Member States with regard to the maintenance of law and order and the safeguarding of internal security'.

[47] Article K.3 only stated that 'Member States shall inform and consult one another within the Council with a view to coordinating their action'. Article K. TEU scarcely developed the way these areas of common interest should be tackled. There was for instance no clarification of whether the cooperation was intended to provide for and/or encourage legislative initiatives, or whether practical operational cooperation was the objective. Cf. Apap, 2002, p. 46.

[48] This attitude also accounts for the choice of soft law whenever sensible subjects such as harmonization of criminal law was on the agenda. Cf. Joint Action of 17 December 1996 adopted by the Council on the basis of Article K.3 of the Treaty on the European Union concerning the approximation of the laws and practices of the Member States of the European Union to combat drug addiction and to prevent and combat illegal drug trafficking, OJ L 342, 31 December 1996.

[49] Compare 'During the period between the entry into force of the Treaty of Maastricht on 1 November 1993 and the entry into force of the Treaty of Amsterdam in 1999, a considerable number of legal instruments have been adopted by the Council of the European Union in the field of Justice and Home Affairs, including on judicial and police cooperation in criminal matters. In the judicial and police field there are some 17 Conventions (including protocols to Conventions), more than 20 'Joint Actions' and a dozen resolutions and recommendations. Going through these instruments, one notes that questions related to harmonisation or

4.4.4 First observation about the division between pillars conceived by Maastricht

Theoretically the division as conceived in the beginning of the Union, as worked out in Maastricht, is very simple: all Justice and Home Affairs mentioned in the third pillar list have to be dealt with in the third pillar. Improper use of the first pillar, for instance to impose the use of criminal sanctions in a certain area, is from now on forbidden. Any matters falling within the scope of the objectives of the first and third pillars have to be realized in common through the procedures set out in the treaties and with the legal consequences the treaties attach thereto, whereas any matters falling outside the scope of these objectives cannot be realized through such procedures.

If the creators of the Union wish to confer new powers on it, they have to do so by amending the existing treaties, which implies the convening of a conference of representatives of the governments of the Member States, the results of which must be subject to ratification by the High Contracting Parties in accordance with their constitutional requirements.[50] The same procedure has to be followed when the Community institutions want to handle third pillar issues within the first pillar: this is simply impossible without proper amending of the treaties.

In reality this simple representation of the division after Maastricht should be handled with care, since:

- not all Justice and Home Affairs were excluded from the first pillar. It was never the purpose to prohibit the creation and functioning of initiatives such as OLAF within the traditional Community structures or to infringe on other Community powers or policies;[51]
- after Amsterdam the division will be blurred to a further degree through a transfer of Justice and Home Affairs from the third to the first pillar.

approximation of rules in the field of procedural criminal law have hardly been touched' (Schutte, 2000, p. 48).

[50] As provided in Article N TEU in the Treaty of Maastricht version. Cf. Schutte, 2000, pp. 43–4.

[51] According to Article K.I. in the Maastricht version of the TEU, cooperation in the areas listed has to be conducted 'without prejudice to the powers of the European Community'. However, and notwithstanding this provision, did the third pillar list give way to policies that occasionally clashed and overlapped with Community policies? Should drugs issues fall into the net of health policy (Community) or that of CJHA (trafficking, drug dependency)? Should not questions of asylum, immigration and external frontiers be dealt with in the context of freedom of movement of persons, in a Community framework?, in *Cooperation in the Field of Justice and Home Affairs*, *loc. cit.*, pp. 7–8.

- the division of competence within the third pillar between European and national competences is far from clear-cut. The third pillar is a typical area of mixed powers. This mix has been remixed by the Amsterdam and Nice treaties, with a partial intergovernmentalization of the first pillar as a remarkable result.[52]

4.4.5 A short comment on the working methods in the pillars

The first pillar is designed and implemented according to a well-proven decision-making process that starts with a Commission proposal. Following detailed examination by experts and at the political level, the Council of Ministers may adopt the Commission proposal, amend it or ignore it. The Treaty of Maastricht strengthened the role of the European Parliament in this context by creating a co-decision procedure. As a consequence, a wide range of legislation (such as that pertaining to the single market, consumer affairs, trans-European networks, education and health) has been adopted by both the Parliament and the Council.[53]

The Community's forms of action under Article 249 TEC are regulations, directives, decisions, recommendations and opinions. Recommendations and opinions have no binding force and do not establish any rights or obligations for those to whom they are addressed. Community measures, whenever they are intended to be binding take the form of regulations, directives or decisions.

The Treaty of Maastricht did not implement cooperation in the third pillar in the same way. Given the great sensitivity of matters relating to justice and home affairs, the Maastricht Treaty accorded very great weight to the Member States and to the bodies of the European Union in which they participate directly. The powers of the European Commission, the European Parliament and the Court of Justice have been limited for the same reason (see De Hert 1995).[54] From this viewpoint, implementation of Justice and Home Affairs was very different from the implementation of Community policies.

[52] See on Title IV TEU in the Amsterdam version, 'Visas, Asylum, Immigration and other Policies related to the Free Movement of Goods'.

[53] The social partners and other interest groups are consulted via the Economic and Social Committee and local and regional authorities represented in the Committee of the Regions in a number of fields.

[54] As far as the decision-making machinery of the third pillar under Maastricht is concerned, the key decision-making body was the Council, comprising the Ministers of Home Affairs and Justice. It acted unanimously, under Article K.4 (3) TEU. The Committee of Permanent Representatives and a Coordinating Committee of senior civil servants, the 'K4 Committee', prepared its decisions under Article K.4. The right of initiative lay, depending on the sector, either with the Member States or the Commission, which had to be fully associated with all such work under Article K.3 TEU. They informed and consulted Parliament in certain areas, as its views had to be 'duly taken into consideration'.

Moreover, under the Treaty of Maastricht, the third pillar lacked the legal instruments such as 'directives' or 'regulations' which exist for Community policies. It used only instruments that were specific to the third pillar.

To create a new Area of Freedom, Security and Justice under a new Title IV of the Treaty establishing the European Community, the Amsterdam Treaty moved a good deal of the Maastricht third pillar into the Community sphere, although the decision-making procedures and the powers of the Court of Justice do not strictly speaking comply with Community rules. The decision-making machinery and the instruments of the third pillar, now confined to police and judicial cooperation on criminal matters, were enriched with some Community aspects (see Flore 1999, and Den Boer 1997).

However, the Treaty of Amsterdam did not touch upon the fundamental intergovernmental logic behind the third pillar and the newly rewritten Title VI in the EU Treaty on 'police and judicial cooperation in criminal matters' still preserves intergovernmental procedures, requiring unanimous decisions. This is partly softened by the consultation procedure. This procedure requires an opinion from the Parliament before the Council can adopt a legal measure (the Council is not obliged to accept the amendments listed in the opinion of the Parliament). This consultation procedure has become the common rule in first pillar areas such as agriculture (price review), taxation, competition, harmonization of legislation not related to the single market, industrial policy, aspects of social and environmental policy (subject to unanimity). For the purpose of the approximation of laws and regulations, this procedure also applies to a new framework-decision instrument created by the Amsterdam Treaty under the third pillar.

Before discussing the changes brought in with the Treaty of Amsterdam in more detail, it is useful to ask why changes to the third pillar were needed that speedily after Maastricht. The European Parliament strongly criticized the choice of the 'intergovernmental method' for the third pillar, which it considered ineffective and preventing Parliament and the Court from exercising any scrutiny in the area.[55]

Others insisted on the tedious working structure of the pillar, the relatively high number of soft law instruments and the weak implementation record of the third pillar instruments in the Member States (Den Boer 1997). Observers foresaw a number of frictions potentially arise from the political decision-making processes – non-ratification of third pillar conventions; decisions by the European Council not followed up by practical measures; legislative fatigue/blockages. In this perspective all arguments (efficiency, democratic and judicial control) seem to be in favour of transferring justice and home

[55] 'Justice and Home Affairs: general aspects', fact sheet 4.11.1, published 16 November 2000, www.europarl.eu.int p. 5.

affairs to the first pillar (optimal alternative) or of modelling the third pillar after the first pillar (second best alternative).[56] Both alternatives were in fact proposed by the Treaty of Amsterdam, which has been refined in turn by the Treaty of Nice.

4.4.6 Changes to the first pillar brought in with the Amsterdam Treaty

The third pillar has been decisively reorganized by the Treaty of Amsterdam – areas have been changed, new legal instruments added, the role of the Community bodies defined and enhanced cooperation clarified. The most remarkable change seems to be the remix of the division between the two pillars. The transfer of competence of the third pillar towards the first pillar is impressive (Apap 2002). With the entry into force of the Treaty of Amsterdam, civil law matters, asylum and immigration became community matters, with police and judicial cooperation in criminal matters remaining within the third pillar.

Hence, cooperation in civil matters is no longer an intergovernmental power.[57] Some of the other transferred elements of the previous Title VI, namely policy on visas, asylum, immigration and other policies connected with the free movement of persons, were lifted to the new Title IV of the Amsterdam version on European Union, entitled 'Visas, Asylum, Immigration and other Policies related to the Free Movement of Goods' (see Apap 2002 and Cholewinsky 2002). As a result, measures pertaining to the abolition of internal border controls, external borders, visa policy, asylum, refugees, immigration policy and legally resident third-country nationals, and judicial cooperation in civil matters now form part of EC law.[58]

The idea behind this transfer is that questions of asylum, immigration and external frontiers are better dealt with in the context of freedom of movement of persons, which is a Community framework. The highly sensible nature of these powers leaves no doubt.[59] The decision-making procedures for these

[56] Later on we will argue that this presentation truncates democratic reasoning.

[57] The issue was not only transferred to the first pillar, but also deepened. According to the new Article 65 TEC, measures may be adopted in the field of judicial cooperation in civil matters with cross-border implications and where necessary for the proper functioning of the internal market. On this basis an opening has been made for the adoption of Community rules governing civil proceedings in national courts, which was not accepted before. More in detail: Schutte, 2000, pp. 45–6.

[58] According to the new Article 63, paragraph 1 point (d) TEC the Council is to adopt 'minimum standards on procedures in member states for granting or withdrawing refugee status', which opens the door for the establishment of certain common provisions governing administrative procedures in immigration matters.

[59] A privacy related issue such as the Eurodac database system was adopted on the basis of a Community regulation, Council regulation EC 2725/2000 concerning the establishment of Eurodac for the comparison of fingerprints for the effective application of the Dublin Convention, OJ L 316, 11 December 2000.

issues and the powers of the Court of Justice do not strictly speaking comply with Community rules.[60] The transfer is no more than a partial communitarization operation (Pastore 2000).[61] With regard to the judicial powers, it is however important to note that where areas brought under the Community are concerned, the Court is competent to interpret the new Title of the Treaty and to decide on the validity and interpretation of acts done by the Community institutions when an issue is raised before a national court whose decisions are not subject to appeal under national law and which requests the Court to rule on a question of interpretation or acts done by the Community institutions.

Another provision, newly introduced by the Amsterdam Treaty, might confer even greater powers on the Community in the area of Justice and Home Affairs. Article 280.1 TEC states that:

> The Community and the Member States shall counter fraud and any other illegal activities affecting the financial interests of the Community through measures to be taken in accordance with this Article, which shall act as a deterrent and be such as to afford effective protection in the Member States.

According to paragraph 3, the Member States will organize 'together with the Commission, close and regular cooperation between the competent authorities' and according to paragraph 4, the Community 'shall adopt the necessary measures in the fields of the prevention of and fight against fraud affecting the financial interests of the Community with a view to affording effective and equivalent protection in the Member States'. Enforcement of Community law stops being an exclusive prerogative of the Member States (see Veld Foglia 2002[62]).

[60] The Treaty of Amsterdam lays down that, for a transitional period of five years following its entry into force, the Council will in general act unanimously on a proposal from the Commission or on the initiative of a Member State and after consulting the European Parliament. After this period, the Council will act on proposals from the Commission, which will henceforth acquire sole right of initiative. However, the Commission must examine any request by a Member State that it submit a proposal to the Council. With regard to the decision-making procedure, it is laid down that the Council, acting unanimously after consulting the European Parliament, may take a decision with a view to making all or part of the areas covered by this Title subject to the co-decision procedure. As regards the procedures and requirements for the issue of visas by the Member States and rules on uniform visas, the Treaty provides for the co-decision procedure to apply after the transitional period without the Council having to take a decision. See: Apap, 2000, p. 47.

[61] Some even suggest that the whole operation comes down to the introduction of intergovernmental actors and logic in the first pillar.

[62] On the more important role of the Community due to Article 280 TEC, the extensive interpretation of this role by the Commission and the correct interpretation of paragraph 4. In addition, the need to afford 'equivalent protection' in all the Member States may require an assessment of the procedural rules applicable in these states. However Article 280 TEC does not allow for measures by the Community aimed at the approximation of criminal and other judicial

The clearest examples of new Community powers in matters relating to public order have to do with police and border control activities. Under a new Article 135 in the EC Treaty, the Treaty of Amsterdam strengthens cooperation among national customs administrations and between them and the Commission. Even more meaningful is the incorporation of the Schengen acquis into the framework of the European Union. This incorporation became a fact when the Treaty on European Union entered into force on 1 May 1999 and was accompanied by a partial communitarization process, in which some elements of the Schengen machinery were lifted to the Community sphere (see Den Boer 2000).[63]

By way of conclusion we can say that the Community method now applies to some major areas which hitherto came under the third pillar such as asylum, immigration, crossing external borders, combating fraud, customs cooperation and some of the cooperation under the Schengen Agreement, which the EU and Communities have endorsed in full.

4.4.7 Changes to the third pillar brought in with the Amsterdam Treaty

As regards Title VI of the Treaty on European Union, i.e. areas still covered by the third pillar (police and judicial cooperation in criminal matters), the treaty lays down that the Union is to provide citizens with a high level of safety within an area of freedom, security and justice by developing common action among the Member States in the fields of police and judicial cooperation in criminal matters and by preventing and combating racism and xenophobia. Article 29 (ex Article K.1) Treaty on European Union states that:

> Without prejudice to the powers of the European Community, the Union's objective shall be to provide citizens with a high level of safety within an area of freedom, security and justice by developing common action among the Member States in the fields of police and judicial cooperation in criminal matters and by preventing and combating racism and xenophobia. That objective shall be achieved by preventing and combating crime, organised or otherwise, in particular terrorism, trafficking in persons and offences against children, illicit drug

proceedings, since Article 280, paragraph 4 goes on to say that these measures 'shall not concern the application of national criminal law or the national administration of justice', Cf. Schutte, 2000, p. 46.

[63] See Protocol (No 2) to the TEU integrating the Schengen acquis into the framework of the European Union (1997). The Schengen acquis consists of the following elements: Agreement signed in Schengen on 14 June 1985; Implementation Convention signed in Schengen on 19 June 1990; Accession Protocols and Agreements; and Decisions and declarations adopted by the Executive Committee as well as acts adopted by the organs upon which it has conferred decision–making powers. According to the Protocol only those provisions of Schengen relating to policing and criminal judicial cooperation are moved into the third pillar, whereas all the other provisions, including a part of those regarding the Schengen Information System, are integrated into the first pillar.

> trafficking and illicit arms trafficking, corruption and fraud, through: closer cooperation between police forces, customs authorities and other competent authorities in the Member States, both directly and through the European Police Office (Europol), in accordance with the provisions of Articles 30 and 32; closer cooperation between judicial and other competent authorities of the Member States in accordance with the provisions of Articles 31(a) to (d) and 32; and approximation, where necessary, of rules on criminal matters in the Member States, in accordance with the provisions of Article 31(e).[64]

The three objectives (police cooperation, criminal cooperation, approximation of criminal law) in the second paragraph of Article 29 TEU are spelled out more in detail in the subsequent Articles. Article 31 gives a good feel of the wideness of the domains covered, but Article 31(e), especially, shows that not everything is 'given' to European forum.[65] A harmonization of criminal law, for instance, per se is not envisaged.

A similar message is sent out by Article 33 TEU (ex Article K.5)[66] and the provision in Article 280, paragraph 4 TEC safeguarding 'the application of national criminal law or the national administration of justice'.

Note the different wording of Article 29 compared to ex Article K.1. Under Article K.1 the forms of cooperation listed were considered as matters of common interest 'for the purpose of achieving the objectives of the Union, in particular the free movement of persons'. In the new formulation 'security' is no longer a flanking instrument to this objective, but a self-standing objective of the Union. According to Article 2 TEU (ex Article B):

[64] Note that after the ratification of the Nice Treaty by the Member States, Article 29, second paragraph will also mention the possibility of cooperation through Eurojust. In Article 29, second paragraph, the second indent will be replaced by the following: 'closer cooperation between judicial and other competent authorities of the Member States, including cooperation through the European Judicial Cooperation Unit (Eurojust), in accordance with the provisions of Articles 31 and 32'. Eurojust is a unit constituted of judges, magistrates, prosecutors and legal experts from the Member States, with responsibility for coordinating criminal investigations in matters pertaining to the interests of the EU and/or of several Member States.

[65] Article 31: '1. Common action on judicial cooperation in criminal matters shall include:

> (a) facilitating and accelerating cooperation between competent ministries and judicial or equivalent authorities of the Member States, including, where appropriate, cooperation through Eurojust, in relation to proceedings and the enforcement of decisions;
> (b) facilitating extradition between Member States;
> (c) ensuring compatibility in rules applicable in the Member States, as may be necessary to improve such cooperation;
> (d) preventing conflicts of jurisdiction between Member States;
> (e) progressively adopting measures establishing minimum rules relating to the constituent elements of criminal acts and to penalties in the fields of organised crime, terrorism and illicit drug trafficking (...)'.

[66] 'This Title shall not affect the exercise of the responsibilities incumbent upon Member States with regard to the maintenance of law and order and the safeguarding of internal security'.

> The Union shall set itself the following objectives: (...) to maintain and develop the Union as an area of freedom, security and justice, in which the free movement of persons is assured in conjunction with appropriate measures with respect to external border controls, asylum, immigration and the prevention and combating of crime (see Schutte 2000).

This different wording underlines the purpose of the Amsterdam modification of the third pillar: 'strengthening of the intergovernmental cooperation in the areas of police and judicial cooperation'. This new wording aiming at defining the objectives of the third pillar has not only strengthened the cooperation; new legal instruments have been created, similar to Community instruments,[67] and existing provisions have been enriched. This time the provisions contain a list of very precise tasks indicating how the (new) objectives of the Union in the area of justice and home affairs (now 'Freedom, Security and Justice') have to be met. A closer look at the newly formulated provisions of the third pillars can illustrate our point. Article 29 *in fine* TEU refers to the provisions of Article 31(e). This Article states that common action on judicial cooperation in criminal matters shall include: 'progressively adopting measures establishing minimum rules relating to the constituent elements of criminal acts and to penalties in the fields of organised crime, terrorism and illicit drug trafficking'.

Hence, harmonization of criminal law forms one of the tasks serving the objectives of the new Union.[68] Harmonization of rules of criminal procedure is not explicitly mentioned as one of the tasks of the pillar-actors, but, provided that such a measure would improve judicial cooperation, the possibility of such a harmonization cannot be excluded, since some of the provisions of Articles 30, 31 and 32 TEU address problems of criminal procedure (see Schutte 2000).[69]

[67] We will come back to these new instruments below.

[68] Not everything, of course. The provisions underline the importance of fighting organized crime. Provision is only made for coordinating the national rules on offences and penalties applicable to organized crime, terrorism and drug trafficking.

[69] See for instance: Article 30, paragraph 1(d), and Article 31(c)1. 'Common action in the field of police cooperation will include:

> (a) operational cooperation between the competent authorities, including the police, customs and other specialized law enforcement services of the Member States in relation to the prevention, detection and investigation of criminal offences;
> (b) the collection, storage, processing, analysis and exchange of relevant information, including information held by law enforcement services on reports on suspicious financial transactions, in particular through Europol, subject to appropriate provisions on the protection of personal data;
> (c) cooperation and joint initiatives in training, the exchange of liaison officers, secondments, the use of equipment, and forensic research;
> (d) the common evaluation of particular investigative techniques in relation to the detection of serious forms of organized crime'.

4.4.8 Second observation about the division between the first and third pillar

In our first observation about the division between pillars, we gave the following 'simple' representation of the division of competences after Maastricht:

1. all Justice and Home Affairs mentioned in the third pillar list have to be dealt with in the third pillar.
2. if the creators of the Union wish to confer new powers on it, they have to do so by amending the existing treaties; and
3. the same procedure has to be followed when the Community institutions want to handle third pillar issues within the first pillar: this is simply impossible without proper amending of the treaties.

The method of division between the first and the third pillar is based on the idea or principle of attribution of powers, and not on the more flexible principle of subsidiarity. One could ask if this principle of subsidiarity still has a meaning in the light of points 2 and 3. Before Maastricht the treaties told us only what was in the Community. After Maastricht we also know from the treaties what is in the Union, but not in the Community. With the advent of a large political construct wherein almost all aspects of public life are covered by one of the three pillars, the principle of subsidiarity loses much of its meaning.

The advantage of the principle of attribution of powers is clear: the division is more clear-cut. One only has to consult the third pillar list, to know its competencies. In this respect, the formulation of areas of common interest in the third pillar does not only represent a broadening of European competencies, but also a tool for Member States to control European dynamics.

The Member States' willingness to 'limit their sovereign rights' by recognizing a role for Europe in second and third pillar matters was only possible in the first place, and has only been expanded over time, because the Member States wrote themselves into the supranational game, firstly as the ultimate arbiters of what should or should not bind them, secondly as those responsible in the final analysis for providing the Union 'with the necessary impetus for its development' and thirdly, in large and ever larger areas of public policy as the 'executive arm' of the Union. The result of this strategic move is a *sui generis* system of 'supranational intergovernmentalism' (see Ludlow 2001[70]).

[70] The EU's supranational system is founded on intergovernmental agreement and is only effective because the Member States themselves have become, collectively in the Council, and

Hence, the analogy with a federal system becomes less appropriate. This also accounts for the principle of subsidiarity, traditionally conceived to protect a degree of independence for a lower authority in relation to a higher body or for a local in relationship to a federal body. In the new European system based on a division list or on the principle of attribution of power other kinds of guarantees are needed, this time for all parties involved and not only for the 'lower' bodies. Hence, the formulation of new guarantees to the benefit of the Community structures such as the rule that all forms of cooperation possible within the Union structures cannot affect the policies and forms of cooperation foreseen in the Community treaties.[71]

At least from a national perspective this full restoration of the principle of attribution of power has the advantage of transparency in the power division. The possible disadvantage, i.e. lack of flexibility, is avoided in practice by the 'Monnet method', the process of the permanent reworking of the institutional arrangements through amendment of the relevant provisions in subsequent

severally at the level of administration, central elements in it. 'To relegate the states to a relatively minor role in a European Bundesrat would not only be impossible, it would also be self-defeating. The EU system, though supranational, is shot through with inter governmentalism' (ibid). On the other hand, the Council may be intergovernmental in composition, it is however supranational in the way in which it works and in the effect that its decisions have on the Member States. As for the latter, they are at one and the same time sovereign actors and agents of a supranational authority.

[71] This follows from the new Article 47 of the TEU, which states that '(....) nothing in this Treaty (i.e. the TEU) shall affect the Treaties establishing the European Communities or subsequent Treaties and Acts modifying or supplementing them'. Echoes of this provision are to be found in Article 43 TEU on the enhanced cooperation: 'Member States which intend to establish enhanced cooperation between themselves may make use of the institutions, procedures and mechanisms laid down by this Treaty and by the Treaty establishing the European Community provided that the proposed cooperation.

(a) is aimed at furthering the objectives of the Union and of the Community, at protecting and serving their interests and at reinforcing their process of integration;
(b) respects the said Treaties and the single institutional framework of the Union;
(c) respects the acquis communautaire and the measures adopted under the other provisions of the said Treaties;
(d) remains within the limits of the powers of the Union or of the Community and does not concern the areas which fall within the exclusive competence of the Community;
(e) does not undermine the internal market as defined in Article 14(2) of the Treaty establishing the European Community, or the economic and social cohesion established in accordance with Title XVII of that Treaty;
(f) does not constitute a barrier to or discrimination in trade between the Member States and does not distort competition between them;
(g) involves a minimum of eight Member States;
(h) respects the competences, rights and obligations of those Member States which do not participate therein;
(i) does not affect the provisions of the Protocol integrating the Schengen acquis into the framework of the European Union;
(j) is open to all the Member States, in accordance with Article 43b'.

treaties. The introduction of Eurojust in Article 29 TEU by the Nice Treaty illustrates this.

Within the third pillar, the real debate seems to concern the involvement of the Commission in the policy making. In practice Article 41 (ex Article K.13) TEU plays a very important role in this regard. According to the second and third paragraph:

> Administrative expenditure which the provisions relating to the areas referred to in this Title entail for the institutions shall be charged to the budget of the European Communities...[O]perational expenditure to which the implementation of those provisions gives rise shall also be charged to the budget of the European Communities, except where the Council acting unanimously decides otherwise. In cases where expenditure is not charged to the budget of the European Communities it shall be charged to the Member States in accordance with the gross national product scale, unless the Council acting unanimously decides otherwise.

Therefore, one veto is sufficient to make the Community institutions pay for the operational costs of a third pillar initiative. That may look like an uninteresting arrangement, but in practice it can allow for some more involvement by the Commission in third pillar initiatives. The authority of the actor that pays the money blurs the division of competences.

4.4.9 Changes to the legal instruments brought in with the Amsterdam Treaty

The third pillar structure is very often criticized for all sorts of reasons. Lack of effective instruments compared to the first pillar instruments is a popular critique, which can even be found on European websites.[72] Advocates of

[72] Cf. Chapter IV in *Cooperation in the Field of Justice and Home Affairs, loc. cit.*, pp. 7–8. This chapter deals with the following question: 'Is cooperation in the field of justice and home affairs effective?' We read amongst others that: 'The consistency of cooperation in the field of justice and home affairs must also be viewed in relation to Community policies, which involve the institutions of the European Union intervening differently by means of separate instruments (such as regulations and directives)'. Also that 'the legal instruments proposed in the CJHA framework have proved difficult to use. No precise description of the effects of a common position or a joint action had been contemplated in the Treaty on European Union. Other tools such as resolutions, decisions and declarations have been introduced. As for conventions, they have proved to be a very unwieldy instrument, as States have to submit them for ratification at national level. Although numerous conventions have been signed, their implementation is still awaited, whereas circumstances often call for rapid responses'. And finally that 'the roles of the Commission, European Parliament and Court of Justice, which are weaker than in the Community framework, have often been highlighted. The Commission, the European Parliament and some member states were in favour of copying, to some degree, the Community decision-making process, which was considered more effective, in the field of justice and home affairs.

Europeanization use it to plead for more Community logic in the area of Justice and Home Affairs. Especially after the modifications brought by the Amsterdam Treaty, one should however be very careful while using this critique grounded on the nature of the third pillar instruments. Article 34 (ex Article K.6), second paragraph TEU is a key provision with regard to the new instruments.[73]

Because we assume that the reader is not acquainted with all the implications of the third pillar instruments, we briefly recall some of their characteristics, the essence of which is contained in Article 34, second paragraph TEU. With regard to those areas remaining within the third pillar, the Treaty provides for the following legal instruments: common positions, framework decisions, decisions, resolutions, recommendations, declarations, and conclusions. Most of these instruments were already in use before Amsterdam, but only after the face-lift operated by the Amsterdam Treaty did their importance and effects became more widely known. This can be partly explained by some of the amendments made by the Amsterdam Treaty. The (soft law) instrument of joint actions is no longer provided for by the TEU in the Amsterdam version.[74] Conventions are a traditional instrument of

The question of moving from unanimity to the qualified majority voting rule has also been raised in order to improve the effectiveness of CJHA'.

[73] It states in paragraph 2 that: 'The Council shall take measures and promote cooperation, using the appropriate form and procedures as set out in this Title, contributing to the pursuit of the objectives of the Union. To that end, acting unanimously on the initiative of any Member State or of the Commission, the Council may:

> (a) adopt common positions defining the approach of the Union to a particular matter;
> (b) adopt framework decisions for the purpose of approximation of the laws and regulations of the Member States. Framework decisions shall be binding upon the Member States as to the result to be achieved but shall leave to the national authorities the choice of form and methods. They shall not entail direct effect;
> (c) adopt decisions for any other purpose consistent with the objectives of this Title, excluding any approximation of the laws and regulations of the Member States. These decisions shall be binding and shall not entail direct effect; the Council, acting by a qualified majority, shall adopt measures necessary to implement those decisions at the level of the Union;
> (d) establish conventions which it shall recommend to the Member States for adoption in accordance with their respective constitutional requirements. Member States shall begin the procedures applicable within a time limit to be set by the Council. Unless they provide otherwise, conventions shall, once adopted by at least half of the Member States, enter into force for those Member States. Measures implementing conventions shall be adopted within the Council by a majority of two-thirds of the Contracting Parties'.

[74] Prior to 1 May 1999, the Council of the European Union was able to adopt joint actions. For example, it adopted such an action in 1996 to create a directory of specialized competences, skills and expertise to combat terrorism. The same year a joint action was adopted concerning the approximation of the laws and practices of the Member States of the EU to combat drug addiction and to prevent and combat illegal drug trafficking.

international law and they kept their function and intergovernmental nature within the Union.[75] Contrary to the other third pillar instruments, they have to be ratified by the national parliaments of the Member States. Since the entry into force of the Treaty of Amsterdam, conventions enter into effect, unless otherwise provided, once they have been adopted by at least half of the Member States.

The Council of the European Union can adopt common positions unanimously. These common positions define the European Union's approach on a given question. Thus, a common position was decided upon, prior to the entry into force of the Treaty of Amsterdam, for the harmonized application of the definition of the term 'refugee' in asylum matters. This definition enables national administrations to follow the same guidelines when granting a person refugee status.

The Council of the European Union may take framework decisions to approximate the laws and regulations of the Member States. While these legal instruments are binding on the Member States as regards the result to be achieved, they remain free to choose the means by which to do so. The Council may also adopt decisions in the area of Justice and Home Affairs. These decisions, which cannot have direct effect, are then supplemented by implementing measures.

The Council has resorted to a whole series of instruments to express its political will, such as resolutions, recommendations, declarations, conclusions etc.[76] These instruments are very often used for their 'flexibility' – unlike the other instruments mentioned above, they are not binding upon the Council and the Member States. The remarkable thing about these soft law instruments is their legal basis, or rather, the absence of such a basis. Indeed, they are not provided for in Article 34 TEU or any other provision of the third pillar. On the contrary, Article 39, paragraph 3 TEU seems to suggest that 'recommendations' are tools available to the European Parliament, not to the Council.[77]

4.4.10 A critical comparison of the instruments of both pillars

We saw that as regards areas brought under the Community, Article 249 TEC provides for recourse to the following forms of action: regulations, directives,

[75] After this, the Maastricht's version of the TEU, the Council of the European Union may draw up conventions in the field of Justice and Home Affairs, which it may recommend to the Member States for their adoption.

[76] It has, for example, adopted a resolution on the protection of witnesses in the fight against organized crime, or a recommendation to prevent disturbances likely to occur at football matches, or even a declaration about motorcycle gangs.

[77] The European Parliament may ask questions of the Council or make recommendations to it. Each year, it shall hold a debate on the progress made in the areas referred to in this Title.

decisions, recommendations and opinions. Recommendations and opinions have no binding force and do not establish any rights or obligations for those to whom they are addressed. Regulations have general application, are binding in their entirety and are directly applicable in all Member States.[78] Directives are binding, as to the result to be achieved, upon each Member State to whom they are addressed.

However, the national authorities are left the choice of form and methods to achieve their objectives. Directives may be addressed to individual, several or all Member States. In order to ensure that the objectives laid down in directives become applicable to individual citizens, an act of transposition by national legislators is required, whereby national law is adapted to the objectives laid down in directives. Hence, directives are not directly applicable, in principle.[79]

[78] Regulations apply directly in all the Member States, without requiring a national act to transpose them, on the basis of their publication in the Official Journal of the European Community.

[79] Upon the applicability: 'Sources and scope of Community law', fact sheet 1.2.1., published on November 16, 2000, www.europarl.eu.int, p. 6. The European Court of Justice has ruled that individual provisions of a directive may, exceptionally, be directly applicable in a Member State without requiring an act of transposition by that Member State beforehand (see case-law in *ECR* 1970, pp. 1213 et seq.) where (1) the period for transposition has expired and the directive has not been transposed or has been transposed inadequately, (2) the provisions of the directive are imperative as to their substance and (3) the provisions of the directive confer rights on individuals. Accordingly, if these requirements are fulfilled, individuals may cite the provisions of the directive against all agencies in whom State power is vested. Such agencies include organizations and establishments which are subordinate to the State or on which the State confers rights that exceed those arising from the law on relations between private persons (Court judgment of 22 June 1989 in Case 103/88 *Fratelli Costanzo* ECR 1839 at 31). The agencies must then automatically comply with the directly applicable provisions of the directive. But even when the provision concerned does not seek to confer any rights on the individual and merely constitutes objective law, so that only requirements (1) and (2) are fulfilled, the Court's current case law says the Member State authorities have a legal duty to comply with the non-transposed directive (see [1995] *ECR* I-2189, p. 2224). This case law is mainly justified on the grounds of '*effet utile*', the penalization of violations of the Treaty and legal protection. Finally, when requirements (1) to (3) are fulfilled, an individual may not cite the direct effect of a non-transposed directive where the direct effect is to the detriment of another private person (the 'horizontal effect') (case law, cf *Faccini Dori* [1994] *ECR* I-3325 et seq. at point 25). According to Court case law (*Francovich* case, [1991] *ECR* I-5357 et seq., *Faccini Dori* op. cit. at point 27 et seq.), an individual citizen may be entitled to claim compensation from a Member State which has not transposed a directive or has done so inadequately where (1) the directive is intended to confer rights on individuals, (2) the substance of the rights can be ascertained on the basis of the directive and (3) there is a causal connection between the breach of the duty to transpose the directive and the loss sustained by the individual. Fault on the part of the Member State is then not required in order to establish liability. If the Member State has powers of discretion in transposing the law, the violation must also, in addition to the three above criteria, qualify as defective or non-existent transposition: it must be substantial and evident (*Brasserie du Pêcheur/Factortame* judgment of 5 March 1996, Cases 46/93 and 48/93, *ECR* I-1029).

Finally, decisions are binding in their entirety upon those to whom they are addressed. These may be Member States or natural or legal persons. Decisions serve to regulate actual circumstances vis-à-vis specific entities addressed thereby.

A comparison with the instruments of the third pillar in the Amsterdam version shows many similarities. True, there are neither conventions in the first pillar, nor regulations in the third pillar. There is also nothing about resolutions, recommendations, declarations or conclusions in the third pillar, but this has not stopped the Council from applying them in the third pillar context. This difference does not seem to be the result of a conscious decision. Moreover, the legal character of first pillar directives and third pillar framework decisions is strikingly similar (both are binding upon the Member States with respect to the objective, leaving the choice of form and method of the implementation to the national authorities) and this may also be the case for certain decisions to be taken in both pillars.

Hence, both pillars allow for the use of binding instruments.[80] The only difference lies in the absence of any direct effect comparable to the effect of regulations and, to a certain degree, directives (see Schutte 2000).[81]

Since the Amsterdam Treaty, the Council has adopted most first pillar instruments by qualified majority and in conjunction with the European Parliament under the co-decision procedure. Most of Justice and Home Affairs is still firmly in the grip of the unanimity rule, with little or no room for parliamentary involvement or co-decision and much room for initiative for Member States: the Council may indeed adopt common positions, framework decisions and establish conventions on an initiative of any member state or of the Commission. Again, there is almost no difference in terms of complexity. On the contrary: it is not unreasonable to expect more intimacy between the representatives of the Member States and the members of the Council than between the representatives of the Commission and members of the Council. In terms of efficiency the decision-making machinery of the third pillar has all the advantages (see Faria 2002),[82] and therefore it does not come as a surprise that since Amsterdam there has been an unprecedented, increasing flood of third texts (see Monar 2002 and Schutte 2002).

What cannot be stressed often enough is the political 'twist' that has been operated in the Union structures. Indeed, the Council is the European Union's

[80] Note that the soft law instruments of the third pillar (resolutions, recommendations, declarations, conclusions, etc.) are not binding upon the Member States.

[81] It should also be noted that first pillar measures, in the event of conflict with other legal rules, take precedence over such other rules.

[82] Proof of this can easily be given. The events of 11 September resulted in pushing forward to police and judicial cooperation in criminal matters. Besides the new actions called for, also the instruments and measures already scheduled to be approved were achieved and approved more quickly than had previously been the case.

main decision-making institution. But who or what is the Council? It would be more respectful to Western political tradition to refer to the Council systematically as the Council of Ministers. Members of the executive power jump scales and become the legislative power. Without shame or remorse, the European websites refer to this institution as 'the final legislative authority'.[83] Those familiar with the traditional Community working methods could retort 'Nothing new under the sun', but they fail to see that Community policies on agriculture, transport, environment, energy, research and development are less sensitive to human rights than policies on police and criminal law.[84]

The current arrangement of the third pillar allows for a situation in which a council of members of the executive power in the Member States coordinates the activities of the Member States and adopts binding measures in the field of police and criminal matters. This paradox – executive power dictates legislative power – is worsened by several factors. The decision-making machinery of the third pillars shows that firm control by the Member States remains over the complete procedure, with only very little initiative for the Commission or the Parliament and almost no room for judicial review.

This fundamental difference in nature between first and third pillar areas explains why in the current situation not one single issue can be entrusted to the third pillar structure. This position will be defended in the next section.

4.4.11 Reasons why all current use of the third pillar should be avoided for reasons pertaining to democracy and human rights

Within the third pillar, the Court of Justice does not have the authority that it wields in Community policies. As regards the areas that remain within the third pillar (police and judicial cooperation in criminal matters), any Member State may acknowledge the competence of the Court to give a preliminary ruling on the validity and interpretation of framework decisions and decisions, on the interpretation of conventions and on the validity and interpretation of their implementing measures.[85]

The Court has jurisdiction to review the legality of framework decisions and decisions when proceedings are instituted by a Member State or by the Commission on grounds of lack of competence, infringement of important procedural requirements, infringement of provisions of primary law or misuse of powers, or when proceedings are instituted by the Parliament for the

[83] 'Key players in EU legislation', fact sheet consulted in December 2002 via http://europa.eu.int/eur-lex/en/about/, sub 3 ('the players in the EU legislative process').

[84] 'All this has to be regarded as a serious problem since measures in JHA can have far more direct implications for the rights of individuals than those in other areas of EU policy-making', Monar 2002, p. 163.

[85] Article 35, paragraph 1 and 2 TEU.

purpose of protecting its prerogatives.[86] There is no ground for the Court to review the legality of common positions, although this instrument has also to a certain degree binding force and has been used in the past in a way that obliged Member States to implement it with national measures (see Schutte 2002). Individuals cannot bring in actions. Moreover, the Court has no jurisdiction to review the validity or proportionality of operations carried out by the police or other law enforcement services of a Member State or the exercise of the responsibilities incumbent upon Member States with regard to the maintenance of law and order and the safeguarding of internal security.[87]

The co-decision procedure, which strengthens the role of the European Parliament (EP) as co-legislator, applies to a wide range of issues, such as the free movement of workers, consumer protection, education, culture, health and trans-European networks, but not to third pillar issues. Parliament wants co-decision powers extended to the 'third pillar',[88] but this has not been granted, at least not within the framework of the Nice Treaty. There is a consultation procedure whenever framework-decisions are considered,[89] but the Council is not obliged to accept the amendments listed in the opinion of the EP. Once the EP has given its opinion, the Council can adopt the proposal without amendments or adopt it in an amended form.

Due to the increase in number of texts agreed, both European Parliament and national parliaments have been struggling to cope with the increasing flood of texts and to develop effective mechanisms of parliamentary control (see Monar 2002). Further, specialized agencies such as Europol and Eurojust are not subject to any direct parliamentary control.[90] In practice, some countries such as the Netherlands have instituted mechanisms allowing for a priori consultation before binding third pillar measures are taken, but it would be misleading to call this a general practice. The result is in direct contrast with traditional Western political thought and the social contract idea.[91]

The most troublesome aspect of the current institutional arrangement of the third pillar regards the use of instruments (see Schutte 2002). Article 34 TEU does not say much on when a given instrument should be used. Europol

[86] Article 35, paragraph 6 TEU.
[87] Article 35, paragraph. 5 TEU.
[88] See the Maastricht and Amsterdam Treaties' provisions in that concern.
[89] The consultation procedure requires an opinion from the EP before the Council can adopt a binding legislative measure.
[90] *Ibid.*
[91] 'Laws alone can decree punishments for crimes, and that this authority resides only with the legislator, who represents the whole of society united by the social contract. No magistrate (who is a member of society) can justly establish of his own accord any punishment for any member of the same society', Beccaria, 1995, Ch. 3.

was given a convention, Eurojust (only) a decision,[92] while both institutions collect and process extremely sensitive personal data (see Schutte 2002).

Controversial and far-reaching measures concerning terrorism and the European arrest warrant are introduced by framework decisions, without a proper parliamentary debate in the Member States.[93]

At any rate, there seems to be room for much discretion. Not only can Member States easily put all kinds of issues on the third pillar agenda, they can without many difficulties turn these agenda items into legal instruments. When a certain country meets resistance within the third pillar, it can avoid objection by proposing the use of soft law instruments of less heavily binding instruments. In this respect the use of resolutions, recommendations, declarations or conclusions, not grounded on any provision of the TEU, cannot be accepted pragmatically with reference to their non-binding nature. These instruments have a specific function, i.e. agenda setting. They can pave the way for further European actions or can be used to manipulate or prepare public opinion in the Member States. In 2001 the Council adopted a framework decision on the status of victims in criminal proceedings. Proponents of victim rights immediately hauled this decision as a breakthrough in an ongoing debate about the legitimacy of such rights in criminal procedure (see Groenhuijsen 2001).

In 2000 a team of researchers investigated the possibility of using the Schengen system for combating hooliganism. They concluded that the Schengen Conventions did not allow for the inclusion of hooligans in the Schengen Information System due to the wording of Article 96 of the Convention (see De Schutter, Caronez and De Hert 2000). Moreover, they noted a lack of consensus on the importance of this issue. Not all Member States had experienced public order problems with this kind of behaviour to justify a European policy.[94]

On 25 April 2002 the Council adopted a decision concerning security in connection with football matches with an international dimension.[95] The initiative was taken by the Kingdom of Belgium, a country with a very bad reputation on security in connection with football matches. The preamble is

[92] Council Decision of 14 December 2000 setting up a Provision Judicial Cooperation Unit, *Official Journal*, L 324, 21 December 2000; Council Decision of 28 February 2002, *Official Journal*, L 63/1, 6 March 2002.

[93] The framework decision on combating terrorism does not include a definition on 'terrorism' but it defines terrorist aims and offences and establishes minimum penalties. The European arrest warrant replaces the lengthy procedures of extradition and, in respect of listed offences, without verification of the principle of double criminality. See for more details and the decisions: www.europa.eu.int.

[94] Cf. Ministry of Interior, International Seminar on the prevention and fight of violence in football matches, Palais des Congrès of Brussels, 22 and 23 May 2001.

[95] *Official Journal*, L 121, 8 May 2002, 1–4.

worth reading. It learns that one joint action and two resolutions were needed to prepare the climate for this binding decision.

Following Article 1, all Member States are bound to set up national football information points. These points are to engage in the exchange of personal and police data before, during and after football events (Article 3, paragraph 1). The data may 'involve details of individuals actually or potentially posing a threat to law and order and security' (Article 3, paragraph 3). Compared to the privacy provisions in the Schengen Convention there is very little information. The decision only states that 'personal data shall be exchanged in accordance with the domestic and international rules applicable' (Article 3, paragraph 3).

In the 1990s the Schengen Conventions were criticized because government officials prepared them without much transparency. Contrary to common positions and other decisions, conventions have to be ratified by the national parliaments of the Member States. Schengen was ratified by 15 parliaments. The Council decision on football security, having only one purpose, i.e. to amend the Schengen Convention considered too restrictive to combat hooliganism, was thrown into the Official Journal without proper consultation. It is legitimate to ask whether the third pillar actors will completely forsake the use of Conventions, in the light of the advantages offered by the other instruments. Even when human rights issues, such as data protection and privacy, are dealt with, there seems to be no impediment for not choosing a Convention. No mechanism has been designed to monitor the way in which the Member States implement framework decisions and decisions adopted by the Council. The Council decision on football security states that the Council must evaluate the implementation within two years of its adoption.

From a human rights perspective we are not really comforted in terms of recognizability. Due to the Council decision, we do not exactly know if data with regard to football security is passed around, when we cross borders. Individuals actually or potentially posing a threat to law and order and security have to consult the domestic legislation to verify whether this allows for the exchange of data between football points. We are very far from the idea that privacy-infringing law must have a certain quality to be compatible with the rule of law. On the contrary, on the sole basis of one measure decided by members of the executive power, personal data is allowed to be passed freely around.

Belgian officials have 'jumped scales' with considerable success. It may be clear from the foregoing that the idea of introducing qualified-majority voting in the Council in order for this to become the normal method of decision-making in the third pillar, as proposed by the European Parliament,[96] may be very problematic. The rule of unanimity is in the current situation one of the few democratic guarantees available. The corresponding veto guarantees that all Member States are involved in and support decisions affecting human rights. Qualified-majority voting is not appropriate for such decisions, unless additional democratic guarantees are built in.

4.5 CONCLUSION: THE EUROPEAN UNION AS A POLICE STATE

The division of competence within the third pillar between European and national competences is far from clear-cut. The third pillar is a typical area of mixed powers. The principle of subsidiarity in its current formulation is not capable of safeguarding a strict division between the national and European sphere.

The power of judicial review is limited and much is left to political interplay. This is especially true in the third pillar where almost no action is taken without involvement of the Member States. Apparently many arguments (efficiency, democratic and judicial control) seem to be in favour of transferring Justice and Home Affairs to the first pillar (optimal alternative) or of modelling the third pillar after the first pillar (second best alternative).

Both alternatives were proposed by the Treaty of Amsterdam, which has been in turn refined by the Treaty of Nice. The method of division between the first and the third pillar is now based on the idea of 'the principle of attribution of powers'. With the advent of a large political construct wherein almost all aspects of public life are covered by one of the three pillars, the principle of subsidiarity loses much of its meaning.

The current arrangement of the third pillar allows members of the executive to dictate legislative power in Member States by jumping to the European scale, with very little initiative for the Commission or the Parliament and almost no room for judicial review.

The most troublesome aspect of the current institutional arrangement of the third pillar is regarding the use of instruments. Article 34 TEU does not say much on when a given instrument should be used and in practice this legal vagueness is used to replace or supplement conventions with more flexible instruments that are inferior in terms of political legitimacy and the rule of law. The same legal vagueness and the practical arrangements of the instruments open the door for strategies of jumping of scales.

[96] 'The Maastricht and Amsterdam Treaties: prospects for the European Union,' *l.c.*, 5.

UWE LIBRARY SERVICES

4.5.1 The modern police state

De Tocqueville held that whenever people have political power to influence a given situation, they will refrain from binding regulations and from imposing a line of conduct laid down in advance.[97]

Law and politics are and should be two distinct realms of thought and actions that are closely or intimately interrelated (see MacCormick 1999). Political power is the power to direct social agencies and individuals to certain defined ends presumptively for the common good, to dispose of available goods among persons and groups, and to protect the group against interference from agencies external to others. Law interacts with politics in many ways. Sometimes it is an object over and through which political power is exercised and sometimes it is a control upon the use and abuse of power.[98] The latter interaction is part of the institutional side of law. In a *Rechtsstaat* the question concerning what exercises of executive (or legislative) power are valid is a question of law (see MacCormick 1999) or more precisely of the rule of law. Failure to adhere to any of the canons of legal morality is a symptom of legal pathology (Golding 1999).[99] A police state, then, is a state that ignores the canons of the rule of law (see MacCormick 1999) and suffers from a high degree of legal pathology.[100]

Well-conducted politics are necessary to the maintenance of the inner morality of systems of positive law.[101] Political power, be it democratic or not, can give way to negligence concerning the rule of law. The police state is a constant threat to democracy perverted by the belief in the possession of political power. For political purposes it is enough to indicate the goal to be aimed for and to leave the magistrates free to choose their own means, De

[97] 'In limited monarchies power is divided between people and prince. Both have an interest in the stability of the position of the magistrates. The prince does not wish to place the fate of public officials in the people's hands for fear that they may betray his authority, whereas the people are also afraid that magistrates completely dependent on the prince might be used against their freedom. Thus, in a sense, they are left depending on nobody. The same cause which leads prince and people to make officials independent induces them to look for guarantees against the abuse of this independence, so that it cannot be turned against the authority of the one or the liberty of the other. Hence both agree on the necessity of restricting officials to a line of conduct laid down in advance, and both find it to their interests to impose upon him rules that he cannot disregard', in De Tocqueville, 1835, p. 191.

[98] As an institutional order, law therefore connects necessarily to politics and is in part constitutive of the political.

[99] Because of problems in implementing the conditions of the rule of law, every legal system suffers from some degree of legal pathology. For instance, one of the canons states that rules must remain relatively constant over time, but time can reveal that changes are needed in the law. The point is that differences in degree are morally significant.

[100] For example, by drafting laws containing unclear rules or introducing evil modes of law-enforcement. Cf. MacCormick, 1999, p. 122.

[101] MacCormick, 1999, pp. 136–7.

Tocqueville observes.[102] Habits form in freedom that may one day become fatal to freedom. One of these habits consists of learning to live with legal pathologies, e.g. when the authorities exercise power against the citizens in ways that are not congruent with declared law.[103] Concern for political pathology seems to overrule concern for legal pathology.

The political aspects of the Union have brought both partisans of the intergovernmental and supranational method to a system that is clearly lacking legal morality. In matters that are highly sensitive from a human rights perspective, there are no efficient legal guarantees to prevent abuse of the European construct. Especially after 11 September, the possibility to jump to the European scale to realize certain goals, has become evident. Representatives of interest groups that have gained power in Member States can dictate a European human rights agenda. Within Europe, borders cannot protect us any longer against those willing to live with legal pathologies.

Fortunately, awareness about these pathologies is developing. An important 2001 conference of academics and officials held in Bruges agreed on the fact that there has been recently a rapid proliferation of policy instruments and legal regulations in the area of police and justice cooperation, as well as in data protection. Consequently, the rules have become dense, complex, entangled, occasionally overlapping and they may, thus, create confusion.

Moreover, the rapid succession of agreements and regulations in the field of Justice and Home Affairs has resulted in an under-use of the existing range of instruments and in the absence of any in-depth assessment of the current Justice and Home Affairs acquis (see Thwaites 2002).

Attention was also paid to the big discrepancy between parliamentary control in purely national matters and in matters relating to European issues. While the former are subject to more or less strict democratic scrutiny, there is a lack of transparency, an absence of democratic scrutiny and undue haste as far as decision making in the third pillar is concerned (see Jurgens 2002). The point was made that if decisions taken in the sensitive field of Justice and

[102] 'In the United States that omnipotence of the majority which favours legal despotism of the legislator also smiles on the arbitrary power of the magistrate. The majority, being in absolute command both of lawmaking and of the execution of the laws, and equally controlling both rulers and ruled, regards public functionaries as its passive agents and is glad to leave them the trouble of carrying out its plans. It therefore does not enter by anticipation into the details of their duties and hardly takes the trouble to define their rights. It treats them as a master might treat his servant if, always seeing them act under his eyes, he could direct or correct them at any moment', in De Tocqueville, 1835, p. 234.

[103] 'In general, the law leaves American officials much freer than ours within the sphere marked out for them. Sometimes the majority may even allow them to go beyond that. Assured of the views and strengthened by the support of the greatest number, they then dare to do things that astonish a European, accustomed though he is to the spectacle of arbitrary power. Thus habits form in freedom that may one day become fatal to freedom', in De Tocqueville, 1835, p. 234.

Home Affairs are not based on broad and informed consensus among citizens, they run the risk of backfiring and upsetting the acquis of the Union (see Klages 2002).

In 2004 a new intergovernmental conference is to be convened to consider a more precise delimitation of competencies between the European Union and the Member States, the status of the Charter of Fundamental Rights, simplification of the treaties and the role of the national parliaments. With regard to the latter, one of the suggestions is to add a new chamber to the Union's institutional system composed of national parliamentarians.

The emphasis on national parliaments is seen as a means to ensure respect for subsidiarity and to strengthen the link between the EU and national political life (see Best 2002). Our recommendation would be to organize a complete standstill of legislative activity with binding effects within the third pillar as long as these significant proposals are not put to a test (see Jurgens 2002).[104]

Our second recommendation would be that serious attention is paid to the many recommendations forwarded from the Bruges Conference with regard to the necessity to strengthen national and European parliamentary and judicial control and to assess the current use of third pillar instruments.

REFERENCES

Apap, J. (2002), 'Transfer of Competence: Between Sovereignty and Supranationality', in M. Anderson and J. Apap (eds), *New European Borders & Security Cooperation. Promoting Trust in a European Union*, Centre for European Policy Studies, CEPS, Brussels, pp. 46–47.

Beccaria, C. (1995), *On Crimes and Punishments*, trans. by R. Davies in R. Bellamy, Beccaria: *On Crimes and Punishments and Other Writings*, Cambridge: Cambridge University Press, Ch. 1.

Best, E. (2002), 'The Treaty of Nice: Not Beautiful but it'll do', *Eipascope*, No. 1, European Institute of Public Administration, EIPA, Maastricht, pp. 2–9.

Bleeker, K.A.M. (1993), 'Verantwoorde communautaire sanctionering van het gemeenschapsrecht', *Nederlands Juristenblad*, pp. 1009–13

Buruma, Y. (1995), 'De Repressieve Kant van de Europese Unie', *Justitiële verkenningen*, **1**, 41–4.

Cholewinsky, R. (2002), 'Borders and Discrimination in the European Union', in M. Anderson and J. Apap (eds), *New European Borders & Security Cooperation.*

[104] Compare proposition 6 formulated by Jurgens: 'As long as the Third Pillar has not been integrated into the First Pillar and to support the development of parliamentary scrutiny in JHA affairs, national parliaments should be given the power (as in the Netherlands) to decide which decision their governments take in the JHA Council insofar the Council takes decisions that are binding on Member States', Jurgens, 2002, p. 88.

Promoting Trust in a European Union, Centre for European Policy Studies, CEPS, Brussels, pp. 83–100.

Cloos, J., G. Reinesch, D. Vignes and J. Weyland (1993), *Le Traité de Maastricht. Genèse, analyse, commentaires*, Brussels: Bruylant.

Council Resolution on traffic safety, 26 June 2000, *Official Journal*, C 218/1, 31 July 2000.

Directive 91/308/EEC, *Official Journal of European Communities*, L 166 of 28 June 1991, p.77.

De Hert, P. (1995), 'La Commission Européenne sur la Voie D'une Police Supranationale', *Revue de droit de police*, **1** (2), pp. 21–9.

Demanet, G. (1985), 'De L'utilisation Franduleuse des Cartes Bancaires. Une Nouvelle Incrimination est-elle Necessaire?', *Revue de Droit Pénal et de Criminologie*, **65** (2), pp. 915–32.

Den Boer, M. (1997), 'Justitie en Binnenlandse Zaken in het nieuwe Verdrag van Amsterdam', *Nederlands Juristenblad*, **72** (35), 1625–30.

Den Boer, M. (2000), 'The Incorporation of Schengen into the TEU: A Bridge too Far?', in J. Monar, and W. Wessels (eds), *The Treaty of Amsterdam: Challenges and Opportunities for the European Union*, London: Continuum, pp. 297–319.

De Schutter, B., K. Caronez and P. De Hert (2000), *Bestrijding van het Voetbalvandalisme in het Licht van het Vrij Verkeer van Personen*, Brussels: VUB-onderzoeksrapport.

Denayer, W. (2001), 'Urban Governance, Workfare, and the Conservative Revolution against the Welfare State', *Ethiek & Maatschappij*, **3** (2), 59–79.

Faria, C. (2001), 'Post-Laeken Assessment Justice and Home Affairs', *Eipascope*, No. 1, European Institute of Public Administration, EIPA, Maastricht, pp. 7–9.

Flore, D. (1999), 'Une Justice Pénale Européenne après Amsterdam', *Journal des Tribunaux. Droit Européen*, **7** (60), 121–8.

Framework decision of 15 March 2001 on the status of victims in criminal proceedings, *Official Journal*, L 82, 22 March 2001, p. 1.

Golding, M. (1999), 'My Philosophy of Law', in L. Wintgens (ed.), *The Law in Philosophical Perspectives*, Dordrecht: Kluwer Publishers, pp. 55–79.

Groenhuijsen, M.S. (2001), 'Hervorming van het Strafprocesrecht met het Oog op de Belangen van het Slachtoffer: We ain't seen nothing yet', *Delikt and Delinkwent*, pp. 645–53.

Guild, E. and D. Bigo (2002), 'The Legal Mechanisms–Collectively Specifying the Individual: The Schengen Border System and Enlargement', in M. Anderson and J. Apap (eds), *New European Borders & Security Cooperation. Promoting Trust in a European Union*, Centre for European Policy Studies, CEPS, Brussels.

Jurgens, E. (2002), 'National Parliamentary Control on Justice and Home Affairs Policy Making', in *Integrated Security in Europe. A Democratic Perspective*, Special Edition of Collegium, News of the College of Europe, **22**, pp. 84–9.

Kaptein, P.J.G. and P. Verloren Van Themaat (1995), *Inleiding tot het Recht van de Europese Gemeenschappen na Maastricht*, Deventer, Kluwer.

Klages, R. (2002), 'Final Report on Constitutional and Ethical Principles of Democratic Control on National and European Institutions', in *Integrated Security in Europe. A Democratic Perspective*, Special Edition of Collegium, News of the College of Europe, **22**, pp. 128–30.

Klip, A. (1997), 'Uniestrafrecht is op hol geslagen', *Nederlands Juristenblad*, **15**, pp. 663–71.

Ludlow, P. (2001), 'A Commentary on the EU', *A View from Brussels*, Brussels: Centre for European Policy Studies, CEPS Commentary.

Monar, J. (2002), 'The Problems of Balance in EU Justice and Home Affairs and the Impact of 11 September', in M. Anderson and J. Apap (eds), *New European Borders & Security Cooperation. Promoting Trust in a European Union*, Brussels, Centre for European Policy Studies, CEPS, Brussels, pp. 158–74.

Pastore, F. (2000), 'Justice and Home Affairs: Decision-Making after Amsterdam', *European Law Review*, **25** (2), pp. 190–191.

Pastore, F. (2002), 'Reconciling the Prince's Two Arms. Internal-External Security Policy Coordination in the European Union', in M. Anderson and J. Apap (eds), *New European Borders & Security Cooperation. Promoting Trust in a European Union*, Centre for European Policy Studies, CEPS, Brussels, pp. 57–82.

Peck, J. and A. Tickell (1994), 'Searching for a New Institutional Fix: the after-Fordist Crisis and Global–Local Disorder', in A. Amin (ed.), *Post-Fordism*, London, Blackwell, pp. 280–315.

Pisuisse, C.S. and A.M.M. Teubner (1999), *Elementair Europees Gemeenschapsrecht*, Groningen, Wolters-Noordhoff.

Protocol on the application of the principles of subsidiarity and proportionality, *Official Journal*, C 340, 10/11/1997 p. 0105.

Resolution by the European Parliament about the action plan to combat drugs (2000-2004), *EP*, C 189, 19 November 1999.

Rousseau, J.J. (1762), *Du Contrat Social*, Book 2, Chapter I, p. 368.

Schutte, J. (1995), 'Aard en Werking van de Europese Instellingen. Een Overzicht', *Justitiële verkenningen*, No. 1, 94–9.

Schutte, J. (2000), 'Unification and Harmonisation of Criminal Procedures in the European Union', in J. Nijboer and W. Sprangers (eds), *Harmonisation in Forensic Expertise. An Inquiry into the Desirability of and Opportunities for International Standards*, Amsterdam, Thela Thesis, pp. 43–55.

Schutte, J. (2002), 'De Rechtsinstrumenten van de Europese Unie voor de Ontwikkeling van Gezamelijk Optreden van de Lidstaten op het Gebied van Politiële en Justitiële Samenwerking in Strafzaken', *Delikt en Delinkwent*, No. 5, pp. 84–115.

Stessens, G. (1994) 'De bevoegdheid van de Europese Gemeenschap tot het vaststellen van sancties: op weg naar een communautair strafrecht?', *Rechtskundig Weekblad*.

'Subsidiarity', Fact sheet 1.2.2., 16 November, 2000, www.europarl.eu.int, p. 5.

Swyngedouw, E. (1997a), 'Neither Global nor Local: Globalization and the Politics of Scale', in K. Cox (ed.), *Spaces of Globalization. Reasserting the Power of the Local*, New York: Guilford Press, pp. 137–66.

Swyngedouw, E. (1997b), 'Excluding the other: the Production of Scale and Scaled Politics', in R. Lee and J. Wills (eds), *Geographies of Economics*, London: Arnold, pp. 167–77.

Thomas, F. (1993), *De Europese Rechtshulpverdragen in Strafzaken*, Story-Scientia.

Thwaites, N. (2002), 'Final Report on Police and Judicial Cooperation in the European Union', in *Integraded Security in Europe. A Democratic Perspective*, Special Edition of Collegium, News of the College of Europe, No. 22.

Van Der Net, C. (2000), *Grenzen stellen op het Internet*, Deventer: Gouda Quint, pp. 133–46.

Veld Foglia, M. (2002), '(Nog) geen strafrecht in de Eerste Pijler?', *SEW*, **5** (5), pp. 162–69.

Wright, V. (1998), 'Intergovernmental Relations and Regional Government: A Skeptical View', in P. Le Gales and C. Lequesne (eds), *Regions in Europe*, London: Routledge, pp. 39–49.

PART II

SCENARIOS FOR CRIME, LAW AND JUSTICE IN AN ENLARGED EUROPEAN UNION

5. Law Enforcement in a Broader Europe: The Council of Europe's Strategy Intervention

Jörg Polakiewicz

5.1 INTRODUCTION: THE COUNCIL OF EUROPE – A FORUM FOR WIDER DEMOCRATIC CONTROL

The present chapter will evaluate the Council of Europe's contribution to the creation of an Area of Freedom, Security and Justice, as well as the most relevant treaties and legal instruments concluded within this institution, which form part of the EU's acquis. In the final section a set of practical recommendations will be presented.

As a way of introduction, it is necessary to recall that, created in 1949 to 'achieve a greater unity between its members for the purpose of safeguarding and realising the ideals and principles which are their common heritage', the Council of Europe now unites 44 European states in a common adherence to the values and principles of pluralist democracy, human rights and the rule of law. These include all EU member and candidate countries, as well as all other European states that have committed themselves to the same concept of a democratic society.

The Council of Europe provides a unique forum where representatives from the whole of Europe at parliamentary, governmental, local or regional level come together to discuss questions of common concern on an equal footing – a Europe without dividing lines.[1] In the past ten years, the Council's structure and working methods have been radically adjusted to meet new cooperation needs and the challenges of enlargement, which is almost completed as far as the Council of Europe is concerned (the only remaining candidate states being Belarus, Monaco and the Federal Republic of Yugoslavia).

[1] 'For a greater Europe without dividing lines', The Budapest Declaration of the Committee of Ministers (7 May 1999) on the occasion of the Council of Europe's 50th anniversary.

The Council of Europe uses the following means of action:

- the intergovernmental programme of activities, which is adopted by all Member States; on this basis, almost 200 conventions and agreements and hundreds of recommendations have been drawn up and adopted;[2]
- a series of mechanisms of monitoring and mutual evaluation, either treaty-based or established directly under the authority of the Committee of Ministers (e.g. the European Committee for the Prevention of Torture and Inhuman or Degrading Treatment or Punishment (CPT) or the Group of States against Corruption (GRECO); and
- assistance and cooperation activities to strengthen the rule of law, involving the Council of Europe and one or more member or applicant States.

5.2 THE CONVENTIONAL ACQUIS IN JUSTICE AND HOME AFFAIRS

Many treaties concluded within the Council of Europe have contributed to the creation of an Area of Freedom, Security and Justice, a common goal of the Council of Europe and the European Union. They form part of the European Union's acquis on the basis of which closer cooperation within the Union is being developed.[3]

The Council of Europe's standard-setting role has been most successful in the field of human rights. The European Convention on Human Rights (ECHR, ETS 5, 1950) and its protocols guarantee basic human rights and fundamental freedoms common to all European States. Law enforcement authorities all over Europe must respect in particular the fair trial guaranteed by Article 6 of the ECHR and the right to liberty by Article 5 of the ECHR. The Convention for the Protection of Individuals with regard to Automatic Processing of Personal Data (ETS 108, 1981) formulates basic standards of data protection that are applied in the context of Justice and Home Affairs. The Convention is directly referred to in the Europol and Schengen conventions.

[2] The text of all treaties concluded with the Council of Europe, their explanatory reports, the chart of signatures and ratifications as well as the reservations and declarations made are available on the Internet at http://conventions.coe.int.

[3] See 'Acquis of the European Union in the field of Justice and Home Affairs (Title IV of the TEC and title VI of the TEU, consolidated version, Update first half of 2002)', http://europa.eu.int/comm/justice_home/acquis_en.htm; 'The Council of Europe's contribution to the enlargement of the European Union' (8 March 2002), see also: http://www.coe.int/T/E/Legal%5FAffairs/About%5Fus/Activities/6Contribution_EU.asp.

The conventional acquis in the criminal law field comprises some 25 treaties, including the conventions on extradition (ETS 24, 1957) and mutual assistance in criminal matters (ETS 30, 1959), each complemented by two protocols, the conventions on terrorism (ETS No 90), money laundering (ETS 141, 1990) and the transfer of sentenced persons (ETS 112, 1985). The multilateral conventions replace hundreds of bilateral treaties between the Member States.

The European Committee on Crime Problems (CDPC) regularly examines the operation and implementation of the conventions, with a view to adjusting them and improving their practical application whenever this proves necessary. A Reflection Group, 'New Start', has just presented its analysis of the current status and possible improvements in Council of Europe conventions. It will now be examined how their conclusions will be best implemented.

On the basis of the draft submitted by the CDPC, the Committee of Ministers adopted Recommendation (1999) 20 concerning the friendly settlement of any difficulty that may arise out of the application of the Council of Europe Conventions in the penal field, which is intended to strengthen international cooperation and help states to overcome these problems.

5.2.1 Corruption

Following the second summit of heads of state and government on corruption, organised crime and money laundering, the proceeds of crime were considered as new threats to the security of citizens and the foundations of democracy.

The Multidisciplinary Group on Corruption (GMC), set up in 1994, drew up a number of major legal instruments:

- Resolution (97) 24, including 20 guiding principles to fight corruption, which defines the priority activities for a comprehensive, serious and efficient action against corruption.
- the Criminal Law Convention on Corruption (ETS 173, 1999) which aimed to harmonise national laws on the definition of corruption offences, to set up complementary penal measures (such as the liability of firms for corruption facts) and to improve international cooperation in bringing offenders to justice; the convention entered into force on 1 July 2002 and has so far been ratified by 16 States and signed by 26 States.
- the Civil Law Convention on Corruption (ETS 174, 1999) which covers the definition of corruption, compensation for damage, liability (including state responsibility), contributory negligence, limitation

periods, validity of contracts, protection of employees, accounts and audits, interim measures and international cooperation.

- Recommendation (2000) 10 on codes of conduct for public officials, which complements Resolution (97) 24 on the 20 guiding principles for the fight against corruption, which includes in its appendix a model code of conduct for public officials.

The adoption of this arsenal of legal instruments was coupled with the setting-up of a monitoring body, the Group of States against Corruption (GRECO) in May 1999 (34 states have so far become members of the GRECO, including Bosnia and Herzegovina and the United States of America). The GRECO was conceived as a flexible and efficient mechanism, to monitor, through a process of mutual evaluation and peer pressure, the observance of the guiding principles in the fight against corruption and the implementation of international legal instruments adopted in pursuance of the Programme of Action against Corruption. Full membership of the GRECO is reserved for those who participate fully in the mutual evaluation process and accept the process of being evaluated. The aim of the GRECO is to improve its members' capacity to fight corruption by monitoring the compliance of states with their undertakings in this field. In this way, it contributes to the identification of deficiencies and insufficiencies of national mechanisms against corruption, and to the prompting of the necessary legislative, institutional and practical reforms in order to prevent and combat corruption more effectively.

For its first evaluation round which began in 2000, the GRECO selected the implementation of guiding principles 3, 6 and 7 for the fight against corruption, which deal with the institutions in charge of fighting corruption (independence, impartiality, investigation system, gathering evidence, training, etc.), of their specialisation and the immunities concerning investigation and prosecution.

5.2.2 Anti-money laundering measures

The Convention on laundering, search, seizure and confiscation of the proceeds from crime (ETS No. 141, 1990) has greatly facilitated international cooperation in this field. Forty states, including Russia and Australia, have ratified it. Taking into account the experience and more recent instruments of the Financial Action Task Force (FATF) and the European Union, the CDPC is currently considering a complete review of the convention with a view to strengthening and supplementing its provisions in particular regarding the financing of terrorism, preventive measures, the setting up of financial intelligence units, the return of confiscated and recovered proceeds of crime and asset sharing.

The 1990 Convention and the EU Directive on money laundering are the main parameters for the work of the Select Committee of Experts on the Evaluation of Anti-Money Laundering Measures (PC-R-EV). The Committee uses a mutual evaluation and peer pressure system to review the anti-money laundering measures adopted by the Council of Europe Member States, which are not members of the Financial Action Task Force (FATF). Its aim is to harmonise legal, financial and punitive measures throughout the Member States, relying on the relevant international standards for this purpose. It gives every state a highly detailed set of recommendations on ways of optimising its anti-laundering measures. In the future, the PC-R-EV will give special emphasis to the monitoring of compliance with the recommendations relating to the financing of terrorism, as approved by the FATF.

5.2.3 Organised crime

The Council of Europe prepares annual reports on organised crime, analysing the characteristics, activities, resources, methods, geographical coverage, influence and trends of organised criminal groups operating in Europe. These reports complement the Europol reports at the pan-European level. In addition, groups of experts prepared a series of 'best practice' studies on action to combat organised crime. This work also served as the basis for the Guiding principles for the fight against organised crime, which are included in Recommendation (2001) 11, adopted by the Committee of Ministers on 19 September 2001.

5.2.4 The fight against cybercrime

The Convention on Cybercrime (ETS 185, 2001) was opened for signature in Budapest on 23 November 2001. It has so far been signed by 32 states, including all four non-Member States of the Council of Europe that participated in its elaboration (Canada, Japan, South Africa and the United States). The Convention on Cybercrime is the first international treaty on crimes committed via the Internet and other computer networks, dealing particularly with infringements of copyright, computer-related fraud, child pornography and violations of network security. It also requires states to implement a series of powers and procedures such as the search of computer networks and interception.

At its June meeting, the CDPC approved a draft additional protocol concerning the criminalisation of acts of a racist or xenophobic nature committed through computer networks. After consultation of the Parliamentary Assembly, the Committee of Ministers is expected to adopt this treaty in November 2002.

5.2.5 The fight against terrorism

The terrorist attacks of 11 September 2001 have tragically shown that there is a need to go further more rapidly and to develop instruments of international cooperation that are more efficient and more adapted to this unprecedented form of terrorism. At their ministerial session held in Vilnius on 3 May 2002, the Council of Europe's Member States stated that the respect for human rights is not an obstacle to an effective fight against terrorism. The Committee of Ministers adopted a set of guidelines on human rights and the fight against terrorism, which had been prepared by the Steering Committee for Human Rights (CDDH).[4]

The Multidisciplinary Group on International Action against Terrorism (GMT) was set up in November 2001 with a view to coordinating and strengthening the legal action of the Council of Europe in the field of the fight against terrorism. The GMT contributes to the international action against terrorism, by making use of the added value of the Council of Europe. Its current work focuses on the preparation of a protocol updating the European Convention on the Suppression of Terrorism (ETS 90, 1977), which will include a flexible follow-up mechanism to work on questions related to terrorism (e.g. special investigative techniques, protection of witnesses, etc).

5.2.6 Functioning and operation of justice

The Council of Europe and its Member States attach special importance to questions relating to access to justice and the functioning of judicial systems, which are to guarantee that the rule of law will be respected. These subjects figured prominently on the agendas of recent conferences of European Ministers of Justice in London (June 2000) and Moscow (October 2001).

In March 2000, the Committee of Ministers adopted a global action plan to promote the independence and impartiality of judges, and decided to set up the Consultative Council of European Judges (CCJE). One of its aims is to strengthen the role of judges in Europe, and advising the competent intergovernmental committees on the need to update the Council of Europe's legal instruments. The CCJE is the first body consisting solely of judges, ever set up within an international organisation. The Committee of Experts on the Efficiency of Justice (CJ-EJ) has the task of identifying practical steps that Member States can take to improve the functioning of their judicial systems and the effectiveness of justice. The CJ-EJ is also examining mediation as an alternative to 'traditional' procedures for the settlement of civil disputes, having already considered its role in the fields of family, criminal and administrative law. The CJ-EJ takes a special interest in the 'players'

[4] At the 804th meeting of Ministers' Deputies on 11 July 2002.

involved in court trials – hence the adoption of Recommendation R(2000)21 on the freedom of exercise of the profession of lawyers, covering a whole series of measures and schemes essentially designed to improve the service provided for the public.

In September 2002, the Committee of Ministers adopted Resolution (2002) 12 setting up a European Commission for the Efficiency of Justice (CEPEJ).[5] Its aim will be to improve the efficiency and the functioning of the justice system and to ensure that everyone can enforce their legal rights effectively, thereby generating increased confidence of the citizens in the justice system.

5.2.7 Cooperation and assistance activities

The cooperation programmes are flexible and activities are organised in a country-specific manner. Contents are defined by the authorities concerned together with the Secretariat, taking into account the priorities defined by the government concerned, the results of previous activities as well as the results of monitoring exercises.

Recent work comprised in particular the following activities:

- multilateral or regional seminars, expert meetings and expert missions bring together representatives from all the countries interested (for instance: status of judges, enforcement of court decisions, ethics of lawyers, access to legal norms, control of administrative acts, European prison rules, fight against crime and corruption, status of NGOs, the role of the associations of local authorities, transfrontier cooperation);
- legislative expertise aimed to check the compatibility of legislative reforms with Council of Europe standards. The drafters are advised on the basis of the various European experiences and the realities of their country. The expertise concerns the main codes: civil codes and codes of civil procedure, criminal codes and codes of criminal procedure, administrative codes; of particular importance is the work with Russia which, with the Council of Europe's assistance, is realising a complete reform of its legal and judicial system;
- study visits offer members of the judicial and legal professions the opportunity to analyse the situation and working methods of other European countries and to have exchanges with their European colleagues during the exercise of their daily tasks.

[5] Adopted at the 808th meeting of Ministers' Deputies on 18 September 2002.

Apart from this programme of legal cooperation, some specific cooperation programmes co-financed by the European Commission and the Council of Europe have been set up (in particular in Albania, Armenia, Azerbaijan, Georgia, Moldova, the Russian Federation, Turkey and Ukraine).

5.3 CONCLUDING REMARKS AND POLICY RECOMMENDATIONS

Even after completion of the EU enlargement process currently under way, almost half of the states of Europe will remain outside the European Union. An ever more integrated European Union even runs the risk of creating a sense of exclusion among those states which will remain for the time being outside the Union. The Council of Europe will continue to be the only truly European organisation in which all European states cooperate on an equal footing.

The fight against major threats to our democratic societies such as social exclusion, corruption, drug abuse, violence, racism and xenophobia, as well as organised crime, human trafficking, money-laundering and terrorism cannot stop at the borders of the European Union. These are ideal areas for close cooperation and synergy between the Council of Europe and the European Union. A solid framework for such cooperation already exists, in particular through the presence of the European Commission in all intergovernmental structures, including ministerial sessions. With the Joint Declaration on Cooperation and Partnership signed in April 2001, the two institutions confirmed their determination to deepen the existing partnership.[6]

The European Union and the Council of Europe should make optimum use of the complementary nature of their work, contributing together to the realisation of an Area of Freedom, Security and Justice for the whole of Europe by:

- building closer cooperation within the European Union on the solid foundations of the Council of Europe's existing instruments and institutions;
- active participation of the European Union in the preparation of Council of Europe treaties and accession to them;

[6] See the Annual Reports on relations and cooperation between the Council of Europe and the EU. Available on the Internet at: <http://www.coe.int/sg/e>; References: SG/Inf(2002)7 and SG/Inf(2002)12.

- join development of pan-European responses to major challenges (terrorism, organised crime, corruption, money laundering, drugs and human trafficking, etc.); and
- using the forum of the Council of Europe for EU foreign policy in the field of Justice and Home Affairs towards its immediate neighbours.

6. Good Administration: a Fundamental Right

Jacob Söderman

6.1 INTRODUCTION: THE EUROPEAN OMBUDSMAN – CREATION AND PURPOSE

This chapter will study the European Ombudsman's role and the results of his work. Since the European Ombudsman's establishment, the treatment given by the European Institutions to the EU citizens and the whole administration system in the European Union has been improved considerably. However, further improvements are needed in order to achieve true protection of human rights and civil liberties, with the Convention on the Future of Europe the perfect scenario for this aim to be achieved.

The proposal to establish an Ombudsman for the European Union was first made by the European Parliament back in 1979. The idea resurfaced during the discussions about 'Citizens' Europe' and the right to complain to the European Ombudsman was finally included in the Maastricht Treaty.[1]

The first European Ombudsman was elected by the European Parliament in 1995 and started work in September of that year. The office has now been up and running for more than seven years and has received almost 11 000 complaints from citizens, associations and enterprises.

The Ombudsman investigates maladministration in the institutions and bodies of the European Community, such as the Commission, the Council and the European Parliament. Only the Court of Justice and the Court of First Instance acting in their judicial role fall outside its jurisdiction. Any citizen of the Union or any natural or legal person residing or having its registered

[1] Article 195(1) of the EC Treaty states that: 'The European Parliament shall appoint an Ombudsman empowered to receive complaints from any citizen of the Union or any natural or legal person residing or having its registered office in a Member State concerning instances of maladministration in the activities of the Community institutions or bodies, with the exception of the Court of Justice and the Court of First Instance acting in their judicial role'.

office in a Member State can lodge a complaint with the Ombudsman about maladministration by mail, fax or e-mail.

6.2 GOOD OR MALADMINISTRATION?

6.2.1 What is maladministration?

In 1998, the European Parliament agreed with the Ombudsman's definition of maladministration as follows; 'Maladministration occurs when a public body fails to act in accordance with a rule or principle which is binding upon it'. This means that the EU institutions must apply the rules and act lawfully, including the respect of fundamental rights.

6.2.2 A fundamental right to good administration

The European Charter of Fundamental Rights[2] that was proclaimed at the Nice Summit in December 2000 outlines the rights that European citizens are entitled to. The Charter represents a big step forward for citizens. For the first time ever, an international agreement on human rights includes a right to good administration.

Article 41 of the Charter is entitled 'the right to good administration'. The inclusion of this article follows a proposal that the Ombudsman made to the Convention responsible for drafting the Charter during a public hearing in February 2000.[3] Article 41 states that every person has the right to have his or her affairs handled impartially, fairly and within a reasonable time by the institutions and bodies of the Union. The Article outlines further basic elements of good administrative behaviour including the right of citizens to be heard, the right for them to have access to their own file and the obligation for the administration to give reasons for its decisions. Article 41 contains an obligation for the administration to make good any damage caused by its institution, or by its servants in the performance of their duties. The final provision in Article 41 gives citizens the right to use any one of the languages of the Treaties in their communications with the EU administration.

6.2.3 The European Code of Good Administrative Behaviour

Article 41 of the Charter is not an exhaustive list of the principles of good administration. To clearly define what good administration means in practice, the European Ombudsman drafted a Code of Good Administrative Behaviour.

[2] The Charter is available in http:// www.europarl.eu.int/charter/default_en.htm.
[3] See http://www.euro-ombudsman.eu.int/speeches/en/charter1.htm.

This tells citizens what they have the right to expect from the EU administration and gives guidance to officials for their dealings with the public.[4]

The Code contains rules on how officials should behave in their relations with the public.[5] It includes an article on fairness, providing for proportionality, impartiality and independence, the right to be heard and the absence of abuse of power and discrimination. The Code obliges officials to state grounds for decisions so that citizens understand why a particular decision has been taken. It contains provisions to ensure that the institutions function properly, specifying that officials should send an acknowledgement of receipt, indicate the competent official, transfer a file – where necessary – to the competent service, point out the possibilities of appeal and keep adequate records.

The European Parliament approved this Code in September 2001 on the basis of a special report the Ombudsman submitted to it in April 2000. The special report included a recommendation to the Parliament that in order to have rules of good administrative behaviour that apply equally to all Community institutions and bodies, a European administrative law should be adopted in the form of a regulation. Endorsing this recommendation, the Parliament called on the Commission to submit a proposal for a regulation for a European administrative law. Unfortunately, the European Commission has not yet come forward with a proposal.

6.2.4 Investigating maladministration

The Ombudsman examines the complaints he receives and conducts all the inquiries he considers justified, clarifying any suspected maladministration. In its resolution of September 2001, the European Parliament called on the Ombudsman to follow the European Code of Good Administrative Behaviour in his work. The Ombudsman now uses the Code to examine whether maladministration has taken place.

In carrying out his inquiries, the Ombudsman has wide powers of investigation. The Community institutions and bodies must supply him with the information he requests and give him access to the files concerned. The Member States must also provide him with information that may help to

[4] The Ombudsman has published the European Code of Good Administrative Behaviour on his website in eleven languages at: http://www.euro-ombudsman.eu.int/code/en/default.htm, a brochure version of the Code is available from the Ombudsman's office.

[5] Article 12 of the Code entitled 'Courtesy' states that: '1. The official shall be service-minded, correct and courteous and accessible in relations with the public. When answering correspondence, telephone calls and e-mails, the official shall try to be as helpful as possible and shall reply as completely and accurately as possible to questions which are asked. (...)'.

clarify instances of maladministration by the Community institutions and bodies.

When the Ombudsman tells the relevant institution about a complaint he has received, it can take steps to resolve the problem. This is called 'settled by the institution'. If the case is not resolved satisfactorily during the course of the inquiries, the Ombudsman will try to find a 'friendly solution' which puts right the case of maladministration and satisfies the complainant. If the attempt at conciliation fails, the Ombudsman can make recommendations to solve the case. If the institution does not accept his recommendations, the Ombudsman can make a special report on the matter to the European Parliament. In the event that a 'friendly solution' is not possible due to the circumstances prevailing, the Ombudsman can address a critical remark to the institution concerned.

While most inquiries are initiated on the basis of complaints, the Ombudsman sometimes decides to conduct inquiries on his own initiative. The first own-initiative inquiry was begun in June 1996, after the Ombudsman had received a number of complaints about public access to documents held by the institutions and bodies of the European Community. Other own initiatives launched by the European Ombudsman concern the Commission's dealing with complaints from citizens concerning Member States' failure to fulfil their obligations under Community Law (i.e. the Commission in its role as 'Guardian of the Treaty'), the running of open competitions and, as described above, the establishment of a code of good administrative behaviour.

6.2.5 Results of the Ombudsman's work

From 1 January 2000 to 31 October 2002, the European Ombudsman received 5508 complaints and launched seven own-initiative inquiries. The complaints concerned administrative delay, lack of transparency, work relations between the institutions and their agents, recruitment of staff and the running of competitions. Contractual disputes between the institutions and private firms also gave rise to complaints, as did the European Commission in its role as 'Guardian of the Treaty'.

During this same period, the Ombudsman carried out 622 inquiries. More than 80% concerned the European Commission, almost 8% targeted the European Parliament and 3% were directed at the Council of the European Union; 208 of these cases were settled by the institution after the inquiry was opened, while 35 led to a draft recommendation to the institution concerned. The Ombudsman addressed 102 critical remarks to the Community institutions and bodies and presented four special reports to the European Parliament.

Each case resolved has meant one more satisfied citizen. More generally, the Ombudsman's inquiries have helped improve the way the institutions function. When I first took Office in 1995, many EU institutions applied an age limit of 35 on recruitment competitions. Largely as a result of my own-initiative inquiry based on the anti-discrimination provisions in the EU Charter of Fundamental Rights, the European Commission and the Parliament abolished the use of age limits, while most of the other EU institutions and bodies reassured me that they did not use them. The Administration Board of the recently created European Communities Selection Office looks set to reaffirm this commitment not to use age limits in future recruitment procedures, in line with the promises made to citizens in the Nice Charter. A further example of improvement in the functioning of the institutions is the Ombudsman's own-initiative inquiry into late payments by the European Commission opened in 1999. This inquiry helped to reduce the time that it takes for the Commission to pay its creditors. For some small- and medium-sized enterprises, this has meant that they are now facing healthy financial futures rather than bankruptcy. In 1997, because of the many complaints received regarding lack of transparency, the Ombudsman proposed that the EU institutions and bodies should implement rules on access to documents. All of them, including the European Central Bank and Europol, accepted the Ombudsman's proposal. These improvements bring us closer to realising the fundamental right of every European citizen to good administration, as laid down in the Nice Charter.

6.2.6 National and regional ombudsmen and similar bodies

The European Ombudsman's mandate is limited to the Community institutions and bodies. As a result, the Ombudsman cannot investigate quite a number – almost 70% – of the complaints sent to him. In these cases, the Ombudsman advises the complainant, wherever possible, of another body that may be able to help.

In cases involving Community law in the Member States, it is often a national or regional ombudsman, or committee on petitions, that can deal with the complaint. To better safeguard the rights of citizens under Community law, the European Ombudsman and his colleagues work in close collaboration. This cooperation works through a network and involves regular seminars, a newsletter and a website for exchanging information. In this way, the Ombudsman and his national and regional colleagues aim to ensure that complaints about the wrong application of Community law in the Member States are handled efficiently.

It is my view that more can be achieved by this kind of cooperation than by extending the mandate of the European Ombudsman to all administrative levels of the Union where Community law is applied. Such a wide-reaching role was in fact the very aim of the original Spanish governmental initiative to set up a European Ombudsman in the early 1990s, but is not the most efficient solution in my opinion. We have to put the important principle of subsidiarity into practice whenever possible and must respect it.

It is for this reason that I recently called for the network of ombudsmen and petitions committees in the Member States to be strengthened. The rule of law is primarily upheld by either the judiciary or the administration. But the services of the European Ombudsman and his colleagues in the Member States should continue to play an important role in this respect.

6.3 CONCLUSION: PROTECTING CITIZENS' RIGHTS

For European citizens to fully believe in the Union, they must feel that their rights under Community law are protected. Strengthening the network of ombudsmen and similar bodies in the Union would go some way to ensuring this. However, the ombudsman solution is just one of a number of remedies. Unfortunately, the remedies available to citizens to protect their Community law rights are not set out in the current Treaty. In my role as Observer to the European Convention, which is currently debating the future of Europe, I called for a chapter on remedies to be included in the future Constitutional Treaty.[6]

The chapter on remedies would set out the possibilities for judicial and non-judicial redress when Community law rights are not respected. It should inform citizens that they have the right to:

- go to national courts to defend their rights under Community law;
- petition the European Parliament about infringements of Community law by Member States; and
- complain to an Ombudsman or similar body in each Member State.

The remedies would also protect fundamental rights, assuming that the Charter of Fundamental Rights is made binding when applying Community law. If the Charter is made binding, the European Ombudsman would be willing to deal with cases of principle involving fundamental rights. It could be responsible for referring such cases to the Court of Justice, if a normal ombudsman investigation does not bring about a solution.

Since the European Ombudsman started work in 1995, there have surely been positive changes in the way that the EU administration is run and in how

[6] The Ombudsman's proposal to the Convention is available on his website in all 11 EU official languages at: http://www.euro-ombudsman.eu.int/letters/en/20020712-1.htm.

the institutions treat European citizens. Much remains to be done but the European Convention offers the chance of real progress.

In my view, the Constitutional Treaty that the Convention will present in 2003 should:

- establish openness and subsidiarity as fundamental principles;
- contain a legal basis for ensuring an open, accountable and service-minded administration through a European administrative law; and finally
- inform citizens of the remedies available if their rights, including fundamental rights, are not respected. These remedies include courts, ombudsmen and committees on petitions at all levels in the Union. Thus, citizens can be assured that their rights - including fundamental rights - will be fully respected. Only in this way can European citizens truly have confidence in the Union.

7. The European Convention and its Implications for Justice and Home Affairs Cooperation

Monica den Boer

7.1 INTRODUCTION: OBJECTIVES OF THE EUROPEAN CONVENTION

Despite the urgency for reform on how the European Union works, it has been difficult for Member States to agree on any profound change of its institutions and procedures. Infused by the ongoing enlargement process, the need for institutional reform has remained ever present on the agenda. The Treaty of Nice, which was concluded at the end of 2000 and which was supposed to introduce various changes, turned out to be a disappointment to many, to such an extent that it gave rise to expressions such as the 'Nice left-overs', and even worse, 'Nice hangovers'.

The Nice Summit in December 2000 decided that a debate about the future of Europe had to be initiated, buttressed by the general wish that the EU would have to undergo further reform after enlargement. As a consequence the European Convention was established by the Laeken European Council in December 2001. The Laeken Declaration also defined the mandate of the Convention. This mandate focuses on four issues, which had already been put forward at Nice:

- a more precise delimitation of competences between the European Union and the Member States, taking account of the principle of subsidiarity;
- the status of the Charter of Fundamental Rights which had been adopted at the Nice Summit;
- simplification of the EU Treaties, in order to make them more clear and understandable, without changing the content of the Treaties; and
- the role of the national parliaments within the European structure.

Furthermore, the Laeken Declaration put forward that the Union ought to become more democratic, transparent and efficient, singling out four main questions, namely:

- a better division and description of the competences within the Union;
- simplification of the instruments within the Union;
- more democracy, transparency and efficiency within the Union; and
- the way to a Constitution for EU citizens.

The President of the Convention, Valérie Giscard D'Estaing, and the Vice Presidents, Jean-Luc Dehaene and Giuliano Amato, expressed the ambition that the Convention ought to be closed in the spring of 2003 with a new Constitution for Europe. In the meantime, a draft EU Constitution was presented on 28 October 2002.[1] Throughout the process, many opinions have been voiced. All EU Member States and the 13 candidate Member States have been represented within the Convention. They have been joined by 56 national parliamentarians, 16 members of the European Parliament, and two Members of the European Commission.

On the occasion of the opening session of the Convention on the future of Europe,[2] President of the European Commission, Romano Prodi, proposed that a genuine reform of the Union would be required. First, Europe has to give itself a Constitution, which would mark the birth of Europe as a political entity. Second, a European democracy, 'harmonious model of supranational democracy', is needed; [3] this ought to be based on the people and the states of Europe, resting on basic democratic principles such as the separation of power, majority voting, public debate, elected representation, and the approval of taxes by Parliament. Third, the Union's decision-making system ought to be overhauled with simpler and more transparent procedures for taking and implementing decisions. Underneath all this rests the wish of the Commission to extend the Community method, which by definition would come at the expense of intergovernmentalism in the Council. It would, in effect, amount to the consolidation of power in the European Commission's role of initiator.

Vice President of the Convention, Jean-Luc Dehaene, declared that the European Union would face a severe crisis if a complete revision of the Treaty on European Union could not be reached. He proposed that the European Convention allow the achievement of a certain level of consensus about constitutional issues, such as the clarification of EU competences and the institutional instruments. Dehaene also implied that it would be possible

[1] CONV 369/02.
[2] European Parliament, Brussels, 28 February 2002.
[3] See also COM(2002) 247 final.

to achieve such a consensus because the deliberations have not been led by the executive or diplomats, but by political representatives (see Dehaene 2002).

The contribution below specifically focuses on the opinions and proposals that have been raised concerning one specific field of cooperation within the EU, Justice and Home Affairs Cooperation.

7.2 THE STATE OF JUSTICE AND HOME AFFAIRS COOPERATION: AN INSTITUTIONAL–PROCEDURAL PERSPECTIVE

The objectives of the Area of Freedom, Security and Justice (AFSJ) are twofold, at the very least. One of the principal rationales at the time of creating the AFSJ was to enhance the legitimacy of the EU in the eyes of its citizens. In view of this necessity, the Tampere Summit that was convened in October 1999 and devoted exclusively to JHA, produced proposals of a highly politically symbolic nature. On the other hand, though, Tampere was mainly meant to fix policy objectives for the longer term. When we focus on the proposals that were raised in the security domain, the Tampere Conclusions paved the path for further institutionalization (Eurojust, European Police College, Joint Investigation Teams, Task Force of Chiefs of Police). The creation of new bodies and agencies gave rise to new questions of coordination and competence. Institutions new and old seek to expand their interests by gaining wider competencies, a behaviour that often occurs at the expense of other institutions. In this context, it may be instructive to look at the already hazy demarcation of competencies between OLAF and Europol, or between Eurojust and the national prosecution agencies.

Justice and Home Affairs cooperation in the EU is a dynamic and expanding area of EU policy making. It currently occupies one of the most prominent places in the Commission's legislative agenda. The continuous generation of policy initiatives and agency structures has been dictated by the logic of abundant incrementalism, marked by the hurried launch of policy initiatives at very short intervals. The main causes of this unproductive haste include the relatively short terms of EU Presidencies, ad hoc regulatory reactions to internal security crises (such as the Dutroux case in Belgium), almost uncontrollable illegal immigration, and, of course, the terrorist attacks of 11 September 2001.

Often, however, ad hoc decision-making tends to be succeeded by painstaking negotiations on legal instruments within the multilateral Council bureaucracy. Moreover, the Commission's scoreboard repeatedly reveals that the implementation of legal instruments may be cumbersome, which is mainly due to the adoption of non-binding legal instruments and slow ratification procedures.[4]

An Area of Freedom, Security and Justice (AFSJ) is gradually being built, but this process lacks a precise description of legal objectives and institutional mandates. The lack of a detailed design has frequently caused friction between EU Member States; this has been illustrated by the numerous reserves in draft documents and by the protocols that are attached to various legal instruments.

Despite the common political will expressed by the government leaders at the Maastricht Summit in 1991, the construction and progression of the third pillar has frequently been hampered by the stubborn sovereignties of the Member States. But, vice versa, Member States have also been known for their efforts to 'Europeanize' their domestic interests, which have occasionally resulted from restricted national problem-solving capacities. Moreover, national sovereignty instincts have not prevented Member States from committing themselves to several Action Plans (e.g. Action Plan on organized crime, Vienna Action Plan) and the Tampere 'Milestones'.

Amidst these ambivalent developments, it is difficult to predict how solid the AFSJ construction will become in ten or twenty years' time. There is general consensus that more intra and inter-pillar consistency is required, e.g. in the area of judicial cooperation.[5] There is also a need to embed AFSJ in the encompassing patterns of European integration. Meanwhile, the Justice and Home Affairs arena has become involved with a myriad of actors, mainly because of the multiplicity of political and institutional representatives that have been included in the decision-making process. This development is best illustrated by the creation of several horizontal groups, such as the Strategic Committee for Immigration, Frontiers and Asylum, and the Horizontal Group on Drugs to coordinate anti-drug efforts. But we have also seen a growth in the number of Working Parties and Expert Groups within the Third Pillar, a development largely due to the enlargement process and the incorporation of the Schengen acquis into the Treaty on the European Union (TEU).

In short, the building of the AFSJ seems to be exposed to contrastive dynamics. On the one hand, we witness a process of deepening, which expresses itself through the building of agencies and the gradual consolidation of existing institutions and (binding) regulatory frameworks. On the other hand, we may observe a process of widening: this expresses itself in the expansion of agency mandates, the mobilization of flexible responses to new

[4] See e.g. the Laeken European Council, which was unhappy with the slow adoption of instruments in the field of asylum and immigration, and argued that progress had been slower and less substantial than expected. CONV 69/02, p. 7.

[5] 'While some progress has been made, many consider that cooperation in the judicial field lacks overall coherence: measures are adopted with no reference to an overall plan; the split between the first and third pillars adds to the confusion', CONV 69/02, p. 6.

security challenges, and the transposition of normative expectations from the EU to candidate countries.

The ultimate question about the future construction of the AFSJ concerns the direction of progress. The time has come to insert the future of AFSJ more affirmatively into a wider process of European integration. When issues, such as the AFSJ, concern blueprints for future European integration, Member States may have very different views.[6] It remains to be seen whether this also applies more specifically to the JHA domain.

7.3 THE EUROPEAN CONVENTION AND ITS RELEVANCE FOR JHA

Within the Convention, considerable attention has been devoted to the area of Justice and Home Affairs cooperation. In some of the initial contributions of the Convention it was even regarded as the main theme, or at least one that deserved mention alongside the discussion of other topics.[7] A special session of the European Convention focused on the issue of Justice and Home Affairs Cooperation (6–7 June 2002). Meanwhile, non-governmental organizations such as Statewatch and ILPA have jointly submitted recommendations to the special Working Group X ('Freedom, Security and Justice') of the Convention (Curtin and Peers 2002). The lack of progress on a common immigration and asylum policy has been one of the most persistent subjects of complaint within the European Convention.[8] Moreover, the Convention has raised suggestions concerning institutional improvements in the context of Justice and Home Affairs cooperation. It is especially vital to enhance the role of national parliaments[9] in the area of JHA, as this area of cooperation is still marked – despite improvements – by a significant democratic deficit. Other aspects of the Convention also have an impact on JHA matters. With regard to the debate about widening versus delimiting EU competences (see De Búrca and De Witte 2002),[10] several questions may be raised regarding tasks in the AFSJ. Should governmental authority on free movement of persons and justice be transferred to the European level, given the present international environment and the aspirations of EU citizens? A majority of Convention members that presented their views at the plenary meeting on 15 and 16 April

[6] *European Voice*, 6–12 December 2001, p. 2.

[7] Justice and Home Affairs - Progress report and general problems, The European Convention, The Secretariat, Brussels, 31 May 2002, CONV 69/02.

[8] See http:// www.euractiv.com/cgi-bin/cgint.exe/.

[9] See also CONV 74/02, Brussels, 30 May 2002.

[10] CONV 75/02.

2002[11] argued that the Union should be enabled to act more decisively, whether against terrorism, organized crime, illegal immigration, drugs or trafficking in human beings. This stands as opposed to, for instance, combating poverty and social exclusion, public services and social security, about which opinions differed widely. In this context, opinions were voiced in favour of the creation of a Common European Border Guard and the insertion of the Fundamental Rights Charter into the Community Treaties.[12] The large majority of speakers supported a flexible system for the delimitation of competencies, allowing for some adaptation of the Union's missions and for citizens' expectations to be met optimally. Within the Convention, broad support can be found for a clear-cut division of power and a focusing of European action within the transnational dimension of the criminal activity ('Euro-crimes').

Other different questions of the Convention relate to the following issues:[13]

- *Social legitimacy and support from civil society:* What do the citizens of Europe expect with regard to freedom, security, and justice, and what types of criminal activities may necessitate a closer cooperation at the European level? These questions were also underlined at the Laeken declaration:

  > There have been frequent public calls for a greater European role in justice and security, action against cross-border crime, control of migration flows and reception of asylum seekers, especially those refugees from far-flung war zones.

  Eurbarometer surveys confirm that European citizens are concerned about organized crime and drug trafficking, which rank third after peace and security and the reduction of unemployment.[14]
- *Transparency and comprehensibility*: Is there a need to clarify and simplify the instruments available to the Union in the area of Justice and Home Affairs? In a preparatory document, the Convention states that Third Pillar instruments are not necessarily appropriate to pull off

[11] Note on the plenary meeting, Brussels, 15 and 16 April 2002, The European Convention, The Secretariat, Brussels, 25 April 2002, CONV 40/02.
[12] See recommendation of WG II on the insertion of the Charter / accession to the ECHR, CONV 354/02, WG II 16, Brussels, 22 October 2002, which the EU Charter on Fundamental Rights should become legally binding and acquire a constitutional status.
[13] Convention meeting on 6 and 7 June 2002 – Strengthening the Area of Freedom, Security and Justice, The European Convention, The Secretariat, Brussels, 31 May 2002, CONV 70/02.
[14] CONV 69/02.

ambitious legal projects along the lines of the Tampere conclusions.[15] The legal tools, most of which originally stem from the second pillar, are hardly suitable for a sustained legislative programme.[16]

- *Practical functionality of structures and procedures*: To what extent should structures and procedures currently in place be simplified?[17] The Convention notes that JHA has become one of the most complicated working areas. Consistency and efficiency are under pressure because the division of competences between the pillars is not always clear. Furthermore, there are dual regimes for international agreements on Community matters (Article 300 TEC) and Third Pillar matters (Article 38 TEU). Finally, JHA is the domain with the most abundant application of flexible cooperation initiatives, including the highly complex opt-in arrangements for the UK, Ireland and Denmark with regard to Schengen and Title IV matters. The present institutional and procedural complexity is counterproductive to the achievement of transparency as expected by European citizens.[18]
- *Democratic control on JHA*: How can democratic legitimacy in decision-making in the JHA sphere be bolstered or strengthened? How do national parliaments intend to exercise their powers in the area of justice and security, largely under the third pillar and thus subject at most times to intergovernmental decision-making? Many observers within the Convention attribute the delays in decision-making to the unanimity rule and the difficulty in arriving at compromises.[19] One of the main issues of concern is the limited amount of parliamentary control that can be exercised on Europol's activities. Moreover, there are legal instruments such as common positions that do not require prior consultation of the European Parliament. Different avenues have

[15] See also: Final report of Working Group X 'Freedom, Security and Justice' to the Convention, CONV 426/02 gar/PM/md 1, Brussels, 2 December 2002.

[16] The document CONV 69/02, p. 10, notes that the convention between Member States is no longer used as a legal instrument because of its inertia and the uncertainties involved in the ratification procedures (ratification alone takes 4 to 5 years); also new instruments which were introduced by the Amsterdam Treaty have been suffering from a lack of direct effect (a legal instrument like the European arrest warrant takes a long time to enter into effect as Member States have to transpose it into their domestic law word by word). See also: Final report of Working Group X 'Freedom, Security and Justice' to the Convention, CONV 426/02 gar/PM/md 1, Brussels, 2 December 2002.

[17] The Commission proposed a radical simplification of how the European Union works, amongst others by abolishing the unanimity rule in the Council of Ministers. IP/02/1802, Brussels, 5 December 2002. It also proposed that all European laws, including those in JHA, should be approved by Parliament and Council by co-decision based on a proposal of the Commission.

[18] CONV 69/02, p. 12.

[19] CONV 69/02, p. 8; Opinion of Working Group X on 'Freedom, Security and Justice' in their final report, CONV 426/02 gar/PM/md 4, Brussels, 2 December 2002.

become subjects of exploration: scrutiny at a national level,[20] contacts between MPs and MEPs (e.g. in the form of Parlopol when it concerns parliamentary control on Europol), participation in legislative activities of the Council, enhancement of the role of COSAC, and the possible creation of an independent or second Chamber in the European Parliament.[21]

- *Judicial control on JHA:* Despite the facultative clause introduced by the Amsterdam Treaty, allowing Member States to opt in for a competence exercised by the European Court of Justice, the Court has currently limited control over JHA matters, including those in the fields of asylum and migration. In the meantime, TEU provisions have led to an extremely complex 'variable geometry' arrangement that operates in parallel with the different procedures introduced prior to the ratification of the Amsterdam Treaty. In addition, at Union level, there is no protection against activities performed by Europol; this also applies to activities performed by Eurojust.[22] Meanwhile, Working Group III of the European Convention, which advises on 'Legal Personality', has recommended that the EU Court of Justice should acquire an *ex ante* competence[23] with regard to Titles IV and VI of the TEU and an *ex post* competence in view of prejudicial procedures in certain cases.

One of the more substantial questions also addressed at the European Convention concerns further institutionalization: should there be reflection on the creation of new joint bodies to guarantee border protection and to give Europol an operational role?

[20] See Curtin and Peers (eds) (2002), who in par. 3.4.2, favour 'placing an explicit provision in the EU Treaty that national parliaments must be enabled to exercise effective scrutiny at the national level. The mechanics of that scrutiny must of course remain a matter for national constitutional law. The scope of scrutiny should be wider than EU legislation as narrowly defined at present in the Council's rules of procedure, and could embrace scrutinizing the new Council work programmes as well as the Commission's work programme and the actions of the European Council'. The joint submissions also recommend that scrutiny reserves of national parliaments ought to have far more force and should leave less discretion to a national government to override them.

[21] CONV 74/02.

[22] CONV 69/02, p. 11.

[23] CONV 305/02, p. 17 (WG III 16, 1 October 2002).

7.4 FROM SUGGESTIONS TO BLUEPRINT: POSSIBLE RECOMMENDATIONS OF THE CONVENTION

The above reveals that the three most persistent complaints about the functioning of the JHA decision-making system concern the lack of transparency, the abundance of complexity, and the slow decision-making and implementation. These criticisms are joined by repeated misgivings about the democratic deficit, the judicial deficit, and the sporadic reference to basic principles of human rights.

Several guarantees are thus required for a balanced Area of Freedom, Security and Justice. The European Convention provides more than an excellent opportunity to secure such a balance. The following recommendations could be further explored in terms of political support and practical feasibility:

- The respect for human rights should become the fundamental normative basis for each practice, (legal) instrument, institution and process within AFSJ. The EU Charter on Fundamental Rights ought to become binding in its entirety. Not long ago, JHA Commissioner Antonio Vitorino argued that a constitutional framework of the Union ought to be based on the Charter, and he had in mind the legal position of immigrants within the EU or a European asylum law.[24] The European Convention should also pay attention to the improvement of the Charter of Fundamental Rights and it should consider the inclusion of the EU in the European Convention of Human Rights.[25]
- Securitization ought to be moderated. Participation in the 'risk society' and action against perceptions of threat should not culminate in a European surveillance society and should not be at the expense of fundamental rights, freedoms, or democratic rights. This is a more-than-relevant issue in view of measures that were introduced in the aftermath of 11 September, to include the securitization of the immigration issue, as witnessed at the Seville EU Summit in June

[24] IP/02/750, 'Commission proposes a far-reaching overhaul of the European Union', Brussels, 22 May 2002. See also Andrew Duff's (MEP) presentation to the Convention, 21 March 2002, which says that 'More power at the centre obliges us to build in the safeguard of installing a fundamental rights regime at the heart of the integration process so as to protect the citizen from any abuse of that power. That is why we need to have the Charter enshrined in the basic law'. See also the submission of Human Rights, Democracy and Conflict Prevention NGOs ('Strengthening the Value Base Complying with International Standards Delivering on the Promises', May 2002).

[25] See also Curtin and Peers (2002), who recommend that a legally binding effect of the EU Charter of rights and EU accession to the European Convention on Human Rights and other international human rights treaties is essential to protect human rights related to immigration, asylum, criminal law and policing.

2002. Personal privacy is coming under severe pressure, especially since methods of surveillance are now being employed by both private and public services. Hence, uniform standards of protection should be introduced throughout EU Member States that participate in any international data-exchange systems.

- All strata of civil society ought to be encouraged to participate in the debate about the current and future developments with AFSJ; this will enhance a broad and informed consensus amongst citizens and strengthen the social legitimacy of AFSJ. We have seen that within the European Convention, a genuine effort is made to involve representatives from civil society through the creation of forums. A special session of the European Convention has already been devoted to civil society (24 and 25 June 2002).[26]
- Democratic control should be consolidated at all levels, to the extent that:

  - All Parliaments involved acquire adequate and timely information, e.g. through an Early Warning System.[27]
  - The European Parliament and the National Parliaments should reinforce inter-parliamentary cooperation, for instance in the form of inter-parliamentary conferences[28] or a semi-institution (Parlopol) which would specifically focus on AFSJ matters. A connection should be found with COSAC in this regard.[29]
  - Despite improvements in the position of the European Parliament with regard to AFSJ matters since the inception of the Amsterdam Treaty, co-decision and qualified majority voting should become the general decision-making procedure[30] for all matters through extension of the Community method.[31]

[26] 'The Convention and Civil Society', The European Convention, The Secretariat, Brussels, 13 March 2002, CONV 48/02.

[27] Convention Working Group I, on the principle of subsidiarity, CONV 286/02, WG 1 15, 23 September 2002; See also Working Group IV of the Convention concerning the role of national parliaments, CONV 353/02, WG IV 17, 22 October 2002.

[28] See proposal of Working Group X 'Freedom, Security and Justice', CONV 426/02 lst/PM/md 23, Brussels, 2 December 2002.

[29] See proposals of Working Group IV of the Convention concerning the role of national parliaments, CONV 353/02, WG IV 17, 22 October 2002.

[30] JHA Commissioner Vitorino argued that all legal instruments in the area of Justice and Home Affairs ought to be initiated by the European Commission, by means of a co-decision procedure (Council and Parliament), and they should be subject to legal control by the European Court of Justice (IP/02/750, 22 May 2002; see also IP/02/1802, 5 December 2002). Curtin and Peers (2002) make an exception for the eventual creation of a European Border Guard.

[31] See also Benelux memorandum 'A Balanced Institutional Framework for an Enlarged, More Effective and More Transparent Union', 5 December 2002. See http://www.minbuza.nl/, which proposes extension of the Community method to adoption of legislation in the fight against

- Institutions involving the exchange of sensitive information, such as Europol and Eurojust, should be subjected to (more) democratic control. National models for parliamentary control on policing activities could possibly be elaborated on for a working model at the EU-level.

• Judicial control should be enhanced, e.g. by widening the competences of the European Court of Justice with regard to Title VI matters. Although sensitive in view of the maintenance of national sovereignty, the expansion of EU competences in the field of internal security may be complemented by the gradual establishment of a European *Rechtsstaat*. This can be done by promoting the construction of a European Judicial Area which includes core constituents such as:

  - A European Criminal Court
  - A European Public Prosecutor[32]
  - A European Penal Code, limited to crimes which are categorized as European (transnational 'Euro-crimes')
  - A European Code of Criminal Procedure
  - An extended competence of the European Ombudsman, namely to bring his own cases before the ECJ.[33]

  These are fundamental prerequisites, for instance, in view of a future operational mandate of Europol.

• Agencies and institutions should function effectively and efficiently:

  - Mandates of institutions such as Europol and Eurojust should be clarified through inter-organizational agreements;
  - The Council working methods should be revised and/or rationalized (Haga process, Laeken Summit);
  - Higher levels of transparency should be introduced at all levels of decision-making, to include even the earliest policy-making stages;
  - Inter-pillar cooperation should be further encouraged (e.g. in view of roles and responsibilities concerning crisis management, drugs and data-protection); eventually, the pillars

crime, and complete application of the Community method to legislation in the field of asylum, migration and judicial cooperation in civil matters.

[32] See in particular the Commission's Green Paper on the establishment of a European Public Prosecutor for the criminal law protection of the Community's financial interests, 11/12/01, IP/01/1794 (http://europa.eu.int/olaf/livre_vert).

[33] See also Curtin and Peers (2002).

should disappear,[34] a view shared by the European Commission itself.[35]

- Performance indicators should be developed for institutions like Europol and Eurojust, which may enhance their accountability.

- *Legal instruments* should acquire a higher level of mutual legislative coherence, e.g. in the area of border management and data protection (Title IV and Title VI). The adoption and implementation of Community instruments ought to be considered for all AFSJ matters.[36] Moreover, EU Member States should be encouraged to implement legally binding and non-binding EU-instruments. Parliaments ought to gain the competence to monitor such implementations.
- *Subsidiarity*[37] should remain an important rationale for the distribution of competencies between EU institutions and national, regional or local law enforcement authorities. Within the Convention, the principles of subsidiarity and proportionality form an essential part of the delimitation of competence between the EU and the Member States.

7.5 CONCLUSION

A gradual extension of Community competence – also in the field of police and judicial cooperation in criminal matters – may help to achieve the transformation of some of these normative cornerstones into reality. Given the importance of free movement of persons, security and justice, there is a serious case for embroidering these issues into the wider debate about a possible 'constitutionalization' of the EU. The challenge of the Convention is to draft a blueprint for the future of JHA cooperation in the EU, and to develop a phase-wise implementation process.

[34] CONV 69/02. This is also the opinion of Working Group X of the European Convention on 'Freedom, Security and Justice', CONV 426/02 gar/PM/md 1, Brussels, 2 December 2002; See also Curtin and Peers (eds); (2002): par. 2.3 and 2.4, who argue that the pillar structure should be abolished, but recommend the maintenance of two separate titles within the EU as a whole, as also suggested in the Praesidium's Preliminary Draft Constitutional Treaty.
[35] IP/02/750, Brussels, 22 May 2002.
[36] Opinion of Convention Working Group X, 'Freedom, Security and Justice' (CONV 426/02 gar/PM/md 7, Brussels, 2 December 2002).
[37] See also CONV 71/02, Mandate of the Working Group on the principle of subsidiarity, 30 May 2002. The application of the principle of subsidiarity has also been discussed in the final report of Working Group X of the European Convention, in particular with regard to crime prevention (CONV 426/02 gar/PM/md 13, Brussels, 2 December 2002).

The danger lurking around the corner is, however, that the proposals of the Convention may be short-term and piecemeal in nature. But now that the Convention increasingly gains political importance, it is hard to believe that the IGC 2004 would ignore the results of the Convention. Judging by the first blueprint of a European Convention, which was presented on 28 October 2002,[38] the achievement of a variety of ambitions may be feasible. The text is both promising for the creation of the EU constitutional framework and for management of internal and external policies to optimize EU performance.

With regard to more substantive issues within the field of Justice and Home Affairs cooperation, opinions within the Convention are not divided about the need for a closer cooperation in view of cross-border crime, asylum and immigration policy. The lack of consensus concerns the way in which this closer cooperation ought to be achieved, either by means of the Community method or the intergovernmental one. Therefore, it remains unclear at this point in time what the precise effect of Europe's new blueprint will be for what affects EU citizens most: safety or security.

REFERENCES

Curtin, D. and S. Peers (eds) (2002), *Joint Submissions by the Standing Committee of Experts on International Immigration, Refugee and Criminal Law, the Immigration Law Practitioners Association, Statewatch, and The European Council of Refugees and Exiles to Working Group X*, Utrecht and London.

De Búrca, G. and B. de Witte (2002), *The Delimitation of Powers between the EU and its Member States*, CR 2002/03, Policy Papers, Series on Constitutional Reform of the EU, European University Institute, Robert Schuman Institute of Advanced Studies.

Dehaene, J. (2002), 'Nieuw EU-Verdrag of zware crisis', *Europa van Morgen*, no. 9, 12 June 2002.

[38] CONV 369/02.

8. Rebuilding Police and Judicial Systems in the Stability Pact Countries

Bernard Hemingway

8.1 INTRODUCTION

This chapter is devoted to the assessment of the Stability Pact programmes on Justice and Home Affairs (JHA), looking at its main priorities as well as the different JHA issues and initiatives that are of growing concern in South-Eastern Europe (SEE).

Three years ago the Stability Pact for South Eastern Europe was created by the European Union and endorsed by the G-8, NATO, the OSCE, and other international organisations. Loosely based on the OSCE 'basket' principle, the Pact was organised into three Working Tables:

1. Democratisation and Human Rights;
2. Economic Reconstruction, Cooperation and Development; and
3. Security Issues.

Given the complexity of the last 'basket', the third working table was further divided into two sub-tables: Security/Defence and Justice and Home Affairs.

The overall objective of the Stability Pact programmes on Justice and Home Affairs is to promote national reforms among the countries in South-East Europe, through regional cooperation and closer international links, particularly within Europe. The structure of the Stability Pact and its membership makes it well placed for such a comprehensive strategy.

Adherence to international standards, including an effective judicial system and law enforcement, remains essential for the process of stabilisation of the SEE region and for democratic and economic development.

Important steps of reform have been taken in the field of Justice and Home Affairs, but further reform and capacity-building efforts are needed in a number of key areas, such as asylum and migration, trafficking in human beings, anti-crime and corruption policy, police training as well as border administration. These areas are covered in the JHA programme within the Stability Pact.

Strategies for all the priority sectors of the Stability Pact Programme within the Justice and Home Affairs field have been developed. Together these strategies constitute the basis for the Stability Pact Strategy on JHA, which is now focused on implementation. In this regard the EU Stabilisation and Association Process and the Stability Pact Programme must operate in a mutually reinforcing and complementary manner.

8.2 PRIORITIES

Priorities in the field of JHA derive from four main factors:

1. the need for judicial reform and legislation adhering to international standards;
2. the need to combat organised crime;
3. effective and impartial law enforcement; and
4. a comprehensive system for orderly migration, including measures to combat trafficking in human beings and safeguard asylum systems in line with best European standards.

To address these issues, national reforms, including legislation and institution-building, are key priorities. To be truly effective, the creation of institutions must be comprehensive and cover both required legislation and enforcement mechanisms. Similarly, the formulation of asylum policies and response systems requires a strong capacity to address all migration flows.

Institution-building should also encompass all aspects of administration, including legislation, organisation, training and equipment. No significant progress can be expected without a clear and firm political commitment from governments. This commitment should be the condition set by the international community to finance technical assistance programmes. For the immediate future, priority should be given to institution and capacity building, with particular emphasis on judiciary systems.

Regional cooperation and ownership of the process among countries in the region is the cornerstone of the Stability Pact, also in the Justice and Home Affairs field.

The nature of JHA issues extends beyond national borders and the political role of the Pact is to encourage countries of the region to conclude agreements between themselves on areas of common interest with a trans-national dimension. But it must be emphasised that no regional cooperation can be envisaged without strong and reliable national structures. This is probably the best example to show the complementarity between the European Union's Stabilisation and Association Process and the Stability Pact.

A third priority for countries of the region is the declared perspective of membership in the EU. This perspective provides several important references, either from the acquis communautaire or more broadly from standards applied by the EU Member States.

This set of references is becoming clearer since JHA has become one of the priority areas of the EU, in South-East Europe and elsewhere. The Treaty of Amsterdam adapted the procedures for conducting the European Union's external activities with regard to Justice and Home Affairs. The conclusions of the European Council in Tampere gave the Council the task to develop, in close cooperation with the Commission, specific recommendations on priorities and measures for the Union's external action in JHA.

The conclusions of the European Council of Feira provided that the objective remains the fullest 'possible integration of the countries of the region into the political and economic mainstream of Europe through cooperation in Justice and Home Affairs'. This objective called for intensified cooperation in the region in the field of JHA. Since then, a Multi-Presidency programme for external relations in the JHA field (2001–2002) has been presented.

The methodology applied by the European Union in JHA brings together expertise provided by EU Member States with financial support from the Commission and technical assistance provided by the Commission or other institutions. The specific and important role of the EU must be combined and complemented by other countries and institutions already active in that field. The Stability Pact can usefully bring together all available and willing resources.

In concrete terms the Pact is involved in the following priority areas:

1. *Police forum.* In order to strengthen regional police cooperation in South-Eastern Europe, a training programme has been developed and co-ordinated by the Association of European Police Colleges (AEPC) in cooperation with the Central European Police Academy and the Nordic Baltic Police Academy. This initiative is designed to build professional relations and effective networks, as well as to provide regional training to increase police skills, enhance democratic policing and cross-border cooperation, aiming to create a sustainable system of regional police training.

2. *Asylum and migration policies.* Asylum and migration issues are quite obviously of growing concern in the region. The overall goal with the Stability Pact Migration and Asylum Initiative (MAI) is to develop national and regional programmes and strengthened regional cooperation for orderly migration in line with European standards. The initiative covers five areas: asylum, legal migration, illegal migration, visa policy, and border management. It is based on the twinning idea forming teams for Albania, Bosnia and Herzegovina, Croatia, FYRO Macedonia and the FR Yugoslavia.

3. *Organised crime and corruption.* The Stability Pact initiative to combat organised crime (SPOC) aims at the adoption of policies and strategies, multi-disciplinary coordination mechanisms, legislation, cooperation between national agencies and the establishment of specialised units, and regional and international cooperation. Furthermore, it works closely with the Crime Fighting Centre in Bucharest for the exchange of operational data and the compliance of its legal basis with the Europol convention.

The Anti-Corruption Initiative (SPAI) has developed a political dialogue between countries and international experts, national programmes and joint monitoring procedures and is now becoming focused on providing and co-ordinating technical assistance. SPAI aims at a comprehensive set of actions including: adoption and implementation of European and other international instruments, promotion of good governance and reliable administration, strengthening of legislation and integrity in business operations, and promotion of an active civil society.

4. *Trafficking in human beings.* The Task Force, composed of international organisations and NGOs with relevant experience and expertise, has developed a three-year Action Plan on combating trafficking in human beings. The aim of the comprehensive anti-trafficking strategy is to counter, through concrete action involving all sectors and actors whose intervention is necessary, the activities of traffickers and to assist and protect victims. The focus of the Task Force is on awareness raising, training and exchange programmes, and cooperation in law enforcement, victim protection programmes, return and reintegration assistance, relevant legislative reform, protection and prevention.

8.3 CONCLUSION

As a way of conclusion, it seems clear that it is not possible to create an Area of Freedom, Justice and Security inside the Union without looking into our closest neighbourhoods. With the enlargement process the EU has given a number of countries a concrete perspective. Complementing this, the Stability Pact along with the Stabilisation and Association process, helps countries of the region on their way towards 'European integration'.

9. Eurojust vis-à-vis the European Public Prosecutor

Jorge Costa

9.1 INTRODUCTION: AN AREA OF FREEDOM, SECURITY AND JUSTICE

By way of introduction, as this was an event impossible to circumvent in the European scene, mostly in the field of justice, the Tampere European Council made a significant political assertion when it established that '...[it] is determined to develop the Union as an area of freedom, security and justice; (...) sends a strong political message to reaffirm the importance of this objective and has agreed on a number of policy orientations and priorities which will speedily make this area a reality'. Tampere can thus be considered very much like a port of arrival as well as departure.

It is a port of arrival, following the voyage begun in Rome with the signature of the Treaties establishing the European Communities, and passing by Maastricht and Amsterdam, which were the precursors of the Union and the Area of Freedom, Security and Justice.

It is a port of departure for the course of the voyage whose stop in Nice and Laeken is rather obligatory, along with a guide named Scoreboard. As far as an area of judicial cooperation in criminal matters is concerned, before Tampere, one spoke about cooperation and making efforts towards the settlement of national entities which would be competent to carry out criminal investigations. The word cooperation reigned throughout. In Tampere, however – and with Tampere – a new concept appeared: coordination. And one can affirm that since Tampere everything changed.

It was in Nice that the European Commission presented its proposal to create a European Public Prosecutor for the Member States. The main innovative aspect of this new body would be that it would act neither simply on the basis of cooperation between the Member States, nor only on the basis of coordination achieved by an entity beyond the Member States (though still in the spirit of the intergovernmental method). It would rather constitute a 'common entity'. Moreover, Laeken further stimulated the Council to analyse the Commission's Green Paper on the matter.

Such is the scenario offered by the 'short feature film' on the creation of an Area of Freedom, Security and Justice. My intention hereby is to provide some pictorial highlights of this 'short film' and the present debate, as well as to provide possible trails, which could lead to 'the end of history'.

9.2 EUROJUST

The institution of Eurojust followed the track of ideas presented within the framework of the negotiations which led to the setting up of Europol, by translating the need for coordinating legal proceedings at the European level. To this end, Tampere asked the Council to adopt a legal measure by the end of 2001.

Such a matter was part of the reinforcement progress of the European provisions concerning the fight against organized crime, by introducing something into the overall philosophy that was different from the previous actions which were based more on the legal framing of cooperation as implemented by pre-existing entities (e.g. European Judicial Network, liaison magistrates).

Tampere defined, in political terms, what was expected to be achieved through the establishment of Eurojust:

- To enable an adequate coordination between the national prosecution authorities;
- To establish its competence in relation to criminal investigations on organized crime; and
- To cooperate closely with the European Judicial Network, in particular regarding the simplification of the implementation of rogatory letters.

However, looking at the recent history, and in particular at the issue of judicial cooperation in criminal matters, the core achievement of Tampere has been the creation of a permanent structure aimed at coordinating the authorities which are competent to carry out criminal proceedings and investigations. These authorities have an intergovernmental legal personality, combined with some supranational aspects. Indeed, it is already possible to find some 'disconnection' from the Member States, since for instance, Eurojust enjoys autonomy from them in the following areas: on management – whose competence lies in the board of directors elected among its members (although this election needs to be ratified by the Council); its decisions do not have to be submitted to trade unions within the Member States; and also, its own budget.

Generally speaking, these 'autonomous features' are closely related to the judiciary, which means that they guarantee an independence of action such as that provided by the theory of separation of powers.

Neither the politicians in Tampere, nor the negotiators at that time considered the establishment of an European Public Prosecutor as a high priority policy. It is doubtful whether they also realized on the importance of establishing a body close to the national public prosecutor model, including the material and procedural competences, power of investigation, judicial control, independence, etc.

The idea of establishing such a model was rejected consciously and internationally. The institution of a public prosecutor was not yet a desired goal. This is the reason why a unit was considered, in general terms, as a European body and enjoying legal personality, with still some intergovernmental patterns. Its competences will not include research. Its relevant mandatory competences will operate in two ways, either through a unanimous position of all its members acting collectively or, individually, along with a defined status at national level and enjoying material competence somewhere in between organized criminality and criminality. This reality led to the creation of Eurojust by Council Decision on 28 February 2002 with a view to reinforcing the fight against serious crime. Nevertheless, the features of something different had already started to emerge.

We will see how the provisions on Eurojust within the project of European Constitution, Volume II, Part II, Article III-169 (ex Article 19), presented by the Praesidium of the European Convention, will be considered by the Council.

9.3 THE PROJECT OF A EUROPEAN PUBLIC PROSECUTOR: THE GREEN PAPER

Following its initiative presented at Nice on the creation of a European Public Prosecutor, the European Commission finally decided to issue the Green Paper on the establishment of a European Public Prosecutor for the criminal-law protection of the Communities' financial interests.

The Commission advocates for the centralization, at European level and within the European Public Prosecutor body, of the competences to direct and manage investigations related to the European Communities' financial interests. This centralization would guarantee a more efficient fight against crime across Europe. The legal status and organization of the body would ensure the equal respect of, on the one hand, fundamental rights and freedoms, and on the other the Justice and Home Affairs policy priorities.

It would be therefore desirable to:

- Overcome the existing diversities within the European judicial criminal area;
- Modify the inherent rigidity of the classic methods of judicial cooperation between Member States;
- Attribute a judicial character to administrative investigations; and
- Strengthen the organization as well as efficiency of investigations and gathering of evidence within the European institutions themselves.

The specific competences of the European Public Prosecutor would be limited to the protection of the Communities' financial interests, and it would exercise its powers in the whole European area. Also, it would direct and coordinate prosecutions, and the gathering of evidence, as well as direct the investigation activities.

A fundamental feature of the European Prosecutor would be its independence with respect to the parties of the proceedings as well as the Member States and European Institutions.

The European Prosecutor would be appointed by qualified majority at the Council, being first proposed by the European Commission, and after obtaining the favourable opinion of the European Parliament. It would enjoy, being the head of the European Public Ministry, competences over internal organization, instructions, and the deputy European Public Prosecutors, as well as the power to define the legal framework of the code of behaviour in relation to judicial criminal matters.

Thus, the whole architecture of the European Prosecutor would be based on the division of its competences and those belonging to the Deputy European Public Prosecutors. The Deputy European Public Prosecutors would carry out all the acts that the former would have been responsible for during both the gathering of evidence and the criminal proceedings, and this being either on national territory or on the territory of another Member State, in this case in cooperation with the delegated European Public Prosecutor in charge.

9.3.1 Procedure

The European Public Prosecutor's *modus operandi* would presuppose the definition of a procedural framework which would co-exist with the different national judicial systems.

In addition, the Public Prosecutor would direct and coordinate the gathering of evidence as well as criminal prosecutions in order to fully protect the financial interests of the European Communities on the basis of the information provided by any national of the EU or, compulsorily, at the request of any national or European authority. Therefore it is expected that this body would carry out acts of investigation directly or by delegation, when requested.

Again, the vote by the Council of Ministers on the project of European Constitution will decide the future evolution of the proposal presented by the Praesidium of the European Convention in Article III-170 (ex Article 20).

9.4 SIMILARITIES AND DIFFERENCES

At this stage, in our view it is important to look at the relationship between Eurojust, as a judicial coordination unit already functioning, and the European Public Prosecutor, which is still a project to be considered as a real Public Ministry at European level.

9.4.1 Nature of the organization

(a) Eurojust is still strongly influenced by the Member States. Its appointment has a purely intergovernmental character, as symbolized by the fact that its members are elected at national level by each Member State. This 'link' to national spheres, or sometimes rather dependence on them, brings some ambiguity or uncertainty to the exact legal nature of Eurojust as an independent judicial institution.

(b) The proposal for the establishment of a European Public Prosecutor, however, undoubtedly qualifies it as a judicial body for two reasons:

- The independence with respect to either the parties of the proceeding as well as the Member States and the European Institutions, would constitute a fundamental feature of the organ; and
- It would enjoy a truly judicial competence, i.e. the competence to carry out the investigation as well as to coordinate and direct prosecutions.

9.4.2 Territorial competence

(a) As we have already mentioned, Eurojust still presents obvious intergovernmental features, these being:

- The appointment of its members by the Member States at national level;
- The core goal of Eurojust is above all to simplify as well as facilitate the coordination between the competent national authorities; and
- This implies the existence of national areas/territories.

(b) The European Public Prosecutor is considered as a European body since:

- Its appointment would be subject to European rules and procedures (list of candidates provided by the Commission; assent of the European Parliament and final appointment by the Council acting by a qualify majority); and
- Its territorial jurisdiction would cover all the European Union's territory, which is thus considered as a unique territory in order to carry out the gathering of evidence and criminal proceedings.

9.4.3 Competences

In that concern, the first comment to be made is rather obvious: there is a structural difference between the two bodies - the European Public Prosecutor would be competent to initiate the investigation activities deemed to be necessary, whereas Eurojust is exclusively entitled to contribute to the coordination of the investigations, while the investigations remain purely national in character, i.e. the competent national authorities will always be the ones actually carrying out the investigations. A second difference that needs to be highlighted is the fact that Eurojust has been created to act within the framework of the international judicial cooperation, although with a higher qualitative standing in relation to its coordination functions. Eurojust will not be entitled to carry out investigation except in those cases when one national member has been given these particular powers by her/his own state, as provided by Article 99.3, first paragraph. There are, however, two exceptions to this rule: the power attributed to the national member by the Member State will be limited exclusively to the judicial competence over its own territory; – and the power will not cover Eurojust. The European Public Prosecutor, however, is competent to carry out the investigations and to exercise public action.

9.4.4 Material scope

The decision which established Eurojust provided its competence, among other types of crime, over fraud or corruption against financial interests of the European Communities. Looking at the Green Paper on the establishment of a European Public Prosecutor, the material scope of this body would comprise the same types of financial crimes. Thus, would it be correct to say that the areas of competence overlap between the two organizations?

It is not our intention to define all the categories included within the broad criminal sphere which would be covered by the material scope of the European Public Prosecutor. However, two precautions must be taken as a point of departure: the first is related to the fact that one of the organizations has the competence to investigate and the other to coordinate investigations. This would mean that every crime not covered by the competence of the European Prosecutor would fall within Eurojust's area of competence. Indeed, some breaches of law, which although they fall within the material scope of the European Public Prosecutor, would be addressed to the national jurisdiction. Therefore, the necessary coordination will fall to Eurojust.

(a) The material competences falling within Eurojust's potential fields of action are broad in character (including different sorts of crimes, which are in our view too diverse).
(b) The material scope of the European Prosecutor deals specifically with the protection of the financial interests of the European Communities.

9.4.5 Authority

(a) Eurojust depends, to a great extent, on the goodwill of the Member States. As a matter of fact, they may decide unilaterally whether or not to follow Eurojust's requests, although the Member States have to communicate their decisions and reasoning in that respect. Also, the Member States may even be exempted in certain cases from justifying themselves (on grounds of internal security, security of the person involved, good progress of investigations, etc). It is striking to see that the situations mentioned, which are closely related to, for instance, the start of investigations, approval or denial of evidence, provision of the necessary information to initiate the functions of Eurojust, show the fragility of the powers exercised over Eurojust.
(b) On the other hand, the European Public Prosecutor enjoys a rather 'coherent framework of competences and powers'. Its acts will be valid and recognized within the whole European territory and they will be subject to judicial control (by the national judge involved). These concrete competences would be the following:

- To direct and coordinate the proceedings or prosecutions;
- To manage the activities of investigation or gathering of evidence; and
- To exercise the public action (conviction/acquittal); as it is mandatory to inform the European Public Prosecutor, the achievement of such an objective would be favourable.
- The obligation to inform the European Prosecutor.

9.4.6 Guarantees / Protection

(a) Eurojust has devoted a set of rules related to data protection, allowing it to deal with personal data of an electronic or non electronic nature, within the framework of its competence, and to effectively carry out its functions.

(b) On the other hand, the projected European Prosecutor is not allowed to deal with this sort of data. In our opinion this is not coherent. Access to this sort of information would be needed in order to carry out investigations effectively.

9.4.7 Complementary character and functioning of both bodies

In addition to what has already been explained, it is interesting to assess the potential practical combination and complementary character of both bodies at European level. Thus, in practice one of the most typical situations in which their activities would need to be combined would be the so-called 'trans-pillar case', that is a case falling within the scope of both first and third pillars, and thus both entities would be required to intervene: the European Public Prosecutor would act in those matters within the first pillar, and Eurojust in those belonging to the third pillar structure.

In these particular situations, a rather deep dialogue between both bodies would be required in order to ensure a good level of efficiency and coherence in dealing with those 'trans-pillar' situations in which the two entities will be competent to intervene. Therefore, a fundamental requirement would also be to settle a common dialogue between them in order to determine the definition of common investigation strategies and the priority given to them.

Another situation which needs to be mentioned is the one dealing with elements of personal scope. The Green Paper proposed that the Deputy European Public Prosecutors would also be part of the European Public Ministry structure. As far as Eurojust is concerned, the Council, through its Decision of 28 February 2002, established it with a view to reinforce the fight against serious crimes. Article 12 of the Council Decision stipulates that each Member State may appoint 'national correspondents'. Neither the exact number, nor the precise functions of this category are limited or defined in the legal provision. We may say, however, that the idea was initially to establish one or several privileged counterparts for the national member of Eurojust (and outside the territory) in order to establish regular contacts among them without jeopardizing the direct contact between the national member of Eurojust and the competent national authorities. Another feature is the rule which provides that 'when a member State appoints a national correspondent, the latter may be a contact point of the European Judicial Network'. This is not a mandatory rule, but must be interpreted as a (strong) recommendation.

On the other hand, since the creation of the so-called Deputy European Public Prosecutors is also under way, it would be necessary to provide the same kind of competences and functions to these entities as those given to the national correspondents of the Eurojust/European Judicial network.

The main difficulty appears to be the significant amount of effort and work provided by the accumulation of functions, which can lead to the practical impossibility of defining clear and key policy priorities. Another obstacle would be the one related to the difficulty in defining the internal status of these entities, however, in our opinion, this is a rather technical issue which would be easily overcome.

9.5 WHAT COULD THE FUTURE BRING?

Thus, we have explained which attitude will be adopted concerning the relationship between Eurojust and the European Public Prosecutor. The following policy choices, however, remain open to discussion:

- To establish the European Prosecutor together with Eurojust, while maintaining their respective competences;
- To develop Eurojust at the cost of undermining the European Prosecutor; or rather
- To establish a European Prosecutor in a way that it will be integrated within the body of Eurojust.

We have to admit that, due to its recent creation, Eurojust has not been able yet to prove all its functional capabilities and its real value in practice. However, the nature of Eurojust, as defined at present (following one of the Tampere policy orientations), is limited to the 'coordination' of any investigation, within the inter-state framework. Nowadays, as a matter of urgency this organization needs a more diversified and broader intervention capacity on combating crime.

The basic equation is thus of a political nature: what do we want to do with respect to the reinforcement of the fight against criminality?

(a) To maintain that fight exclusively at national level, by adopting the instruments necessary to reinforce the cooperation between the Member States.

(b) To carry out the fight, instead, through a common intervention (common interest).

(c) To create the necessary European framework and structures which would enjoy operational competences over the whole European territory in an equivalent manner.

The politicians are the ones to answer these questions. We may, however, contribute to the debate by submitting our opinions and suggestions. Therefore, in relation to the potential co-existence of Eurojust/European Public Prosecutor, we think it may be useful to examine the model existing in Portugal for the repression of serious crimes:

(a) Recently, the Central Department of investigations and penal proceedings was created in Portugal (1999). This national body is dependent on the General Prosecutor of the Republic.
(b) The Central Department is in charge of the direction and coordination of investigations as well as the prevention of violent criminality, which is strongly organized and complex in nature.
(c) The material scope – within the framework of the direction and coordination of investigation – comprises the most representative violations: crimes against peace and humanity, terrorism, drug trafficking, money laundering, financial crimes having international or transnational effects, etc.
(d) When the criminal activities involved fall within the above type of violations the Central Department will be in charge of the direction of the investigations and will initiate the public action.
(e) Finally, it carries out preventive actions.

We may conclude from the Portuguese case that the three main aspects inherent in the implementation of criminal law policies are present, these being: prevention, coordination (of gathering evidence), investigations and public action.

Finally, we may wonder whether the European Union will in the future adopt this 'integrated' model which centralizes within the same organ the competence to carry out preventive actions, coordination/cooperation (Eurojust) as well as investigations and criminal proceedings (European Prosecutor).

10. Policing in a European Context

Willy Bruggeman

10.1 INTRODUCTION

Safety and security are among citizens' main concerns. They are also major issues for both local and national authorities, and at the European Union level. For this reason the legitimacy of the police is closely related to the position of law enforcement. A precarious relationship exists between police powers and the democratic control of the police in all democratic states.

The growing unification of the European countries, the growth of organised crime and terrorism, migration movements and the severity of crime problems as such, are some of the major challenges for states and the European Union. In particular international policing is becoming increasingly complex, which starts to have a limited focus on the identification of misbehaviour or dysfunction. Very diverse and fragmented monitoring and accountability systems are in place (Van den Wyngaert 1997).

10.2 POLICE AND POLICING AT EUROPEAN UNION LEVEL

All modern state theories are based on the trinomial: sovereign state – power of coercion – police (Recasens 2000). Until recently it was sufficient to keep the control mechanism ultimately in the hands of the sovereign nation, which should control the state, which should in its turn control police forces.

Particularly during the last two decades the main problem encountered in Europe is precisely the breakdown of that trinomial. The emergence of new elements transcending the concept of state and sovereignty such as those observed from the European unification process as well as those elements originated in the privatisation of some security sectors, have plunged the traditional model into a probable irreversible change.

Seen from the perspective of the 1990s, European police cooperation is an opaque and complex patchwork of institutions which aim to promote different forms of cooperation.

The birth and development of a European police/law enforcement sphere is, in an increasingly pressing way, demanding the handing over of state sovereignty to European institutions and instances in all areas, including police powers. Despite the reluctance of some states, police/law enforcement spheres seem to be increasingly 'communitarised' as they move forward, according to the Trevi action programme, the Schengen agreement, the Maastricht Treaty on European Union and reforms which were introduced in the Amsterdam Treaty on the European Union (TEU).

We are now witnessing an era in which the legitimate monopoly of policing society was born, developed, and is finally about to collapse. The era began with the Declaration on the Rights of Men and Citizens of 1789, and has lasted, in general terms, until the constitution of OLAF (end of 2001); Europol (in force since October 1998 and implemented in July 1999), and the creation of Eurojust (2002). If such trends are consolidated it is likely that this coming century will be a time of profound change regarding the patterns (Recasens 2000), structure and dependency of what we know in Europe today as 'the police'.

This is generating a specific European space and a void in each nation state that will undoubtedly affect police functioning and powers as well as the control of mechanisms of police activity, which will be created in the various gaps that will appear or that will be modified in a European, as well as a nation state context.

Similar to this, deep transformations are also taking place in the laws' spaces, which also implies in itself important changes in the role played by the social actors involved. For example, European codes of law allow us to contemplate how citizens and victims in particular are claiming their own space. The model is also shifting towards partnership (IHESI 1998) where the police are irreversibly becoming one of many actors in the game together with citizens, victims, aggressors, other institutions, other services, and so on.

The main relationships are now: liberties, security and safeguard-efficacy. If greater security is recognised then certain liberties must be sacrificed. Especially, in order to safeguard the enjoyment of liberties an efficient protection is necessary, and to obtain it, those charged with that protection must be empowered with the adequate means and possibility of action.

The balance is now increasingly as follows: more security implies less freedom; more efficient means fewer safeguards. Within the European Union, some are of the opinion that there is a 'security deficit' and are claiming greater security measures.

The European Parliament has warned[1] against a 'democracy deficit' within the European institutions, which affects the protection of rights and liberties, which – among other things – prevents the full achievement of a Europe of citizens or of the people (Duverger 1994).

The emergence of a European police/law enforcement space generates doubt as to whether traditional police powers are going to be mimetically repeated in the new European structure, or whether new powers are going to emerge from the new functions and structures. What seems clear is that when these European executive structures (e.g. OLAF) emerge, the pattern of the traditional division of powers of the liberal state is being unevenly reproduced, generating what the European Parliament has labelled in several reports as a 'democratic deficit'.

Before developing this item further, it is interesting to examine what changes have occurred recently. The basic principles are now changing as follows (Bruggeman 2001):

- moving from an informal to a formal form of cooperation, mostly based on intergovernmental law enforcement (Schengen, Europol);
- moving from locally oriented cooperation towards a global police/justice (Eurojust) form of cooperation;
- showing a rising influence of new interests such as human rights in general and principles of personal privacy in particular;
- from a thematic (drugs, terrorism) towards a more general (organised crime) oriented approach;
- from a national (principle of sovereignty) towards a horizontal supranational law enforcement level. Vertical enforcement (e.g. UN Yugoslavia Tribunal) still remains the exception; and
- parallel growth of the need for supranational political/democratic control mechanisms.

Therefore the European Union is having specific interests in a tendency to build up a network or framework, basically to set up a data exchange through a powerful information system (Schengen/Europol). In addition, Europol has other tasks: crime analysis, support, research and training and just recently the right to ask the joint investigation teams to operate on its behalf.

Other ideas concerning cooperation models launched at EU level thus far include:

- A gradual harmonisation of national criminal laws involving a harmonisation of minimum penalties for certain offences (initially perhaps even in absence of harmonised constituent elements) and

[1] In Resolution A3-01/23/92 of 8 April 1992.

(perhaps later) a harmonisation of the constituent elements of certain offences. These offences could include organised crime, drug trafficking, money laundering and terrorism;

- Improving cooperation between police and judicial authorities in the areas of prevention, investigation, prosecution, court proceedings and enforcement;
- A further strengthening of the role of Europol, for instance by making it obligatory for the Member States to supply Europol with operational powers, which has proved to be very controversial;
- The creation of a Eurojust composed of national prosecutors or magistrates vested with certain powers to prosecute cross-border criminal activities. National liaison officers could be seconded to this body, each of which would have the task of initiating and directing investigations within his national territory according to national law;
- The conclusion of agreements with third countries (the candidate countries, the USA, Switzerland or Russia, for instance) on matters of police cooperational and criminal justice; and
- The creation of EU border police.

Therefore, international cooperation in criminal matters takes different forms. Some of them have a long tradition while others are of recent origin.

Some of them are relatively complicated and only granted when many different conditions have been met, others are more easily obtained. Some of them involve police authorities only while others require the intervention of public prosecutors and courts.

Roughly speaking there are four different forms of international cooperation in criminal matters subject to recent developments: extradition, mutual assistance in the investigation and prosecution of criminal offences, transfer of criminal proceeding and transfer of the enforcement of criminal justice. Horizontal enforcement is the rule. Horizontal enforcement means enforcing criminal law on the national level. The advantage is obvious; the entire machinery of national criminal law can be used for enforcement purposes.

Nevertheless, the two main obstacles to horizontal enforcement are the following: possible 'political' hesitation to prosecute and the necessary criminalisation of the act in order to permit prosecution (Mueller and Besharov 1999). An international tribunal directly enforcing an international norm is vertical enforcement.

The only possible fora where direct prosecution is possible so far have been three:

1. the tribunal(s) provided for under the 1919 Treaty of Versailles (which in the end resulted in national prosecutions in Leipzig);

2. the International Military Tribunal for the Far East (the Tokyo trials) at the end of World War II; and
3. the International Criminal Tribunal for the Former Yugoslavia in The Hague (Yepes-Enriquez 2001).

Some initiatives can be identified as belonging to a mixed model, which merges two logics to a certain extent (such as the Lockerbie Tribunal), and which appears to be the most preferred logic until now.

Based on the horizontal approach especially in the United Nations and in the European Union there has been an exponential growth in the numbers of international instruments with various aspects of international criminal law (Van den Wyngaert 2000). A growing number of national courts are confronted with questions of international criminal law. As indicated before, the police were first in facing the practical difficulties of investigating transnational cases, but a new generation of judges, prosecutors and lawyers are gradually waking up to the fact that international criminal law exists.

Many important new international criminal law conventions have been opened for signature, including: the Rome Statute for an International Criminal Court (1998); the Conventions on Terrorist Bombings (1994); the Financing of Terrorism (2000); the EU Convention on Mutual Assistance in Criminal Matters (2000) and the UN Convention against Transnational Organised Crime (2000). The two last conventions especially reveal a trend of focusing on organised/serious transnational crime, rather than on specific crime areas.

When analysing the horizontal and/or vertical enforcement model the development of universal jurisdiction is also interesting. All this influences the accountability models, which were previously based on national sovereignty, but which are nowadays dramatically affected by new models for international transborder cooperation. We can easily state that almost no new initiatives – not even the Europol concept – include sufficiently enforceable accountability needs.

Universal jurisdiction refers to the assertion of jurisdiction over offences, regardless of the place where they are committed or the nationality of the perpetrators. It applies to a range of offences when repression by all states is justified, or required as a matter of international public policy.

Certain offences are regarded as being subject to universal jurisdiction as a matter of customary international law. A key distinction must be made between those offences in relation to which states are obliged to assert universal jurisdiction (mandatory universal jurisdiction) and those offences in relation to which a state may, if it so chooses, assert universal jurisdiction (permissive universal jurisdiction).

10.3 NEW POLICE REALITY AT EUROPEAN LEVEL

10.3.1 Europol's objective

The objective of Europol is the improvement of the effectiveness and cooperation of law enforcement authorities of Member States in combating and preventing drug trafficking, other serious forms of international organised crime and terrorism. This should mainly be achieved through the facilitation of information exchange between Member States and through obtaining, collating and analysing information. Europol is only competent when a case affects two or more Member States and cross-border criminal investigations are necessary.

The fact that the Convention limits Europol's tasks basically to crime analysis, information exchange and coordination shows that Europol has only a limited function compared with the wide range of functions entrusted to the police forces of the Member States. Europol has no executive powers: it has no power to conduct wire-tapping, house searches or arrests.

These executive police powers potentially infringe the fundamental rights of citizens and thus have to be subjected to an adequate legal basis and have to be monitored by public prosecutors and/or a democratically accountable authority.

The Europol Convention describes in detail what Europol is allowed to do and how it should operate in performing its functions. Two main aspects should be briefly discussed:

- protection of personal data; and
- the central role which has been assigned to the Management Board, in which all Member States and the Commission are represented, in supervising Europol.

The only fundamental right of citizens affected by Europol's work is the right of access to personal files (knowledge of the existence and content of personal files). Therefore it was particularly necessary to create instruments for the control of Europol in this respect. As a result the Europol Convention provides a great number of articles dedicated to the handling of personal data and data protection.

There are so many that there is no time to mention them all. One of the most important provisions is the establishment of the Joint Supervisory Body (JSB) in Article 24. This is an independent body responsible for the constant monitoring of the activities of Europol in order to ensure that the rights of individuals are not violated by the storage, processing and utilisation of data by Europol.

Europol has the obligation to assist this body in carrying out its tasks successfully, in particular to allow free access to all its premises, to supply requested information, to give access to all kind of data and to carry out the JSB decisions on appeals.

Each individual has the right to request the JSB to ensure that the treatment of personal data by Europol is lawful and accurate. The instrument of the JSB is completed by the introduction of National Supervisory Bodies in the Member States.

These ensure at national level that the handling of personal data received from or sent to Europol does not violate individual rights in accordance with the respective national law.

Last but not least, very detailed regulations are provided – in the Convention itself and in several complementary Council decisions – which lay down the rules on the use of data and the communication of data to third states and third bodies. This is an essential requirement for the full implementation of close cooperation between Europol and the police forces of candidate countries.

As regards the day-to-day work of Europol the main role in steering the organisation is played by the Management Board (Article 28), which is composed of one representative of each Member State. The Commission also attends its meetings.

The Management Board meets at least twice a year, but in practice about six times a year. Its tasks are, amongst many others to:

- prepare the implementing rules governing data files;
- approve orders to open data files;
- take part in the appointment and dismissal of the Director and Deputy Directors;
- take part in the drawing up of the budget;
- adopt the five-year financing plan;
- appoint the financial controller and oversee the performance of his duties; and
- take part in any amendment to the Convention.

This shows that Europol's functioning is monitored very closely by the Management Board. Member States' authorities are informed in great detail about Europol's functioning through their representatives in the Management Board. Decisions are taken by unanimity.

The detailed provisions on data protection, including the appeal procedures, assure that EU and Member States data protection regulations are adhered to. All this constitutes a high-level of control of Europol.

UWE LIBRARY SERVICES

From our point of view, all these controls taken together may even reach further than the controls that apply to national police services, realising that their powers are much wider than those of Europol.

10.3.2 Europol and parliamentary control

Concerning parliamentary control, the starting point is the Europol Convention itself, which was adopted by the Council by unanimity. The responsibility for the functioning of Europol belongs to the Management Board composed of 15 representatives of the Member States, who report to the Member competent for police matters in each Member States. Each of them can be held accountable before his/her national Parliament on national policy as regards Europol. Through their Ministers responsible for police matters, the national Parliaments can remain informed about the functioning of Europol.

The first and most important provision regarding possible control by the European Parliament can be found in the Treaty of the European Union (TEU) itself. Article 39 lays down an obligation for the Council to consult the Parliament before the adoption of legally binding measures, such as framework decisions, decisions and conventions. This provision also applies to Europol. In quite a number of articles the Europol Convention itself stipulates that decisions have to be taken by the Council in accordance with the procedures foreseen in Title VI of TEU. This means that the above-mentioned obligation of Article 39 TEU to consult the Parliament applies. Thus it is ensured that the European Parliament participates in many important decisions as regards the development of Europol, e.g. any amendment to the Convention.

These provisions of the Amsterdam Treaty improved the role of the European Parliament. Even if these improvements are considered to be modest, they apply not only to Europol, but to all provisions in the field of EU police and judicial cooperation in criminal matters.

The Europol Convention also contains provisions on the European Parliament. Article 34 stipulates that the Presidency must forward each year a special report on the work of Europol to the European Parliament. In addition to Article 39 TEU, the Convention lays down that the European Parliament has to be consulted before any change of the Convention. Furthermore, through the acting Presidency of the Council and the Commission, the Parliament is able to remain informed about the work of Europol. It has to be emphasised that the Commission does not take part in the decision-taking process in Europol structures, nor has it any power of control over it.

Before continuing the debate on whether parliamentary control should cover more of the work of Europol than it currently does, we should remember that Europol is a police office which is working above all in a highly sensitive area: 'organised crime and terrorism'.

The main challenge is to find the right balance between a high level of parliamentary control and the need for confidentiality and discretion of a police body working in such a highly sensitive area.

The European Parliament has raised the subject of democratic control several times. In April 1999 it adopted a Recommendation to the Council on the extension of the powers of Europol and the reinforcement of parliamentary control over it. In October 2000 it adopted a Report on the Portuguese initiative to extend Europol's competence to money laundering in general. More recently, in October 2001, it has adopted a report on the joint Belgian–Swedish initiative to extend Europol's competence to all forms of crimes listed in the Annex to the Europol Convention.

In its 1999 Recommendation, which was approved before the entry into force of the Treaty of Amsterdam, the Parliament stated that existing parliamentary control arrangements were too cumbersome and, as a result of the intergovernmental nature of decision-making procedures in the police cooperation area, ineffective. It does not relate to the way in which information on Europol's activities is given to the European Parliament as representing an adequate form of parliamentary control.

However, the Parliament also argued that Europol's new powers, based on its support role in the coordination of police deployment made possible by the Amsterdam Treaty, did not fundamentally alter the system or imperatives of parliamentary control.[2]

In particular the Parliament:

- calls on the Council to incorporate into the Treaty provisions on full parliamentary and judicial scrutiny of Europol at the level of the European Union and not to give any operational powers to Europol without providing for adequate scrutiny by the European Parliament. The Parliament urges the Council to take account of the already established rights of the European Parliament to be informed and consulted;
- proposes to incorporate Europol's budget in the Community budget;
- suggests that, in the event of Europol's evolving into a police organisation with cross-border operational powers, the Council should look into setting up a European public prosecutor's office or some other judicial body. In this case Europol should be given a basis in

[2] See consideration Q and S of the 1999 Recommendation.

Community law and should be placed under the responsibility of a member of the Commission; and

- calls on the Parliaments of the Member States to take consistent account of their right and duty to supervise the actions of their national Council member responsible for Europol and the Member States' representatives appointed to the Europol Management Board. This should happen in close cooperation with the European Parliament.

On the occasion of its Report on the Portuguese initiative adopted on 14 November 2000, the Parliament repeated its earlier criticism and proposed additional ideas on how to enhance the democratic accountability of Europol (e.g. the appearance of the Europol Director before the competent Parliamentary Committee; the right of the Parliament to request an exchange of views on the special annual report; making the European Court of Justice competent to rule on any dispute or conflict between Member States regarding the interpretation or application of the Europol Convention).[3]

The suggestions which were raised by the European Parliament on the occasion of the report on the joint Belgian–Swedish initiative (which related to the extension of Europol's mandate to all serious forms of crime listed in the Annex to the Europol Convention adopted on 13 November 2001) also mainly aimed at increasing the control of the European Parliament over Europol. Thus the Parliament requested for example that the Commission should present by the end of 2001 a proposal to revise the Europol Convention following best practices and methods of democratic control of police services in the Member States:

> A proposal for the comprehensive reform of the instruments of police and judicial cooperation, including revision of the Europol Convention to bring it into line with higher standards and methods of democratic control of the police forces of the Member States is to be submitted by the Commission by the end of 2001; that comprehensive reform should aim gradually to communitarise those instruments, to strengthen judicial control by the court of Justice and to fund those instruments through the Community budget.[4]

At the time the Parliament put forward this request the Council had already made an inventory of the amendments to the Europol Convention that were considered necessary to make Europol function more effectively. Member States judged it useful to postpone a fundamental discussion on the question of democratic control over Europol until the Commission's Communication on the subject. The Communication can be considered as an important first step in the process of gradually improving democratic control

[3] Report of the European Parliament; A5-0312/2000, pp. 6–8.
[4] Report of the European Parliament; A5-0370/2001 final, p. 6.

over Europol: much of it is devoted to clarifying some basic questions concerning the exact tasks and functions of Europol as compared with those of the police services of the Member States as well as the currently existing types of control over the organisation.

It is interesting to observe the organisation of a conference on the subject of parliamentary and judicial control on Europol (The Hague, 8 June 2001), which brought together representatives from all EU Member States and from the European Parliament. JHA Commissioner Antonio Vitorino stated at this conference:

> That formally speaking there does not seem to be an urgent need for further parliamentary control. But even if this is formally correct, I think that this would have to be considered as quite unsatisfactory and short-sighted in light of some of the developments taking place around Europol. Assuming that Europol, in the coming years will get more powers, I am of the opinion that it is only reasonable to launch the debate now and to start a process of gradual enhancement of parliamentary control.

The meeting appeared to set out a network for the exchange of information and taking of initiatives, under the name of Parlopol, where those parliamentarians concerned with police and judicial affairs will be subject to forms of European Information Exchange with the Council of Ministers or with the governing bodies of Europol and Eurojust.

A second Parlopol meeting was organised during the Belgian Presidency (October 2001) and the general need to enhance parliamentary control was confirmed.

The analysis of the existing controls of Europol indicates that the current system cannot be regarded as legally insufficient, given the limited nature of the powers attributed to Europol by comparison with those of national police forces. The existing controls (through the Parliaments, the national Supervisory Bodies, the Joint Supervisory Body and the management Board) are, however, exercised in an indirect, fragmented and not easily understood manner. This gives rise to a general feeling – as widely expressed at the 7–8 June Conference in The Hague – that something clearer and more transparent is needed.

What is felt to be missing at the moment is first of all an institutionalised and regular information exchange between those responsible in national parliaments and the European Parliament. If all the provisions and procedures regarding parliamentary control existing at national or EU level were made known to all the other parliaments, the situation would already be improved considerably. In addition, there are no regular formal exchanges foreseen between the Parliament and Europol and there is also room for improving the information basis of the European Parliament.

In the Commission's view, such improvements would be achieved through a limited number of amendments to the Europol Convention itself, together with the establishment of a mechanism enabling national Parliaments and the European Parliament to examine and coordinate their respective roles.

However, if in the future Europol were to be entrusted with investigative powers, farther-reaching measures would become necessary. In the meantime the Commission offers the following recommendations for consideration in its Communication:

1. establish a formal mechanism for information exchange and coordination between national Parliaments and the European Parliament. The current fragmented, and thereby less effective, control, would be gradually transformed into a structured and unified control at European Union level, based upon an enhanced cooperation between the Member States' Parliaments and the European Parliament;
2. to this end a joint committee, consisting of members of both the Member States' and European Parliaments committees responsible for police matters could be established. This joint committee could meet twice a year to exchange information and experience and to discuss matters relating to Europol;[5]
3. amend Article 34 of the Europol Convention, so as to come to a single annual report on Europol's activities for information for both the European Parliament and the Council;
4. amend Article 34 of the Europol Convention, so as to give the European Parliament the formal right to request an exchange of views on the Europol annual report with the Presidency;
5. amend Article 34 of the Europol Convention, so as to give the European Parliament the formal right to request the Europol Director to appear before the competent committee; and
6. amend Article 24 (6) of the Europol Convention, so as to make it obligatory for the Joint Supervisory board to draw up its activity report on an annual basis and to forward it to the European Parliament. It could be envisaged to include, in these reports, information on the controls carried out by the National Supervisory Bodies.

Hence, for the time being, the system of external controls seems inefficient. The deficit is partly due to the fact that there is no institutionalised judicial control in place yet, despite the recent advances of the Treaty of

[5] An example might be the conference of the Community and European Affairs Committees of the Parliaments of the European Union (COSAC). COSAC was established in 1989 to reinforce the role of national Parliaments in the community. The aim of this conference is to intensify the exchange of information between the various committees in national Parliaments specialising in European affairs and to meet twice a year to discuss issues of common concern.

Amsterdam and the agreement reached in the Tampere Summit (15–16 October 1999), with the creation of Eurojust by the end of 2001. Likewise the lack of common European codes and the still far from possible penal code leads us to think about stability of a common deontological code. The publication of Recommendation 1402 (1999) on the control of Member States' Internal Security Services of the Council of Europe is a great advance in this area.

Last but not least, operative activities (even while limited at the moment) should be subject to judicial authority with clear conditions on systems of accountability, and improved and more effective democratic control must be organised.

10.3.3 Other EU institutions

Several other third pillar organisations (as for instance Eurojust, CEPOL, etc) are in creation. Eurojust was set up by Council Decision of 28 February 2002 inviting it also to establish and maintain close cooperation with Europol in so far as relevant for the performance of its tasks and for achieving its objectives, the essential elements of this cooperation being determined by an agreement, as for Europol nothing is foreseen on parliamentary control. Subsequently, the control mechanism to be put in place covers Europol as well as other intergovernmental institutions which operate in the area of police and judicial cooperation in criminal matters.

The agreement to be concluded between on the one hand Europol and Eurojust, and on the other hand Europol and CEPOL will be an ideal opportunity to further explore the creation of common control instruments. At the time of writing, these agreements were planned to be achieved during the first semester of 2002.

10.4 CONCLUSION

The globalisation ('global village') of many sectors of social life is one of the characteristics of our modern world. Considering that this globalisation concerns many sectors of our economic and social life, it is evident that it also affects the world of crime. In the European and Mediterranean areas (but this phenomenon concerns the whole world), criminal organisations are joining to do business in the field of drugs, arms, prostitution, trafficking in stolen cars, and trafficking in human beings and to invest the proceeds of crime where it is more convenient. Hence, there exists an extreme danger of a global criminal system for the economic systems, the financial markets, our public institutions and the people.

If this is true, then no one can say that organised crime does not exist in one's country. Modern organised crime is present everywhere, although in different forms, according to traditions, social, economic and political circles and type of business handled. One must not confuse the presence of criminal organisations which the manifestation of serious crimes against assets (burglaries and extortion) or against individuals (murders, kidnappings); consequently it is wrong to say that organised crime does not exist in a country when no Mafia-style murders are committed there. Many crimes committed by organised crime are in fact committed for the survival itself of criminal organisations (intimidation, corruption, money laundering, and investment of criminal profits), and many of these crimes are not 'visible'.

I would like to make it clear that this is not solely an Italian point of view, but it is shared by many states who are in the forefront in the fight against organised crime or in the development of appropriate instruments to combat it (as is the case of the United States, Germany, The Netherlands, Belgium and Spain).

In addition, in 1993 the French National Assembly approved a report stating that:

> Three levels of activities in the Mafia industry have been established by the experts: the first concerns violent exactions and traffics that ensure the Mafia's control over a territory and the production of proceeds; the second is constituted by money laundering; the third is the investment of laundered capitals in legal activities.

The main instrument through which organised crime associations and Mafia-type organisations operate is not violence, but corruption and intimidation. Corruption and intimidation are directed towards individuals and both private and public institutions. Criminal organisations resort to violence only as a last resort, because through violence they make themselves visible, they show their danger, they generate concern within the public opinion, and oblige to accomplish the same results with less risk, and it threatens the public institutions from within.

Today, organised crime tends to expand at an international level and engages in any traffic or business that can boost its profits. The main objective of organised crime is to make profits and to acquire as much power as possible.

It should be emphasised that the internationalisation of the major criminal organisations has come about regardless of the treaties on the free movement of goods and persons. They have been helped in this internationalisation process by the gaps in, and inadequacy of, international treaty rules and by the difference in national legislation and by the gaps in, and incompleteness of, the criminal laws of many countries.

Europe is fighting against a unified organised crime in its objectives and modus operandi with forty different criminal codes and as many police and judicial authorities as there are countries. And it is this difference which nurtures organised crime.

Experience, in fact, has shown that organised crime is attracted both by countries where investments are convenient, those that lack or do not have strong rules regarding the financial world, and by countries lacking strict laws against organised crime.

REFERENCES

Bruggeman, W. (2001), 'International Law Enforcement Cooperation: a critical assessment', *European Journal on Criminal Policy and Research*, **9** (3), 283–90.

Council Decision setting up Eurojust with a view to reinforcing the fight against serious crime, 28 February 2002.

Den Boer, M. (ed.) (1997), *Undercover policing and accountability from an international perspective*, European Institute of Public Administration, EIPA, Maastricht.

Den Boer, M. (ed.) (2002), *Organised Crime: A Catalyst in the Europeanisation of National Police and Prosecution Agencies?*, European Institute of Public Administration, EIPA, Maastricht.

Duverger, M. (1994), *Europa de los hombres: una metamorfosis inacabada*, Madrid: Alianza.

European Parliament Recommendation to the Council on Europol: reinforcing parliamentary controls and extending powers; A4-0064/1999 adopted on 13 April 1999.

European Union Convention on Mutual Assistance in Criminal Matters, 2000.

IHESI (1998), *Les partages de la securité: médiation, partenariat et sécurité*, Paris.

Mueller, G. and D.J. Besharov (1999), 'Evolution and enforcement of international Criminal Law', *International Criminal Law*, vol. I, pp. 257–67.

Recasens, A. (2000), 'The control of police powers', *European Journal of Criminal Policy and Research*, **8** (3), 247–69.

Report on the initiative from the Portuguese Republic with a view to the adoption of a Council Act on the drawing up on the basis of Article 43 (1) of the Europol Convention of a protocol amending Article 2 and the Annex to the Convention: A5-0312/2000 adopted on 14 November 2000.

Report on the initiative of the Kingdom of Belgium and the Kingdom of Sweden with a view to adopting a Council decision extending Europol's mandate to deal with the serious forms of international crime listed in the Annex to the Europol Convention.; A5-0370/2001 Final of 24 October 2001 adopted on 13 November 2001.

Storbeck, J. (1997), 'Coordinating the flow of European Intelligence: Europol's Accountability Mechanisms', in M. Den Boer (ed.), *Undercover policing and accountability from an international perspective*, Maastricht: European Institute of Public Administration, EIPA.

UN Convention Against Transnational Organized Crime, 2000.
Valkeneer, D. De (1991), *Le droit de la police*, Brussels: De Boeck.
Walker, N. (1997), 'Deficient weaponry, reluctant marksmen and obscure targets', in M. Den Boer (ed.), *Undercover policing and accountability from an international perspective*, Maastricht: European Institute of Public Administration, EIPA.
Wyngaert, C. Van den (2000), *International Criminal Law*, The Hague: Kluwer.
Wyngaert, C. Van den (1997), 'Organized crime, proactive policing and international police cooperation in criminal matters: Who controls the police as an international context?', in M. Den Boer (ed.), *Undercover policing and accountability from an international perspective*, Maastricht: European Institute of Public Administration, EIPA.
Yepes-Enriquez, R. (2001), 'Enforcement of the prohibition of chemical weapons in its wider perspective', in R. Yepes-Enriquez and L. Tabassi (eds), *Treaty Enforcement and International Cooperation in Criminal Matters, with Special Reference to the Chemical Weapons Convention*, The Hague: T.M.C. Asser Press.

11. OLAF and its Cooperation with the Institutions of New Member States

Luc Schaerlaekens

11.1 INTRODUCTION: OLAF'S MISSION

The main objective of this chapter is to assess the European Anti-Fraud Office's (OLAF) role and activities for law enforcement in the fight against fraud and corruption, as well as the Anti-Fraud Coordination Service's operational activities (AFCOS) of the candidate countries towards accession.

OLAF is a relatively new service, which was created in 1999 to fight fraud against the financial interests of the Community. It has already investigated fraud and other irregularities in candidate countries and will continue to do so after the accession. So, rightfully, OLAF has a place on this list and stands grateful for its inclusion in the present discussion.

Let us recall first the mission of OLAF, a service of the Commission, which can initiate and perform investigations to discover irregularities and fraud against the budget of the Community in a fully independent way. OLAF's investigators have no police powers, only administrative ones; our interventions are based on secondary legislation of the first pillar. This could reflect the relative weakness of the service; on the other hand Member States are obliged, according to first pillar secondary legislation, to fully co-operate with the Commission' services.

Thus the fight against organised crime can be widened to the extent that it affects the Community budget. This constitutes only a small fraction of all organised crime, but the means we use to affect this portion are quite effective. OLAF doesn't exercise 'normal control' on proper application by Member States of the community legislation; instead its investigations are oriented to specifically detect fraud and other serious irregularities.

OLAF is presently combating, for example, international cigarette smuggling. As customs duties are at stake, use of the full investigative capacity of the Commission is not only justified: it is legally required.

Member States are obliged (and collectively willing) to transfer relevant information to OLAF. On the basis of all the information received, OLAF co-ordinates the Member States' actions on the ground. Rapid information exchange is easily facilitated because we know very well the structural and functional competencies of the different services of the Member State. If you know, then, that every seized lorry of cigarettes represents € 1 million on value added taxes, it is not so surprising that organised crime has found a profitable venture in smuggling cigarettes. OLAF helps Member States to uncover smuggling lines and bring the smugglers before the court.

The organisation also aids in the recovery of money, even when the process must be taken before American courts, since we claim enough evidence exists that some American manufacturers are also involved in some of the relevant smuggling activities.

Organised crime is also heavily involved in the smuggling of alcohol, a highly taxed good. If you want to make high profits in these kinds of markets you have to be represented in different Member States avoiding considerable start-up capital in the form of, for example, establishing 'truck-parks'. In this field OLAF uses more of its own investigative power than in the black market cigarette industry, where more coordination takes place with the activities of Member State services.

Smuggling investigations are all, at large, conducted with the willing cooperation of the Member States, even when Community budgets stand as the primary concern of those investigations. It seems clear why it is so:

- Firstly, organised criminal groups that smuggle alcohol, cigarettes, and other commodities into the Union do the same in candidate countries; common financial interests are being safeguarded;
- Second, we have a solid legal basis for cooperation, based on the 6th protocol of the association arrangements, which created the possibility to provide mutual assistance in Customs matters; this has proved to be quite an effective tool.

11.2 OLAF AND THE NEW MEMBER STATES

On-ground cooperation with the customs services of candidate countries has been very successful, to date, from the perspective of OLAF. This international customs cooperation mainly works well because customs regulation has had a long tradition in international cooperation.

In addition to this, we feel that there exists a will to proactively co-operate and that the necessary competent people are present, even though Eastern Europe customs services also have to struggle against a 'brain drain' from the public sector to private firms. Candidate countries often urged us during our visits to help with the fight against organised crime in the VAT sector. OLAF is not only protecting the resources of the Community but also the expenditure and subsidies, including those that are already allocated to the candidate countries.

What we call the pre-accession funds (PHARE funds, ISPA and SAPARD-funds) are all destined to help applicant countries reach the standards of the acquis by investment and institution building. Because these subsidies go to projects co-financed by the candidate countries, one might expect a mutual interest in and thus capacity for fighting fraud, corruption and irregularities. While this may be true, the countries' capacity to react and to combat this fraud in an effective way is not always so apparent and efficient; cooperation, then, becomes more difficult. The obligation to co-operate, though, is manifestly part of the acquis that candidate countries will apply from the first day of accession.

We must refrain from recalling all of the legal provisions that accession countries must undertake, even though there are not so many in the anti-fraud field. Limiting myself to the obligations of Article 280 of the Treaty, without referring to secondary legislation, candidate countries should ensure by appropriate measures an effective protection of the financial interests of the Community. The principle of equivalence should be respected; this means protecting the financial interests of the Community as they would their own financial interests. They must, accordingly, organise cooperation between themselves and the Commission.

As the Communities' financial interests cover both income and expenditure, why does cooperation with regard to expenditure seem more difficult than cooperation in the customs field? Here we will operate under some generalisations that do not apply to all candidate countries. It does not seem that misappropriations of public money gained their necessary attention in the recent history of these countries. Defrauding public money was not likely recognised as a significant or soluble problem in the former communist household; neither was corruption, as capital was rarely registered as a production factor.

When, after the bloodless revolution, Europe began dispensing financial aid via PHARE programmes, this money was spent largely on priorities that these countries decided freely themselves at a time when the principles of financial control and audit were not yet effectively in place.

Within the new context of becoming a full member of the European Union, the candidate countries could no longer decide so freely on the destination of Europe's financial support. The subsidies (which now amount to € 3.3 billion) have to be used 'specifically' to facilitate the ongoing process of enlargement. Projects are approved by the Commission and have to be formulated more precisely; also, stronger control procedures are imposed and audits can be performed afterwards. Before, this was occasionally perceived by some countries as interference in national sovereignty.

Cooperation with OLAF and the willingness to fight against fraud and corruption in subsidy programmes remained less clear to national authorities than the management of their 'own resources'.

OLAF had already detected fraud in these pre-accession funds; as the budget spent in this area has increased, fraud has also increased. It is not simply that organised crime is the main perpetrator of this fraud. It is more a matter of not following, mostly intentionally, the rules of public procurement procedures to get more money for the delivered services.

In order to combat this fraud OLAF has tried, beside efforts aimed at encouraging the candidate countries to take over the legislative anti-fraud acquis, to convince applicant countries to create a central structure or service responsible for coordinating all national anti-fraud efforts that OLAF can co-operate with efficiently. This is, strictly speaking, not an obligation under community law but rather an institution-building measure.

Nevertheless, Article 280 § 3, which reads that Member States must co-ordinate their actions aimed at protecting the financial interests of the Community against fraud, legitimately displays the Community recognition of organisational necessity. Countries that cannot effectively integrate and streamline their own national responses to fraud should not be reasonably expected to do so with other countries.

We have carefully avoided putting too much emphasis on the importance of structural change or competency relocation for these countries; instead, we suggested that this function could be facilitated inside existing governmental services. In that capacity all applicant countries committed themselves to create co-ordinated anti-fraud services or structures. And as they did, most of these structures were created, or are in a process of being created, inside the Ministries of Finance. In some candidate countries these services will depend directly on the Prime Minister's office (Romania and Slovakia). In the Czech Republic this service depends on the public prosecutor's offices.

Notwithstanding, the organisational solutions for anti-fraud coordinating structures (AFCOS) were chosen by each respective country. AFCOS should itself have at least the mandate and means to oversee and facilitate:

1. coordination within the country of all legislative, administrative and operational aspects of the protection of the Community's financial interests; and
2. cooperation between the Commission and the Member States as required by Article 280.

The tasks of an AFCOS may therefore include:

- ensuring that the competent authorities launch the appropriate administrative or criminal proceedings when well-founded suspicions of irregularities or fraud detrimental to the Communities financial interests are brought to light;
- taking the lead in formulating, disseminating and implementing an anti-fraud strategy for each respective country, aimed at reinforcing the protection of national and the Community's financial interests;
- responsibility for the coordination within national administrations of all legislative, administrative and operational/investigative activities related to the protection of the Community's financial interests. This includes cooperation with the Commission (OLAF) in customs matters;
- facilitating the cooperation in investigative activities concerning suspected fraud or irregularities affecting the Community's financial interests between national investigation authorities and prosecution services, to include the efforts of national authorities and OLAF;
- ensuring the exchange of relevant information on detected fraud and irregularities at all levels inside the national administration and in relation to the Commission/OLAF; and
- ensuring that appropriate training for the success of the fight against fraud takes place in the national administration.

11.3 CONCLUSION

It is indeed crucial that other institutions or bodies involved in the protection of the Community's financial interests support the AFCOS coordinating activities. It is also necessary that the candidate country's legislative or administrative framework allows the AFCOS to fulfil its role.

Where necessary, binding agreements should be concluded between the AFCOS and the other institutions involved in the protection of the Community's financial interests.

There does not seem to be a real resistance against the creation of such services but there has not been real enthusiasm either, except maybe from Bulgaria and Romania.

It was certainly true that competencies had to be reshuffled and a competent leading service had to be appointed that made it difficult for candidate countries to take the necessary decisions. As a matter of fact the situation of applicant countries is not so different from that of the current

Member States; both are regularly confronted with these kinds of competency battles inside their administrations.

The European Commission needs to prioritise even more strongly the institution-building aspects of enlargement to ensure that candidate countries do form stable administrative structures with competent and well trained staff and continue in their fight against any potential fraud and economic crisis.

PART III

TOWARDS AN IMMIGRATION AND ASYLUM POLICY FOR EUROPE

12. Recent Developments as regards European Migration Policy in view of an Enlarged Europe

Joanna Apap

12.1 INTRODUCTION: A HISTORICAL OVERVIEW

During the 1990s, Justice and Home Affairs reached, in an unexpected way, centre stage in the European debate. Growing concerns about immigration policy, since the Maastricht Treaty institutionalised the third pillar of the European Union, have been stimulated by several factors – the persistence of irregular migration and tragic incidents, such as the one in Dover in July 2000 in which 58 Chinese nationals trying to enter illegally into the United Kingdom lost their lives, the need for immigrant workers in some sectors, and the spectre of an ageing European society.

More generally, the Treaty of Amsterdam, since its entry into force in 1999, represents a major development in overall Justice and Home Affairs policy, and the implementation of the treaty provisions in Justice and Home Affairs was described as the next major EU initiative after the single currency.

Moreover, the Conclusions of the European Council in Tampere (15–16 October 1999) gave an additional push for the adoption of the measures considered necessary for the realisation of an Area of Freedom, Security and Justice, reaffirming traditional and integrating new principles in these fields.
In fact, the European debate had until then already taken consistency in the European Act of 1986. Article 7a (Art 14) of the Single European Act stated the following: 'The internal market shall comprise an area without internal borders in which the free movement of goods, persons, services and capital is ensured in accordance to the provisions of this Treaty'.

This Article gave rise to different interpretations of who has freedom of movement rights, and on the methods, including the compensatory measures involved, of implementing free movement of persons.

The Single European Act did not clarify the question of the institutional framework of the compensatory measures for free movement of persons. Whilst the programme of the Commission in this area had to be carried out according to Community standards and by the 'Community method', some Member States considered that only the intergovernmental method was acceptable in matters at the core of national sovereignty. Progress has been made, however, in that Member States have agreed on a common approach to foreigners' rights.

Omissions and ambiguities in the Single European Act led to conflict between the Commission and certain Member States on the competence of the Community Institutions with the result that Member States decided policy by the intergovernmental method; a good example of the latter was the Schengen Agreement of 14 June 1985 followed by a Convention of 19 June 1990. Various episodes of the conflict about competence even provoked disagreement between Community Institutions. Worn down by these disputes and the systematic blocking by the Council of Ministers, the Commission for the most part conceded the intergovernmental method in the field of Justice and Home Affairs, in the hope that a pragmatic stance would make progress possible in this sensitive field. The European Parliament suffered most because it was for the most part excluded from the decision-making process.

The Maastricht Treaty signed in 1992 gave comfort to the partisans of the intergovernmental method over those who were in favour of a more communitarian/supranational approach. The new Title VI called: 'Cooperation in the fields of Justice and Home Affairs' was nothing other than the formalisation of very slightly modified intergovernmental cooperation. The policy sectors covered by Title VI were referred to simply as 'matters of common interest' (Article K.1). This weak statement of intent was scarcely developed by Article K.3, which stated only 'Member States shall inform and consult one another within the Council with a view to coordinating their action'.

There was no clarification of whether Justice and Home Affairs cooperation is intended to provide for and/or encourage legislative initiatives, or whether practical, operational cooperation was the objective (Den Boer 1996). Rather than a clear distinction between supranational or intergovernmental cooperation, the third pillar occupied (and, what remains of it, still occupies) a halfway house, struggling to reconcile two very different institutional patterns, neither with primacy.

In the Maastricht Treaty, Member States seemed happy to have a reference to the principle of subsidiarity included in the Treaty. The EC will act (Article 3b [now Article 5]): 'Only if ... the objectives of the proposed action cannot be sufficiently achieved by the Member States and can therefore, by reason of the scale or effects of the proposed action be better achieved by the Community'.

With the Amsterdam Treaty (1998), the transfer of competence of the third pillar towards the first pillar seemed impressive. All the matters listed under Article K.1 of the Maastricht Treaty were transferred to Pillar 1, except for the police and judicial cooperation in penal matters which remains in the third pillar. The new Title IV 'Visas, asylum, immigration and other policies related to free movement of persons', which brings together the most important provisions, is subject to a special institutional mechanism providing for derogation on numerous points from the supranational approach (Article 67) and allowing for a transition period – 5 years after the entry into force of the Treaty before majority voting is introduced. Policy towards third-country nationals until Amsterdam was one clear example of the limits of European integration. Amsterdam tries to address the various lacunae by assigning to the Community objectives to be achieved within a fixed timetable. Parliament may eventually be involved if the Council of Ministers accepts the co-decision procedure. Furthermore, the transfer of competence to the first pillar implies recognising the authority of the European Court of Justice (ECJ) in the new areas of Community competence.

12.2 SUPRANATIONAL AND NATIONAL COMPETENCIES AND THE STATUS OF THIRD-COUNTRY NATIONALS

In the provisions of the Treaty of Amsterdam, third-country nationals have finally found their place in Community law. Certain categories of third-country nationals already benefited from the protection of Community law. These are:

- members of the family of an EU national;
- nationals of states connected to the EU by an association or cooperation agreement; and
- workers of a company on whose behalf they carry out services in another Member State (according to the Van der Elst principles)[1].

These three categories of third-country nationals were 'privileged' – the provisions of Community law did not cover other third-country nationals until the entry into force of the Amsterdam Treaty.

The heading of the new title IV is significant. It does not mention a common immigration policy, but provides a partial inventory of elements of

1 Case C-43/93, *R. Van der Elst and Offices des Migrationes Internationales*, judgement of 9 August 1994.

such a policy: 'Visas, asylum, immigration and other policies connected with free movement of persons', whereas Article K.1.3 of the Maastricht Treaty aimed at 'immigration policy and policy with regard to third-country nationals' before listing 'measures concerning immigration policy within the following areas'. In three sectors (Article 63.3), the more detailed specification of these sectors and the level of competence accorded to the EU in migration matters do not live up to the statement of the intent to introduce a comprehensive and coherent immigration policy. Also the second subparagraph of Article 63 indicates that: 'Measures adopted by the Council pursuant to points 3 and 4 shall not prevent any Member State from maintaining or introducing in the areas concerned national provisions which are compatible with this Treaty and with international agreements'.

The tendency in recent years by the Member States to interpret restrictively the competences of the European Union, contributes to a genuine doubt about when the European level of decision-making applies. Only recourse to Article 308 (ex Article 235) of the Treaty makes it possible to avoid a purely intergovernmental approach, by transferring the provisions concerning immigration policy from the third to the first pillar (Hailbronner 1998).

Despite the significant progress that the Treaty of Amsterdam represents for the European Union, it is only the beginning of a move towards a genuine European immigration policy. It remains uncertain whether, at some time in the future, it will become a supranational competence. Article 61 stipulates that the Council will adopt: 'Within a period of five years after the entry into force of the Treaty of Amsterdam the measures aiming to ensure free movement of persons in compliance with Article 14'.

This illustrates the resistance of the Member States to further European integration in this field. Article 14 is a re-statement of Article 7A of the (1986) Single European Act, which instituted an area without internal borders and with free movement of persons by 1 January 1993. The Treaty of Amsterdam complements the Single Market by security and justice supports for free movement. The compensatory measures intended to complement free movement of persons, alluded to in the Single European Act, became explicit in Article 61(a) of the Amsterdam Treaty.

Before examining the actual debate on immigration as well as the possibilities opened by the New Title IV of the Amsterdam Treaty, it seems necessary to describe and analyse the developments in immigration policies between the Maastricht Treaty (1992) and the Amsterdam Treaty (1998).

12.3 DEVELOPMENTS BETWEEN MAASTRICHT AND AMSTERDAM

12.3.1 Entry in the European Union

Article 62.2 deals with 'measures concerning the crossing of the external borders of the Member States'. The practical question is whether or not third-country nationals need a visa to enter the European Union. Article 62.2 (b) stipulates that the Council may adopt 'rules on visas for the stay envisaged of a maximum of three-month duration' with regard to:

1. the list of the third countries the nationals of which are subject to the visa to cross the external borders and those whose nationals are exempt from that obligation;
2. the procedures and conditions of issuing of the visas by the Member States;
3. a standard visa; and
4. rule model as regards uniform visa.

This aspect of migration policy was already communitarised by the Maastricht Treaty, which introduced Article 100C into the TEC. The new provisions may resolve the serious difficulties of interpretation within the Council of Ministers of Justice and Home Affairs during the discussions on the implementation of Article 100C.

The adoption of Regulation 2317/95 of 25 September 1995 determined which third-country nationals must be in possession of a visa when crossing an external border of the Member States. However, this was preceded by Byzantine discussions about the limits of the jurisdiction of the European Community on the basis of Article 100C. The only power explicitly granted to the Union was to draw up a list of those third-country nationals who require a visa to enter the Union. However, the Council of Ministers then decided that only the Member States could decide which third-country nationals were exempt from visa requirements. This implied that Member States reserved themselves the power to add to this joint list.

The situation is, in principle, much clearer since 15 March 2001 when the Council of the European Union adopted Regulation No 539/2001 to make a common list of those third-countries whose nationals '*de jure*' should require a visa and those third countries whose nationals are exempt from visa requirements. This regulation eliminated the previous 'grey list', thus abolishing the discretion of Member States to add other countries which were not on the Common Visa list.

12.3.2 Residence in the European Union

Article 63.3 lists, in a restrictive way, two competencies of the European Community with regard to third-country nationals staying for more than three months in a Member State.

Point (a) of Article 63.3 covers 'conditions of entry and residence, and standards on procedures for the issue by Member States of long term visas and residence permits, including for the purpose of family reunion'. This provision is both more complete and less specific than Article K.1.3 (b) (Maastricht) which stated: 'The conditions of entry and residence for third-country nationals on the territory of the Member States, including for family reunification and access to employment'.

In the absence of Community competence, the procedures for the granting of visas and long-term residence permits create recurring implementation problems within the Member States, despite some case law of the Court of Justice. In addition, no mention (probably deliberately) is made in Article 63.3 of immigration for employment. The phrasing 'including for the purposes of the family reunion' suggests that other forms of immigration are envisaged, including for reasons of employment. However, what exactly is included in the first pillar and what remains in the third pillar is unclear. The harmonisation which appeared in the text submitted in December 1996 during the intergovernmental conference during the Irish presidency as well as in the plan proposed in October 1996 by the Commission concerning an area of freedom, security and justice (CONF 3912/96 of 18 September 1996), also disappeared from the text adopted in Amsterdam. [2]

Point (b) of Article 63.3 is of a repressive nature; it covers 'illegal immigration and illegal residence, including repatriation of illegal residents'. This point differed from the original point (c) of Article K.1 that defined as a question of common interest 'the fight against illegal entry, residence and employment of third-country nationals on the territory of the Member States'. It is difficult to tell whether these differences in drafting represent significant differences. The disappearance of the reference to the illegal employment of third-country nationals cannot be fortuitous. As there are at stake essential questions of regulation in certain Member States, the common European labour market is undermined. The addition of repatriation of persons without authorised residence is also significant, as individual Member States have never managed to control undocumented immigration.

[2] See the text 'The European Union today and tomorrow: to adapt the European Union in the interest of its citizens and prepare it for the future, general Framework for a draft revision of the treaties', published by the Secretariat-General of the Council under the title *An Intergovernmental Conference for the amendment of the treaties, the Irish presidency's Six-month period, Compilation of texts,* Luxembourg, Office for Official Publications of the European Communities, 1997, p. 32.

12.4 THE CURRENT POST-AMSTERDAM DEBATE

In March 2000, a very controversial report of the United Nations based on demographic considerations was published (UN Secretariat ESA/P/WP.160). Resting on the analysis of the current population trends in the world and projections for the period 1995–2050, this report pleaded for 'replacement immigration' in order to compensate for the inevitable population decline in Europe and in other parts of the world. According to this report, the number of immigrants necessary to avoid a decline of the total population of the EU in the 50 years ahead is approximately comparable with the immigration rate of the 1990s, i.e. average annual net migration of 857 000 persons. However, the report stipulates that, in order to prevent a labour force decline, the number of migrants entering each year should double.

The 'provocative' observations of the report stimulated an intense public debate on this question in the European press, but they also contributed to the re-opening of the issue on immigration in the European institutions and Member States at a time of reflection on how to implement the new Amsterdam provisions.

One of the first post-Amsterdam initiatives proposed by the Commission on the ground of migration is the draft Directive on the right to family reunification, submitted to the Council on 1 December 1999 but which has not been approved yet. This initiative is the first of a series of draft Directives on the admission of third-country nationals for various purposes, which represent the 'communitarisation' of the draft Convention on the admission submitted by the Commission to the Council before the entry into force of the Treaty of Amsterdam. This project was followed by a draft Directive on the status of third-country nationals who are long-term residents in the Union, presented on 13 March 2001.

A proposal for a Directive dealing with the conditions of entry and residence of third-country nationals for the purpose of paid employment and self-employed economic activities was published on 11 July 2001, the same day as the publication of a Commission Communication on an 'open method of coordination' for the Community immigration policy. Furthermore, the Commission has prepared a draft Directive on the admission of third-country nationals for study and vocational training purposes. Two other directives approved by the Council, respectively in June and November 2000, are closely connected with the questions of migration, but deal more specifically with the fight against discrimination, racism and xenophobia.

With respect to the 'fight against illegal immigration' and to the management of migratory flows, a particularly important instrument is the draft framework-decision of the Council on the fight against the trafficking of human beings that the Commission presented in December 2000. In addition, a Communication proposal from the Commission to the Council and to the

European Parliament covering the common fight against illegal immigration is currently being prepared. Several proposals have also been submitted by the Member States, which share with the Commission a right to take initiatives in this field (Article 67.1 TCE). The French Presidency, in particular, presented several initiatives in the second half of 2000 covering primarily the means of preventing and of fighting illegal immigration. These initiatives, already approved by the Council, comprise the following Proposals of directives on, respectively;

- the definition of the assistance at the entry, residence and the irregular stay;
- the harmonization of the legislations of the Member States as regards liabilities imposed to the carriers for the territory of the Member States of the nationals of third countries stripped of the documents required to be allowed there;
- the mutual recognition of the orders of expulsion; as well as
- a Framework Decision on the reinforcement of the penal framework for the prevention of facilitation of unauthorised entry and the stay of third-country nationals.

Moreover, the French Presidency was particularly active in reviving the general debate on immigration which had been started by the above-mentioned report of the United Nations: discussions on this subject were held at the informal ministerial meeting in Marseilles (July 2000) and at three conferences on co-developments and migrants (6–7 July), on Illegal Migration Networks (20–21 July) and on the Integration of Immigrants (5–6 October).

The Commission intervened in this discussion in November 2000 with a Communication analysing the state of the debate on immigration. In this Communication on a Community immigration policy, the Commission states as a starting point that 'there is a growing recognition that the zero immigration policies of the past thirty years are no longer appropriate' in the current economic and demographic context of the European Union and of the countries of origin, and argues for a 'new approach of immigration', according to which channels for legal immigration should be made available, especially for labour migrants.

However, the Communication clearly takes its distance from the adoption of a policy of 'replacement migration' as proposed by the UN report on Replacement Migration as a possible scenario to counteract demographic decline. The Commission believes that 'while increased legal immigration in itself cannot be considered in the long term as an effective way to offset demographic changes, since migrants once settled tend to adopt the fertility patterns of the host country'.

Nevertheless, it considers that many 'economic migrants have been driven either to seek entry through asylum procedure or to enter illegally. This allows for no adequate response to labour market needs and plays into hands of well organised traffickers and unscrupulous employers'. It stresses the need for an approach based on the recognition that these migratory pressures will continue. Moreover, it stresses the fact that 'the opening up of channels for immigration for economic purposes to meet urgent needs for both skilled and unskilled workers has already begun in a number of Member States'.

In this context, the Commission underlined the need to have a 'proactive immigration policy', i.e. a policy which instead of focusing on vain attempts aiming to prevent and stop immigration by creating a 'Fortress Europe', would try to control immigration according to needs of the European labour market (see the proposal of directive of 11 July 2001). Moreover, the Tampere Council itself stressed the need for an 'Approximation of national legislations on the conditions for admission and residence of third-country nationals, based on a shared assessment of the economic and demographic developments within the Union, as well as the situation in the countries of origin' (paragraph 20 of the Presidency conclusions).

The Commission does not propose any quota system on a European scale, which would be 'impracticable', but rather some 'indicative targets', a system based on periodic reports of the Member States, re-examining the impact of their immigration policies during the past period and making projections on the number of economic migrants they would need in future (including their qualification levels). These indicative objectives would not only take into account the labour market needs of each Member State, but would also take into consideration the agreements in place with countries of origin of the migrants, the public acceptance of additional migrant workers in the country concerned, the resources available for reception and integration, the possibilities of cultural and social adaptation, etc.

This process should take into account the development of the general employment situation in the EU, and in particular the progress achieved in the implementation of the European Strategy for employment, defined by the European Councils of Luxembourg (1997) and Lisbon (March 2000). The mechanism proposed by the Commission therefore leaves the last word on the admission of the migrants to the Member States, but the various migration policies will however be coordinated at European level.

It is obvious that the approach defended in these texts represents a clear rift with former immigration policies at EU level. The question is whether Member States will follow the Commission in this way, considering the sensitivity of the question at the national level as well as the differences of approaches and policies in this field.

In presenting its proposals, the Commission intends to establish a coherent framework that would determine the basic conditions and procedures to be applied. This framework approach would be based on the following principles:

- the granting of a working permit should be simple, rational, flexible, on the basis of verifiable and objective criteria, delivered within a short time and the procedure should be transparent;
- applicants should preferably have an employment contract or a recruiting promise. However, this should not be an obligation;
- Member States should have the opportunity to establish quotas responding to their specific needs;
- the response on the request for the work permit should be delivered in a 180-day maximum delay. (Although this period is certainly not optimal for industry);
- reasoning for refusals should be clear; and
- working permits should not be limited to only one employer, but should be related to the sector of specialisation of the migrant worker or even to the region of his/her residence for a 3-year duration, with a possibility of prolongation.

The question of competence to grant or refuse a permit then arises: according to the principle of subsidiarity, this should be delegated to the Member States. This will give more coherence between the employment and immigration policies.

The objective would be to give a secure legal status for temporary workers who intend to return to their countries of origin, while at the same time providing a pathway leading eventually to a permanent status for those who wish to stay and who meet a certain number of criteria.

The proposal for a Directive of 13 March 2001 on the status of third-country nationals who are long-term residents supplements the other initiatives. The idea is a differentiation of the rights according to the length of stay. The principle that the length of residence has an influence in the rights of persons has a long tradition in the Member States and is referred to in the Tampere conclusions. Within five years, they will be allowed to move freely in the territory of the Union with the aim of seeking employment in another Member State.

12.5 FREEDOM OF MOVEMENT OF WORKERS FROM THE CEECS

On the other hand, clear demonstration of the reserve of the Member States in this field is the attitude towards the separate but related question of the extension of freedom of movement for the workers coming from the Central and Eastern European countries (CEECs) after enlargement. On this topic, which one cannot develop fully here, a plethora of studies and reports have already been produced, presenting rather different figures, forecasts and scenarios (and sometimes even contradictory). The German government for instance, proposed a seven-year transitional period before extending to the nationals of the CEECs the right to freedom of movement for the workers, although the Commission had submitted an 'information Note' in March 2001, which concluded that there would be no spectacular increase in East–West migration and that the overall impact on the European labour market would be limited, even though certain Member States could be affected more than others.

This document suggested five possible options to deal with this issue:

- a total closure of the Community labour market for a limited period to the workers of the CEECs;
- a complete liberalisation from the adhesion on; and
- three intermediate hypotheses: a quota system, a safeguard clause and a flexible system of transitional schemes.

The option retained ultimately by the Commission envisages a general transitional period of five years, with a possible individual extension by each Member State for a maximum period of two years. However, after the first two years, an automatic review is envisaged, resting on a report submitted by the Commission to the Council: at that moment, it would be possible to decide to shorten or extend the transitional period, while leaving to the Member States the possibility of maintaining a more restrictive procedure if they wish to. The discussions on the question remain open and the result of the debate will depend without any doubt on the overall agreement on the package deal of adhesion.

One must bear in mind that the end of the Cold War precipitated a new liberalised era for the free movement of people; not only between Eastern and Western Europe, but within Central and Eastern Europe itself. The open borders policy within CEE has helped to break down stereotypes and hostilities in the region, as between Poland and Russia, has helped foster contacts between national minorities, such as between Hungarians in Ukraine, and has generated spheres of economic activity and cooperation within the region. The EU accession of Baltic and Central European States threatens this. In February 2000 the Czech Republic announced visa regimes for citizens of the Ukraine, Russia and Belarus, with Slovakia following suit. In September Estonia introduced full visa regimes for Russian citizens, following the termination in March of the two countries' agreement on simplified border crossings. Lithuania has warned that it may have to rule out its agreement allowing for visa-free travel of Kaliningrad citizens by 2003. And while the implementation of the Schengen acquis creates tensions between candidate countries and their eastern neighbours, candidate countries will only be able to reap the benefits of freedom to take up employment in present member countries after a 'transition' period of several years.

It is clear that the present implementation of the Schengen criteria will have an adverse effect on the free movement rights of citizens along the EU's future border; both in the freedom to travel and the freedom to reside and work. Meanwhile the question of whether visa regimes could have the effect of not curbing crime while making travel and work difficult for most normal citizens remains unanswered. Moreover, the new security agenda in the wake of 11 September will in all likelihood make the process of obtaining a Schengen visa even more difficult, and could exacerbate existing tendencies in the lack of transparency in the administration of visas. Increasingly the obtaining of a visa could become a privilege, not a right. Keeping in mind that the border regions are not only linked through economic ties, but often through family and national identities – as with the Russian population living on both sides of the Narva–Ivangorod border between Estonia and Russia – it is clear that a hostile visa regime could infringe the basic rights of citizens.

These opposing tendencies have highlighted an existing contradiction in the EU's eastern policy. On the one hand, EU external relations have focused on encouraging cooperation between the EU and its future Eastern neighbours; on the other, the logic of EU enlargement and the demands made on candidate and accession countries to adopt the Schengen criteria lead to an exclusionary situation on the EU's future border. The incorporation of Central European and the Baltic States in the EU has the marked potential of drawing new dividing lines across Europe, undoing the progress which has been achieved over the last decade. One must not forget either, that the future members of the EU have also started to experience demographic problems similar to those of the current EU members. Therefore they too will be thinking of participating in a controlled open immigration policy addressing their own needs.

12.6 A COMMON EUROPEAN POLICY ON IMMIGRATION: THE WAY FORWARD

The topic on immigration is very sensitive, as it has an impact on a wide range of areas (social, cultural, economic and legal). It is therefore difficult to reach an agreement on this debate. Although the latest developments and the partial change of attitude on a European level can give rise to moderate optimism on the future of a European policy on immigration, the principal following points remain highly controversial:

Firstly: Is Europe ready to be defined as an area of immigration?

If this question is answered in the affirmative, then we need to bear in mind that the definition of an area of immigration does not necessarily involve the granting of free and generalised access to the labour markets, as the examples of the United States of America and Australia show. However, it would probably be the first step towards a clear and coherent policy of management of migratory flows, which should supplement the measures intended to fight against illegal immigration, smuggling and the drafting of human beings.

Secondly: Is the European Union willing to grant to third-country nationals who reside legally in the territory of one of the Member States rights which are 'as near as possible to those enjoyed by EU-citizens'?

The importance of fair treatment of third-country nationals has been underlined by the European Council in Tampere, in which the need of an 'approximation of the legal status of third-country nationals to that of the member States' was acknowledged (Para. 21), and the objective that 'long-term legally resident third-country nationals be offered the opportunity to obtain the nationality of the Member State in which they are resident' was endorsed. However, EU immigration policy has not, so far, incorporated steps to ensure that migrants benefit from comparable living and working conditions to those of nationals.

12.7 BY WAY OF CONCLUSION…

It is undeniable that the EU advances towards a common migration procedure. However the question is when and, one could add, how, such a system will be set up. Although the Treaty of Amsterdam, the Vienna action Plan and the Tampere Conclusions fix precise deadlines for the adoption of the majority of the measures, this process knew some delays and encountered a number of difficulties. One can only hope that the new attitude towards the immigration of third-country nationals combined with the new competencies of the Community in the field of immigration will reflect the 'good intentions' expressed in several documents and action plans in policies that would be at the same time concrete, effective and human.

REFERENCES

Den Boer, M. (1996), 'Police Cooperation', in J. Monar, N. Neuwahl, D. O'Keefe and W. Robinson (eds), *Guide to the EU*, London: Butterworths, pp. 247–49.

European Commission (2000), Communication from the Commission to the Council and the European Parliament *on a Community Immigration Policy*, Brussels, 22/11/2000.

European Commission (2001), Proposal of directive concerning *the status of third-country nationals who are long term residents* of 13/3/2001, COM (2001)127 final.

European Commission (2001), Proposal for a Council Directive *on the conditions of entry and residence of third-country nationals for the purpose of paid employment and self-employed economic activities*, COM (2001) 386 final.

European Commission (2001), Communication from the Commission to the Council and the European Parliament *on an open method of coordination for the Community immigration policy*, 11/7/2001, COM (2001)387 final.

European Union Council (1997), 'The European Union today and tomorrow: to adapt the European Union in the interest of its citizens and prepare it for the future, general framework for a draft revision of the treaties', published by the Secretariat-General of the Council under the title *An Intergovernmental Conference for the amendment of the treaties, the Irish presidency's Six-month period*, Compilation of texts, Luxembourg, Office for Official Publications of the European Communities, p. 32.

Federal Ministry of the Interior (2000), *Policy and Law Concerning Foreigners in Germany*, Berlin, August.

Glover S., C. Gott, A. Loizillon, J. Portes, R. Price, S. Spencer, V. Srinivasan and C. Willis (2001), *Migration: an economic and social analysis*, London: Research, Development and Statistics Directorate, Home Office.

IOM (1998), *Migration Potential in Central and Eastern Europe*, IOM, Geneva.

IOM (2000), *World Migration Report 2000*, IOM, Geneva.

Ministry of Foreign Affairs, Sweden (2001), *Sweden in 2000 – A Country of Migration Past, Present, Future*, Stockholm: Department for Migration and Asylum Policy.

OECD (1991), *Migration: The Demographic Aspects*, Paris: Organisation for Economic Cooperation and Development.

OECD (1998), *Ageing Populations: The Social Policy Implications*, Paris: Organisation for Economic Cooperation and Development.

OECD (1999), *Trends in International Migration*, Paris: Organisation for Economic Cooperation and Development.

OECD (2000), *Trends in International Migration*, Paris: Organisation for Economic Cooperation and Development.

Salt, J. (2000), *Current Trends in International Migration in Europe*, Strasbourg: Council of Europe.

Van Het Loo M., S. DeSpiegelaire, G. Lindstrom, J. Kahan and G. Vernez (2001), *A Comparison of American and Dutch Immigration and Integration Experiences: What lessons can be learned?*, The Hague: WRR, Working document, 120.

13. Immigration and European Immigration Policy: Myths and Realities

Giuseppe Sciortino and Ferruccio Pastore

13.1 INTRODUCTION

The promises of Tampere have quickly begun fading away. Cashing in on the spaces opened up by the Amsterdam Treaty, the EU meeting in Tampere (1999) called for a fully-fledged 'common EU migration policy'. On this basis, waves of ambitious communications and proposals were proffered by the Commission. Soon after, however, the political climate changed. The scoreboard that the Commission – perhaps over-confidently – had set up immediately after Tampere has since revealed that long delays have already accumulated for several key proposals. Meanwhile, various press agencies have informed of open conflicts about proposals. In the Laeken summit, the former incremental approach and restrictive orthodoxy have again taken centre stage, while the dream of a comprehensive common immigration policy has faded deep into the shadows. This fundamental trend has not only been confirmed but reinforced in the subsequent Seville summit.

Such a change in the prospects of a European immigration policy may be explained in several ways, contingent upon the level of analysis selected. In the short term, developments may be explained by looking at the changing political environment. The political environment has changed significantly since Tampere; with the recent rise in popular support for centre-right governments, xenophobia and immigration panic have moved again to the forefront of the political agenda while waves of populist movements gain success in both the media and the ballot box. In more structural terms, this change may be explained by the difficulties associated with institution building or by the power of networks engendered in past intergovernmental developments. This analysis remains by and large correct, though it falls short of our objective of telling the full story. Instead we must understand this shift as the latest swing in the pendulum-like oscillation that EC immigration policy has exhibited in recent history. To explain the unfolding pattern, it is necessary to focus heavily on the conceptual framework that has been embedded in the long history of attempts to construct immigration as a 'European' issue. We will argue that the tensions between the 'intergovernmental' and the 'European' approaches are not simply an organizational issue; they have produced an entirely new set of rhetorical structures and binary oppositions that have become embedded in the institutional debate. In the next step, we describe the conceptual framework that has triggered the (re)construction of European migration as a common policy issue. We outline how this framework is grounded in a number of mythical assumptions that one can confront with some readily available data. Altogether these steps bring to light key elements of the difficulties of establishing fully Europeanized immigration policies; any attempt to create a common immigration policy must directly face the challenge of overcoming the myths of the European vision of immigration. The political difficulties involved in the process, we will argue, are intrinsic – as yet unacknowledged – stumbling blocks in the way of European policy development. In the conclusions we then suggest a few – and rather modest – policy actions that may help in shaping a more reasonable – and thus feasible – European policy on the issue.

13.2 EUROPEAN MIGRATION POLICY BEFORE TAMPERE: A BRIEF HISTORICAL BACKGROUND

Throughout the continent, the immigration debate contains plenty of references to 'Europe'. In most public opinion, it is commonplace to hear the argument that immigration is a 'European' problem while complaining about the shortcomings of the European immigration policy. In the southern European countries, politicians argue that immigration reforms are necessary to bring them up to the 'European' standard, while opposition parties claim the same reforms are bringing their countries 'out of Europe'. In other European countries, it is a common charge that Europhile politicians discuss or accept immigration decisions against national interests. According to public opinion data, European citizens, overall, are deeply dissatisfied with their representative immigration policies. Still, the numbers of citizens that consider useful some kind of European policy are fairly high. In other words, the fact that 'European immigration policy' remains a highly conflicted and contested field should not blind us to the truth that the boundaries of such a field – the assumption of its existence, peculiarity and significance – firmly establish it as a political object. Dwelling on frequent opposition to specific

European immigration policy proposals should not deter the European Community from the idea that a common European answer to immigration problems is both desirable and achievable (Eurobarometer 1989).

For a long part of post-war European history, thirty glorious years of economic recovery and state reconstruction, European countries experienced impressive migratory flows (Bade 2000). This era did not, however, imply any kind of coordination among receiving countries. While a web of treaties were established to create a link between sending and receiving countries, the relationships among governments of the European receiving countries were absent or openly competitive. The first steps toward the construction of a 'European immigration policy' took place only in the early 1980s, when the consequences of the 'immigration ban' of the mid-1970s had destroyed both the delusions and hopes of the previous era for separate, unilateral solutions (Pastore 1999). The construction of the 'European immigration policy' field – the synthesis of the idea that the control and management of migratory flows should be considered a European problem – has been facilitated by several factors. First of all, clashes with the embedded liberalism regimes – experienced by many countries in their post-1973 attempts to restrict immigration with country-based measures – made appealing the existence of a forum where Member States could bypass their internal constraints in the attempt to regulate forms of migration that their policies defined as unwanted (Geddes 2001). Second, a certain measure of European policy coordination easily fits with the technical problems of the establishment of an increasingly integrated common market. Third, policy responses to certain historical events – such as the Turkish asylum-seekers' upsurge in 1979 and 1980 – had taught that the control of unwanted migration could require measures (such as the introduction of visa requirements and agreement with neighbouring states) whose efficacy was almost entirely contingent upon coordination with other receiving states of close geographical proximity. There is also reason to believe that an intrinsic factor in the establishment of a common European immigration field was the very same adoption of 'banning policies' in the mid-1970s. Although the migratory regimes of the European receiving states were quite varied, the adoption of a number of similar decisions suggested possible alternative methods, simply from the perspective that similar solutions could be inferred from the presence of similar problems. At the root of the European immigration policy process, then, one may find the methodical emergence of a common vision of a European immigration system.

The shared construction of 'Europe' in reference to immigration, however, would leave open a question of which 'Europe', particularly with respect to the institutional framework of a newly constructed policy field. Since the beginning, there has been a tension between attempts, by the European Commission, to establish immigration policy as a fully-fledged field of

Community competency, and several states and state structures, interested instead in a dense network of intergovernmental bodies. In 1985, we witnessed both the seedling establishment of the Schengen system – bound to become the quintessential symbol of the intergovernmental approach – and an attempt by the Commission to establish a somewhat binding coordination of Member States in matters of entry, residence, working permits, contrast of irregular migration and cooperation with sending countries. While the Schengen system would find success and gain strength in subsequent years, the Commission's attempt was quickly defeated by a challenge in the European Court of Justice as introduced by several Member States.

A similar conflict appeared during the negotiations of the Single European Act of 1986, where the Commission's inclusion of Article 8(a) was defeated by the Member States, unwilling to reduce their powers of discretion in the treatment of third-country nationals. Disagreement came again in 1990, when at the Council meeting in Rome the Commission's rather mild proposals were defeated in favour of an incremental coordination on control measures (Coordinators Group on Free Movement of Persons 1989–1990; Commission of the European Communities, 1990).

In the aforementioned events one can discern a pattern that will be encountered again and again; the slow condensation of organizational energies and rhetorical resources in the hands of the proponents of an EU immigration policy, a decreasing satisfaction with the achieved level of coordination on immigration control, the attempt by supranational bodies to seize the resulting opportunities, and the production of apparently successful proposals, only to be followed by a severe defeat at the end, characterized by rapid Commission retreat and a return to the perspective of incremental coordination on strictly defined immigration control measures. As a matter of fact, the pattern manifests itself again in the early 1990s regarding the fate of the two 1991 communications on asylum and immigration, and again in the mid-1990s with the communication on immigration and asylum policies (Commission of the European Communities 1991a; 1991b; 1994).

There is, then, some evidence in favour of the existence of a pendulum-like pattern, biased in favour of loose coordination among Member States on a limited and control-based list of issues. Circumstances do create differentiation between these predictable and repetitive behaviours. Cycle by cycle, the institutional and organizational options have become charged with a variety of symbolic meanings, related both to their overall characteristics and to the values and priorities that each 'European' policy should embrace (Table 13.1).[1] This set of rhetorical binary oppositions is often more sharply

[1] The table has been constructed starting from a (surely non probabilistic) sample of official documents, scholarly papers and press cuttings. It should be assumed consequently as a sensitizing device, not as a factual description of the situation.

polarized than the actual policy measures advocated. The rhetorical structure adopted, however, has some consequences also for the actors that adopt it: their agenda and options becomes – at least partly – constrained by symbolic attributes they employ to carve out a space for themselves (DiMaggio 1997 and Nash 2001). After every downturn, the Commission aimed and proposed structures that have found themselves more and more identified with the aim of a 'global, complementary, comprehensive and realistic' immigration policy (Commission of the European Communities 1991b).

Table 13.1 The rhetorical structure of institutional options

Intergovernmental	Supranational
Control	Control and integration
State-centred	EU-centred
Short-term	Long-term
Incremental	Comprehensive
Restrictive	Enlightened
Fragmented	Systemic
Lowest common denominator	Up to the task
Unaccountable	Accountable
Fortress Europe	Area of Freedom, Security and Justice
Rights-reducing	Rights-enhancing
Pragmatic	Ideological
Realistic	Grandiose
Common sense	Elitist

13.3 SCHENGEN II: THE REVENGE?

The Amsterdam Treaty seemingly marked the end of the pattern previously identified. The Treaty provided the institutional resources for a full 'communitarization' (contingent upon a unanimity vote in 2004) of the main structures of the intergovernmental approach. This outcome was made possible by, again, the success of intergovernmental coordination. From one side, Schengen was by then basically covering all the external southern frontiers of the Union. Its main engine – the exchange between the willingness to play the role of a buffer state and the symbolic recognition granted by the Schengen membership (Sciortino 1999 and Pastore 1999) – was beginning to run out of fuel. On the other side, communitarization appeared, even to those supporting the intergovernmental approach, a reasonable way of avoiding the increasingly costly shortcomings of intergovernmentalism: the extensive dependency on unanimity decisions (producing painfully slow and weak decisions), the unequal distribution of financial and control burdens that would derive from a real application of the Dublin Treaty (producing widespread delays and endemic subterfuges) and interest in presenting accession countries with a take-it-or-leave-it package of immigration control. Regardless, the restrictive orthodoxy seemed to be breaking down; the need for foreign labour was starting to be openly recognized in several European political systems, and some Mediterranean countries had already introduced a basic set of active immigration policies.[2]

The Tampere Council of 1999 – with its emphasis on the adoption of an 'integrated approach' (Commission of the European Communities 2000) – seemed to many to hold the promise that a 'communitarized' immigration policy would be something different from Schengen in sum (Pastore 1999). On the basis of the decisions taken in Tampere, the Commission has issued several communications and legislative proposals addressing a variety of key issues and, more importantly, launching an integrated, medium-term strategy for immigration policy in Europe. To elaborate on the established metaphor, the pendulum began to swing decidedly towards a supranational Europe with both practical and symbolic implications.

It did not last long. Already at the end of 2001, it was clear that measures intended to expand and revise the Schengen tradition stood likely to succeed, while the measures targeted to deal with regular immigration – a key dimension of the Commission's strategy – seemed doomed to fail. The dynamic of the Laeken summit brought the main sources of contention to light; some Member States responded to integrative Commission approaches with open resistance, others expressed a more residual concern. The same summit produced a fairly strong scaling-down of the strategy, giving full priority to control issues and to the standardization of procedures only in the field of humanitarian acceptance. The collective change of attitude became even clearer in Seville.

Given the aforementioned trend, there is more than a fair chance that the 'new communitarized' approach will assume most of the three main features of the former intergovernmental mindset: restricting issues to those managed according to a search for lowest common denominators, focusing nearly exclusively on control issues and pursuing objectives in a fragmented rather than systemic way. The choice seems to be between a communitarized immigration policy that follows rather closely the immigration strategy and approach of the previous intergovernmental stream – thus basically

[2] All the talk of 'zero immigration' notwithstanding, no EU Member State has ever stopped labour migration completely. All Member States have actually a variety of programmes for the entry of foreign labour (ECOTEC 2001).

renouncing the aura identified in Table 13.1 – and an overarching chance of failure in 2004.

This trend shows that the previous dominant explanation of European immigration policy – centred on the institutional level – needs to be qualified. Opposition to 'communitarization', in other words, could prove to be less connected with institutional design and fears for loss of sovereignty than previously assumed. On the contrary, the systemic, comprehensive, medium-term policy stance, strictly associated with that project, could turn out to matter more.

Our argument is that – beside the obvious importance of the competing institutional projects and of the power networks associated with them – an adequate understanding of the issues involved requires paying due attention to the conceptual frame embodied and employed in the very same construction of an 'European immigration policy'. This frame is embodied in a few assumptions that have been fuelled since the beginning of the growth of the 'European immigration policy' field, thus gaining a kind of taken-for-granted status. They are, unfortunately, largely mythical, being the last poisoned fruit of the delusions of the 1960s and early 1970s. The evolution of European immigration policy cannot be understood without taking into consideration the growing tension between the migratory practices of most European states and the mythical frame that has coalesced in a restrictive orthodoxy, a set of beliefs only to be challenged – from the political and electoral point of view – at great risk. Increasingly, states seem not to be practising what they have preached. We argue that such a divide gives competitive advantage to incremental and fragmented policy-making over the kind of approach traditionally associated with 'communitarization'. As this chasm would be much more difficult to uphold within the context of a comprehensive immigration policy, the political pressure to maintain the framework – no matter the growing feeling of unreality – forces the policy process towards negotiations restricted to control issues.

13.4 MYTHS AND REALITIES

From the point of view of its cognitive framework, the European immigration policy debate shows a fairly strong continuity. Reading the available planning document at length, it is striking how stable and consistent the set of basic assumptions is revealed to be. This set of assumptions may be summarized as follows:

- Western Europe is a single, albeit internally varied, migration system;
- EU Member States have (at least) a set of common migratory problems, that can (and should) be managed in similar ways;

- in Western Europe, there is no structural demand for unskilled foreign labour;
- the main factors behind irregular immigration are inadequate control systems;
- irregular migration toward EU countries is mainly push-driven;
- the integration of immigrants is difficult and it poses several challenges. To be able to integrate the foreigners already present, a tight control is necessary;
- to regulate restrictively the mobility of third-country nationals (TCNs) is necessary given their high mobility potential. Without such restrictions, foreigners would move to the most generous welfare states; and
- European societies are highly homogeneous and most citizens feel culturally threatened by immigration. Consequently, xenophobic backlashes are an ever-present possibility to be constantly monitored and accounted for.

All these assumptions may be questioned and – indeed – are questioned by several researches. We will restrict ourselves to public-use, easily accessible data, just in order to show that such premises are not inference from factual knowledge, but rather a kind of moral discourse – evolved as a reaction from the 'guestworkers' era delusions – that is continually reinforced by its assertion as a realistic frame for policy-making.

Let's start with the first crucial assumption. In the last 20 years there has been a remarkable process of convergence among the immigration policies of the EU Member States, at least as far as migratory control is concerned (Brochmann and Hammar 1999). Can we say the same for the de facto migratory flows such policies are meant to regulate? Comparative data are scarce and less reliable than they could be.

However, if we have a look at the available data (Council of Europe 2000; Eurostat 2000 and OECD 1999), we easily discover that:

- there exists little debatable evidence of convergence among European countries as far as migrants' countries of origins, destinations and individual characteristics are concerned;
- there is very weak evidence of convergence among migratory trends, with only a few countries experiencing in the last decade structural changes in the composition of migration flows;
- there is even scarcer evidence of convergence among migratory stock trends, both in reference to the stock of resident foreign population and its labour market participation rate or sectoral employment;

- sub-regional homogeneities are very limited and hardly ever exist among contiguous units; and
- attractive capacities of countries, and increasingly of their regions, appear to be highly uneven.

A point that should be stressed is that such results are not surprising from the point of view of contemporary migration theory (Massey et al. 1998). On the contrary, they are precisely what a sophisticated theory of migration would lead us to expect. The convergence among control policies is perceived as a reaction but is empirically a construction (Sciortino 2000).

From the first assumption in the European policy debate, it usually follows that EU Member States have at least some common migratory problem that could and should be managed in a coordinated way. At first glance, it may appear obvious. Compared with 30 years ago, all Western European countries – actually most European countries *tout court* – have become receiving countries. All public opinions are concerned with a set of apparently similar issues such as irregular migration, security and the migratory consequences of international crisis. Indeed, the agenda is much more similar today across European countries than it used to be 30 years ago. At a closer look, however, such similarities do not tell us the full story. The clearest example is the 'control crisis' of the early 1990s, a main triggering factor in the development of European immigration policy as a policy field (Cornelius et al. 1994 and Freeman 1994). Most European coordination at the time had been targeted to bring crises under control, identified mainly with the upsurge of asylum-seekers and refugees (introduction of visa requirements, externalization of border controls, sanctions to carriers, involvement of Eastern European countries, the safe haven concept, temporary and discretionary protection programmes). By and large, these policies have been successful. Though on the rise again, the number of asylum applications in Europe was in 2001 only slightly more than 50% of the 1992 peak and the Kosovo war has shown that even the flows of displaced persons may be contained effectively. In retrospect, however, it has become clear that the 'crisis' was hardly 'European': it was a German (as well as partly French, Swedish and British) crisis, rooted in medium-term patterns already well established before the late 1980s. Not surprisingly, the policies enacted in the period have changed the situation in terms both of volumes and regional distributions.

In the last few years, Germany has received less than a quarter of all European applications and the absorption rate of the four major countries of the 'crisis period' has lowered from 86% to 63%. It may be questioned whether the measures adopted and the policy stances taken have really answered to an European-wide problem: southern European countries, that in the same years were experiencing a large influx of foreign labour, would have presumably benefited much more from the development of an active entry policy, by a more liberal visa regime, by programmes for seasonal work and tailored employer sanctions. Such items were in fact on the European table, but they were given low – if existent – priority. The latter point is closely connected to the third myth we have identified: the lack of a structural demand for unskilled – or low skilled – foreign labour. Such an assumption was born in the years prior to the great immigration ban of the early 1970s, and it has since fossilized into permanence. Historical records do indeed show to the contrary that the ban on immigration was more for political reasons than economic ones. In fact, it took place while employers were frantically recruiting abroad, resorting in Germany even to chartering flights. The immigration ban was entirely a political decision, aimed at establishing a political control over the composition of the population, based on the perception that the situation was producing benefits for the entrepreneurs and costs for the political system.[3]

The era of large manufacturing plants simultaneously hiring thousands of steelworkers has indeed ended. But a large demand for low-skilled and unskilled work still exists in European manufacturing. Moreover, given that European welfare states (with the exception of the Scandinavian countries) are service-lean and transfer-based, European households need to acquire a large volume of personal services on the market, producing an additional demand for low-skilled jobs.

Agriculture still requires a number of jobs shunned by locals. According to the most recent estimates, more than one agricultural seasonal worker out of ten is a foreigner (Table 13.2). As one can see from the table below (Table 13.2), in the absence of a heavy proletarization of the native population, such large demand for unskilled or low-skilled work will almost always require the presence of a large number of foreigners. Not surprisingly, we find across Western Europe immigrants over-represented in the manufacturing, construction and service sectors (OECD 2001). The same sectors are supposed to harbour most of the undocumented migration jobs, with an even larger presence in the personal services (OECD 2000).

[3] This was openly recognized in the very first SOPEMI report, written in 1979: the decision to ban immigration is presented as motivated 'strictly by political reasons' and it is argued that the oil shock had been an occasion for pushing forward 'restrictive decisions grounded in the political and social situation rather than in the economic one'. See also Sciortino, 2000.

Table 13.2 Foreign seasonal employment in the agricultural sectors (2000)

Country	Number of Workers
Germany	250 000
Austria	28 421
Greece	120 000
Finland	2 502
Sweden	2 835
Netherlands	6 328
Italy (2001 data)	30 328
Spain	32 315
Portugal	–
France	7 100
Denmark	50
Belgium	–
Partial total	522 685

Source: Coldiretti calculation on GEOPA data, 2002, and Caritas-Migrantes, 2002

As matter of fact, hundreds of thousands of the migrants that, in the last two decades, were said to 'migrate into unemployment' appear actually to be by now firmly employed. All in all, the market participation rate of male foreign workers is frequently above that of natives in European labour markets, more remarkably in the younger countries of immigration such as Italy or Spain. Although immigrants may face difficulties in entering the labour market in the short term, they seem to receive and produce beneficial effects in the medium term (Glover et al. 2001).

A final consideration may be made by looking at what the EU Member States do, rather than what they preach; in recent years, a variety of seasonal worker programmes have been opened or strengthened in some European countries, employing hundreds of thousands of temporary workers (OECD 2001). If we review current political discussions, we may even suspect that a new 'guest-worker era' is starting. It is just too early to say if such programmes will turn out to be effective or if they will nurture a new historical delusion about their impermanence.

This brief summary of the information available points to the existence of a large demand of unskilled foreign labour, originating both in small and medium sized firms and in households. Large industrial plants were the key actor in traditional corporatist immigration planning. Today, however, policing the boundaries of the labour market is a much more complicated matter. It is not surprising then that at least sections of the European migratory system have, rather than stopping, turned from regular to irregular, from documented to undocumented. As irregular migrants are, by definition (in Europe, at least), excluded from the official labour market, the existence of a sizable irregular migration system is largely contingent upon the size, structure and strength of the informal economy in the different economic systems. According to IMF estimates, the contribution of the informal economy to the official GDP is estimated as ranging from a minimum of 9% (Switzerland) up to 27% and 30% respectively in Italy and Greece (Schneider and Enste 2000). Given this context, the assumption that irregular migration is produced (or made possible) by weak external controls appears to be rather mythical too.

Since the late 1980s, most European governments' attentions have been devoted to the reform of external controls. Visa requirements have been introduced for nearly all sending countries and significant investments have been made on border police authorities (International Centre for Migration Policy Development 1999). With a remarkable degree of creativity, 'borders' have been expanded and enlarged, buffer states and buffer areas have been identified, and a growing number of actors have been made subject to control duties (Lahav and Guiraudon 2000). Such efforts have had a remarkable degree of success in the control of the flows of asylum-seekers and, more generally, in managing the growing demand for admission. This success is perhaps best witnessed by the surge of illegal entries recorded in recent years and the development of a specialized transnational smuggling industry (Pastore et al. 1999). Such a large investment on external controls could be highly effective if the migratory flows were a flood, a multitude of atomized persons pushed out from their countries desperately. The previous points, however, have shown how such vision is deeply mistaken, at least for the mainstream of the flow. Most irregular migrants have both connections and some kind of job prospects in the receiving countries. And precisely for this reason a number of them can, given the strength of the demand for foreign labour, circumvent a system focused nearly only on external control.

Here we again encounter a myth that the main channels of irregular migration are those based on clandestine entry. Such a sub-myth, functional to the overemphasis on border controls, does underplay the complexities of visa regulations in a highly interconnected world. As matter of fact, even tight visa requirements still allow for overstaying. A survey carried out on a large sample (7 692) of foreigners in Lombardy in 2001 shows that more than a third of the interviewees had entered the country with a short-term visa, and had since subsequently overstayed (Blangiardo 2002). This cannot be attributed to a lax implementation of visa requirements by Italian authorities. The number of visas issued by Italian consulates in the sending countries is quite reasonable and perhaps lower than international trade and tourism flows would lead one to expect (Table 13.3).

Table 13.3 Visas granted by some Schengen countries (1998–2000)

Country	1998	1999	2000	Var. % 1999/2000
Germany	2 498 000	2 264 131	2 607 012	15.1
France	2 053 443	1 940 000	2 113 632	8.9
Italy	741 077	834 776	1 008 999	20.9
Spain	660 359	542 000	670 949	23.8
Greece	–	462 748	–	–
Austria	419 700	433 867	449 035	3.5
Netherlands + Luxemburg	415 420	369 665	320 847	-13.2
Belgium	147 684	122 761	–	–
Portugal	111 859	106 565	122 002	14.5
Total	7 047 542	7 076 513	–	–

Source: Ministero degli Affari Esteri, Repubblica italiana

An effective system of immigration control in western Europe should be then focused on reducing the availability of informal, undocumented jobs, thus dealing indirectly with the main pulling factor. Western European states, however, do not place the contrast of irregular work at the top of the policy priority (Robin and Barros 1999), though it has been present in the planning document since the beginning. A further assumption is that the influx of new immigrants would put a heavy strain on the integrative capacities of western European societies, thus threatening already-present situations. The connection between integration of already-present immigrants and tight control of new entries is the hard core of the European vision of immigration. Actually, the whole restrictive orthodoxy is defended as a condition for managing integration successfully. It is said that contemporary conditions for immigrants' integration are markedly different from the previous ones, that integration is slower and more painful, that immigrants display a stronger feeling of resistance, that transnational links make their 'foreignness' more foreign and lasting. Unfortunately, again, this assumption does not seem to fit well with the available evidence. Far from being characterized by their active 'resistance' to assimilation, contemporary migratory flows are repeating familiar steps. Socio-economically, it has been seen how immigrants tend in the long term to acquire a profile similar to natives (OECD 2001). Socially, the evidence seems to point to a reasonable process of 'assimilation'; most of them learn the language of the new country within their lifetime and very few of their offspring fail to do so.[4] After a decade of litanies on the failures of

[4] When and where reality seems to diverge from such a pattern, we usually find policies that, keeping immigrants uncertain about their settlement, make such a goal more troublesome and

assimilation, the now available research shows quite a different story (Modood et al. 1994; Tribalat 1996). In Europe difference-based arguments over immigrants seem to be more popular with – and full of implication for – receiving societies' élites and public opinions, than they are with the immigrants themselves (Rath 1993; Schain 1999; Silverman 1992). Would such processes be modified by a flow of new entries? It would surely make a difference from the point of view of the observer: continuing migration does indeed create a perception of enduring ethnic visibility. But most such processes operate at the micro level over time, largely independently from the flows of new arrivals. Plus, it should be considered that the 1990s have already been a decade of heavy new inflows.

The issues of immigrants' integration is somewhat linked to the issue of third-country nationals' (TCNs) mobility within the union. The Commission has several times launched, and failed to secure, attempts to include TCNs among the beneficiaries of free movement. Most states, however, have assumed that such freedom of movement would be a great risk, with large number of TCNs admitted in a country but more than willing to move quickly to another. According to this logic, freedom of movement for TCNs would basically be a renouncement of state control over the size and characteristics of new entries. Now, there is for sure a certain degree of intra-European mobility in the irregular migratory system. As far as legally resident immigrants are concerned, however, the matter seems more complicated.

Most resident foreigners and denizens – the target of TCNs' freedom of movement – have settled for many years. And economic conditions across EU Member States are by and large similar or vary within a limited range. The only simulation available for international mobility within a free movement space with such conditions – developed using Scandinavian data – would lead any analyst to a safe bet that, if such freedom were granted, the movements would be pretty much frictional (Muus 1998). This also has great implications for the assumption that generous welfare conditions do work as a welfare magnet, attracting migrants where they may enjoy the most liberal conditions. Prima facie, the theory of the welfare magnet seems more than reasonable: studies in Germany, Sweden and Denmark have documented an increase in the rates of welfare dependency of foreign populations, in absolute terms and relative to the native population. At the same time, however, such analyses document how such difference disappears once controlled for observable characteristics and taking into account the large number of asylum-seekers who are made 'welfare dependent' by design (Brücker et al. 2001). In contrast to the US, in western Europe welfare dependency decreases with the length of stay: foreigners assimilate out of welfare assistance. A strain on the

less desirable. Such is the case of most of the contemporary European policies for refugees and asylum-seekers.

welfare purse does indeed exist, but it is largely linked to the management of asylum-seekers, for whom in most countries it is forbidden to work. Such data provide a fertile ground for questioning both the assumption that 'generous' welfare countries will exhibit increased immigration and that migrants are attracted to generous welfare states (Baldwin-Edwards 2002). The last mythical assumption we identified concerns the risk for xenophobic backlashes in the European populations worried by the loss of cultural homogeneity. Such problems make the headlines in many European media, and in the aftermath of 11 September such worrisome attitudes have taken a distinct religion-specific emphasis. Racism and xenophobia do exist. And it is true that in most western European countries the national narratives tell a story of similar people bound by the enactment of similar lifestyles. The enduring, constitutive cultural and social heterogeneity of most European populations is precisely one of the dimensions of their identity that each national narrative, to quote Renan, *doit avoir oublié*. This notwithstanding, it is important to stress that many opinion polls of the European public opinion do document an attitude, at least at the declaration level, much more open than that which public discourse would lead us to predict (Eurobarometer 1989, 1997). A survey carried out on behalf of the Vienna-based EUMC in 2000 shows a fairly negative vision of immigration among European public opinions. The answers, however, are mainly concerned with unemployment, welfare intake and personal security rather than with 'ethnocultural' issues. Actually, a majority of respondents display what the analysts label a 'multicultural optimism'. Only in three countries – Belgium (50%), Germany (69%) and Greece (45%) – do respondents feel that cultural diversity may weaken the country fabric. The same data document how in every EU member country a majority of the respondents – ranging from 79% to 54% – disagree with any strongly assimilationist programme (Thalhammer et al. 2000). On the whole, the actual negative vision of immigration that we detect in European public opinion is based much more on functional than ethnocultural reasoning. Western Europe, of course, appears unfortunately to have a fairly large number of 'bigots'. But for the majority of its citizens, the trouble lies more in the balance between costs and benefits, and in their distribution. In this sense, an openly functional argument could turn out to be much more important and relevant than a paternalistic attitude.

13.5 SOME POLICY IMPLICATIONS

The arguments developed in the chapter have been focused mainly on the policy consequences of a largely mythical framework within which most European policy elaboration has taken place in recent decades. This should not be taken to imply a cynical or necessarily pessimistic attitude toward the possibility of a European immigration policy. On the contrary, we think that such a policy could be quite beneficial, and we hold that the target set in Tampere should be considered not only as the outcome of a cultural maturation's phase in western European attitudes towards international migration. We argue, however, that such goals cannot be achieved without a deep restructuring of the European immigration policy field, both in its cognitive frameworks and in its bargaining context.

As far as the cognitive framework is concerned, we have argued, following an old Zen understanding, that the problem of European immigration policies is less connected with the contemporary migratory flows than the delusions embedded in the framework employed to interpret them. We have also noted that such a framework is running against both theoretical wisdom and empirical evidence easily available in the field of migration studies. The first policy implication has then to do with the learning mechanism operating in the field. It is correct to note that the various EU bodies do indeed produce a significant amount of research. It should be stressed, however, that most such research is policy-oriented. While such emphasis on policy-oriented research may appear reasonable at first glance, it should not be forgotten that such research does adopt, by definition, the cognitive framework of policy-making that causes it to reproduce itself in a circular logic. Such research, moreover, has to adopt a time frame that hardly matches that of most migratory processes. We would then suggest that even a comparatively small amount of investigation dedicated to classical descriptive and explanatory research could well work wonders. This kind of research would help define immigration as a normal structural phenomenon, would differentiate among different flows and different migratory systems, and would identify specific activation mechanisms. It would identify the structural boundaries of policy action instead of inflating them. While apparently less useful in the short run, it could rather contribute a great deal to the development of a humbler but realistic immigration policy (Massey et al. 1998).[5]

A second policy implication may be derived from our argument, concerning the institutional structure of collective decision-making. We have argued that Europe is involved in a variety of migratory systems, with different structures and scope. We have consequently acknowledged that the intergovernmental approach has more than a grain of truth in its emphasis on national specificities and plural priorities.

[5] Talking about the cognitive basis of a common European migration policy, it should also be stressed that the degree of coordination (and transparency) of national statistical systems is still insufficient, that Eurostat migration statistics, although improving, are not yet satisfactory, and that the 'virtual European Migration Observatory', under discussion for years (see the Commission's Scoreboard, COM(2002) 261 final, § 2.4.), remains still much too 'virtual'.

At the same time, it should be stressed that such country-level divergences produce quite a long list of reciprocal externalities that cannot be dealt with adequately only within a comprehensive approach. If this assessment is correct, it may imply that the main weakness in the post-Tampere development has been to try to develop a comprehensive package employing the old bargaining structure of writing separate proposals for each item, and triggering separate negotiations on each proposal. That kind of bargaining structure has impeded the development of a real compromise among the diverging sets of structural interests and favoured the return to incremental decision-making. How to reform institutions and procedures in order to clear the way to a really comprehensive (and still effective) decision-making: this remains the obvious and tremendous challenge for the future of the Union, not simply of its migration policy.

REFERENCES

Bade, K. (2000), *Europa in Bewegung*, Munchen: Beck Verlag.

Baldwin-Edwards, M. (2002), *Immigration and the Welfare State: a European Challenge to American Mythology*, Universita Pompeu Fabra, Conference on Europe-Mediterranean Immigration Policy: Barcelona.

Blangiardo G. (ed.) (2002), *Report on Migrations in Lombardy*, Milan: Fondazione Ismu

Brochmann, G and T. Hammar (1999), *Mechanisms of Immigration Control*, Oxford: Berg.

Brücker, H., G. Epstein, B. McCormick, G. Saint-Paul, A. Venturini, and K. Zimmerman (2001), 'Managing Migration in the European Welfare State', in T. Boeri, G.H. Hanson and B. McCormick (eds), *Immigration Policy and the Welfare State*, Oxford: A Report for the Fondazione Rodolfo Debenedetti.

Caritas-Migrantes (2002), *Immigrazione*. Dossier statistico 2002, Roma: Nuova Anterem.

Commission of the European Communities (2000), Communication from the Commission to the Council and the European Parliament *on a Community Immigration Policy*, COM(2000)757 final.

Communication from the Commission to the Council and the European Parliament on an Open Method of Coordination for the Community Immigration Policy (2001), Brussels, COM(2001) 387 final.

Communication From the Commission to the Council and the European Parliament on Immigration and Asylum Policies (1994), Brussels, COM(94)23 final.

Communication from the Commission to the Council and the European Parliament on the Right of Asylum (1991a), Brussels, SEC(91)1857 final.

Communication to the Council and the European Parliament on Immigration (1991b), Brussels, SEC(91)1855 final.

Coordinators' Group on Free Movement of Persons (1989), *Free Movement of Persons*, Report to the European Council by the Coordinators' Group (Palma Document) Coordinators' Group, CIRC 3624/89.

Cornelius, W., P.L. Martin, J. F. Hollifield (1994), *Controlling Immigration: A Global Perspective*, Stanford: Stanford University Press.

Council of Europe (2000), *Recent Demographic Development in Europe 1999*. Strasbourg: Council of Europe.

DiMaggio, P. (1997), 'Culture and Cognition', *Annual Review of Sociology*, **23**, pp. 263–87.

ECOTEC Research and Consulting Ltd (2001), study on the *Admission of Third-country nationals for Paid Employment or Self-Employment Work.*

Eurobarometer (1989), Racism and Xenophobia, Brussels: Commission of the European Communities.

Eurobarometer (1997), Eurobarometer Opinion Poll 47.1, Bruxelles: Commission of the European Communities.

Eurostat (2000), *Pattern and Trends in International Migration in Western Europe*, Bruxelles: European Commission.

Freeman, G. P. (1994), 'Can Liberal States Control Unwanted Immigration?' *Annuals of the American Academy of Political and Social Sciences*, 534, pp. 17–30.

Geddes, A. (2001), 'International Migration and State Sovereignty in an Integrating Europe', *International Migration*, **39**(6), pp. 21–41.

Glover S., C. Gott, A. Loizillon, J. Portes, R. Price, S. Spencer, V. Srinivasan and C. Willis (2001), *Migration: an Economic and Social Analysis*,. London: Research, Development and Statistics Directorate (RDS), Home Office.

Guidelines for a Community Policy on Migration (1985), Luxembourg: Bullettin of the European Communities, Supplement 9/85.

International Centre for Migration Policy Development (1999), *Border Management in Europe*. Vienna: ICMPD.

Lahav, G. and V. Guiraudon (2000), 'Comparative Perspective on Border Control: Away From the Border and Outside of the State', in *The Wall around the West*, P. Andreas and T. Snyder (eds), Lanham: Rowman & Little, pp. 55–80.

Massey, D. S., J. Arango, G. Hugo, A. Kouaouci, A. Pellegrino and J. E. Taylor (1998), *Worlds in Motion, Understanding international migration at the end of the millennium*, Oxford: Claredon Press, pp. 254–74.

Modood, T., R. Berthoud, J. Lakey, J. Nazroo, S. Virdee and S. Beishon (1994), *Ethnic minorities in Britain: Diversity and disadvantage*, London: Policy Studies Institute.

Muus P. (1998), *A Study on the Expected Effects of Free Movement for Legally Residing Workers From Third Countries Within the European Community, Migrants, Minorities and New Forms of Citizenship in the European Union*, Florence: EUI.

Nash, K. (2001), *'The "Cultural Turn" in social theory: Towards a theory of cultural politics'*, Sociology, **35**(1), pp. 77–92.

Pastore, F. (1999), *Verso Una Politica Migratoria Comune?*, Rome: CeSPi.

Pastore, F. (2001), 'La Rotta Di Enea. Relazioni Euromediterranee e Migrazioni', *EuropaEurope*, no. 1, pp. 165–79.

Pastore, F., P. Romani and G. Sciortino (1999), *L'Italia Nel Sistema Internazionale Del Traffico Di Persone*, Roma: Commissione per le politiche d'integrazione degli immigrati, working paper 5.

Policies on Immigration and the Social Integration of Migrants in the European Community (1990), Experts' Report on Behalf of the Commission of the

European Communities, Brussels: Commission of the European Communities, SEC (90)1813.

Presidency Conclusions (1999), Tampere Meeting of the European Council 15–6 October 1999, Brussels: SI (99) 800.

Rath, J. (1993), 'The Ideological Representation of Migrant Workers in Europe: a Matter of Racialization?', in J. Wrench and J. Solomos (ed.), *Racism and Migration in Western Europe*, Providence: Berg, pp. 212–38.

Robin, S and L. Barros (1999), 'Measures Undertaken to Prevent and Combat the Employment of Foreigners in an Irregular Situation in Certain OECD Member Countries', DEELSA/ELSA/MI(99)4, Paris: OECD.

Schain, M. (1999), 'Minorities and Immigrant Incorporation in France. The State and the Dynamics of Multiculturalism', in C. Joppke and S. Lukes (eds) *Multicultural Questions*, Oxford: Oxford University Press, pp. 199–223.

Schneider, F. and D. Enste (2000), *Shadow Economies Around the World: Size, Causes and Consequences*, Washington, DC: International Monetary Fund, working paper WP/00/26.

Sciortino, G. (1999), 'Le Politiche Migratorie nel Contesto Europeo', *Diritto, Immigrazione e Cittadinanza*, **1**(3), pp. 21–40.

Sciortino, G. (2000), *L'Ambizione Della Frontiera. Le Politiche Di Controllo Migratorio in Europa*, Roma: FrancoAngeli.

Sciortino, G. (2000) 'Towards a Political Sociology of Entry Policies', *Journal of Ethnic and Migration Studies,* **26**, pp. 213–28.

Silverman, M. (1992), *Deconstructing the Nation: Immigration, Racism and Citizenship in Modern France*, London: Routledge.

Thalhammer, E., V. Zucha, E. Enzenhofer, B. Salfinger and G. Ogris (2000), *Attitudes Towards Minority Groups in the European Union*, A Special Analysis of the Eurobarometer Year 2000 Survey, Vienna: European Monitoring Centre on Racism and Xenophobia.

Towards a Common Asylum Procedure and a Uniform Status Valid throughout the Union for Persons Granted Asylums (2000), Brussels: Commission of the European Communities, COM (2000) 755 final.

Trends in International Migration (1999), Annual Report 1999, Paris: OECD.

Trends in International Migration (2000), Annual Report 2000, Paris: OECD.

Trends in International Migration (2001), Annual Report 2001, Paris: OECD.

Tribalat, M. (1996), *De L'Immigration à L'Assimilation: Une Enquete sur les Immigrés et Leur Enfants*, Paris: La Découverte.

14. Mechanisms of Exclusion: Labour Migration in the European Union

Elspeth Guild

14.1 INTRODUCTION

Labour migration in Europe has been a field of policy characterised by great fluidity over the past 50 years. The policies and politics of the European Union Member States in this area have moved from one extreme of general inclusion to the other extreme of substantial exclusion and back again in very short time periods (Guild 2003).

Changes in policies have been fuelled by employment levels in the Member States and transformations of industry requiring different skills from the work force. In other fields of cross-border movement such as goods and capital, the possibility of extreme variations in policies and politics has gradually been diminished through multilateral agreements. This has been a process undertaken at numerous supranational levels, most notably the European Union (EU), but also the World Trade Organization and others at the regional level.

The assumption of competence at the European Union level regarding external cross-border movements as regards goods and transport has been very much the heart of the development of the EU's commercial policy, to the exclusion of separate commercial policies at the national level (Macleod et al. 1996). However, as regards the movement of workers from outside the Union into the Member States, there has been a fierce struggle of competence in the past 15 years, where the justice and interior ministries within the Member States have sought to retain control of movement of persons (Guild 2001).

Following the entry into force of the Amsterdam Treaty amendments to the EC and EU treaties, the power to adopt binding rules on labour migration from outside the EU was granted to the European Community. However, the power does not give rise to direct rights in law but rather must be implemented through measures adopted by the Union. On 11 July 2001 the European Commission presented a proposal for a Directive on the conditions of entry and residence of third-country nationals for the purpose of paid employment and self-employed activities. This proposal is made under Part III Title IV of the Treaty Establishing the European Community, using Article 63(3) as a legal base.[1] The proposal, when adopted, will replace the national rules of the issue of work permits for employment and self-employment in the Member States, substituting a Community system. One of the central questions that such a transfer of competence engenders is whether it will bring forth a change to the basic assumptions in the policy area.

In other fields of economic activity over which the Union has acquired competence, principles of economic liberalisation have been dominant (Notaro 2001). Protectionism in economic terms has come under attack from the EU institutions (Craig 2002).

In order to evaluate whether labour migration is being integrated into the central ethos of Community law on economic activity, it is first necessary to consider what the mechanisms are of the Member States at the national level to retain control over labour migration. What are the stated objectives and what are the legal tools used to achieve those objectives? Secondly, a review of the models of state regulation of labour migration must be undertaken, followed by an assessment of the choices made by the European Commission in its first proposal on harmonisation in this field.

In this chapter I will review briefly the common aspects of the rules in the 15 Member States regarding labour market tests and skills levels which apply to third-country nationals coming to the state to take up employment. I will provide only a summary of the original research that I carried out in the Member States over 2001–2002 (see Cholewinski 2002).[2] This is followed by an analysis of the models of regulation of international labour migration, which have been used in Western Europe over the past 50 years.

There are four main models and against them, in the light of the results, I will consider the Commission's first steps towards exercising its new powers over economic migration for employment.

As labour migration is a field where the use of exceptions is commonplace, it is perhaps useful to start with the groups of classes to which the general rules apply. These rules do not apply to the following:

- European Economic Area (EEA) nationals and their third country national family members;
- nationals of third states who enjoy preferential treatment in accordance with agreements between their state and the EC (except Turkey);
- students, who are outside the scope of this study;

[1] This means that the Irish and UK Government have the choice whether to opt into the measure or not in accordance with the opt-out protocols to the Treaty.

[2] Unpublished manuscript, prepared for the European Immigration Lawyers Network.

- refugees who have a right to employment under the Geneva Convention once recognised as such; and
- long-term resident third-country nationals who in all cases (except Austria) have free access to the labour market. Similarly, diplomatic, seasonal, agricultural and maritime workers are not included.

In all Member States the main purpose of the work permit schemes is to protect jobs for the domestic and EC labour force while allowing business to bring employees from abroad only when justified on strict economic and employment grounds.

The essence of all work permit schemes is related to how assessment of the labour market happens. As the main ground for limiting access to the territory and employment for foreign nationals is the domestic labour force, the justification for refusing any application must be based on an assessment of needs. Only then can the decision be taken whether to apply an exception to the rule, bearing in mind that the exceptions in the case of many countries in fact account for the majority of the work permits issued.

A second layer of protection of the domestic labour force can exist in the form of a minimum skills level below which work permits will not be issued. In light of the Community proposal now on the table and the increasing cross-border movement of third-country nationals, it is timely to look at national laws and practices and how they fit into the classical neo-liberal approach towards trans-border movement of economic actors adopted at the European Union level.

14.2 THE PROTECTED GROUP

The main criterion which applies to the authorisation of third-country nationals to work in any Member State is the existence of a job which has been offered to the individual and for which there is no domestic or EC national available. The purpose of the work permit rules is without exception stated to be the protection of employment possibilities for persons within a specified group beginning with own nationals and Community nationals.

The system of authorisation for the employment of third-country nationals is designed to ensure that the third country national are not discriminated in their labour market participation of the host Member State. Thus as the purpose is to place obstacles in the way of movement of labour across some borders, the application of those rules of obstacles varies in the strictness with which they are applied.

In all Member States the protected group includes nationals of the state itself, as well as nationals of the other Member States and the EEA.

In practice the test of the labour market is either limited to the region, as in the cases of Belgium and Germany, or to the response of notification to the labour exchange, as in Sweden and Denmark. These tests include other markets, such as advertising in the UK and Ireland. In no case does it include a serious attempt to test the labour market in a Member State other than that where the job is. Thus as a protected group, the EC labour force is more fictional than real. The limit of the test to the region appears in countries where there are substantial divisions between regions such as in Germany and Belgium. Promoting movement of own nationals across regional borders does not appear to be a high priority. However, even in such cases where the labour market test is regional, the intention is to include the whole of the EEA labour market in the test.

In a number of Member States the protected group specifically includes various categories of third-country nationals already resident in the territory. The most detailed list appears in Austria. All Member States appear to assimilate the position of long-term resident third-country nationals on their territory to that of own nationals, thus bringing them within the priority group. Such protection also appears to apply to third-country family members of own nationals. This category is also likely, in practice, to benefit from protection: refugees once recognised as entitled under the Geneva Convention to access to employment on a non-discriminatory basis. In most states they even appear to be assimilated again to the position of own nationals.

However, it is by no means clear that those states which include in legislation the most detailed lists of groups to be included in the protected status are in fact the most successful at protecting employment for them. This of course begs the question as to whether the regulatory system protects employment for anyone.

The second priority of the EC labour market, Turkish nationals within the Member States, does not appear to find explicit reflection in most legislation. While this group may be subsumed into the general category of third-country nationals resident in the Member State, thus coming within the protected group definition of most States, it is not singled out as a second preference as required by the subsidiary legislation to the EEC Turkey Association Agreement.

14.3 CARRYING OUT THE TEST: A STATE OR PRIVATE RESPONSIBILITY?

The degree to which the exercise of the labour market test is carried out by the company or the state changes the relationship of the parties (in no case is there an active role of the individual third country national in this part of the procedure). In states that have moved towards substantial de-regulation of the market, notably the UK and Ireland, the onus of proving the absence of an EC worker for the job rests mainly on the company seeking to employ the third country national.

In states where the role of the state in labour regulation is greater, such as France or Belgium, specialised state authorities are responsible for carrying out most of the steps to check the labour market. The differences in the participation of the company, individual and state in the evidence used for deciding whether or not to authorise a third country national's employment have important consequences for all of the actors. The balance of power changes, i.e. the degree of control over the decision making process, and with it the role of lawyers advising the actors changes as well.

14.3.1 The individual, the company and the state

Without exception the rules on the labour market test are applied without the participation of the individual. Notwithstanding the rules in most Member States, which require third-country nationals to be in (or go to) the country of origin to collect the work permit and apply for any necessary visa before returning to the state of employment, the most important criterion does not involve the individual.

The question of whether the job can be filled by someone already within the state is determined by agreement or discord between the employer and the company. Where the state has a very substantial degree of control over the process to the exclusion of the company, as in the case of Belgium, an appeal right appears to be used to assist the company to achieve its aim against arbitrary exercise of administrative power. However, the appeal rights of individuals, where they exist at all, appear to be limited to questions of visas and do not approach issues at the heart of the authorisation procedure.

14.3.2 Bending the rules – the exceptions

All states have at least one system for excluding some companies and posts from the labour market test rules. A number of countries use more than one system. The most common system is the designation of certain posts as not subject to the labour market test rules. The most high profile of these exceptions is the highly publicised German green card scheme for technology staff where there is a general decision by the authorities that there is a shortage of labour, thus an individual test of the labour market in each case is waived. In Finland a mechanism is favoured which waives the work permit requirement altogether for certain categories and groups of employees. This system is also used in most other countries for various groups, often in low skill categories such as domestic workers.

In France and the UK a salary level is used – if the post carries a monthly salary equal to or above a set amount the labour market test is not applied. This excludes the high end of the labour market from the labour market test rules. In Luxembourg if the company is willing to place at the disposal of the state a bank guarantee of a specified level this will facilitate the issue of the work permit. The sum is forfeited if the conditions of the permit are not respected.

In both cases, either by the exception of the rules or by their deemed satisfaction by a salary criterion, the state permits a rapid decision on the applications, as the time-consuming search of the labour market does not take place. Thus it facilitates the movement of senior executives and their personal staff.

14.3.3 Skills tests

There is a much divided practice with regards to work permits and skill tests. In some countries the work permit system is limited to specialist and managerial staff that may be defined in a sufficiently flexible way so as to resemble a balloon. When unemployment is low a much lower threshold of specialist skills is applied than when unemployment is high (for instance as in the UK).

In other countries, such as France, formal discrimination between the well educated and 'the others' is not reflected in the rules, though it appears elsewhere in the form of the salary exception. In Luxembourg it appears that a skills test applies only with respect to some groups subject to the work permit scheme, but not to all. Meanwhile, in Portugal, the expectation is that most third-country nationals who come to work will be eligible for work permits whatever their skills level. The differentiation depends wholly on ministerial decisions.

14.3.4 Globalisation – the exceptions for transnational corporations

Most countries also exclude the labour market test where the third country national is being moved from one company within a group to another. Many of these systems have various peculiarities, such as the Dutch system, which requires the company group to be based in at least three countries and to have a share capital/turnover exceeding a specified amount. In Italy not only does a scheme exist for intra-company transferees to be preferred, also there is a relaxation of the rules on the basis of nationality, for US and Japanese nationals.

14.3.5 The main features of the national level

The most striking element revealed by an examination of the labour market test and skills test is the purpose – protection of the domestic labour market. The seriousness with which this intention is pursued varies substantially. In those countries where the state has continued to accepted a responsibility to manage employment for the purpose of reducing unemployment, the rules applied appear at least on the surface to be very strict, for instance in France, Spain and Austria. In those countries where the state has changed its position from one of management of the employment market to facilitating the growth of businesses, for instance the UK and Ireland, the link between the labour market test and the issue of work permits has become less strict. The emphasis, then, is on letting companies carry on their business as they wish with a minimum of direction from the state.

After that initial difference, the convergence is equally surprising. Although the official position is the exclusion/strict limitation of third country national employees, all states have at least one, if not more, mechanisms that permit companies to circumvent the rules. Some mechanisms are directed at particular skills groups such as IT specialists.

Other mechanisms relate to income levels or the size of the company or group. The observer is left with the distinct impression that while there is a political discourse, which favours exclusion of foreign workers except in highly circumscribed situations, there is equally an administrative reality, which facilitates the opposite but at the express demand of companies based within the state.

14.4 MODELS FOR THE REGULATION OF INTERNATIONAL LABOUR MIGRATION: THE OPTIONS FOR THE EUROPEAN UNION

There are four models at the supranational level for the regulation of international labour migration. I shall deal with them in order of their comprehensiveness: the International Labour Organization (ILO), the World Trade Organization (WTO); thereafter I will move to the regional level in Europe – the Member States' intergovernmental cooperation through the 1980s and 1990s – and finish with the European Community (EC) model.

14.4.1 The International Labour Organization model

The International Labour Organization (ILO) model is based on an agreement between the sending state and the receiving state regarding the movement of workers. The sending state is under a duty to permit and make available workers to the receiving state; the receiving state is under a duty to place those workers in suitable jobs and secure certain basic rights for them. This model is not particularly well adapted to the needs of labour migration of the European Union in the 21st century.

The nature of labour migration is no longer one where the state is the primary determinant of the need for labour. In the 1950s and 1960s the State was also the main employer of labour, thus the labour ministries, which were responsible for labour migration, were in fact responding to the needs of the industry ministries to provide workers for nationalised industries and state service sectors.

This relationship is no longer primary. Many of the fields which were within state control in the 1950s and 1960s have been moved to the private sector through privatisation and the re-definition of the core functions of the state which has taken place in all EU Member States over the last 20 years. It is now primarily the private sector that is determining the need for migrant workers (though some service sectors within the responsibility of the state are still in need of migrant workers, such as the health services particularly as regards nurses, and in some Member States education).

Collective state recruitment, which is the foundation of the ILO model, is no longer effective in fulfilling the labour needs of Europe because of the fundamental restructuring of the economy that has changed the relationship of industry to government. However, the emphasis in the ILO model on guaranteeing equal treatment in working conditions, remuneration and dismissal is still of critical importance. Not only does the right to equal treatment protect the migrant, it also protects the labour standards achieved in the host state and diminishes the risk of 'social dumping'.

14.4.2 The World Trade Organization model

Under the World Trade Organization (WTO), a new framework for labour migration has been created in the General Agreement on Trade in Services (GATS). This model gives the company or business the right to move personnel in the form of service providers from one GATS state to another in order to carry out service provision.

The GATS concept of service provision includes the Community law concept of establishment – i.e. the long-term settlement of personnel in the territory of another state in order to establish a commercial presence for the main business in that state.

Although the GATS model is still subject to many horizontal and sectoral limitations placed by EU Member States, the intention is that these restrictions will slowly be removed and a liberalisation of the movement of services and service providers will be achieved. The Doha round of negotiations on the WTO, which opened in 2001, has emphasised the need for progress in this area. The GATS principles are that providers of foreign services will have most-favoured-nation access to the national markets of other states and parties; once in the market, there will be no discrimination between service providers from other states and those of the host states.

There must also be transparency in the rules that apply to the scheme. This model is, in some ways, the mirror image of the ILO model except that the privileged recruitment is that of private companies, not the state. While the European Community is a party to the WTO it has at least mixed competence with the Member States for GATS. While the system provides clear rules (in principle at least leaving aside the practice of limitations), rights are given to the business, thus leaving the individual who is employed by the business to carry out service provision locked in a position of dependence on the economic activity. Companies are given an undue amount of power over their employees where the company is the arbiter of whether the individual can continue to reside in the host state or not.

This may be termed a form of 'privatization' of immigration rights geared towards expanding rights of companies at the expense of rights for individuals. Moreover, there is no right to equal treatment to protect the worker or service provider.

14.4.3 The intergovernmental cooperation model

The intergovernmental model was used exclusively by the Member States of the Union before the introduction of Community competence in the field. Following the 1985 European Commission White Paper on completion of the internal market, the justice and interior ministries began to exchange information and gradually to seek to approximate their rules in the field of movement of persons (Guild and Niessen 1996). This approach was used in the drafting of the two Resolutions of the Third Pillar, one on exclusion of labour migration and the other on the exclusion of the self-employed.

The overriding feature of the two Resolutions is that the principle employed is one of exclusion with exceptions permitted on the basis of an exercise of state discretion. The discretion of a state to admit an individual is only marginally circumscribed. The duty to prevent and exclude labour migration is the underlying principle. This model does not adapt itself easily to Community law. First, it fails to provide a consistent standard, which will result in similar outcomes across the Member States.

By starting with a principle of exclusion, against which exceptions may be made on individual cases at the discretion of the state, a complex and unwieldy system has been created which by its very nature is inconsistent. The wider the exercise of discretionary power by an administration, the greater the burden on the administration in terms of hours of assessment and the levels of management involved in each decision.

Every decision to grant a work permit must involve an appreciation by a senior officer to exercise a discretionary power against the principle of exclusion. This makes the process cumbersome, inconsistent and expensive. It is not a model that easily adapts to the Community framework. Further, it leaves both the individual worker and the employer in uncertainty about any particular application. The lack of clear rules, which could permit a degree of foresight, increases the cost to the individual, the business and the Community of the benefit of labour migration.

14.4.4 The European Community model

The European Community (EC) has used a model for labour migration that has worked particularly well. It has permitted the creation of rights to move for economic purposes, rights that have been given to the individual and guaranteed by the Community.

The Member States have implemented the rights, affording the individual a right of residence provided that he or she is also exercising the right of economic activity. The rules have been drafted in clear, precise and unconditional terms, thus simplifying the job of the national administrators responsible for their application. These administrators can check against the rules who is entitled to a right of movement or residence and who is not.

This Community model has been extended to third-country nationals through provisions on natural persons and movement in agreements with their states. It is found in the EEA Agreement, concluded between the European Community and the EFTA Member States that all nationals of the EC and all nationals of the non-EC EFTA States (a separate agreement with Switzerland came into force in June 2002) have the right to move to and reside in the territory of the other parties for economic purposes. It is also the foundation of the implementing Decisions under the EEC Turkey Association Agreement regarding Turkish workers.

While the relevant Decision (No. 1/80) does not deal with first access to the territory of the Union, it provides that after one year's employment Turkish workers are entitled to an extension of their work (and hence residence) permits provided their job is still open to them. After four years they are entitled to free access to the labour market. Again, the rules are clear, precise and easy for the national administrator to apply.

In the Europe Agreements concluded between the European Community and the Central and Eastern European countries, the Baltic States and Slovenia, it appears that a similar approach has been followed, this time limited to self-employment and establishment of companies.

In these agreements nationals of the respective parties are entitled to exercise self-employed activities within the territory of the other. Four cases are currently pending before the Court of Justice on the exact meaning of this right.

14.5 CONCLUSIONS

The interests of the three main actors in the question of labour migration – the state, the economic actor (i.e. the company), and the individual – coincide in many respects and diverge in others. The state has a legitimate interest in knowing who resides in the territory and seeks to provide protection to the people resident there.

The meaning of the concept of protection and the degree of the engagement of the state in economic choices of companies and individuals is increasingly under examination. In the framework of the European Union this engagement has been subjected to substantial limitations in favour of commercial choices, by companies, and life choices of individuals. The company has an interest in engaging or retaining the services of individuals best able to supply the services that the company needs.

The individual is primarily concerned with access to the labour market, security of employment and residence, to include protection from expulsion. Depending on the length of time that individuals may stay in the state, family reunification may become relevant. The balance of these interests is and will be the key to the model chosen for the European Union.

Too often the question of economic migration becomes entangled with issues of policing and security. Then the economic foundation of this form of migration is obscured. However, economic migration is primarily about the achievement of economic objectives and thus needs to be informed by consistent principles that apply to the economic policy of the Union. Already the European Commission has chosen, as the starting place for the exercise of its new powers in this field, another intergovernmental model. This may turn out to be a mistake, needing rectification in due course.

The fundamental problem with the intergovernmental model in this field is that it does not lead to harmonisation of the field of activity but instead permits a further divergence of national rules under the guise of common policy.

The need for a harmonised Community measure on access to the territory for labour migration and self-employment is underlined by the fact that, until there is such a measure, Member States will have difficulty agreeing on other measures of common immigration policy. The argument could always be raised that there is no common bottom line on who gets access to the territory of the Member States. Unless there is a firm and consistent common position on labour migration, progress on other aspects of the treatment of third-country nationals will remain hostage to Member State confidences, or lack thereof, in one another's national rules.

By giving privilege to the power of justice and interior ministries over businesses seeking labour and individuals seeking to come to the Union to take up employment, the Commission has adopted a position at odds with the spirit of the internal market and the principles of market liberalisation. Whether this will be sustainable in the longer term is unclear.

The centrifugal force of the market integration approach of Community law is unlikely to leave this field untouched. The arguments for security to be controlled nationally, both in forms of employment security for nationals (at the expense of security of employment for non-nationals) and national security (border-crossing by foreign nationals being a manifestation of potential state security risks), will need substantial reinforcement if they are to withstand the present political and legal culture of the Union.

Even the additional emphasis that international concerns about terrorism after 11 September 2001 have brought to the field may, in the longer term, be insufficient to withstand the pressure to harmonise through market liberalisation. Market liberalisation, and the creation of individual rights of access to the territory and employment for individuals, will subject the use of the concept of public security by the state to ever more severe limitations.

REFERENCES

Cholewinski, R. (2002), *The Legal Status of Migrants Admitted for Employment: A Comparative Study of Law and Practice in Selected European States*, Strasbourg: Council of Europe.

Craig, P. (2002), 'The Evolution of the Single Market', in J. Scott and C. Barnard (eds), *The Law of the Single European Market*, Oxford: Hart, pp. 1–41.

Guild, E. (2003), 'Intersecting Worlds? Understanding the Legal Framework of European Labour Migration in Susan Strange's Modern World', in D. Bigo and E. Guild (eds), *Controlling Frontiers: Free Movement into and within Europe*, Aldershot: Ashgate.

Guild, E. (2001), 'Primary Immigration: The Great Myths', in E. Guild and C. Harlow (eds), *Implementing Amsterdam: Immigration and Asylum Rights in EC Law*, Oxford: Hart, pp. 65–94.

Guild, E. and J. Niessen (1996), *The Developing Immigration and Asylum Policies of the European Union, Adopted Conventions, Resolutions, Recommendations, Decisions and Conclusions*, The Hague: Kluwer Law International.

Macleod, I., I. Hendry and S. Hyett (1996), *The External Relations of the European Communities*, Oxford: Clarendon Press.

Notaro, N. (2001), 'The EC and WTO Trade and Environment Case Law: Procedural Aspects, Legal Principles and Institutional Matters', in A. Dashwood, J. Spencer,

A. Ward and C. Hillion (eds), *The Cambridge Yearbook of European Legal Studies*, **3**, Oxford: Hart, pp. 327–50.

15. The New German Immigration Law

Doris Schmidt

15.1 INTRODUCTION

Regarding the question – 'Are we on the way towards a more open immigration policy in Europe?' – it might be of interest to look at the recent immigration legislation of the largest EU Member State: the Federal Republic of Germany.

For the first time in history the German government and all political parties agreed that a new legislation on immigration to Germany was needed. This new law has to fit into the frame of a future European Immigration policy. Also, it has to assure that Germany continues to fulfil its responsibility and obligation as a member of the international community of states. In addition, the Geneva Refugee Convention and the European Human Rights Convention must not be forgotten.

First let us present a short overview on the development of immigration issues in Germany over recent years. With the turn of the century a paradigmatic change of position in all German political parties occurred. Unison – the Christian Democrats (CDU/CSU), the Social Democrats (SPD), the Greens (Bündnis 90/Die Grünen) and the Liberals (FDP) all proclaimed suddenly that 'Germany needs immigrants,' and 'Immigration to Germany has to be structured'. This fundamental chance in policy was instituted when the so-called 'Green Card' was introduced in the year 2000 to allow temporary work permits for specialists in information and communication technology. For the first time the ban on recruitment of third-country nationals that had been in force since 1973 was put into question. In addition, Germany changed its outdated law on nationality, making it possible for children born in Germany to become German citizens, if their parents are legally residents. Asylum seekers were given limited rights to work because of the labour shortage.

In the past, the political and normative guiding principle was 'Germany is not a country of immigrants'– a source of discussion and arguments in the Parliament, the German Bundestag. This definition was based on the political fact that Germany was not in principle welcoming foreigners to immigrate to Germany and to integrate into society. On the other hand – because of some exceptional rules concerning the banning of recruitment and because of family-unification – immigration into the country was a reality. The Federal Republic of Germany has actually been a country of immigrants for a very long time. Since 1954, about 31 million ethnic Germans and foreigners have immigrated. Over the same period, 22 million people have left the country.

In 1992 there were over 555 000 third country citizens seeking political asylum in the Member States of the European Union. Germany received almost 80% of all these asylum-seekers. At present, 7.3 million foreigners are living officially in the Federal Republic of Germany – that is almost 9% (8.9%) of the entire population. Germany is in third position in the EU ranking – after Luxembourg in first position with 35.6% of foreigners, and Austria in second position with over 9% (9.1%). Out of the 7.3 million foreigners living in Germany today almost 40% have been living here for more than 15 years. The 2 million 'Aussiedler' who immigrated to Germany from the Eastern countries in the last decade are German nationals and are not shown as foreigners in the official German statistics.

15.2 'ZUWANDERUNG' AND 'EINWANDERUNG'

The German language makes a difference between the words 'Zuwanderung' and 'Einwanderung'. Both are translated as 'immigration' because there is no direct equivalent for the term 'Zuwanderung' in the English language. However, they have a significant different (political) meaning. The term 'Zuwanderung' has a temporary character, in the sense that people are immigrating for a (shorter) period to Germany and leaving the country after some time. It should be translated as immigration to Germany. The word 'Einwanderung' is understood as permanent settlement – in the meaning of nation building.

But this may lead to confusion, because the word 'Zuwanderung' with its temporary character is however used in the German title of the new immigration law. Its full title can be translated as: 'Law for controlling and limiting immigration (to Germany – *Zuwanderung*) and for regulating the stay and integration of union's citizen and foreigners.'

15.3 WHAT WAS THE STATE OF PLAY IN JANUARY 2003?

The new immigration law continues to be controversial. The Social Democrats and Greens are in favour of it, and the opposition – the Christian Democrats – withdrew its support.

The bill went through the Bundestag, the lower house, on 1 March, 2002 with a hefty majority. By a disputed vote in the Bundesrat, the upper house, where Germany's constituent states are represented, the controversial immigration bill went through at the end of March 2002. The Christian Democrats called the way it was voted a 'violation of the constitution'.

The 'joker' was the Land of Brandenburg, run by a coalition of Social Democrats and Christian Democrats. The two parties could not reach an agreement. In addition, Germany's constitution allows no split vote; therefore a state must cast all its votes one way, or abstain. In the oral vote the state's Bundesrat members would normally have abstained, however the leader of the state Social Democrats said 'yes' while a Christian Democrats junior partner confirmed 'no'. The Bundesrat's chairman, Mr Wowereit (SPD), announced that Brandenburg had voted in favour. This is the reason why the bill went through the Bundesrat.

The central-Right stated that if Germany's President, Johannes Rau (SPD), would put his signature on the document, it would appeal to the Constitutional Court. However, Mr Rau signed the law at the end of June 2002. After the general elections on 22 September, six union-run Länder – Bayern, Baden-Württemberg, Hessen, Saarland, Thüringen and Sachsen – called upon the Constitutional Court. On 18 December, 2002 the country's highest Court pronounced judgment on the disputed Bundesrat vote. The Court in Karlsruhe agreed with the union parties, that last March's Bundesrat vote was unconstitutional and so invalid. The Court struck down the law on procedural but not substantive grounds. The ruling by the Federal Constitutional Court means that the new law could not come into force on 1 January, 2003 as planned, but the law has to pass again through the Bundesrat, the upper house, in March 2003. A majority voting in favour for the new immigration law is unlikely even if Brandenburg approve it, because the red-red (SPD-PDS) Länder's government in Sachsen-Anhalt was recently removed. A new draft of the German immigration law will have to be discussed in the Bundestag, the lower house. Otto Schily (SPD), the Federal Minister of the Interior, confirmed he will attempt to reach agreement with the CDU/CSU on a revised bill.

15.4 THE NEW GERMAN IMMIGRATION LAW

The new German Immigration Law, which should have come into force in the beginning of 2003, is being prepared on the basis of the recommendations of the Independent Commission on Migration to Germany. This Commission was set up in the year 2000 by the Federal Minister of the Interior, Mr. Otto Schily (SPD). He appointed Prof. Rita Süßmuth from the CDU as the chairperson. The Commission's main task was to present an overall concept for the future structuring of the German immigration and asylum policy. Its report with the title 'Structuring Immigration – Fostering Integration' was presented to the Bundestag mid 2001.

The central conclusions of the Süßmuth Commission were as follows:

- The need to structure immigration to Germany as well as integration;
- In relation to the labour market the following three challenges must be met:

  1. The German population is becoming older and will decrease considerably in the 21st century. This will not only seriously affect the labour market, but will also affect the innovativeness of the economy and society. Young immigrants are needed.
  2. The increasing internationalisation and globalisation of the world economy. The qualifications and knowledge of people are important growth factors in order to ensure Germany's competitiveness. Immigrants as experts are needed.
  3. A large number of highly as well as less qualified employment positions cannot be filled even though 4.3 million people are registered as unemployed. Working-immigrants are needed.

- The need to structure immigration to Germany is seen only in combination with urgently needed internal reforms, particularly in education and training, family policy, scientific and technological policy as well as in labour market and social policy; and finally
- The new immigration policy should reflect the interests of society as a whole. Germany's obligation to protect victims of political persecution is not affected by this.

The report summarises as the main point that 'Germany needs immigrants', and the structuring of immigration to Germany and integration is one of the most important tasks of the next decade. It requires a policy with a long-term vision. The commission equally recommends the creation of a German Federal immigration and integration law.

This clearly opened the door for groundbreaking new legislation. Thus based on these conclusions, five main goals are set to be reached by the new Immigration Law:

a) Structuring the future immigration policy regarding the way in which the need for immigrants to Germany can be determined and how immigration can be managed and limited.
b) Implementing a concept for the integration of immigrants to Germany.
c) Structuring the asylum procedure so that it is fairer and more effective and addresses how abuses can be counteracted while observing Germany's humanitarian obligations.
d) Implementing a concept in organisational, institutional and legal terms.
e) The new German Immigration law has to fit into the overall European picture.

Four of these goals are examined below.

15.4.1 Structuring the future immigration policy

'Law for Residence, Employment and Integration of Foreigners in the Federal Republic' is the full title of Article 1 of the new immigration law. It completely restructures the 'Aufenthaltsgesetz' (residence law) in order to simplify the present complicated system of residence titles for greater comprehensibility and transparency.

The existing five types of permits such as 'Aufenthaltsberechtigung' (Right of unlimited residence); 'Aufenthaltserlaubnis' (Residence permit), 'Aufenthaltsbewilligung' (Residence title for specific purposes), 'Aufenthaltsbefugnis' (Residence title for exceptional circumstances), and 'Aufenthaltsgestattung' (Permission to reside) will be reduced to only two, these being: The 'befristete Aufenthaltserlaubnis' (limited Residence permit), and the 'unbefristete Niederlassungserlaubnis' (unlimited Settlement permit).

The new law focuses on: the flexible controlling of immigration to Germany in relation to the labour market – and the creation of attractive conditions for residence of foreign students and specialists – in order to ease mobility.

This is a milestone on the way towards a more open immigration policy in Germany: the paradigmatic change from the ban on recruitment to the controlled immigration of foreign workers to Germany. While the need for immigrants cannot be determined by numbers alone, it must be seen in terms of qualifications. The idea is that immigrants to Germany, who are brought into the country for economic and demographic reasons, must be chosen in such a way that their integration into society and into the labour market proceed smoothly.

As far as Article 1, par. 20 is concerned, it deals with immigration by competition. This is a new concept for controlling and managing the immigration of skilled workers, experts and specialists. It is based on a 'system of points' ('Punktesystem'). Candidates scoring the highest number of points should be chosen from the applications that meet the minimum point requirements. The criteria are for example: age and health of the candidate, qualifications, work experience, civil status, knowledge of languages, relation to the Federal Republic of Germany, country of origin, etc. Special account will be taken of nationals from the candidate countries for EU membership. What should be achieved by this new legislation?

- to solve the labour shortage in areas where there is no domestic supply of workforce.
- to find (highly) qualified labour with the view to creating additional employment opportunities for the domestic workforce.
- qualified worker immigrants should contribute to stabilising the social security systems.
- to find highly qualified labour to enhance the competitiveness of the economy.

Par. 38 of Article 1 provides a new regulation for German 'Spätaussiedler', so called 'ex-Germans' – foreigners of German ancestry from East European successor states from the former Soviet Union. Article 1, par. 38, line 2 says that a residence title will only be given to an ex-German living in a third country if he or she has a 'satisfactory level of knowledge of the German language'. Each applicant has to pass a language test in his country of origin.

Having no command of or an unsatisfactory command of the German language led in the past to serious integration problems for repatriates and their family members. This new law regulates and limits the immigration of ex-Germans in the light of their integration potential. Only those who have a chance of integrating into society, should be given admission as well as German nationality.

In addition, a new regulation was set regarding the age of children as latecomers joining their parents in Germany. At present, children have the right to follow their legally immigrated parents up to the age of 16. Now the new Article 1, par. 32, 2 limits this right to children up to the age of 12. Older children have to prove a 'satisfactory level of knowledge of the German language.' The new regulation aims at the better integration of foreigners' children. At a younger age they are still able to learn the new language quite quickly, and have a better chance of fitting into the new society. But Line 4 opens the door for unmarried minor children to follow their parents to

Germany – up to the age of 18 years – if the family situation requests a family unification or if it is in the child's interest.

15.4.2 Implementing a concept for the integration of immigrants to Germany

Article 1, par. 43 to 45 concerns the fostering of integration of foreigners into the German society. It represents something new in the history of the Federal Republic of Germany.

Immigrants have the right and the obligation to participate in integration seminars. The integration programme provides intensive language courses, seminars on German law, society, culture and history. Child-care is also provided for. The right of participating in an integration programme is held by every foreigner in possession of a Residence Permit – for work reasons, for family unification, or for humanitarian reasons.

For the first time in German history, immigrants – including the descendants of German ancestors – have to study the German language. These immigrants groups will be able to integrate well and quickly into German society because of their language skills and their understanding of German culture. They should feel as if they are part of their new home country.

15.4.3 Structuring the asylum procedure

Based on Article 16a of the German Basic Law in force since 1993 and the obligations incumbent on the Federal Republic of Germany under international law, article 3 of the new Immigration Law will speed up the asylum procedure, taking effective measures against abuse as well as optimising the return and repatriation of asylum applicants whose applications have been rejected.

At present, the asylum procedure can take years; asylum applicants whose applications have been rejected won't return and abuse the social security system by staying.

The Süßmuth Commission concluded in its report that: 'The deficits in this area discredit the entire asylum practice; they undermine measures for acceleration, limit the scope for controlled immigration to Germany and encourage the smuggling of illegal immigrants. For these reasons, obstacles preventing the return and removal of persons must be eliminated'.

In order to accelerate procedures and to make abuse of the system more difficult it is necessary to take measures safeguarding the identity of a person during the visa procedure. This must be combined with better data collection and data transfer.

On the other hand, the situation of recognised persons seeking protection or of refugees who cannot be deported will improve with a new regulation for admission and for guaranteeing the right to stay because of humanitarian obligations.

This includes the recognition of the need for protection of persons, because of gender-specific and non-governmental persecution. For the first time a German law affirms the need to protect women who are being persecuted due to their gender. The same applies to people facing risks to their life and freedom in situations in which state structures do not exist or in which states can no longer meet their obligations to protect their citizens.

The new regulation will improve the right to stay and the right to work for recognised persons seeking protection.

14.5.4 Implementation of a concept in organisational, institutional and legal terms

A German Federal Office for Immigration to Germany and Integration (Bundesamt für Migration und Flüchtlinge) is to be created in order to handle the permanent immigration to Germany and to foster integration. The new Federal Office is to emerge from the German Federal Office for the Recognition of Foreign Refugees (Bundesamt für die Anerkennung ausländischer Flüchtlinge). Inside this office an independent scientific institution should be established.

15.5 THE CONTROVERSY BETWEEN THE FEDERAL GOVERNMENT AND THE OPPOSITION

The main objective of the new law should be to structure and to limit immigration to Germany in general. It is not a question of a more open immigration policy in the sense that 'everyone who wants to come can come'. The new immigration policy should reflect the interests of society as a whole while guaranteeing Germany's obligation to protect victims of political persecution who are seeking asylum.

The Federal Republic of Germany wants immigration for demographic and economic reasons. The new option of work-migration will open an additional door for legal migration and reduce illegal immigration and abuses of the asylum procedure. Uncontrolled and illegal immigration flows weaken the economic growth and the social security systems. That's the common opinion of the political parties in Germany.

The criticism of the Christian Democrats is based on their opinion that this new immigration law will rather encourage immigration of people who might have difficulties in integrating in society. The new immigration law does not seem to structure or limit immigration.

The main points of their criticism are the following:

- The new regulation for the age of children as latecomers joining their parents who are living in Germany will encourage immigration and might create problems for integration. Because of Article 1, par. 32, young people who grew up in their home country's culture are able to immigrate to Germany up to the age of 18. Right now the limit is set at the age of 16;
- Furthermore, the demand of a 'satisfactory level of knowledge of the German language' might not be sufficient. Having no command of or an unsatisfactory command of the language led in the past to serious integration problems for children as latecomers as well as for repatriates and their family members. A better criterion might be 'satisfactory command of the German language';
- Foreigners who have already been living in Germany for a longer time will not have the right to participate in integration seminars and language courses. This is counter to the need to foster integration of all immigrants; and
- Amongst the 7.3 million foreigners living in Germany more than 20% were registered in January 2002 as unemployed. This is quite significant. In view of the 4.3 million unemployed the ban on recruitment should be maintained. The new law about 'immigration by competition' based on a point system without a concrete job offer might reinforce the unemployment situation on the German labour market.

15.6 BY WAY OF CONCLUSION…

Thus, we can ask the same question once again, are we on the way towards a more open immigration policy in Germany? It is obvious that the German immigration policy is being upgraded. The country will be open for work-immigration of less qualified as well as highly qualified third-country nationals. The new policy of welcoming immigrants because of an economic and demographic need, promotes the political will to foster integration. This will be to the benefit of the immigrants and their families as well as to the domestic society.

The new naturalisation law should be mentioned. It allows a child born in Germany of parents who are legally residents to obtain the German nationality in addition to the parent's nationality. This is a big step away from the '*jus-sanguinis*' principle towards the '*jus-soli*' one. This might be also a first step in the direction of a future European consensus on naturalisation.

We can also answer the question concerning whether we are on the way toward a more open German asylum policy in the affirmative. It will be generous towards those who rightly deserve protection and help. Germany will always meet its humanitarian responsibilities. With the new law, the protection of persons who are political persecuted in the sense of the Geneva Convention is extended to people who suffer from persecution because of their gender or from non-governmental persecution.

On the other hand immigration will be structured and limited. This includes prevention against illegal immigration, trafficking in human beings and abuse of the asylum procedure. Germany wants to play its part in tackling the problems facing Europe at large.

Looking to Seville, to the conclusion of the presidency of the European Council in June 2002, the future European immigration and asylum policies will concentrate on the Union's action which should be based on two principles. The new German Immigration Law corresponds to that:

- Immigration flows have to be structured and limited within the reception capacity of the Union and its Member States. Immigration must pass through the legal channels provided for it. The integration of immigrants lawfully present in the Union entails both – rights and obligations in relation to the fundamental rights recognised within the Union.
- And second, in accordance with the Geneva Convention, it is important to afford refugees swift, effective protection, while making arrangements to prevent abuse of the system. It is to ensure that those whose asylum applications have been rejected are returned to their countries of origin more quickly.

The overall shift we are witnessing in Europe is to better structure immigration flows. The German law is a good example of how European countries can regulate immigration as well as foster integration – and provide for the necessary economic and social stability and security that their citizens are calling for. With reforms like those happening in Germany, Europe can demonstrate that it does not turn its back on its global responsibility.

16. The Future Common Asylum System: Between a Closed-Circuit and an Open-Ended Scheme?

Johannes van der Klaauw

16.1 INTRODUCTION[1]

The European dimension of EU Member States' asylum policies and practices has been in the limelight for some time now. This is not only the result of legal and institutional developments – Article 63 of the Amsterdam Treaty calls for the adoption of a number of Community legislative instruments – but also because a solution of Member States' problems in the management of their asylum systems has been expected for some time now from increased European cooperation based on a common legal framework.

Yet hopes for an early solution of these management problems through European harmonisation and cooperation have been dashed lately. This has resulted in disenchantment with the asylum harmonisation process in a number of Member States. Nevertheless, Member States continue to construct the building blocks of the common asylum system although with a main focus on accommodating domestic concerns in any agreed common standards. They are also increasingly engaged in efforts to strengthen cooperation with third countries in order to be able to 'externalise' some of their asylum responsibilities. In ongoing negotiations on proposals for legislative instruments, Member States have shown reluctance to develop an open, rights-based and forward-looking asylum policy reflecting an ambitious level of harmonisation and based on a comprehensive set of common standards, tools and mechanisms. Rather they have aimed at preserving the particularities of their domestic systems increasingly dominated by concerns to control access to territory and to stem abuse of the asylum procedure. The

[1] The views expressed in this article are those of the author and do not necessarily reflect the positions of the United Nations.

States' reflex to review the various draft Community legislation in the light of national laws and administrative and judicial practice has been the dominating factor during recent negotiations.

Since the various proposals have to be adopted with unanimity, the end result of negotiations has been the adoption of the lowest common denominator due to a lack of agreement. Provisions as finally agreed often show a large margin of administrative discretion for states. They are often marked by emphasis on deterrence of real or perceived abuse of the asylum system rather than by a genuine attempt to set comprehensive standards for a fair and efficient determination of those in need of protection. The modest number of instruments adopted so far, aimed at regulating admission for legal or humanitarian purposes, as well as the length and complexity of negotiations which preceded their adoption, stand in marked contrast with the plethora of measures – as well as the short time span in which they have been adopted – aimed at controlling irregular migration and human trafficking.[2]

This contribution will analyse recent developments in the construction of the common asylum system within the broader framework of continuing efforts at European level to address the challenges of managing migratory movements. In negotiating asylum instruments, states have tried to accommodate domestic concerns on controlling abuse and excluding undeserving claims by restricting the application of principles rather than by tackling the procedural and managerial problems of their asylum systems.[3]

We shall have a closer look at the change in attitude by Member States from a stated policy to work towards an open, forward-looking common asylum policy in favour of a system which provides broad latitude for Member States to pursue restrictive national policies and practices. This chapter will also comment on the linkages between the migration and the asylum debate, not only by exploring to what extent the former informs the latter, but also by comparing progress made in the adoption of migration control measures and that achieved in the area of legal admission and asylum policy.

[2] A good example is the latest version of the Road Map for the follow-up to the Conclusions of the European Council in Seville on combating illegal immigration, integrated management of external borders, integration of immigration policy in the Union's relations with third countries and speeding up of the legislative work in framing a common policy on asylum and immigration (6023/4/03/REV 4 JAI 27 ASILE 8 MIGR 8 FRONT 9 VISA 25), 5 May 2003. This reveals a dominant focus on control and repressive measures whose adoption and implementation is taken on energetically in comparison to agreement on relatively few asylum and admission instruments.

[3] This has been, for instance, the case with negotiations on the Directive on minimum standards for reception conditions for asylum applicants (compare the final version as published in OJEC L 31 of 6 February 2003, p. 18 with the text as originally proposed by the Commission as published in OJEC C 213 E of 31 July 2001, p. 286).

Finally, the recent emphasis on developing the external dimension of the common European asylum and migration policy needs some comment. Developments in this area to a large extent are prompted by a desire to reduce the numbers of asylum applications lodged in the European Union and to design tools and mechanisms aimed at containing refugee movements in regions of origin – rather than by placing Europe's responsibilities as asylum region within a global system of responsibility – and burden-sharing.[4]

16.2 EUROPEAN STANDARDS AND DOMESTIC CONCERNS

Following the entry into force of the Amsterdam Treaty on 1 May 1999, the European Council in Tampere on 15–16 October that year provided the key orientations and political guidance for developing *inter alia* a common asylum and immigration policy. The Summit Conclusions were forward-looking and put the asylum issue up-front. The conclusions stopped short of calling for the establishment of a single system based on a common asylum procedure and uniform status valid throughout the Union – the latter should be the subject of a Commission Communication to be submitted within one year.[5]

The common asylum system would be part of a four-prong approach to migration and asylum: first, other tracks focused on strengthening partnership with countries of origin and transit – in order to address migratory and refugee flight problems closer to the source; second, a vigorous integration policy by approximating entry and residence conditions for legally admitted third-country nationals to those of EU citizens; third, the adoption of measures aimed at improving the management of migratory flows at all their stages. The fourth approach would include measures to tackle irregular immigration and human trafficking, develop common visa policies, improve border management and establish co-ordinated readmission and return policies.[6]

[4] See Agenda for Protection, Goal 3 on sharing burdens and responsibilities more equitably and building capacities to receive and protect refugees (United Nations General Assembly A/AC.96/965/Add.1 of 26 June 2002).

[5] Presidency Conclusions Tampere European Council, 15–16 October, par. 15. The Communication 'Towards a common asylum procedure and uniform status for those who are granted asylum valid throughout the Union' (COM (2000) 755 final) was published by the Commission on 22 November 2000 and sets out the basic elements for the future harmonisation of the EU asylum policy beyond the transition period covered by the asylum paragraph of the Amsterdam Treaty.

[6] Ibid., paragraphs 10–27.

The spirit of these conclusions was marked by a clear concern to comply with international obligations for refugee protection, by emphasising the 'absolute respect of the right to seek asylum' and the need for the future EU asylum policy to be based on the 'full and inclusive application of the Geneva Convention'.[7] The aim would be an 'open and secure European Union, fully committed to the principles of the Geneva Convention and other international human rights instruments, and able to respond to urgent humanitarian needs on the basis of solidarity'[8] and committed to 'offer guarantees to those who seek protection in or access to the European territory'.[9]

Since the adoption of these conclusions, the Commission has put forward the full package of asylum legislation to the Council and the European Parliament, as well as a number of draft instruments in the migration area, as regards admission, residence and expulsion policy. The latter have been complemented by proposals drafted by Member States, particularly in regard to measures aimed at controlling irregular migration and human trafficking. However, a number of trends during subsequent negotiations testify to the loss of momentum of the Tampere spirit and the increasing dominance of domestic concerns to secure the EU from abuse of its asylum and entry and residence policies, combat the criminal elements of migrant smuggling and human trafficking, and – ever since the tragic events of 11 September 2001 – the terrorist threat. Among the first instruments put forward by the Commission as part of the implementation of the Amsterdam agenda were proposals on a common temporary protection regime and a common family reunion policy. However, Member States' attention was quickly captured by overriding concerns about irregular migration, migrant smuggling, human trafficking, sanctioning carriers for transporting undocumented travellers, visa policy and readmission and return of irregular migrants.

Whether Council negotiations on asylum proposals were taken decisively forward depended to a large extent on the interest and willingness of subsequent Presidencies, notwithstanding statements that this was dependent on the own dynamics of the process and the legacy of preceding Presidencies.

Whereas the Portuguese and French Presidencies during 2000 showed little interest in starting negotiations on draft asylum instruments,[10] the Swedish Presidency, during the first half of 2001, made asylum one of its priorities, culminating in the adoption of the Directive on minimum standards for the granting of temporary protection. This Presidency also showed a

[7] Ibid. par. 13.
[8] Ibid. par. 4.
[9] Ibid. par. 3.
[10] These Presidencies managed to break the political agreement on the establishment of a European Refugee Fund as well as on the initiative to support and to encourage Member States' efforts in receiving asylum-seekers and in integrating or voluntarily returning refugees or beneficiaries of temporary protection.

genuine interest in developing the external dimension of the EU asylum policy, particularly as regards capacity-building in asylum in candidate countries, Eastern Europe and the Western Balkans, as well as in relation to the work of the High Level Working Group on Migration and Asylum (see Van Der Klaauw 2001).[11] This Presidency also organised an important seminar on international protection issues related to material and procedural asylum law in preparation of Commission proposals for a Directive on the harmonised application of the refugee definition and the concept of subsidiary protection, as well as a Commission study on the single asylum procedure.[12]

During the second semester of 2001, the Belgian Presidency focused most of its energies on the issue of migration, by organising, *inter alia*, a high-level conference on the issue.[13] In the asylum field, this Presidency started negotiations on the proposal for a Directive on minimum standards for procedures for granting and withdrawing refugee status – a proposal which had been submitted by the Commission one year earlier. Since this happened in the aftermath of the terrorist attacks of 11 September 2001, negotiations were coloured by a concern to protect asylum procedures from abuse by potential criminal and terrorist elements, to screen out undeserving claims rapidly, develop an extended definition of 'manifestly unfounded' claims, and reduce possibilities for appeal including its suspensive effect. The Belgian Presidency did not succeed in bringing the negotiations to an end; instead Heads of State at the December 2001 Laeken Summit called on the Commission to modify its original proposal, taking into account Council guidelines adopted by the Justice and Home Affairs Council shortly prior to the Summit, calling for more restrictive provisions aimed at accelerating processing, tightening admissibility, and limiting appeal.[14] Out of a similar concern for speeding up the negotiations in asylum and immigration, the Summit also gave the Commission the task of preparing a modified proposal for a Directive on family reunion, which should take into account delegations' requests for more restrictive provisions as regards e.g. eligible family members, qualifying conditions and standards of treatment.[15]

Subsequently, the Spanish, assuming the Presidency in early 2002, announced that the fight against terrorism and combating irregular immigration and human trafficking would be among its key priorities generally.

[11] This body was established in early 1999 as a result of a Dutch initiative. For its terms of reference see 5264/2/99 REV 2 JAI 1, AG 11, 22 January 1999. Its mandate was modified and amplified in 2002 (see 9433/02 JAI 109 AG 20 ASIM 18, 30 May 2002).

[12] See www.migrationsyerket.se.

[13] European Conference on Migration, Brussels, 16–17 October 2001.

[14] See Council Conclusions 15107/1/01 REV 1 ASILE 59, 18 December 2001.

[15] Presidency Conclusions Laeken European Council, 14–15 December 2001, par. 41.

Indeed, much effort was put in preparing a number of initiatives, culminating in the adoption of an Action Plan on combating irregular immigration and human trafficking,[16] an Action Plan on integrated border management,[17] a Council Framework Decision on the European Arrest Warrant to facilitate surrender procedures between Member States,[18] and a Council Framework Decision on combating terrorism.[19] On the eve of the Spanish Presidency the Council had already adopted a number of instruments which should enhance cooperation among EU Member States and between the EU and third countries in the fight against terrorism. These included a Common Position implementing relevant UN Security Council Resolution 1373 (2001), listing a comprehensive package of measures, aimed at, *inter alia*, freezing of assets, establishing early warning systems, providing mutual support in criminal proceedings, strengthening border controls to prevent terrorists from seeking access to territory and the asylum procedure, and improving information sharing. The Council had also adopted on the eve of 2002 a Common Position to combat terrorism in its cooperation with third countries, including the EU's own definition of terrorist acts and terrorist groups, as well as listing of specific groups.[20]

Given the Spanish Presidency's attention to repressive measures, asylum matters were not given much attention, though it managed to obtain agreement on a 'general approach' – i.e. short of political agreement – to the draft Directive on minimum standards for reception conditions for asylum-seekers in April 2002. However, later in the year first the German Minister in June and then the UK Home Secretary in October asked the negotiations on this instrument to be re-opened in order to align certain provisions with evolving national practice by rendering them more responsive to domestic concerns.

[16] The Action Plan was preceded by a European Commission Communication on a common policy on illegal immigration. For a United Nations High Commissioner for Refugees (UNHCR)' critical analysis see UNHCR, Communication from the European Commission on a Common Policy on Illegal Immigration – UNHCR observations, Geneva, July 2002 on www.unchr.ch.

[17] The Council of the EU Plan for the management of the external borders was also the follow-up to a Commission Communication on integrated management of external borders.

[18] The instrument includes a provision stipulating that its implementation shall not impact on respect for fundamental human rights and a paragraph in the Preamble allowing for non-execution of surrender in case there are objective reasons to believe that prosecution by the issuing state may amount to persecution if conducted on account of race, religion, ethnic origin, nationality, political opinion, gender or sexual orientation, or where there is a serious risk that the person to be extradited would be subjected to the death penalty, torture or other inhuman or degrading treatment.

[19] As with the European Arrest Warrant, political agreement on this instrument had been reached already by the end of the Belgian Presidency.

[20] Note that so far no international definition of what constitutes a terrorist act has been agreed to.

While the German delegation wished to subject access to the labour market to conditions to be determined by Member States, the UK delegation argued for an amplification of provisions on withdrawal or ending of reception facilities in order to prevent late applicants from benefiting from the various rights and benefits as provided for in the Directive. Both proposals for amendment were accepted, yet it was striking to note that the UK amendment to the EC Directive was agreed to when a similar amendment to the national asylum bill was still subject to a discussion in the UK Parliament.[21]

The impact of domestic concerns on Council negotiations on the proposed Community asylum system was also noticeable during the Danish Presidency in the second half of 2002, when Member States tried to reach agreement on the draft Directive on minimum standards for the qualification as a refugee or beneficiary of subsidiary protection. While it was expected that it would be difficult for the negotiations to reach consensus on the harmonised application of the refugee definition in situations of persecution inflicted by non-state agents, for gender-related reasons, or committed in situations of indiscriminate violence, it still came as a surprise that the main challenges for the global protection framework resulted from negotiations on the provisions on exclusion, withdrawal and revocation of status. In these discussions Member States raised concern over the limitations of the exclusion clauses of the 1951 Convention which do not allow States to exclude from refugee status persons who, once on their territory, engage in activities which represent a danger to society and to internal security. These persons would still maintain their refugee status even if Article 33 (2) of the 1951 Convention were copied in the text. In the end a compromise was reached to insert an Article on revocation or ending of status, which was interpreted as the revocation of the rights and benefits ('asylum') yet not of the recognition as a refugee ('refugeehood').[22]

The modified proposal for a Directive on minimum standards for asylum procedures as put forward by the Commission in June 2002 upon request by the Laeken Summit is another example of Member States' predominant focus on abuse of procedures. This is reflected in a number of exceptions to the guarantees offered to the asylum-seeker, an emphasis on accelerated procedures to declare applications inadmissible or screen out undeserving

[21] In the course of negotiations during the Spanish Presidency, a number of requests from delegations to lower standards or leave a broad margin of administrative discretion had been accepted already, such as with regard to provisions on family members, freedom of movement, employment, vocational training, the quality of reception and actions to improve the efficiency of the reception system. By modifying the provisions as originally proposed by the Commission, the Council decided not to harmonise or to harmonise at minimum level.

[22] However, this Article was to remain under scrutiny until the very end of the negotiations, in an effort by some Member States to allow for the revocation of not just the refugee rights and benefits but also the condition of being a refugee.

claims quickly, an extension of the grounds to dismiss applications as manifestly unfounded, and the suppression of the suspensive effect of the appeal in accelerated procedures. Considerations of admissibility are to be dealt with in accelerated procedures rather than in separate procedures, and new cases of inadmissibility are introduced. Two new types of accelerated procedures are introduced: one for examining applications at the border (where a number of guarantees governing the regular procedure no longer apply) and one for the treatment of repeat or subsequent applications. The new provisions on detention of asylum-seekers are formulated in broad terms, allowing detention for reasons of efficiency and necessity, rather than by way of a carefully and exhaustively listed set of exceptional measures as was the case in the original proposal, copying the relevant EXCOM Conclusion 44 (XXXVII).

These examples show a tendency in Council negotiations to tinker with the principles of states' asylum policies rather than to address the imperatives of sound asylum management. In so far as Member States believe that Community standards can only be of limited help in addressing their domestic concerns, they continue to introduce reforms to their laws and procedures even if these relate to issues which are simultaneously discussed at European level. In fact, domestic reforms have resulted in Member States taking intransigent positions in negotiations on draft Community instruments.

Having recently amended their national rules and regulations, Member States are not prepared to adopt Community standards which subsequently require modifications of their law and practice once again.[23] Meaningful harmonisation is hampered by a lack of political will of Member States to give up national sovereignty in those areas of asylum where problems are most poignant. This is coupled with a lack of ambition to adopt a consistent and coherent set of common standards – delegations appear to be satisfied with a minimalist approach.

The danger of adopting the lowest common denominator and deleting provisions considered to be too prescriptive and detailed may in future be countered if voting in Council shifts from unanimity to qualified majority. However, even with such institutional change, the substance of policies will not be altered decisively in the absence of a determined push towards the

[23] The most salient example is the recent domestic reform in asylum in Germany: its lengthy negotiations have prevented the German delegation so far from taking clear positions in the Council on EU asylum instruments. This, in turn, has prevented agreement being reached on a number of key provisions of draft asylum instruments, as has been the case notably in regard to the draft Qualification Directive. Other domestic reforms undertaken in parallel with EU negotiations have taken place i.e. in the Netherlands, Denmark, France and the United Kingdom. Such reforms have had a direct impact on these delegations' negotiation mandates for negotiations on draft Community instruments.

adoption of truly common policies, tools and mechanisms, beyond the minimum standards approach prescribed by the Amsterdam Treaty.

The European Commission has sketched the way forward by suggesting elements for a common asylum procedure and uniform status valid throughout the EU – *inter alia* the introduction of a single procedure in each of the Member States, the further elaboration of common tools to streamline the asylum procedure with a view to improved quality and speed of decision-taking, and the development of common mechanisms for a more orderly intake of refugees through protected entry schemes and a common resettlement mechanism. But it seems that Member States are yet to be prepared for this second stage of harmonisation, save where this would be in their domestic interest, such as proposals to establish processing centres and reception facilities in regions of origin, aimed at preventing secondary movement of refugees and asylum-seekers towards the European Union.

Notwithstanding the present lack of enthusiasm among states in the asylum harmonisation debate, the process has its own dynamics and is governed by the Treaty obligations of States to agree on the building blocks of the common asylum system by 1 May 2004. The proper transposition and implementation of Directives in domestic asylum systems will require regular review and, in certain areas, the adoption of legal remedial reforms or supplementary implementing regulations.[24] The establishment by the Commission of the open coordination mechanism facilitates consultation between Member States on the proper application of the various Community instruments.[25]

The creation of the EURASIL forum in July 2002 for the exchange of information and analysis of legal trends and concepts, country of origin situations and the eligibility of particular groups of asylum-seekers will contribute to improvements in harmonised decision-taking.[26] The new areas of competence of the EC Court of Justice under Article 68 of the Treaty are expected to result in further harmonisation and standardisation of asylum processes in EU Member States. Future case-law of national courts and preliminary rulings and decisions of the EC Court of Justice in relation to the interpretation and application of Community asylum instruments will be

[24] An example is the transposition of the Directive on temporary protection which has required the introduction of laws and regulations in *inter alia* Spain and Greece. These processes have been monitored carefully by UNHCR in order to ensure that international standards as included in the Directive are fully adhered to.

[25] This open coordination mechanism was introduced by the Commission in its Communication on the common asylum policy, introducing an open coordination method.

[26] EURASIL, a Commission-led forum, succeeded to CIREA, the Council body which existed from 1992–2002 and pursues similar objectives yet within a Community framework, hoping to achieve more visible results as its predecessor.

another important vehicle towards more enhanced harmonisation of administrative and judicial practice.[27]

The common European asylum system cannot emerge without a minimum of legislative harmonisation, yet the search for communality in States' managerial and administrative tools and mechanisms remains equally important. Member States are fully aware of the significance and potential of strengthened practical cooperation and joint management in some key areas of their asylum systems. The adoption of joint operational strategies is considered as important as the further development of the legislative agenda.[28]

16.3 THE ASYLUM AND MIGRATION NEXUS

As much as Council negotiations on draft EC asylum instruments are indicative of how States' concerns for abuse and irregular movement have prevailed over well-intended efforts to create an open and inclusive asylum area in the EU, negotiations on EC instruments in the area of legal admission and residence of migrants have shown equal preoccupation for control and a lack of willingness to establish an open yet managed common immigration policy. The draft Directive on family reunion has undergone two revisions by the Commission and numerous text amendments brought forward by Member States, all aimed at reducing the personal scope, increasing the number of qualifying conditions, including for refugee families, and reducing the level of rights to be accorded to family members.[29]

Council negotiations on the draft Directive on the status and rights of long-term residents have resulted so far in similar pruning of a number of more progressive elements of the Commission proposal.[30] Commission

[27] UNHCR has proposed the establishment of a review body at EU level as a contribution to the harmonised application of various tools and concepts of material and procedural asylum law. See the Statement of the High Commissioner to the Informal Justice and Home Affairs Council, Copenhagen, 13 September 2002 (www. unhcr.ch).

[28] The Odysseus programme since 1998 (see OJEC L 99, 31 March 1998) and the ARGO programme since 2002 (see Council Decision 2002/463/EC in OJEC L 161 of 19 June 2002) for the training, exchange and administrative cooperation in the fields of asylum, migration, visa and border management have contributed to this practical cooperation and mutual assistance.

[29] The modified proposal on the right to family reunification of 2 May 2002 is marked by a more flexible approach towards certain provisions, the insertion of both a 'standstill' clause and a 'sunset clause/clause *de rendez-vous*', but also stricter qualifying conditions and the possibility for a number of derogations.

[30] The draft of the Council Directive concerning the status of third-country nationals who are long-term residents originally included – albeit implicitly – refugees who would be able to obtain long-term residence status and be allowed to use their right of mobility to take up residence in another Member State preserving their refugee rights and benefits. The refugee

proposals for a common policy on the admission of third-country nationals for labour purposes, self-employment, study or vocational training so far have not even been considered by the Council.[31] The Council approach towards negotiations on instruments regulating entry and residence has been similarly restrictive as the Council attitude to asylum tools: limiting the personal scope, tightening the criteria for entry, restricting the possibilities for long-term residence, and, generally, imposing a number of qualifying conditions on the beneficiaries. The creation of a more open and transparent immigration policy, however, could be an important factor in efforts to alleviate the pressures on States' asylum systems.

The linkages between asylum and migration are nowhere more apparent than in the use, or misuse, of the asylum system by economic migrants, whether skilled or unskilled. Yet they are also present where refugees and asylum-seekers, being part of broader migratory movements, are prevented from access to safety as a result of stringent border control and interception measures. Other areas where the nexus between asylum and migration is to be explored is in measures aimed at combating migrant smuggling and human trafficking, or policies on readmission and return of irregular residents. In addressing the linkages, it has proven to be difficult to factor protection safeguards into instruments aimed at combating irregular migration and migrant smuggling. This, however, is necessary since measures to stem irregular entry and residence do not discriminate between those who are in need of protection and those who are not. Refugees are increasingly part of broader migratory flows, of both forced and voluntary nature, often moving for a mixture of motives, which makes the identification of those with protection needs even more complicated. In addition, refugees may have to resort to the services of migrant smugglers and human traffickers, to escape violence and persecution in their home countries or in countries where they thought they had found asylum. They are often non-documented, being told by smugglers to dispose of their documents or simply not having been able to procure themselves of the necessary travel documents prior to their flight. If migration control and interception measures do not include safeguards for the protection of those in need of it, and acknowledge that refugees may not always be in a position to comply with requirements for legal entry, such measures may represent insurmountable obstacles for refugees to seek safety and protection, and, hence, may result in rejection at the border and, ultimately, *refoulement*.

dimension was excluded in Council negotiations which may result in compromising the need of refugees for longer term stability and security.

[31] A Commission proposal for a Directive on conditions of entry and residents of students so far has also been neglected by Council.

Both the Commission and Council have acknowledged that safeguards to ensure the protection of refugees as well as humanitarian exceptions to penalties need to be included in instruments on carrier sanctions, migrant smuggling and human trafficking. However, the relevant clauses have often been couched in vague and general language, and their application made optional rather than mandatory. An example is the Framework Decision on the facilitation of entry and residence of illegal migrants aimed at 'harmonising' Member States' sanctions regime for smuggling, which is lacking in a reference exempting smuggled asylum-seekers and refugees from criminal liability – although this is compensated to some extent by the inclusion of a general savings clause, stipulating that this instrument shall apply without prejudice to the protection afforded to refugees and asylum-seekers in accordance with international instruments for refugee protection and related to human rights. The accompanying Directive defining the act of migrant smuggling includes a humanitarian clause exempting smugglers from sanctions where they have acted out of purely humanitarian reasons, yet this clause is optional only, and its wording departs from agreed language in UN instruments, such as the Protocol on Smuggling attached to the UN Convention against Trans-national Organised Crime, signed – also by the Community – in Palermo in December 2000.

A similar lack of balance between obligations for the protection and assistance to victims and imperatives of strengthening the criminal liability of perpetrators is noticeable in the Framework Decision on combating trafficking in human beings. This text lacks specific and comprehensive provisions on the protection of and assistance to victims. The reason given is that a separate EU instrument exists on the standing of victims in criminal proceedings yet this does not address the specific vulnerabilities and concomitant needs of victims of trafficking (see Van Der Klaaw 2002).

A third example can be found in the Directive on carrier sanctions. This instrument is aimed at strengthening the implementation of relevant provisions of the Schengen acquis, short of harmonising the level of sanctions. The humanitarian exception in Article 4 (2) does not acknowledge that a person with a well-founded fear of persecution may have to seek illegal entry for lack of valid documents. The Directive also charges companies with the task of verifying the validity of travel documents whereas such should normally be the competence of immigration officers.[32]

[32] Following the adoption of the Directive, the Commission organised a round table process with all stakeholders concerned – regulators, transport sector and humanitarian organisations. A number of expert opinions, including on the humanitarian dimension, can be found on the website of the European Commission Directorate General Justice and Home Affairs, www.europa.eu.int/comm/justice_home/index_en.htm.

The operational strategies developed between EU Member States in order to increase the effectiveness of controls at the external borders have had even less regard for protection considerations. UNHCR's involvement in the implementation of the EU Action Plan on integrated border management has been limited to discussions on the establishment of a core curriculum for the training of border guards, where UNHCR managed, although with some difficulty, to include references to pre-screening of arrivals and subsequent referrals of asylum-seekers to competent authorities, as well as references to international refugee law and human rights law principles. Various initiatives to develop immigration liaison networks to control the external borders of the enlarged Union or the borders of the 'new neighbours' in Eastern Europe or the Western Balkans, the establishment of coordination centres, and the design and implementation of pilot projects aimed at mutual assistance in jointly operating interception measures at the EU external borders, including the high sea, so far have not addressed any specific refugee protection requirements.[33]

The 'externalisation' of the EU's border management to third countries, particularly in Eastern Europe and the Western Balkans, appears to disregard the extra-territorial effects of State obligations to respect international refugee law and international human rights law principles. The common list of third countries whose nationals need to be in possession of a visa in order to enter any of the EU Member States includes countries which are known for serious human rights violations – to mention just a few countries on which the EU is regularly issuing statements condemning ongoing abuses: Belarus, Colombia, Democratic Republic of Congo, Iraq, Liberia, Myanmar, Sierra Leone and Zimbabwe. The Commission's proposals for concluding Community readmission agreements with third countries include only scant references to human rights provisions, and the choice of countries with which such agreements are to be concluded is inspired by the nature and size of migratory flows towards the EU and the partner countries' attitude towards cooperation in migration issues, rather than by these countries' respect of human rights.[34] On the list of countries with which such Community readmission agreements are to be concluded figure the Russian Federation, Algeria, China, Turkey, Pakistan and Sri Lanka, all of which are known for continuing patterns of human rights violations.[35]

[33] See also the Justice and Home Affairs Council conclusions on Illegal Immigration and Human Trafficking by sea of 25–26 April 2002 and the General Affairs/External Relations Council Conclusions on Illegal Immigration of 15 June 2002 (the latter also focusing in particular on migrant smuggling and human trafficking by sea) which include no single reference to refugee protection considerations in the various interception and control measures announced.

[34] See the General Affairs/External Relations Council Conclusions on Intensified cooperation on the management of migration flows with third countries, 18 November 2002, Para. 4.

[35] It has been argued that readmission agreements only concern those residing irregularly and having no protection needs Hwever, such agreements may inadvertently cover asylum-seekers

The EU Action Plan on combating illegal immigration and human trafficking, adopted in February 2002, pays little attention to refugee protection and human rights considerations, except for a reference to the need for balancing control measures with protection concerns. A reference to obligations stemming from international refugee law and international human rights law instruments can be found in the EU Return Action Programme adopted in November 2002 during the Danish Presidency, yet the various measures listed in this Plan do not specify as to how such obligations are to be respected in practice. The Return Action Programme was preceded by a Commission Communication and Green Paper[36] on the subject, which, like the Commission Communication on a Common Policy on Illegal Immigration preceding the relevant EU Action Plan, included additional, albeit general references to refugee and human rights requirements, to be respected while addressing the whole chain of displacement, in countries of origin, transit and destination. The various documents cover both forced and voluntary return as well as the various stages of pre-departure, return and post-arrival and reintegration, and emphasise the cooperation with countries of origin and transit as a prerequisite for the successful implementation of any return operation. The Community effort must create 'added value' to the activities undertaken by Member States bilaterally with regard to the facilitation of the return and reintegration.

The EU Return Action Programme was adopted at the same JHA Council in November 2002 which also adopted a specific Afghan Return Plan, as had been requested by the Seville Summit in June 2002. This plan, which foresees the voluntary and forced returns of Afghans as of mid 2003 onwards, focuses on the pre-departure, travel related and post-arrival measures and the cooperation with international organisations, including in Afghanistan. Given the nature of its framework, and the limited competencies for the Community to be involved in the facilitation of return, which are to be conducted by Member States bilaterally, the plan is lacking in specific standards and tools, as well as responsibilities and roles of stakeholders as normally described in traditional framework agreements for return. The plan also fails in setting standards for the legal, physical and material safety and dignity of returnees once reintegrating in their country of origin. The consistency of this EU return

who have been stopped at the border and are prevented from lodging their application, which risks not being examined. If the asylum-seeker is subsequently returned to a third country pursuant to readmission obligations he or she may be at risk of return to the country of origin. Implementing readmission agreements in such cases may result in cases of indirect *refoulement* of refugees.

[36] For a UNHCR comment on the Green Paper on a Community Return Policy on Illegal Residents see Commission Green Paper on a Community Return Policy on Illegal Residents – UNHCR's comments, July 2002, www.unhcr.ch.

programme with on-going operations for voluntary repatriation from countries in the region also needs to be addressed in more detail.

All these examples show that the EU, in addressing the nexus between asylum and migration, has invested its political and financial dividend increasingly in instruments and operational strategies to control entry, strengthening and harmonising sanction regimes, and common strategies aimed at readmission and return, rather than in creating channels for legal entry, strengthening the position of legally residing third-country nationals, including refugees, and establishing an inclusive asylum policy. While the latter can best be developed with due regard to the imperatives of sound management of broader migratory movements, in recognition of the increasing emergence of 'mixed' flows, sufficient political space should exist to preserve a rights-based approach to asylum and to develop the standards of the common asylum system as a contribution to strengthening of the international protection framework. This also means that protection safeguards must be factored into migration control measures if and where required, in recognition of the vulnerable position of those in need of protection. There should be better identification of and proper response to the needs of asylum-seekers and refugees who are intercepted at land borders or on the high sea.[37] In strengthening efforts to combat migrant smuggling and human trafficking, the needs of victims must be properly addressed, including where trafficked persons may have valid asylum claims. Moreover, where EU Member States are justifiably concerned about so-called secondary movements of refugees from countries of first asylum to their territory, they should invest in measures addressing both push and pull factors of such movements. Action in this area will be successful only if a more articulate understanding of what constitutes effective protection in first countries of asylum is reached and sufficient investments are made for capacity-building measures in such countries. The role and responsibilities of countries of origin, countries of first asylum and countries of destination must be better defined in order to agree on comprehensive arrangements for durable solutions for refugees.

16.4 DEVELOPING THE EXTERNAL DIMENSION

In order to establish the area of freedom, security and justice it was recognised that this could not be limited to a process of setting common policies and strategies for the EU internally. Increasing use of the EU's

[37] See also UNHCR Standing Committee paper 'Interception of asylum-seekers and refugees: the international framework and recommendations for a comprehensive approach', EC/50/SC/CRP.17 of 9 June 2000, www.unhcr.ch.

external relations should be made to integrate migration policies in EU cooperation with third countries. The Tampere Summit called on the EU institutions to develop the external dimension of EU Justice and Home Affairs policies as much as Justice and Home Affairs concerns should be integrated into the definition and implementation of the Union's external relations and development policies.[38] While in no way should a foreign policy specific to justice and home affairs be sought – the external dimension should serve the objective of strengthening the values, freedoms, justice and security within the EU – it was acknowledged that the EU had much to contribute to third countries in defining and implementing their justice and home affairs policies, including the management of migration flows. This would include support for partner countries in improving border controls, aligning visa policies to those of the EU, and enhancing capacities to combat irregular (transit) migration, migrant smuggling, human trafficking and other forms of organised crime, *inter alia*, by support for judicial reform and police training. In so far as this is considered useful, EU assistance to institution-building and practitioner training in asylum can also be provided. However, the focus is on support for control and repressive measures which is a clear indication of the EU's focus on protecting its area of freedom, security and justice from irregular migration, human trafficking and organised crime from and through third countries, with support for asylum institution- and capacity-building based on needs and priorities of partner countries as only a secondary objective.[39]

Asylum issues have become an area of interest in the EU's external relations mainly in the context of the pre-accession strategy for candidate countries. Even if the human and financial resources invested in migration control, border management and combating organised crime outweigh by far support for asylum capacity-building,[40] the fact is that candidate countries have developed functioning asylum systems mainly as a result of the enlargement process, coupled with assistance provided by UNHCR.

[38] Tampere European Council Conclusions, par. 59–62.

[39] See for this imbalance in support for control and protection measures Council of the European Union, (Swedish, Belgian, Spanish) Presidency programme concerning external relations in the JHA field (2001–2002) 5146/01 JAI 2, 11 January 2001, and Council of the European Union, Troika (Danish, Greek, Italian) programme (2002–2003) 10685/02 JAI 159, RELEX 134, 5 July 2002.

[40] A summary of PHARE allocations over 1997–2000 indicates 11 MEURO for asylum capacity-building (and an additional 3 MEURO for a regional programme in asylum for all 10 Central European candidate countries) against 230.5 MEURO for border management. This trend has continued: as part of the EC assistance for a country like Albania in Justice and Home Affairs (48% of the total EC assistance for this country) for the period 2001–2004, 24.5 MEURO (13.5%) is allocated to border management, another 24.5 MEURO (13.5%) to judicial reform, 35 MEURO (19.3%) to police and organised crime and only 3 MEURO (1,7%) to asylum system development.

The new neighbours of the enlarged Union now also benefit from more specific attention from the EU to asylum matters as is the case with assistance programmes to the Russian Federation, Ukraine, and the Western Balkan countries. The geographical position of partner countries, the nature and size of irregular (transit) migratory flows generated by these countries, the number of EU Member States affected by these flows, the attitude towards cooperation in migration matters (readmission, return) and prospects for successful capacity-building in migration and asylum play an important role in this regard.[41] However, the EU's attention to the asylum dimension in its cooperation in justice and home affairs depends to some extent on the priorities of subsequent Presidencies[42] as well as the attitude of partner countries. For instance, cooperation in asylum matters with Northern African countries remains a distant aim, as long as the EU is not prepared to engage these countries in a meaningful asylum dialogue.[43] The lukewarm EU attitude towards asylum system building in this region can be explained by the EU's priority concern to successfully conclude negotiations on the readmission of irregular migrants and improve cooperation in combating irregular migratory flows, including joint interception in the Mediterranean basin. Partner countries are prepared to accept pressure from the EU to conclude such agreements provided they are supported in strengthening their border controls and in facilitating the return of irregular migrants to their countries of origin, whereas they are also offered improved socio-economic integration of their own nationals in EU Member States. Where partner countries are not interested in becoming points of destination for refugees, preferring to continue their status as transit countries, the EU so far has refused to use its arsenal of political, financial and technical instruments to 'impose' cooperation in asylum on these countries, unless it sees a clear need itself such as in the Western Balkans and Eastern Europe.

Notwithstanding this emphasis on support for control measures, Member States' concern for irregular migration, including so-called secondary movements, cannot be addressed effectively without attention to the refugee

[41] See the GAERC Council Conclusions.

[42] Whereas the Swedish Presidency put the asylum issue upfront in its dialogue with Western Balkans countries – see Conclusions of the JHA Troika Ministerial Meeting in Sarajevo, March 2001, the Greek Presidency in 2003 did not discuss asylum in any detail in its JHA dialogue with Western Balkan countries, focusing the dialogue on organised crime, border management and reform of the judiciary.

[43] It required strenuous efforts and, ultimately, the intervention of candidate country Malta, to include in the Regional JHA programme of the EU – Mediterranean, 'Barcelona process', cooperation, a reference to asylum as an issue of future cooperation ('in agreement with the countries concerned' and: 'where appropriate'). See Regional Cooperation programme in the field of justice, in combating drugs, organised crime and terrorism, as well as cooperation in the treatment of issues relating to the social integration of migrants, migration and movement of people – Framework Document, chapter II, 2.c adopted at the Fifth Euro-Mediterranean Conference of Foreign Ministers, Valencia, 22–23 April 2002.

dimension of such flows. A number of refugees and asylum-seekers are resorting to smugglers and racketeers to move onwards to the EU after having tried to find physical safety, legal security and socio-economic well-being first in countries near to their homes. However, for lack of effective protection in these countries of first asylum, refugees and asylum-seekers, often at high cost and with danger for life and limb, make every effort to reach safety in EU territory. The EU would act to the benefit of refugees, as well as in its own interests, if it made a concerted effort to invest in durable solutions for refugee problems in regions of origin. This would help refugees to find safety close to home and render the prospects for voluntary return and reintegration more fulfilling. It would also be one of a series of measures to effectively break the vicious circle in demand and supply created by smugglers and trafficking rings.

Recently the EC Commission put forward a Communication on integrating migration issues into the EU's relations with third countries, commenting on the nexus between migration and development on the one hand, and on the use of the EU financial instruments to address irregular migration in countries of origin and transit on the other. The policy part focuses on key principles, such as the need to respect overall coherence of the EU's external action (i.e. to respect the agreed orientations of the EU's development cooperation), address root causes of forced and voluntary displacement by prioritising poverty eradication, institution-building and conflict prevention, to revisit periodically country strategies, and inject sufficient funding into activities aimed at improved joint migration management with partner countries. Yet these policy priorities mainly focus on the need to combat irregular migration and enhance capacities for readmission and return of those illegally present on EU territory.

There is less attention given to the potential of development cooperation in finding durable solutions for refugee situations, whether in protracted crisis situations or during post-conflict return operations. The emphasis on EU assistance to partner countries in combating irregular movement and support for the readmission and return of illegal migrants from the EU is even clearer in the second part of the Communication. This part analyses the existing EU financial instruments and proposes a more targeted use of these instruments, albeit within the present limits of available funding. Here again, emphasis is laid on funding the readmission and return of irregular migrants, as well as strengthening partner countries' border management and fight against irregular migration.

The nexus between development and migration can be used positively in addressing the challenges for durable solutions for refugee problems. Development cooperation is to target the sustainable reintegration of returnees in post-conflict situations, should address the needs of returnees and the receiving local community alike and focus on measures ensuring sustainable reintegration and preventing a recurrence of factors which would result in renewed flight. Returnees should take part in reconstruction and rehabilitation activity; and in allowing for such participation the donor community can avoid a transition gap between the delivery of humanitarian aid and the provision of assistance for long-term and structural development. In protracted refugee situations, warehousing of refugees can be avoided if they become actors in the process of developing their host country, on the condition that the latter includes refugees in their national development strategies.

Without such choices, however, for a more targeted use of development assistance towards refugee and migratory challenges in countries and regions of origin, the migration dimension of this assistance will be reduced to a narrow approach to combating irregular movement. It will also result in an unhealthy quarrel about the use of development funding for the return of irregular residents from the EU and the threat to cut aid to countries showing a lack of cooperation in taking back their own nationals or third-country nationals, or combating irregular (transit) movement.

The EU has regularly voiced as its stated aim the need to develop an integrated, comprehensive approach to migration and refugee challenges by mobilising political and financial support from foreign, development, humanitarian and social affairs – as can be seen from the mandate of the High Level Working Group on Migration and Asylum, confirmed and amplified in its modification of 2002, as well as from the political orientations adopted by the Tampere Summit. However, in reality attention given to solutions for refugee problems has been little in comparison to political and financial support for measures aimed at combating irregular migration, improving border management, developing immigration liaison networks, facilitating readmission and return policy. Sound partnership with countries of origin and transit, however, should encompass the full spectrum of displacement, including refugee flight, and the various needs to manage population flows, including the offer of effective protection.

In addressing the dilemma to reconcile requirements of migration control with obligations to provide protection to those in need, new avenues for the improved management of asylum can be explored in close cooperation with countries of origin and first asylum. Mechanisms can be developed for the legal and orderly intake of refugees via humanitarian visa schemes, or so-called protected entry procedures,[44] or the establishment of regional processing centres. Any support for external processing which the EU may wish to consider should take into account the many needs for capacity-

[44] See Study on the feasibility of processing asylum claims outside the EU against the background of the common asylum system and the goal of the common asylum procedure, by Gregor Noll, Jessica Fagerlund and Fabrice Liebaut, Danish Centre for Human Rigths, commissioned by DG JHA (See www.europe.eu.int/comm/justice_home/doc_centre/asylum).

building in partner countries and the imperatives of sound burden-sharing and responsibility-sharing.

EU support for bringing asylum procedures and processing closer to countries of origin should be a complement to, not as a replacement of, the EU's responsibility towards asylum-seekers who arrive spontaneously on its territory. If protection is to be offered closer to home, substantial investments have to be made in refugee integration programmes, in asylum states which have to cope with numerous problems of their own, have been guilty of cases of *refoulement* and rejections at their borders, and have been concerned with growing numbers of rejected cases which they have not been able to return.

As part of any comprehensive strategy addressing specific refugee caseloads, EU Member States should participate in resettlement programmes for those with particular vulnerabilities who need special care often only available in industrialised countries. A specific EU resettlement programme, defining the material and procedural criteria and providing direction and assistance during the various stages of the resettlement process, including processing, reception and integration, could be an important tool to be developed as part of the external dimension of the EU asylum policy.

16.5 CONCLUSION

Access to protection in the EU, support for durable solutions for refugees and better responsibility sharing with third countries are among the goals of the Agenda for Protection, the document drafted by States and UNHCR as the outcome of the Global Consultations which were launched on the occasion of the 50th anniversary of the 1951 Convention. This agenda shows the way forward to develop new approaches, tools and standards to underpin the present refugee protection regime. In a recent communication, the European Commission has pledged support for these policy objectives and analysed its forthcoming contribution to the implementation of the Agenda for Protection. Access to protection should be ensured within and outside the Union through the preservation of tested tools and schemes and the development of new avenues to asylum, in an effort to preserve the standards and principles, and, where necessary, modernise the procedures and tools.

The search for durable solutions to refugee challenges remains another main objective for the EU, as well as strengthened partnership with third countries in order to achieve a more equitable sharing of burdens and responsibilities in addressing the plight of refugees. This, however, requires an open and inclusive approach towards the acceptance of refugees in a country's own territory. It asks for the development of a comprehensive set of protection standards which can serve as a model for other regions in the world. It also calls for concluding agreements based on shared responsibilities between partners, among EU Member Sates and between the EU and its partner countries. These agreements, introduced by the High Commissioner as 'Convention Plus',[45] are aimed at bringing the countries of the North and South together in finding durable solutions for refugees, whether in crises of mass influx, protracted refugee situations or secondary movements of migrants and refugees. All these situations require collective and cooperative action by countries of origin, transit and destination, whether in physical or financial terms, whether aimed at providing asylum, facilitating return and reintegration, or preventing causes of future flight.

All this means that the EU should preserve an open attitude towards contemporary problems of forced displacement. It should develop its own asylum space based on standards in accordance with principles of international refugee law: both comprehensive and sufficiently detailed. At the same time, it should improve the management of States' asylum systems by streamlining and rationalising procedures, upgrading tools and improving the cooperation in, *inter alia*, the determination of responsibility for examining asylum applications.[46] Access to protection on EU territory should be ensured, yet the quality of decision-taking in asylum equally merits priority attention. Additional measures will be needed, such as creating avenues for legal entry and residence, *inter alia* on the basis of a common resettlement scheme, and support for pilot projects to improve processing of refugee claims closer to refugees' home countries, coupled with assistance for local integration of those accepted and return of those rejected. Neither a closed circuit nor an open-ended scheme fits in such a picture. What does respond to these imperatives is an open, inclusive and rights-based system, properly managed, and capable of preserving a balance in addressing requirements for migration control and respecting obligations to offer protection to all those entitled to seek and enjoy asylum on EU territory.

REFERENCES

Amended proposal for a Council Directive on the right to family reunification, COM (2002) 225 final, 2 May 2002.

European Commission (2003), Communication on the common asylum policy and the Agenda for Protection COM (2003) 152 final, 26 March 2003.

[45] Used for the first time in a statement delivered at the Informal JHA Council in Copenhagen, 13 September 2002 (www.unchr.ch).

[46] It is hoped that the recently adopted Regulation No 43/2003 of 18 February 2003, together with the Eurodac system for fingerprinting, will be more effective than its predecessor, the Dublin Convention, which in its implementation encountered numerous practical and legal difficulties.

European Commission (2002), Integrating migration issues in the European Union's relations with third countries, COM (2002) 703 final, 3 December 2002.

European Commission (2002), Amended proposal for a Council Directive on minimum standards on procedures in Member States for granting and withdrawing refugee status, COM (2002) 326 final, 18 June 2002.

European Commission (2002), Communication Towards integrated management of the external borders of the Member States of the European Union, COM (2002) 233 final, 7 May 2002.

European Commission (2002), Green Paper on a Community Return Policy on Illegal Residents COM (2002) 175 final, 10 April 2002.

European Commission (2001), Communication on the common asylum policy, introducing an open coordination method (COM (2001) 710 final, 28 November 2001.

European Commission (2001), Communication on a common policy on illegal immigration COM (2001) 672 final, 15 November 2001.

European Commission (2001), Communication on the Community Return Policy on Illegal Residents COM (2002) 564 final, 14 October 2002.

European Commission (2001), proposal for a Council Directive on minimum standards for the qualification and status of third-country nationals and stateless persons as refugees or as persons who otherwise need international protection (COM (2001) 510 final, 12 September 2001.

European Commission (2001), proposal for a Council Directive concerning the status of third-country nationals who are long-term residents COM (2001)127 final, 13 March 2001, in OJEC C 240 E, 28 August 2001.

European Commission (2001), proposal for a Council Directive on the conditions of entry and residence of third-country nationals for the purpose of paid employment and self-employment economic activities COM (2001) 386 final, 11 July 2001.

European Commission (2001), proposal for a Council Directive on minimum standards on procedures for Member States for granting and withdrawing refugee status (COM (2000) 578 final, 20 September 2000, in OJEC C 62 E, 27 February 2001.

European Commission (2000), proposal for a Council Directive on minimum standards for giving temporary protection in the event of a mass influx of displaced persons and on measures promoting a balance of efforts between Member States in receiving such persons and bearing the consequences thereof, COM (2000) 303 final, 24 March 2000, in OJEC C 311 E, 31 October 2000.

European Commission (2000), proposal for a Council Directive on the right to family reunification (COM (1999) 638 final, 1 December 1999) in OJEC C 116, 26 April 2000, p. 66.

Council Common Position of 27 December 2001 on combating terrorism (2001/930/CFSP) in OJEC L344 of 28 December 2001, p. 90.

Council Common Position of 27 December 2001 on the application of specific measures to combat terrorism (2001/931/CFSP) in OJEC L 344 of 28 December 2001, p. 93.

Council Decision European Refugee Fund, 2000/596/EC of 28 September 2000, in OJEC L 252, 6 October 2000.

Council Directive 2001/55/EC of 20 July 2001 on minimum standards for giving temporary protection in the event of a mass influx of displaced persons and on measures promoting a balance of efforts between Member States in receiving such persons and bearing the consequences thereof, in OJEC L 212, 7 August 2001, p. 12.

Council Framework Decision of 13 June 2002 on combating terrorism (2002/475/JHA) in OJEC L 164 of 22 June 2002.

Council Framework Decision of 13 June 2002 on the European arrest warrant and the surrender procedures between Member States (2002/584/JHA), in OJEC L 190 of 18 July 2002 p. 1.

Council of the European Union (2002), proposal for a Return Action Programme, 14673/02 MIGR 125 FRONT 135 VISA 172 of 25 November 2002.

Council of the European Union (2002), Afghanistan Return Plan, 14654/02 MIGR 124 RELEX 248 25 November 2002.

Council of the European Union (2002), Comprehensive Plan to combat illegal immigration and trafficking of human beings in the European Union in OJEC C 142 of 14 June 2002, p. 23.

Council of the European Union (2002), Plan for the management of the external borders of the Member States of the European Union, 10019/02 FRONT 58 COMIX 98, 14 June 2002.

Council of the European Union (2002), Modification of the terms of reference of the High Level Working Group on Migration and Asylum, 9433/02, JAI 109 AG 20 ASIM 18, 30 May 2002.

Council of the European Union (2000), European Union priorities and policy objectives for external relations in the field of Justice and Home Affairs, Presidency report to the Feira European Council, 19–20 June 2000 7635/00 JAI 35.

Council Directive 2001/51/EC of 28 June 2001 supplementing the provisions of Article 26 of the Convention implementing the Schengen Agreement of 14 June 1985. See in particular preambular paragraph (3) and Article 4 (2).

Council Framework Decision of 28 November 2002 on the strengthening of the penal framework to prevent the facilitation of unauthorised entry, transit and residence in OJEC L 328, 5 December 2002, p. 1 – see in particular the non-affection/savings clause in Article 6, and Council Directive 2002/90/EC of 28 November 2002 defining the facilitation of unauthorised entry, transit and residence in OJEC L 328, 5 December 2002, p. 17 – see the optional humanitarian clause in Article 1 (2).

Council Framework Decision of 19 July 2002 on combating trafficking in human beings, in OJEC L 203, 1 August 2002.

Council Regulation (EC) No. 539/2001 of 15 March 2001 listing the third countries whose nationals must be in possession of visas when crossing the external borders and those whose nationals are exempt from that requirement, in OJEC L 81, 21 March 2001, p. 1. Last amended by Regulation (EC) No. 453/2003 of 6 March 2003.

Commission Staff working paper 'Evaluation of the Dublin Convention' SEC (2001) 756 final, 13 June 2001.

Report from the seminar 'International Protection within One Single Asylum Procedure', Norrkoping, Sweden, 23–4 April 2001.

Van der Klaauw, J. (2001), 'Building Partnerships with Countries of Origin and Transit,' in: Clotilde Marinho (ed.), *Asylum, Immigration and Schengen Post-*

Amsterdam, a First Assessment, Maastricht: European Institute of Public Administration, EIPA, pp. 21–46.

Van der Klaauw, J. (2002), 'The Trafficking of Human Beings in the European Union: Specific Problems of Victims and Asylum-Seekers,' in Claudia Faria (ed.), *Managing Migration Flows and preventing Illegal Immigration*, Maastricht: European Institute of Public Administration, EIPA, pp. 29–47.

17. Family Reunification as a Constitutional Right?

Ryszard Cholewinski

17.1 INTRODUCTION

In response to the question of 'family reunification as a constitutional right', it is tempting to take the role of the perennial sceptic about European Union immigration policy and conclude that the evident answer is 'no'; that family reunification[1] cannot be considered as a constitutional or fundamental right, particularly given the current restrictive immigration climate in Europe; and that the EU is turning its back on the development of a more open immigration policy, which was signalled during the heady days of the Tampere European Council summit in October 1999. Moreover, in an attempt to prevent voters drifting towards supporting extremist political parties on the far Right, moderate European politicians are sending out tough signals on immigration policy in a context where illegal immigration and transnational crime are perceived to constitute the main problems, with the result that adoption of a more open immigration policy would seem to be more remote now than ever before.[2]

Indeed, this approach is evident from the recent Conclusions of the Seville European Council, which attached top priority to certain specific measures to combat illegal immigration.

[1] The terms family reunification and family reunion are synonymous for the purpose of this chapter and are used interchangeably.

[2] The editorial in the Financial Times, '*Knocking at the rich man's door*', on 25 May 2002, p. 6, begins: 'The resurgence of the far right and populist parties in Europe has sent mainstream politicians scrambling for ways to sound tough on immigration. Their eagerness to neutralize the issue is understandable, even commendable. Resentment of foreigners mixed with anti-establishment malaise makes for a potent brew easily exploited by demagogues. Yet immigration policy made on the hoof does more harm than good. Europe was beginning to edge towards a more rounded and rational set of migration rules based on labour market needs. Once again, the emphasis has shifted towards pulling up the drawbridge of Fortress Europe'.

But it is surely preferable to answer the question 'family reunification as a constitutional right?' by trying to accentuate the positive rather than the negative features of the development of a common EU immigration policy and its impact on third-country nationals residing in the EU. It would be closer to the truth to argue that family reunification is indeed a constitutional and fundamental right, and that the gap between rhetoric and reality is not as great as might first appear. It is possible to advance such an argument despite the fact that a Council document in April 2000, in a preliminary response to the first proposal of the Commission on this subject, asked the question, 'Is family reunification to be regarded as a right?',[3] as if to cast doubt on whether it ever could be.

The concept of a right to family reunification remains one to which it is easier to agree in principle, but where states find it much more difficult, for a variety of reasons, not least the lack of political will and vision, to determine the contours of this right and to apply it in practice. However, the right is recognized implicitly and explicitly in the legislation of most Member States and candidate countries. For example, the recent Spanish law on the rights of foreigners living in Spain clearly refers to the 'right' of resident foreigners to be reunited with certain family members, while Poland's amended Aliens Law obliges the authorities to issue a resident's permit to the spouse and minor children of the migrant settled in Poland or working there on a temporary basis provided that certain conditions are satisfied.

Despite this general consensus about the existence of a right to family reunification for foreigners at the national level, states have struggled to find a consensus internationally, particularly in respect of the conditions under which family reunion should take place. However, the EU must now come to grips with the issue of family reunification urgently as it is undoubtedly an important building block of the EU's common immigration policy on the treatment of third-country nationals lawfully resident within the EU.

The European Commission was aware of the significance of this question when it advanced its first text on a proposed Directive for the right of family reunification in December 1999, which was also the first substantive law proposal under the new Title IV of Part Three of the Treaty Establishing the European Community (TEC) on 'Visas, Asylum, Immigration and Other Policies Related to Free Movement of Persons'. Unfortunately, progress since this initial bold step was taken has been painfully slow.

This chapter constitutes a brief and critical account of the tortuous attempts of EU institutions and Member States to arrive at a Community consensus on the question of family reunification for third-country nationals.

It starts from the premise of Community Law, where this right is enshrined for EU citizens. What are the background principles underlying this right

[3] Council Doc. 7675/00 (7 April 2000) at p. 2.

within the unique Community legal framework and can they (or should they) also be translated for the benefit of third-country nationals residing in the EU? Is the gulf in treatment that exists between Community nationals exercising their freedom of movement rights, Member States nationals who have not exercised such rights (and to whom Community rules are inapplicable) and third-country nationals justifiable? Or does this difference in treatment merely constitute overt discrimination? How is the EU responding to this challenge and what progress, if any, has been made?

17.2 BACKGROUND PRINCIPLES: COMMUNITY LAW AND A RIGHT TO FAMILY REUNIFICATION FOR MEMBER STATE NATIONALS EXERCISING THEIR FREEDOM OF MOVEMENT RIGHTS

For a long time, the notion of an immigration policy in Europe was effectively a myth, because labour migration to Western Europe in the 1960s and 1970s was largely perceived as a temporary phenomenon. Migrant workers were guest workers and the rationale for their presence was primarily economic. They would come to work for a few years and then return home after the job was done. They were perceived as young unmarried men or fathers who would come alone to work without their families. Their integration into the social and cultural fabric of the host community was unnecessary because they were not going to stay.

The ban on immigration in the early 1970s, which still continues to inform the basis of immigration policy in a number of EU Member States, placed these countries in a dilemma: what should be done with those members of their foreign labour force, who, having worked and lived there for a considerable period of time, did not return to their country of origin but wished to remain and to have their families join them? It was not possible, largely for humanitarian reasons to deny these migrants what nationals took for granted – the right to live with those with whom they had the closest human attachments. After the ban on labour migration, foreign populations in many Western European countries actually increased rather than decreased (see Cholewinski 1997, p. 334). They became a permanent fixture on the landscape and their integration into the host societies became a human, social and political necessity.

Parallel to the ban on immigration to Western Europe after the economic downturn in the 1970s, the European Community had just begun to implement its freedom of movement of workers regime, which extended to the obligation to admit the family members of Member State nationals working in other Member States.

In contrast, therefore, to the restrictive stance adopted in respect of immigration generally, the adoption and development of these Community principles actually furthered it in the specific supranational context.[4] Regulation 1612/68/EEC constitutes the main piece of secondary legislation implementing the principle of free movement of workers in Article 39 TEC. This Regulation recognizes an unequivocal right of Community workers to have their families join them in the Member State of employment. The drafters realized that the right to freedom of movement would ring hollow if the social conditions that Community workers experienced in their home Member State were not replicated in other Member States, including the possibility of living in that Member State with their families.

The necessity for equal treatment in this respect is clearly recognized in the fifth recital of the Preamble to the Regulation alongside the need to foster the integration of the worker into the host community:

> Whereas the right of freedom of movement, in order that it may be exercised, by objective standards, in freedom and dignity, requires that equality of treatment shall be ensured in fact and in law in respect of all matters relating to the actual pursuit of activities as employed persons and to eligibility for housing, and also that obstacles to the mobility of workers shall be eliminated, in particular as regards the worker's right to be joined by his family and the conditions for the integration of that family into the host country.

Consequently, the right to family reunification is designed generously in Regulation 1612/68/EEC. While the concept of family remains the traditional Western nuclear family, the right of workers to have their family members join them extends to the spouse and children in respect of which the age limit is set liberally (21 years of age), or older children if they are still dependent on the worker, as well as relatives in the ascending line of the worker and his or her spouse if they are dependent. In order to facilitate freedom of movement, the Court of Justice has interpreted this principle broadly.

Moreover, the sole condition on this right, possession of accommodation considered as normal by national standards, is understood in the context of adequacy at the time of arrival and is not subject to a subsequent change in conditions.[5]

[4] Nevertheless, non-EU nationals continued to be largest group of migrants immigrating to the EU in the 1990s. See Eurostat (2002), 'Migration keeps the EU population growing', *Statistics in Focus*, Population and Social Conditions, Theme 3 – 7/2002.

[5] Case 249/86, *Commission* v. *Germany* [1989] ECR 1263.

17.3 HUMAN RIGHTS PRINCIPLES

While the driving-force for the Community right is the free movement principle, it should be underlined that the right is not based solely on an economic imperative in the name of the greater good of prosperity for all Community citizens. Clearly, there is also an important human rights element involved, which must be seen as standing alone. Indeed, the Court of Justice already recognized some time before Article 6 (2) of the Treaty on European Union[6] that family reunion is a subject where Community principles engage with the jurisprudence of the European Court of Human Rights under Article 8 of the European Convention on Human Rights (ECHR).[7] This argument is particularly important because it can be used to counteract assertions that the Community is a 'special legal order' justifying a more favourable regime for EU citizens over third-country nationals. Although the latter contention has been articulated by the Court of Human Rights, when considering the application of the non-discrimination provision, Article 14 ECHR, to differences in treatment between Community citizens and third-country nationals in the context of expulsion,[8] it should not be viewed as permitting such distinctions in all circumstances and the proportionality principle should therefore play a critical role in precluding patent discrepancies. Indeed, the Court has recently been bolder in applying Article 8 ECHR to cases of entry by recognizing that state parties are under a positive obligation to admit a family member in a situation where the family unit cannot reasonably be expected to relocate to the country of origin.[9]

Consequently, there is scope for contending under the ECHR that certain differences in treatment between EU citizens and third-country nationals, such as those in respect of family reunion, would not be proportionate in the context of Articles 8 and 14 ECHR.

It is important also to remember that the ECHR is not the only barometer of the protection of human rights as far as family reunion is concerned and that in the social field the Council of Europe's Social Charter (and revised Social Charter), which all Member States and a number of candidate countries

[6] Article 6: 'The Union shall respect fundamental rights, as guaranteed by the European Convention for the Protection of Human Rights and Fundamental Freedoms signed in Rome on 4 November 1950 and as they result from the constitutional traditions common to the Member States, as general principles of Community law'.

[7] *Commission* v. *Germany*, Para. 10: 'Regulation No. 1612/68 must also be interpreted in the light of the requirement of respect for family life set out in Article 8 ECHR. That requirement is one of the fundamental rights which, according to the Court's settled case-law are recognized by Community law'.

[8] *Moustaquim* v. *Belgium* (1991) 11 EHRR 802; *C.* v. *Belgium*, Eur. Ct. H.R., Judgment of 7 August 1996, Eur. Ct. HR Rep. 1996-III.

[9] *Sen* v. *Netherlands* (Application No. 31465/96), Eur. Ct. H.R., judgment of 21 December 2001, available at http://www.echr.coe.int/.

have ratified, is equally pertinent. Article 19 of the Charter draws up a framework of protection for migrant workers from other Council of Europe Member States and includes an explicit provision on family reunion in Article 19(6),[10] which has been interpreted liberally by the Committee of Independent Experts, the body responsible for monitoring State Party compliance with the Charter. Indeed, some of the interpretations of this Committee are clearly at odds with a number of the provisions in the Commission's most recently amended proposal for a Directive on the right to family reunification. For example, the Committee of Independent Experts interprets the family reunion provision of the Charter, Article 19(6), as permitting a waiting period before family members can join the worker in the host State Party but only if it is not excessive. Consequently, the Committee has found that a three-year waiting period is contrary to Article 19(6),[11] which nevertheless remains possible in the Commission's most recent proposal. Moreover, in the Council deliberations on the proposal one Member State would still like to extend this waiting period to at least five years.[12]

Finally, the EU's own Charter of Fundamental Rights,[13] in keeping with other more general international human rights instruments,[14] also protects the right to respect for private and family life (Article 7), recognizes the right to marry and to have a family (Article 9), and declares that 'the family shall enjoy legal, economic and social protection' (Article 33(1)).[15]

The growing gulf between family reunion rights in the EC Treaty, as implemented by Regulation 1612/68/EEC, and what is on offer at the moment to third-country nationals resident in the EU, cannot arguably be justified in any context. Furthermore, it should be underlined that this remains one of those vexing and inconsistent areas of Community law where the rights are only available to those EU citizens exercising their free movement entitlements. Consequently, the discrimination remains at two levels affecting both third-country nationals lawfully resident in the EU and those EU citizens

[10] Art. 19(6) places Council of Europe Member States, which have accepted it, under an obligation 'to facilitate as far as possible the reunion of the family of a foreign worker permitted to establish himself in the territory'. However, this is only an obligation 'to facilitate' and not 'a right' of family reunification, although the complete denial of entry to family members or indeed the application of overly onerous conditions to family reunion would no doubt contravene this obligation.

[11] *Conclusions II* at p. 69, cited in Council of Europe, *Case Law of the European Social Charter – Supplement No. 3*, Strasbourg: Council of Europe Press, 1993, at p. 163.

[12] See Council Doc. 13053/02 (23 October 2002) p. 13 (Austria).

[13] OJ 2000 C 364/1.

[14] See e.g. Art. 23(1) of the 1966 International Covenant on Civil and Political Rights: 'The family is the natural and fundamental group unit of society and is entitled to protection by society and the State'.

[15] However, the latter provision would appear to be rather more limited in scope because it is found in the context of reconciling family and professional life in respect of protection from dismissal for a reason connected with maternity (Art. 32(2)).

who have not exercised free movement rights and who are subject to more restrictive domestic measures in respect of family reunification in their Member State of origin. In such cases, however, overly restrictive national measures can still be subject to a challenge under Article 8 ECHR.[16]

17.4 THE COMMUNITY AND A RIGHT TO FAMILY REUNIFICATION FOR THIRD-COUNTRY NATIONALS: FROM A WHIMPER TO A BANG TO A WHIMPER AGAIN?

The first attempt of the Community to achieve a consensus on the question of family reunion of third-country nationals was disappointing and lacklustre. In the pre-Maastricht period of intergovernmental cooperation, European immigration ministers adopted the Resolution on the harmonization of national policies on family reunification in Copenhagen on the 1 and 2 June 1993, which, as indicated in its title, did not recognize 'a right' to family reunification (see Guild and Niessen 1996).[17] The Resolution was basically an 'agreement to disagree' and laden with restrictive provisions and discretion enabling Member States to effectively maintain their own nationals' policies (see Boeles and Kuijer 1993, and Peers 1998). However, this measure should not be dismissed too lightly. While not strictly speaking about an EU measure as well as constituting 'soft law', it remains the sole measure agreed to date by EU Member State governments on the question of family reunification for third-country nationals. Moreover, it has found its way into the EU acquis on immigration and asylum that has to be transformed by EU accession countries into their domestic legislation (see van Krieken 2000, pp. 83 and 104).[18]

Fortunately, the Resolution is not the sole measure governing legal developments regarding family reunification in the accession states and the jurisprudence of the European Court of Human Rights under Article 8 ECHR has been applied to correct imbalances. For example, the Constitutional Court in Estonia recently ruled that the domestic immigration legislation, partly designed to comply with the EU acquis, and in which an immigration quota also applied to the entry of family members of foreigners, was

[16] E.g. see Case C-60/00, *Carpenter* v. *Secretary of State for the Home Department*, judgment of 11 July 2002, where the Court of Justice had to resort to Article 8 ECHR to prevent the deportation of the Filipino spouse of a UK national providing services in other Member States in accordance with Art. 49 TEC but where the absence of movement by both spouses together meant that the family unity provisions in the implementing legislation (i.e. Directive 73/148/EEC of 21 May 1973) could not apply.

[17] Doc. SN 2828/1/93 WGI 1497 REV 1.

[18] See the TAIEX (Technical Assistance Information Exchange Office) list, considered to be the most authoritative and exhaustive list available of the Justice and Home Affairs (JHA) acquis.

unconstitutional because it contravened Article 8 ECHR.[19] The continued validity of the 1993 Resolution, albeit more by default than by design, and the EU's failure to move forward and adopt an equitable stance in this important policy area is also an indication of the intractable difficulties accession states face in adjusting their national laws to the EU moving target on asylum and immigration.

Further activity in this area, which briefly gave rise to a conditional right of family reunification for third-country nationals in the Commission's proposed 1997 Convention on rules for the admission of third-country nationals to Member States, was effectively curtailed by negotiations at the subsequent intergovernmental conference. Communitarization of asylum and immigration policy by virtue of the Treaty of Amsterdam, albeit in a somewhat fragmented guise, raised hopes that such an equitable policy might be adopted in respect of a right to family reunification of third-country nationals residing lawfully in the EU. Article 63(3)(a) TEC mandates the Council to adopt 'measures on immigration policy within the following areas: [*inter alia*] conditions of entry and residence, and standards on procedures for the issue by Member States of long term visas and residence permits, including those for the purpose of family reunion ...'. Shortly after the entry into force of Title IV TEC, the European Council at Tampere set the following positive agenda regarding the treatment of third-country nationals:

> The European Union must ensure fair treatment of third-country nationals who reside legally on the territory of its Member States. A more vigorous integration policy should aim at granting them rights and obligations comparable to those of EU citizens...[T]he legal status of third-country nationals should be approximated to that of Member States' nationals. A person, who has resided legally in a Member State for a period of time to be determined and who holds a long-term residence permit, should be granted in that Member State a set of uniform rights which are as near as possible to those enjoyed by EU citizens...[20]

To date, however, this promise of near-equality or comparable treatment for third-country nationals, particularly long-term residents, has yet to be realized.

The Commission's proposed Directive relating to the status of third-country nationals who are long-term residents[21] and the proposed Directive on family reunification, as discussed below, remains the subject of tortuous deliberations in the Council working groups. In the meantime, activity has been intense in other areas, which are clearly being viewed by the EU and

[19] Discussions at the IOM-UNHCR Regional Seminar on the Protection of Human Rights in the Context of Asylum Seeking and Migration, 25–26 April 2002, Tallinn, Estonia.

[20] *Tampere European Council: Presidency Conclusions*, 16 October 1999, *Bull. EU 10-1999*, points 18 and 21.

[21] COM (2001) 127 of 13 March 2001.

Member State governments as a priority, such as combating irregular migration and trafficking, with a particular emphasis on cooperation with third countries, the development of EU visa policy and strengthening external borders.[22]

On the whole, the Commission's first proposal for a right to family reunification was well received (see Boeles 2001).[23] The recognition of a 'right' found resonance not only with the earlier proposed Convention in 1997, but more importantly with the Community free movement rubric. As such, therefore, it was grounded on firm principle even though the proposal was also criticized for adopting a narrow concept of family and for attaching too many onerous conditions to the right (Cholewinski 2002). Another important innovation was the removal of reverse discrimination to ensure that third-country family members of EU citizens not exercising free movement rights would be treated in the same way as third-country nationals joining EU citizens residing and working in other Member States. The significance of this particular aspect of the proposal was that its implementation would arguably have swept away any vestiges of a free movement rationale for family reunion and therefore an important justification for the difference in treatment between EU nationals and third-country nationals in this field. Consequently, equal treatment and human rights would have held sway.

The Commission amended its proposal in October 2000 in response to suggestions by the European Parliament, but no consensus could be reached in the Council. A few delegations opposed Community treatment for third-country family members wishing to join Member State nationals not exercising their freedom of movement rights.[24] The concept of family was insufficiently narrow for some and the conditions on family reunion were not onerous enough for others. A number of versions of the Directive were advanced and the last discussed was a compromise proposed by the Belgian Presidency, which outlined different rights for different family members.[25]

It should be recalled at this point that a number of the contrary positions were clearly minority ones, but given the requirement of unanimity in the Council for adopting this kind of measure under Title IV TEC no further progress on the proposal could be forthcoming.

Finally, the Laeken European Council requested the Commission to return to the drawing board and introduce a re-amended proposal.[26]

[22] *Seville European Council: Presidency Conclusions*, above n. 3, par. 30–36.

[23] The author considered this proposal as a development of major importance.

[24] See Council Doc. 8209/01 (2 May 2001), p. 5.

[25] See Council Docs. 10394/01 (2 July 2001), 10992/01 (20 July 2001) and 12022/01 (24 September 2001).

[26] *Laeken European Council: Presidency Conclusions*, 14–15 December 2001, Doc. SN 300/01, para. 41.

The Commission's re-amended proposal was published at the beginning of May 2002. It is an unashamedly compromising text, which appears to have as its purpose prompt acceptance in the Council. On the one hand, it is a significantly watered-down version of the original proposal. Most strikingly, it discards equality of treatment for all EU citizens in respect of the entry of their third-country family members and thus keeps reverse discrimination intact, for the time being at least.[27] The proposal preserves a narrow conception of the family and Member States are only under an obligation to admit the spouse and minor children and retain complete discretion whether to admit first-degree relatives in the ascending line, adult unmarried children and unmarried partners.[28] In addition, the Directive would only apply to third-country nationals with residence permits valid for one year or more who have 'a reasonable prospect of permanent residence'.[29]

The new proposal also introduces a number of optional or 'flexible' provisions (as the Commission in its Explanatory Memorandum prefers to call them) in those areas where there was previously considerable disagreement or deadlock in the Council. Consequently, the conditions on family reunion may now be continued until first renewal of the residence permit[30] and the length of time applicants should have to wait before their family members can join then in the EU Member State can be up to three years.[31] A three-year waiting period is permissible by way of derogation where legislation having regard to a Member State's reception capacity providing for such a period is already in force at the time of the Directive's adoption. This approach, as discussed above, not only contravenes Member States' human rights obligations under Article 19(6) of the European Social Charter, but also conflicts hugely with the Commission's clear and contradictory position on this issue in its original proposal, where it emphasized in the Explanatory Memorandum that 'the qualifying period may not exceed one year, for otherwise the exercise of the right to family reunification would be devoid of substance'. Furthermore, the amended proposal builds in an exception in respect of existing national legislation by virtue of which Member States might deny entry to a child over 12 years of age if the child is deemed not to meet a condition of integration provided in

[27] See Explanatory Memorandum. The Commission explains that it will return to this question once it has recast Community law on the free movement of EU citizens. See COM (2001) 257 final of 23 May 2001.

[28] See draft Arts. 4(1)–(3). See also Recital 11 to the amended proposal: 'Family reunification applies to members of the nuclear family, that is to say the spouse and the minor children. It is for States to decide whether they wish to extend this category and authorize family reunification for relatives in the ascending line, children who are of full age and unmarried partners'.

[29] See draft Art. 3(1).

[30] See draft Art. 7(1)(c).

[31] See draft Art. 8.

that legislation.[32] This approach should be contrasted with the age limit of 21 in Regulation 1612/68/EEC and the European Social Charter.

It is also significantly lower than what is understood by minor children in the revised European Social Charter and the 18 years stipulated in a recent Recommendation of the Council of Europe's Committee of Ministers.[33]

Finally, it is likely to constitute a violation of the International Convention on the Rights of the Child,[34] despite the obligation in the new text where Member States are required to have 'due regard to the best interests of minor children' in accordance with the Convention when examining applications for family reunification.[35]

On the other hand, the Commission's re-amended proposal attempts to regain the moral high ground by including a clause enabling Member States to apply higher standards,[36] a standstill clause in respect of the flexible provisions permitting the derogations described above,[37] and the misleadingly named deadline clause,[38] which requires review of these provisions two years after the Directive's transposition into national legislation but without making any firm commitments to their amendment in the future. In other words, the Commission foresees EU law and policy on family reunion taking shape in stages, although there is no guarantee that the current stage will not be the last. The Seville European Council urged the Council to adopt the family reunification measure, together with the proposed Directive relating to the status of long-term residents, by June 2003.[39] Deliberations on the re-amended proposed Directive have continued apace in response to the

[32] Amended Proposal for a Council Directive on the right to family reunification, above n. 42, draft Art. 4(1) (c), indent 3.

[33] See Recommendation Rec (2002) 4 of 26 March 2002 on the legal status of persons admitted for family reunification, which though not applicable to the admission of family members but only their treatment in the host country, defines child in par. I (2) as 'every human being below the age of eighteen years unless, under the law applicable to the child, majority is attained earlier'.

[34] Art. 9(1) of the Convention reads in part: 'States Parties shall ensure that a child shall not be separated from his or her parents against their will, except when competent authorities subject to judicial review determine, in accordance with applicable law and procedures, that such separation is necessary for the best interests of the child'. Art. 10(1) adds that, in accordance with this obligation, 'Applications by a child or his or her parents to enter or leave a State Party for the purpose of family reunification shall be dealt with by States Parties in a positive, humane and expeditious manner'. For the purpose of the Convention, 'a child means every human being below the age of eighteen years unless under the law applicable to the child, majority is attained earlier' (Art. 1).

[35] See draft Art. 5(5) of the amended proposal.

[36] See Explanatory Memorandum and draft Art. 3(5).

[37] See Explanatory Memorandum and draft Art. 3(6).

[38] See Explanatory Memorandum and draft Art. 19.

[39] Seville European Council: Presidency Conclusions, above n. 3, Para. 37.

promptings of the Seville European Council,[40] but to date have resulted alarmingly in a further lowering of standards. The most significant change concerns the removal of the standstill clause preventing the introduction of less favourable conditions than those already existing in the Member State on the date of the Directive's adoption. This is in respect of the flexible provisions permitting derogations concerning the definition of family members authorized to enter, the condition requiring the possession of stable resources and the period of time applicants must have stayed lawfully in the country before their family members can join them.[41]

The notion of stable resources itself has also been altered and refers now to 'stable and regular resources which are sufficient to maintain [the applicant] and the members of his/her family, without recourse to the social assistance system of the Member State concerned'.[42] The reference to the resources 'being higher than or equal to the level of resources below which the Member State concerned may grant social assistance' has been deleted. With regard to the waiting period for family reunion, the Austrian delegation maintains a reservation insisting on the extension of the maximum duration of this period to at least five years instead of three years. Moreover, a further optional condition on family reunion has now been added to the text, namely that 'Member States may require third-country nationals to comply with integration measures, in accordance with national law'.[43]

Finally, the German delegation wishes to include an optional clause in the Directive, which would enable Member States to impose a further limitation on family reunification by requiring applicants who have held residence permits for less than five years to have been married to their spouse before the issue of the residence permit.[44]

17.5 CONCLUSIONS

The Commission's most recent amendment of its proposal for a Directive on the right to family reunification for third-country nationals leaves much to be desired.

[40] See Council Docs. 10857/02 (9 August 2002), 13053/02 (23 October 2002), 13968/02 (12 November 2002) and 14272/02 (26 November 2002). I am grateful to Professor Steve Peers for bringing these documents to my attention.

[41] Council Doc. 13968/02 (12 November 2002) at p. 5.

[42] Council Doc. 13053/02 (23 October 2002) at p. 12 (draft Art. 7(1) (c).

[43] Council Doc. 14272/02 (26 November 2002), draft Art. 7(2). This provision is supported by Austria, Germany and the Netherlands, but subject to scrutiny reservations from Belgium and Sweden.

[44] This optional clause is supported by Austria, but subject to scrutiny reservations from Belgium, Finland, Italy, the Netherlands, Portugal, Spain and Sweden.

It is a significant climb-down from its original position, which is, however, perhaps inevitable given the opposition to some of the more enlightened provisions by certain Member State delegations in the Council. It would appear though that more political impetus has now been given by the Seville European Council to the adoption of measures in the asylum and immigration field with the result that the proposed Directive on the right to family reunification is likely to be adopted in some form or another (although it would not be the first time that such a deadline – June 2003 – has been missed). But the vexing question is whether the measure that will eventually be adopted will be worth supporting.

Indeed, given the further dilution of its key provisions, both by the Commission in the re-amended text and in the subsequent deliberations in the Council working groups, a danger exists that on adoption the Directive will effectively become a 'free for all' and rather similar to the Resolution adopted a decade earlier by European Immigration Ministers.

The introduction of optional or flexibility clauses, enabling Member States to derogate in particular areas in view of their own national restrictive positions, makes it very difficult to continue speaking of a 'common' policy on immigration in this field.

Can any positive conclusions be drawn from this difficult experience of drafting a Directive on a right of family reunification for third-country nationals?

- one positive statement worth making is that family reunification for third-country nationals is still considered to be a right, although of course there comes a point where the extent of conditions imposed on a right render it ineffectual and very difficult to enjoy as indeed the Commission itself recognized in the Explanatory Memorandum to its original proposal.
- another positive feature is the clear signal that Member States are free to adopt or retain higher standards, although given the other possibilities for reducing overall protection, such higher standards are likely to be the exception rather than the rule. The so-called 'deadline clause' also foresees the repeal of the more restrictive provisions a few years after the adoption of the Directive, although there is no guarantee that this will occur.

Unfortunately, therefore, even these positive remarks are subject to provisos:

- perhaps the most positive conclusion that can be advanced is that a future Directive on family reunification for third-country nationals cannot be the end of the story. Once adopted and implemented, its provisions will be subject to the jurisdiction of the Court of Justice. By then, the Charter of Fundamental Rights may also have taken on a more meaningful legally binding status in Community law.[45]

- finally, the European Court of Human Rights should not of course be left out of the equation. It has already indicated clearly that state parties cannot be absolved from their human rights obligations by entering into agreements among themselves.[46] It would be unfortunate, however, if the Court of Human Rights were called upon regularly to referee on the human rights compliance of Community measures in the asylum and immigration field.

The EU still has time to reverse the recent restrictive trends and to adopt a more visionary measure in respect of family reunification, which can also serve as a worthy milestone of its developing common immigration policy vis-à-vis third-country nationals resident in its territory. Otherwise, an opportunity to improve their social condition will have been alarmingly and sadly missed.

REFERENCES

Boeles, P. (2001), 'Directive on Family Reunification: Are the Dilemmas Resolved?', 3, *European Journal of Migration and Law*, pp. 61–71.

Boeles, P. and A. Kuijer (1993), 'Harmonization of Family Reunification' in H. Meijers, et al., (eds), *A New Immigration Law for Europe? The 1992 London and 1993 Copenhagen Rules on Immigration*, Utrecht: Dutch Centre for Immigrants, p. 25.

Cholewinski, R. (1997), *Migrant Workers in International Human Rights Law: Their Protection in Countries of Employment*, Oxford: Clarendon Press.

Cholewinski, R. (2002), 'Family Reunification and Conditions Place on Family Members: Dismantling a Fundamental Human Right', 4, *European Journal of Migration and Law*, pp. 271–90.

[45] Indeed, the final report of Working Group II in the Convention on the Future of the EU on 'Incorporation of the Charter/accession to the ECHR' has recommended that legal effect should be given to the Charter in a new Constitutional Treaty and that the EU should accede to the ECHR. See Doc. CONV 354/02 (22 October 2002).

[46] Eur. Ct. HR admissibility decision of 7 March 2000, Application 43844/98, *T.I.* v. *United Kingdom*, reproduced in (2000) 12 *International Journal of Refugee Law* 244: 'Where States establish international organizations, or *mutatis mutandis* international agreements, to pursue cooperation in certain fields of activities, there may be implications for the protection of fundamental rights. It would be incompatible with the purpose and object of the Convention if Contracting States were thereby absolved from their responsibility under the Convention in relation to the field of activity covered by such attribution'. *Ibid.* p. 260.

Council Regulation 1612/68/EEC of 15 October 1968 on freedom of movement for workers within the Community, as amended, OJ Sp. Ed. 1968–69, 475, JO 1968 L 257/2.

European Commission (1997), Proposal for a Council Act establishing the Convention on rules for the admission of third-country nationals to the Member States, COM (97) 387 final of 30 July 1997, draft Art. 24(1).

European Commission (1999), Proposal for a Council Directive on the right to family reunification, COM (1999) 638 final of 1 December 1999.

European Commission (2000), Amended Proposal for a Council Directive on the right to family reunification, COM (2000) 624 final of 10 October 2000.

European Commission (2002), Amended Proposal for a Council Directive on the right to family reunification, COM (2002) 225 final of 2 May 2002.

European Commission's Communication, Towards Integrated Management of the External Borders of the Member States of the European Union, COM (2002) 233 final of 7 May 2002.

Guild, E and J. Niessen (1996), *The Developing Immigration and Asylum Policies of the European Union,* The Hague: Kluwer, pp. 251–73.

Law of 25 June 1997 on Aliens (*Ustawa o cudzioziemcach*), amended on 11 April 2001. Official Journal of Laws (*Dzennik Ustaw*) 2001, No. 127, item 1400.

Organic Law 4/2000 of 11 January 2000 on the Rights and Freedoms of Foreign Nationals living in Spain and their Social Integration, as amended by Law 8/2000 of 22 December 2000 (*Ley orgánica 4/2000, sobre derechos y libertades de los extranjeros en España y su integración social, reformada por la Ley orgánica 8/2000*), BOE (Official State Bulletin) of 23 December 2000, Art. 17(1).

Peers, S. (1998), 'Building Fortress Europe: The Development of EU Migration Law', 35, *Common Market Law Review,* pp. 1235–72.

Plan for the Management of the External Borders of the Member States of the European Union, Council Doc. 10019/02 (14 June 2002).

Proposal for a Comprehensive Plan to Combat Illegal Immigration and Trafficking of Human Beings in the European Union, OJ 2002 C142/231; Guidelines for the introduction of a 'common system for an exchange of visa data', Council Doc. 7309/3/02 (7 May 2002).

Recommendation Rec (2002) 4 of 26 March 2002 on the legal status of persons admitted for family reunification.

Seville European Council: Presidency Conclusions, Doc. SN 200/02, 21–22 June 2002, Para. 30.

Van Krieken, P.J. (ed.) (2000), *The Asylum Acquis Handbook,* The Hague: T.M.C. Asser Press.

18. Taking the Bogus out of the Discourse concerning Asylum

Constança Urbano de Sousa

18.1 INTRODUCTION

Pondering the theme 'taking the bogus out of the discourse concerning asylum', as part of a discussion on 'balancing openness with control', some of the ambiguities in asylum policy, stemming especially from its increasing links to immigration, immediately sprang to mind. Although they are related, immigration and asylum are legally separate issues. Nevertheless, amid security concerns, post-11 September, and the success of far-Right parties in France, the Netherlands and Denmark, basing their campaigns around the issue of controlling immigration and its link to insecurity, the EU has been infected by the discourse of fear. In fact, as far as immigration goes, the EU appears to be set on pushing through measures to increase control of external borders and to fight illegal immigration.

This narrow vision of immigration policy may, however, strengthen the dangerous link in the minds of individuals between insecurity and the increase in the number of immigrants. This might foster, in turn, the idea that Europe is being invaded by fraudulent asylum seekers: in other words, that 'the boat is full', to coin Pim Fortuyn's expression.

On the one hand, as pointed out by the Commission in its Social Situation Report 2002, Europe needs immigrants to secure sustainable labour markets and pension systems. In other words, immigration should not be looked at as a problem, but rather as a solution to problems. On the other hand, the number of asylum seekers is falling. According to the data from the Office of the UN High Commissioner for Refugees, the total number of asylum seekers arriving in the European Union last year (384 530) was nearly half the number in 1992 (675 460).

Nevertheless, security concerns are making the discourse on asylum increasingly ambiguous, if not contradictory, especially if we consider the agreement by the European Council at its special meeting in Tampere, to work towards establishing a Common European Asylum System. The system is to be based on the full and inclusive application of the Geneva Convention relating to the Status of Refugees, thus maintaining the principle of non-*refoulement* and ensuring that nobody is sent back to persecution.

In this chapter I focus on three of the ambiguities in the asylum discourse, stemming from asylum policy being subject to premises pertaining to immigration policy, these being the trends towards:

1. a narrower application of the Geneva Convention.
2. making economic and humanitarian immigration synonymous.
3. giving precedence to fighting and tightening up on illegal immigration over humanitarian obligations.

18.2 THE TREND TOWARDS A NARROWER APPLICATION OF THE GENEVA CONVENTION

As far as the first ambiguity is concerned, a tendency can be appreciated to dismiss protection that should be afforded to refugees under the auspices of the Geneva Convention by instead making temporary and supplementary forms of protection more widespread. This notion runs counter to the all-inclusiveness ideal of the Geneva Convention as set out in Tampere. Hence many refugees are erroneously granted only subsidiary protection and not refugee status. Migration concerns clearly influence this trend, since the status granted under subsidiary protection is usually less stable, such as on the issue of family reunification.

Thus, for instance, over recent years, the majority of legal immigrants in EU Member States have immigrated under family reunification provisions. In order to meet the demands of certain Member States that wish to restrict or reduce family immigration, the Commission submitted the 3rd amended proposal for a Council Directive on the right to family reunification, which sets unreasonable limits on the principle of family unity as enshrined in international law. According to the proposal, Member States are only bound to guarantee the right to family reunification with spouse and children to those immigrants with reasonable prospects of obtaining the right of permanent residence and of Geneva Convention refugees. The beneficiaries of subsidiary protection are specifically excluded from the scope of this Directive. Although the European Council of Tampere had agreed that Community rules regarding refugee status should be complemented by measures on subsidiary forms of protection, the fact is that the Community Law being drafted does not guarantee the basic fundamental right to family reunification. This right is directly linked to the right to family unity, protected under international law on human rights and recognised in particular by the Charter of Fundamental Rights of the European Union.

18.3 THE TREND TOWARDS MAKING ECONOMIC AND HUMANITARIAN IMMIGRATION SYNONYMOUS

The second ambiguity arises from the interference of economic immigration policy in the asylum policy of some Member States. Those which have recently adopted a more flexible approach on labour immigration, by creating 'green card' systems or something similar, appear to think that this gives them a legitimate basis for adopting more restrictive asylum policies (see Bontempi 2001). By putting immigration and asylum in the same 'basket' we run the risk of legitimising those who fail to see the differences between the various legal forms of access to EU territory.

This risk manifests itself in the widespread practice of using immigration-related grounds of inadmissibility while handling asylum applications, such as the lack of travel documents or false ones, which often stems from the need to flee the country of origin and seek protection. The green card system or equivalent is only designed to meet sporadic labour market needs and cannot be envisaged as a sufficient replacement for the protection, which according to international law, must be afforded to refugees or others who require international protection.

Above all, these economic immigration systems imply that the immigrant is perceived as a 'disposable good', designed to meet the needs of the labour market. This purely functional view of immigrants is tantamount to denying the system of humanitarian values on which contemporary European society is based, especially the absolute value of human dignity. A comprehensive approach to immigration involves adopting measures to help immigrants integrate into the host societies. This means that immigrants must be given a stable legal status, which also includes being given the right to family reunification. If immigrants are denied a real opportunity to become integrated into host societies, the pattern of exclusion will go on and on; racism and xenophobia will only gain momentum.

18.4 THE TREND TOWARDS GIVING PRECEDENCE TO FIGHTING AND TIGHTENING ILLEGAL IMMIGRATION OVER HUMANITARIAN OBLIGATIONS

The last ambiguity is the one concerning the misleading parallel between immigration and asylum made by European politicians. Indeed, European leaders, shackled by the anti-immigration and anti-refugee propaganda of the far Right, are placing a far greater emphasis on migration concerns and combating illegal immigration than on humanitarian needs and principles.

One can justify and defend measures to regulate migratory flows and combat illegal immigration – issues that are high on the European political agenda. However, such measures cannot ride roughshod over the distinct divide between an immigrant and a refugee. Above all, they cannot and must not sacrifice respect for human rights. Unfortunately this is a fairly typical circumstance, as certain measures taken to tighten up immigration and combat illegal immigration actually prevent refugees and those needing international protection from gaining access to Europe, thereby denying them the fundamental right of seeking asylum.

Examples of this include the Visa Regulation and, above all, the Directive on Sanctions for Carriers Transporting Foreign Nationals into the Territory of Member States without the necessary documents. The sanctions imposed on the carriers, in addition to transferring the responsibility for guarding Europe's external borders to private entities, keeps not only illegal immigrants out but also asylum seekers (see Lluch 2001).

The Visa Regulation, by obliging nationals of countries that are a source of refugees to hold a visa (e.g. Iraq), makes legal entry into countries of asylum far more difficult for those nationals. Neither the guarantee provided in Article 31 of the Geneva Convention, that refugees will not be penalised for illegal entry or stay, nor the protection provided by the principle of non-*refoulement*, are of any use if carriers do not let them on board (see Lluch 2001).

Even if the Directive on Carrier Sanctions will only be implemented without prejudice to the obligations resulting from the Geneva Convention, companies carrying refugees without legal documents will not be sanctioned; in reality, this may not go beyond legal rhetoric.

Firstly, the onus rests not on employees of carrier companies to protect refugees. What is more, they have hardly been trained to distinguish a refugee from an illegal immigrant, and nor should they be expected to make a decision on any related matter (Crepau 1995, p. 203). Secondly, even though employees of carrier companies may come across people who are obviously being persecuted and need international protection, a lack of necessary documentation would prevent the majority of those companies from allowing the persecuted to board. Business interests and the threat of penalisation would be significant deterrents to most acts of benevolence under those circumstances (Crepau 1995, p.203).

Unlike immigrants, refugees and others requiring international protection cannot choose when or how to flee their home countries. As it becomes more difficult to gain access to a country of asylum, the persecuted have no other option than to resort to illegal immigration networks, no matter the degree of danger or illegality. And this is how governments and other political actors get trapped in a vicious cycle that entwines illegal immigration and the fundamental right to seek asylum.

18.5 CONCLUSIONS

Striking a balance between the need to combat illegal immigration and tighter border controls, on the one hand, and obligations regarding the right to seek asylum, on the other, is a very difficult task. Yet the dividing line clearly lies in guaranteeing a fair asylum appraisal for all persecuted people. Full respect for the right to seek asylum and the principle of non-*refoulement*, which the EU Member States underlined at Tampere, implies that legal channels for asylum seekers to enter the EU must be kept open. Otherwise no reason exists for having an asylum system that offers the full range of procedural guarantees and living conditions for asylum seekers. According to the principle of non-*refoulement*, which guarantees that nobody will be sent back to persecution, refugees and people that need international protection have no real chance of exercising the right to seek asylum.

In addition, it would be folly to think that the only way to effectively fight illegal immigration is to strengthen border controls and impose penalties – in short, by creating a 'Fortress Europe'. Such a battle will always be lost, so long as there are glaring development gaps that encourage thousands of people to scrape out a living in Europe. When a thriving black market economy in Europe meets labour needs through use of illegal immigrants and links in the chain of production are not made responsible for exploiting illegal immigrant labour, then hopes for a balanced regulatory border system will remain futile. Clear demarcation between immigration and asylum policies must therefore become a primary goal.

It is therefore high time that measures be taken to create a European asylum policy – a policy respecting international obligations and making the protection of refugees and others seeking humanitarian care its number one priority. Otherwise the EU may be denying 'principles of liberty, democracy, respect for human rights and fundamental freedoms and the rule of law,' which, pursuant to Article 6 of the Treaty of the European Union, are the very bedrock of the European Community.

REFERENCES

Amended proposal for a Council Directive on the right to family reunification COM/2002/0225 final.

Bontempi, R. (2001), 'Hacia una Política Europea de Inmigración y un Régimen Común en Materia de Asilo', *Revista Cidob d'affers Internacionals*, **53**, 123.

Council Regulation (EC) No 539/2001 of 15 March 2001 listing the third countries whose nationals must be in possession of visas when crossing the external borders and those whose nationals are exempt from that requirement, OJ L 081, 21.03.2001 p.1. Amended by Council Regulation (EC) No 2414/2001 of 7 December 2001, OJ L 327, 12.12 2001, p. 1.

Council Directive 2001/51/EC of 28 June 2001 supplementing the provisions of Article 26 of the Convention implementing the Schengen Agreement of 14 June 1985, OJ L 187, 10.07.2001, p.45.

Crepau, F. (ed.) (1995), *'Droit d'asile – de l'Hospitalité aux controles migratoires'*, Brussels: Bruylant.

Lluch, T. (2001), 'Hacia una política común de asilo para la Unión Europea,' *Revista Cidob d'affers Internacionals*, **53**, pp. 144–5.

19. Balancing Openness with Control: Management of Border Controls and the Euro-Border Guard

Marek Adamczyk

19.1 INTRODUCTION

In this chapter an evaluation of the feasibility study of a Euro-Border Guard is carried out, taking as a basis the example of the Polish Border Guard (PBG). Globalisation and the organised character of cross-border crime require that preventative actions be jointly co-ordinated in identifying and combating the source. The process of EU enlargement will bring about significant changes in areas of operation and border service competencies both in the candidate countries and the present EU Member States.

The PBG does not operate in a vacuum; it is not isolated in the struggle against border crime nor in the reform and preparations aiming at adjusting to the EU requirements. Its activities and measures are the result of national plans defined by the National Integration Strategy, and are accompanied by the assistance from Union partners, in particular the German Federal Border Guard (BGS).

The discussion on challenges related to the enlargement process of the European Union, particularly in the area of Justice and Home Affairs, is an important one. Border services represent an important link in the system of institutional protections in all of our countries. Threats related to the spread of world-wide terrorism, illegal migration, large-scale smuggling, money laundering, and drug trade transit – all presently having features of international organised crime – all manifest the different problems that border services have to face. Effectively operating against these unwanted behaviours is one of the criteria of evaluating public and private services, including efforts both by the government and by society at large. Attempting to deal with these problems independently would doom them collectively to failure. The present and foreseen migration situations, especially, require joint and co-ordinated action.

19.2 THE OPINION OF THE POLISH BORDER GUARD: THE COMMISSION'S FEASIBILITY STUDY ON EUROPEAN BORDER SERVICE

The actions undertaken by the Border Guard (BG) of the Republic of Poland in recent years have caused a limitation of transit migration into Western Europe as well as to Poland itself. Polish Border Guard policies have thus contributed to a radical decrease in the number of foreigners readmitted via the Western border. The force carries out its tasked obligations following the Aliens Act that effectively governs the rules of state migration policy.

In 2001, and the first half of 2002, the Border Guard continued actions aimed at the limitation of illegal migration and organised crime of a border character. The effectiveness of reconnaissance, border control, and administrative activities have each been improved, resulting in an increase in the apprehension of migrants attempting to cross the border into Poland illegally; these improvements have particularly affected the Eastern border and particularly the section with Ukraine, where the threat posed by illegal migration is the largest. An additional decrease in the number of aliens readmitted to Germany has been achieved. The realisation of responsibilities imposed on the Border Guard within the national system of alien expulsions has lately been at a very high level.

The Border Guard has now entered into the crucial period of adjustment to the standards of the EU acquis. The conditions for effective protection of the EU external border should all be met by the end of 2003. The works aimed at sealing the state border protection and control system at sections that will become in the future part of the external border of the EU and setting up of the system of security measures, which will compensate the abolition of controls at the internal border, are continuing on schedule. The tightness of the Polish border in the East has systematically grown – for instance in 2001 five new border patrol stations have been introduced to the system, while a further four will be opened by the end of this year (2002). By the end of 2004 an additional nine stations will be established along various points at the Polish border. The main consequence of the new stations will be the shortening of the average section protected by one border patrol station to about 20 km. Preparatory works related to the launch of a technical system of border surveillance are ongoing. Also, development of an Automated Radar System of the territorial sea and internal waters has commenced.

In order to ensure performance of tasks in line with the EU's expectations, the BG has been subject to the process of changes in the area of competencies, organisational structure and human resources. The bases for these changes were the amendments to the Border Guard Act that entered into force in April 2001; these legislative changes have been followed by organisational changes. In relation to the expansion of power to operate on the whole territory of the state, given to the Border Guard, BG structures are now being established inland.

On 1 January 2002 organisational changes in the BG were initiated. Their aim is to define the precise area of competencies and responsibilities of individual departments of the Guard, which should be achieved by the end of 2002. A fully integrated management system is being developed through joining the border traffic control and border protection services into one comprehensive unit. The Polish Border Guard expects to make great strides in efficiency and success through better coordination and supervision of all tasks in direct state border protection, our border zone area and inland.

Furthermore, in May 2002 a new concept of training and vocational improvement has entered into force, the aim of which is to prepare inter-disciplinary officers, having theoretical as well as practical knowledge in border traffic controls and state border protection.

The objective of the Border Guard of the Republic of Poland is the further improvement of mobility and activities related to state border protection; improved cooperation with the border services of neighbouring states is a main part of this goal. The Polish Border Guard structure is indeed aware of the significance of multilateral and bilateral cooperation. A model example of such cooperation can be the interaction with the BGS. A significant step within the process was the signature on 18 February 2002 of the Polish–German Agreement on Cooperation of the Police and Border Services in Border Areas. The ratification process for this legislation is ongoing. The Polish and German border services want to undertake actions so that cooperation will achieve new levels of coordination. In order to do so we have established a working group, whose task it will be to prepare time frameworks and further organisational undertakings, which the parties will eventually introduce into everyday practice. It is also important to mention that the agreement contains significant provisions related to the powers of officers while performing duties on the territory of the second country. They are authorised to wear uniforms, carry weapons and to use measures of direct force. At the same time they are authorised to use the weapons and measures of direct force for self-protection purposes in cases and methods defined by the internal legal regulations of the country where the duty is performed. The agreement also governs the issues of processing and protection of personal data transmission as well as compensation claims in the territorial duties of the states.

The Border Guard (BG) aims at transferring selected forms of cooperation, verified within contacts with the BGS, into actions with the border services of the neighbouring states. Thus, for instance, it should be mentioned that in March 2002 a new form has been added to an already worked-out model of cooperation – the realisation of tasks by officers of both services in a contact and communication scheme. The initiative shows that that model of border protection at the Polish–Lithuanian border is based on modern solutions, verified in the EU and already known to the Polish Border Guard from Polish–German experiences.

The Polish Border Guard is in possession of basic information on the assumptions and plans related to the initiative of setting up of the European Border Service. A Polish delegation participated, along with others, in the conference held on 30 May in Rome.

The Border Guard of the Republic of Poland, as a border service of an EU Candidate Country, fully supports the concept of 'integrated protection' of the external border. Today – as a Candidate Country, and tomorrow, as a Member State – the PBG opts for and will support the need for common actions and practical solutions that aim at the improvement of protection and controls at external European borders. In the light of current and foreseen migration problems, the citizens of our states expect, from border services and other qualified groups, a greater degree of security. A commonality and clarity of concept is therefore needed.

The Polish Border Guard remains extremely interested in the development of cooperation with its counterparts from the EU states both within the cooperation based on twinning projects and through bilateral contacts. At the same time we declare active participation in drafting the unified procedures of a training system for European border services practitioners. A good training base exists in Poland and the participants are ready to develop a common project with EU partners in this area.

The Border Guard, as part of the border service of the future Member States, supports the proposals contained in the report presenting the feasibility study on the European Border Service which are aimed at:

- improvement of border services capabilities in strengthening the state borders' security;
- actions aimed at supporting and assisting introduction and dissemination of unified regulations and procedures on controls;
- drafting a common training system for border services;
- unification of requirements relating to equipment used in border protection and border traffic controls;
- support in the field of investments and modernization; and
- burden-sharing related to border protection and border traffic controls among EU Member States.

The Polish Border Guard follows each step of the discussion on the initiative with great attention. Poland would like to see their experts participating in the discussion as observers with the right to raise their own initiatives. They stand ready to share our experiences and achievements, which will serve well in the improvement of the security level at borders of EU Member States and Candidate Countries.

The Polish Border Guard welcomes the information that one of the recommendations of the European Commission within the common acquis is to draft a new version of the Common Manual on External Borders. It is indeed necessary to amalgamate the experts' work from border services of the Candidate Countries. The opportunity to participate in these works is of essential importance not only to the present EU Member States. It has to be remembered that in the foreseeable future the 'verified practices' contained in the Common Manual will also have to be met by border services of the present Candidate Countries.

The Polish Border Guard also sees the need to establish an institutional forum for chiefs of services responsible for protection and controls of borders of the EU Member States and Candidate Countries. We are in favour of the idea that such meetings would better serve the discussion of concrete issues and problems, of both scenario-specific and systemic types. The process should be given a maximal practical character. The leading subject of sessions should be defined flexibly, depending on needs and observed threats. The meetings should serve all parties well, among others in the context of pace and the challenges of the EU enlargement process, as well as the need to establish a readable coordination and cooperation mechanism among border services.

19.3 CONCLUSION

The proposals contained in the report on the possibilities of setting up a European Border Service have to be discussed widely and openly. There is no need to shy away from the truth that some assumptions and solutions are controversial and difficult to be imagined in practice today. There are various opinions, including the ones that are eagerly undertaken by the media, which tend to distort the initiative negatively. During the initial stages it will remain necessary to focus on those objectives that are to be achieved in the first, short-term period. The dynamics and level of development of these ideas should then indicate further priorities to be achieved at later dates. It will also represent an opportunity to verify and assess the feasibility of these proposals that at present have been indicated as mid-term and long-term objectives.

In the discussion on a possible European border corps the question of state sovereignty has often been raised. It seems that it would also be worth considering a different aspect, which is the role and place of national border services of individual countries in the national system of state security. It is important in the context of NATO membership of most of the EU Member States and Poland, the Czech Republic and Hungary, as well as the planned enlargement of the organisation, in the foreseeable future, by some of the other Candidate Countries. Finally, as far as Poland is concerned, which to the East borders countries that are not Pact members and that in the foreseeable future are not going to be candidates for membership, the Border Guard has tasks in the area of state security that are defined by the law.

20. The Transformation of Border Controls: What is different about Europe?

Malcom Anderson

20.1 INTRODUCTION

The specifics of border controls are often regarded as belonging to the detail of public administration, but they raise very large political questions about the authority of states and the nature of the European Union (Torpey 1999). A consideration of what is specific to Europe and what are shared common features with North America should serve as a background to developing EU border policy. Setting current developments in the EU in a comparative and historical context involves re-visiting some familiar, but crucially important, ground. Although aspects of the changing significance of borders in the last two decades are global phenomena, the ways in which the movement of persons across European frontiers has altered are more far-reaching and complex than elsewhere.

These changes are associated with turbulent and rapid political developments in the various phases of the Cold War leading to the collapse of communism, and from the beginnings of regional economic integration to the inauguration of a 'European Union'. The transformation of border controls in the European Union may give some indications about possible scenarios for other parts of the industrialised world, particularly in North America. There are, however, specific factors in the development of the EU that are not, and may never be, present elsewhere (Anderson 1996).

20.2 A BRIEF HISTORICAL OVERVIEW

The different historical experiences of the North American and the European states have been marked and contribute to stereotypical outlooks that, in present circumstances, diverge and result in mutual incomprehension. These experiences can only be sketched here in a brief, broad brush-stroke fashion.

In Europe, by historic standards, there has been a remarkable shift from the closed borders of the 1940s to the open borders within the EU, and the relatively open borders with the rest of the world, at the end of the 20th century (Anderson 1996). Warfare and threats to physical security from neighbouring states were the overwhelming influence on attitudes towards frontiers until the end of, and in many cases, until after the Second World War. The security, economic and political barriers represented by borders were formidable in the middle of the 20th century. In Western Europe this was evident by the procedures in place at border crossings; persons and their belongings were scrutinised individually and very closely at border posts. Foreigners, even from friendly countries, were treated with suspicion. Borders were patrolled by law enforcement agencies; they were clearly marked by obstacles, very often fences, and there was a strong military presence in frontier regions. Passports and visas were necessary for temporary visitors to other countries, residence permits and work permits were required for longer periods of residence; police agencies imposed reporting systems on aliens, and visits to work sites where they were employed were common. The infringement of any regulation usually resulted in immediate deportation without any right of appeal. The executive authority of the state reigned supreme, reflecting a particular view of state sovereignty in which only citizens had rights.

Running through Central Europe, from the Baltic to the Mediterranean (or Black Sea), was the most closed border in recent European peacetime history. This 'Iron Curtain' shared characteristics with other closed borders, both in symbolic representation and in practical forms of control. The symbolism, exemplified by the propaganda of both the Free World and the Communist bloc, represented a line between good and evil, truth and error, justice and oppression, democracy and dictatorship. In practical terms, the frontier was fortified, lined with watch towers, patrolled by dogs, and guards with orders to shoot to kill, and, over part of its length, lethal automatic firing devices.

The kinds of controls exercised on people by the communist states were draconian. They required exit visas; emigration was not normally allowed; and occasionally exile was used as an instrument of policy. Some communist countries ransomed their own nationals and allowed foreign governments to purchase the right of exit for, in particular, Jews and ethnic Germans. It was taken for granted that states had not only the right but the legitimate authority to control all activities on their territory and to do this they needed, in principle, absolute control of passage across their borders. The states' monopolisation of the right to authorise movement (Torpey 1999) became entrenched.

The contrast with the North American experience is sharp; mentalities about frontiers have been shaped very differently. For a century and a half before 1945, there was, for the USA, no major security threat from any neighbouring state. The burning of the frontier town of Columbus by Pablo Vilar in 1916 and the retaliatory US raid into Mexico was the last spark of a 19th Century conflagration, during which the United States annexed about half of the territory of Mexico. The US–Canada border has never been effectively militarised and was completely undefended in the 20th century. Both borders were lightly policed and were not obstacles to people determined to enter the USA without proper documentation. Physical distance made the territory of the North American states relatively secure from security threats until the arrival of long-range military aircraft and, above all, the inter-continental missile. The United States was reluctantly and belatedly involved in both World Wars, and it was only in the post-Second World War era that the country became convinced that involvement in a system of collective security was essential to its physical safety and the security of its interests. After a flurry of concern, which some considered bordering on paranoia, over the Soviet threat, a sense of physical invulnerability persisted until it was radically and dramatically broken by the events of 11 September 2001.

Another long-term contrast has been the different experiences of migration of people. Although there have been large movements of people in Europe in recent history, no nation in Europe, by contrast with the USA and Canada, has been built on immigration. The contrast between the two continents can be too sharply drawn, particularly as France in 1930 had a higher proportion of immigrants in its population than the USA, but the psychological differences remained profound. Anti-immigrant feelings have been present in the USA at least since the anti-Irish Boston riots of the 1830s and immigration has been controlled since the early 20th century because of fears that too many people of the 'wrong' kind of ethnic and cultural categories were arriving. But there remains a widespread belief, remarkably absent in the Member States of the EU, that immigration is a perfectly normal phenomenon and of benefit to the country. There has, as a consequence, been a widespread tolerance of those who have entered the country illegally. Until 1986, it was not an offence to employ an undocumented immigrant and, even after that date, the penalties were insignificant and rarely imposed. The US has also, with certain notorious exceptions, been more willing to receive refugees and asylum seekers than most Western European states.

The major change, now, in Western Europe is that for 13 of the 15 members of the European Union, there are no border controls on persons (or goods) between the Member States. Any citizens, whether in employment or engaged in any legitimate activity or retired, can freely settle in any other member state of the Union. To achieve free movement of labour the contracting parties first gave social and economic rights to citizens of the other Member States. Barriers to free movement, such as the non-equivalence of professional qualifications and health regulations, were negotiated away. Freedom of movement was finally achieved by the 1991 Treaty of Maastricht, which gave rights of residence to non-active citizens as well as certain political rights to all EU citizens resident in other Member States. In concord the 1996 implementation of the Schengen accords abolished systematic controls on persons at the internal borders between Schengen Member States. The border as a limit of political rights and political activity was eroded; EU citizens resident in other Member States can vote in local and European elections; representation of citizens and of interests through European institutions is now a well-established reality. In the border regions of Member States, trans-frontier cooperation between local and regional authorities became standard practice (Anderson 1998).

In Eastern Europe radical changes in the practices of border controls occurred with dramatic suddenness. When, in 1989, the German Democratic Republic could no longer control its borders, it collapsed. The disintegration of the Soviet bloc and communist regimes resulted in the appearance of about 8000 miles of new international borders in Central and Eastern Europe, mostly drawn along the lines of old internal administrative boundaries. It also introduced a brief moment of euphoria when freedom of movement for all in Europe seemed a possibility. This euphoria quickly disappeared as Western governments became alarmed by the possibility of a mass movement of people, following the precedent of the exodus of East Germans, from East to West. 'Joining the West' was the clear aspiration of the peoples and governments of East Central Europe.

20.3 THE COMPLEXITY OF THE TRANSFORMATION

The changes in European borders in the last half-century have been, therefore, complex. Although no longer militarised and so obviously repressive, frontiers remain crucially important political, administrative, legal, and cultural/linguistic lines of division. They retain basic control functions in Central and Eastern Europe and at the EU external border. The dismantling of border controls within the EU and the increased permeability of borders apparent throughout the highly developed world have led to anxieties, even fears, which are exploited in electoral competition. Frontiers may no longer be threatened by military action in Europe (although the Kosovo case has shown that, in exceptional circumstances, this is possible); nonetheless the inviolability of frontiers remains an essential part of contemporary notions of security.

Anxieties and fears, both among ordinary citizens and among governing elites, about security in Europe are difficult to pin down. They are linked to the great economic and technological transformations of the late 20th century. Feelings of powerlessness and vulnerability produced by international mergers, international financial transactions and new technologies are difficult to assess. Cultural insecurity is triggered by the vast diffusion of popular cultural products and the dominance of the English language. Added to these are insecurities about crime, frequently associated with foreigners, and whether crime is politically motivated terrorist actions or various kinds of organised trafficking, involving the use or the threat of violence. More immediate anxieties concern street crime, often linked (sometimes in an exaggerated way) with immigrant groups. Control of territory is still regarded as important in mitigating some of the effects of these developments but the borders of states are now perceived as much more permeable.

Another kind of anxiety, mainly confined to administrative and political elites, is based on the absence of consensus about the direction and speed of European integration. Borders within the EU remain, with marginal exceptions, the limits of criminal and civil law jurisdictions, executive police powers, public administration, educational systems, tax regimes (excepting tariffs), social security systems and most non-governmental organisations. If present trends continue, breaches in these limits will increasingly be made and there will be progressive integration of public institutions across borders (with systems of coordination characteristic of federal systems), a more rapid integration of social organisations and an increase in the numbers of cross-border mergers. But there is an ever-present risk that some of these trends may be blocked by recalcitrant electorates.

Security, in the more restricted state-centred meaning, has been undergoing a conceptual shift; the boundary between internal and external security has been eroded. The reasons for this shift are threefold. First, and probably the most important, is the disappearance of a direct military threat to Member States of a kind previously represented by the USSR. Second, for a widespread conviction to exist that a basic justification for the coercive power of the state is the ability to defend the security of its citizens – some threat to their security must therefore exist. In practice, in order to try to fulfil this obligation, the police have been obliged to operate trans-frontier networks (Bigo 1996, 1997 and 1998). Third, new areas of policy have emerged in the late 20th century as the problems facing advanced industrial societies change. The effect of these factors is that a new kind of security discourse is emerging. Threats to the security of EU Member States are now perceived more criminal than conventional military threats: mafias, drugs, illegal immigrants, traffic in human beings, and trade in illegal goods (arms, child pornography, body parts, nuclear materials). Also present now are threats to public order by violent elements coming from neighbouring countries (football hooligans, disorderly holiday makers, political demonstrators) or the spill-over effects of conflicts such as those in Algeria, Turkey and ex-Yugoslavia through refugee crises and terrorist action. In addition the concept of security has been extended to 'societal security' – threats to human rights, to the environment, and to cultures.

Conceptions of security have evolved in similar ways in Europe and the US since the end of the Cold War. Fear of crime (organised crime and drug trafficking) and terrorism (politically motivated outrages) has led both in the US and the European cases, to a reorientation of police, intelligence and military priorities. It has also led to a tightening of border checks and security at border crossings. This was a key element in the far-reaching plan, announced by President Bush on 6 June 2002, for reorganising agencies concerned with 'homeland security', with particular emphasis on intelligence services and coordination of the agencies concerned with border controls.

The publicly proclaimed objectives or aims of border management are similar in the European and the US cases. Both the EU and the US aspire to create a system of border checks which effectively control movement of all persons across their frontiers with third countries, exclude undocumented migrants and undesirable persons, and remain important forms of crime control, particularly trafficking in people, drugs and other illegal commodities. There is a broad similarity of results achieved – whatever successes are claimed in terms of exclusion of illegal immigrants or impressive quantities of drugs seized, as measured by the availability and price of drugs and estimates of other kinds of criminal activity, are not commensurate with the resources employed. The response of governments is not, as it may be in other areas of policy, to consider a change of policy but to attempt to achieve better control of borders by the deployment of more resources. This is, from one point of view, understandable because previous attempts to tighten up border controls seem to have foundered on lack of resources. In the early 1950s Operation Wetback succeeded in expelling well over one million Mexican clandestine immigrants but within a maximum of two to three years they were back to their previous numbers.

The celebrated 1986 immigration act IRCOM held up illegal immigration until it was realised that the workplace controls introduced by the act were not being applied because the INS lacked the resources. Similarly, the processing of asylum seekers or illegal immigrants destined for expulsion has been so slow in some North European states that applicants have acquired some title to residence by finding work and raising families whilst the system for processing their dossiers clogs because of the numbers of asylum seekers/clandestine immigrants. They acquired entitlements by residence and establishment. In Southern European states, the situation has become untenable and general amnesties of undocumented immigrants have been promulgated. All these cases suggest that more resources could have made a difference. Similarly the deployment of more personnel and more technology has stemmed the flow of illegal immigrants at some places on the US–Mexican border and the Caribbean as well as on the EU external frontier. Closer examination suggests that the argument is not entirely plausible.

Particular border problems have marked similarities in the US and European cases. The arrival of undocumented immigrants, escaping in unseaworthy boats, is familiar circumstance to both entities. Both penury and political oppression have been features of the Caribbean Sea frontier of the US and the Mediterranean frontier of the EU (Spener 2000). Over the last decade, the Mediterranean has frequently been called Europe's Rio Grande. The migratory pressures and the chasm in the relative per capita incomes on the two sides of the borders are broadly similar in both scenarios. They are economic, demographic and, in some broad respects, cultural frontiers (see King 1998). These examples suggest that there are some basic common features of a global frontier separating the rich from the poor. While these situations pose local problems, the solutions are not local.

20.4 COOPERATION IN BORDER CONTROLS

There is no institutionalised system or arrangement of border control to control movement of persons into the territory of the North American Free Trade Area. There are US pressures on Mexico and Canada to tighten up their border checks with a view to filtering out illegal immigrants and terrorists that may seek to enter US territory. There have been considerable instances of intelligence sharing between the Canadian and US border control authorities, as well as law enforcement authorities, more generally. Some sharing takes place with the Mexicans, especially via the El Paso Intelligence Centre (EPIC), which has an intelligence and coordinating role for the US–Mexican border. There are severe limits to the amount of intelligence sharing on this border because of the prevalence of corruption, which is not limited to the Mexican side but remains a serious problem. There was a severe tightening of checks on this border in the aftermath of 11 September 2001, with long queues developing at border check points and intensified 'inland' checks in the border region and a resultant depressing effect on the economy of the border regions. Commuter traffic was disrupted; goods delayed and new cross-border economic projects were suspended or cancelled.

One effect of 11 September was partially to officially establish the presence of Mexican undocumented immigrants in the US by accepting a card issued by the Mexican consulates as proof of identity. The card has helped to improve relations with the police because it establishes a nationality and a personal identity. This new facility could well have the effect of an incentive to more immigration by Mexicans. This could presage relatively free movement of labour between the US and Mexico. Since there has been a longstanding movement south by well-educated Canadians, qualified free movement between the three members of NAFTA may now be a distinct possibility in the future. If this is the case, the North American equivalent of the Schengen system could compensate for the relative loss of control at the borders between the three members of NAFTA and ensure that their external border is as tightly controlled as possible. With the exception of the abolition of border controls, which will have to remain in place on the US–Mexican border for the foreseeable future, the rest of the Schengen system could be adapted to the rather different conditions of NAFTA, if the political will existed. The fundamental flaw would remain that such a system would inevitably be US-dominated. For cultural, political and symbolic reasons there would be great hesitations by both Mexico and Canada about adopting the system.

For them to accept the proposal for the management of the EU external borders published by the Council of the EU on 31 May 2002, would be unthinkable. The three (out of 25) proposals which are the most radical are the setting up of an external borders practitioners unit, a rapid response unit and the establishment of a European Border Police. The European Border Police remains a vague idea; the relations with Member States' border police, the legal basis and the geographical scope of its operations have all to be worked out. The idea has, however, been placed firmly on the agenda and is likely to be implemented in some form.

20.5 CONCLUSION

Several general propositions and arguments emerge from the remarkable evolution of border control regimes in Europe, which also have relevance for North America.

There is undoubtedly a connection between border controls and the nature of political regimes. Authoritarian, repressive regimes are threatened by open borders and cannot tolerate them. If compelled by circumstances to open their borders, they must either reform or collapse. This was as true of Japan in 1853, when Commodore Perry enforced access to the Japanese market for Western goods. A similar scenario unfolded for the Communist bloc countries after 1989. By contrast, liberal regimes, with a respect for human rights and based on a market economy, cannot impose an exclusive and rigorously enforced border control regime without compromising their basic values. One anxiety in Europe is that an EU regime of tight immigration controls will lead to a more controlled and policed society with increased surveillance of individuals and of certain geographical areas. In the United States, civil liberties concerns, as well as economic interest, have acted as a constraint on certain forms of immigration control; this is likely also to be the case in Europe. However, the reaction to 11 September inaugurated increased surveillance of populations within the US and a closer control of the frontier; these risk the strengthening of authoritarian aspects of American government.

Second, border controls necessarily vary according to the nature of international economic relationships. In simple terms, the full implementation of the 'Four Freedoms' (for movement of capital, labour, goods and services) contained in the 1957 Treaty of Rome inevitably led to the abolition of all border controls. There was an important sub-text to these freedoms – the political ambition, stated in the preamble to the Treaty of Rome, for 'an ever closer union' between the European peoples. A free trade area, such as NAFTA, does not carry with it the same implications or express the same political ambition. But a slow and hesitant introduction of freedom of movement is probable in NAFTA.

Third, there has been a certain de-territorialization of border controls in both Europe and North America. Controls are now exercised in the consulates, by transportation companies through the use of carrier liability legislation, by third countries on transit traffic, by internal controls on identity by police and other public services, and by the Schengen external frontier. Also, immigration diplomacy, seeking the cooperation of countries from which immigrants originate, is becoming increasingly important for the EU and the USA as a means of controlling migration flows. In 2002, Presidents George Bush and Vicente Fox came to agreement on a target for development aid, the poorer regions of Mexico, which provide most of the illegal immigrants to the US. The fundamental difference between Europe and North America is that in the latter region no general agreement exists in NAFTA to cover all aspects of border controls.

Fourth, the effectiveness of border controls on persons is open to question. The USA and the EU share a similar problem of immigration crises provoked by political persecution, penury and violence in other countries. Also, there are large numbers of undocumented immigrants in both the USA and the EU. Ways of dealing with this latter issue have varied across Europe. Uniformly stringent enforcement of controls faces three obstacles – it is too expensive, too disruptive and too threatening to human rights; moreover, it sometimes runs counter to certain powerful economic interests. In the USA, certain economic sectors in particular regions would suffer without illegal Mexican immigration. The amounts of force used and arbitrary action taken by authorities charged with border control are limited by public opinion, to include well-organised human rights groups. In the absence of the reality of controls, a certain myth of control is substituted. This myth is necessary to sustain the legitimacy of the EU and its member states, and maintain political support in America for the Bush administration.

Fifth, the modern state is inextricably bound to a clearly defined territory as well as a clearly defined membership. The clearly delimited territories of the modern state are of recent origin and there is no reason, in principle, why they should persist indefinitely. But we cannot, despite the progress of European integration, envisage a system in which all the security, protections, services and benefits provided by the modern state can be organised without delimited territories. In the EU, by contrast with the NAFTA, this situation is evolving because responsibility for access to territory is being shared and a European security community is being built. The 'decoupling' of police from the state has, in Europe, become an issue for discussion. The nature of the debate in North America is very different because it focuses almost exclusively on the extra-territorial operations of US law enforcement agencies.

Sixth, the concentration of frontier functions on the linear state border is beginning to break down in obvious ways, such as the transfer of national border controls to the EU external border (and where possible to the borders of neighbouring states) and embryonic federalisation of police cooperation. There are also less obvious ways – Thomas Faist has argued that the boundaries of welfare provision no longer correspond with the borders of the state, with the establishment of supra-national rights and the different regimes for third-country nationals within the EU. Different frontiers are being established, in terms of direct or indirect effects of decisions, for different areas of policy. This is also happening in North America because, as Mexicans and Canadians are often sensitively aware, policy decisions taken in the USA within NAFTA have a direct impact on them.

Seventh, the debate has begun on the criteria for admission of persons to the EU, whether immigrants officially resident in the EU should be able to move freely between the Member States, and whether the civil liberties of immigrants should be more adequately protected. Without the implementation of common rules in these areas, EU immigration policy will remain, at the moment, an aspiration. However, EU countries are committed to movement towards a common immigration policy – in NAFTA, this is not considered a possibility.

These seven points show some overlap between European and North American (NAFTA) concerns, but the debate in Europe is both wider and deeper because of the inherent nature of the EU. The main analogy between the EU and North America is the problem of control of persons at the US–Mexico border and the external border of the EU. One feature of the US–Mexico border experience which is almost bound to be reflected in Europe is that drives towards strengthening border controls in some places simply have a displacement effect – illegal immigrants are diverted to those sectors of the border where the enhanced controls are not in place.

The US Caribbean Sea frontier shows precise parallels with the EU Mediterranean frontier – persistent immigration pressure punctuated by crises. What Nevins describes as the 'NAFTA-ization' of the US–Mexico border – the promotion of 'extra-territorial opportunities for national territory-based capital whilst attempting to provide security against the social costs unleashed by globalisation – especially immigration', approximates to what is happening between the EU and its neighbours. Encouraging cross-border economic flows while enforcing strict border controls on persons is, as Andreas observes, a delicate political task shared by the USA and the EU.

REFERENCES

Anderson, M. (1996), *Frontiers: Territory and State Formation in the Modern World*, Cambridge: Polity.

Anderson, M. et al. (1996), *Policing the European Union: Theory Law and Practice*, Oxford: Clarendon Press.

Anderson, M. (1998), 'Transfrontier Cooperation – History and Theory', in G. Brunn, P. Schmitt-Egner (eds) *Grenzüberschreitende Zusammenarbeit in Europa. Theorie–Empirie–Praxis*, Baden Baden: Nomos.

Anderson, M. (2000), 'Transfrontier Cooperation and Assessment', in L. Hedegaard and B. Lindström (eds), *North European and Baltic Integration Yearbook*, Berlin: Springer Verlag.

Bigo, D. (1996), *Polices en Réseaux: l'Expérience Européenne*, Paris: Presses de Sciences Po.

Bigo, D. (1997), 'Security, Borders and the State', in P. Ganster, A. Sweedler, J. Scott and W. D. Eberwein (eds.) *Borders and Border Regions in Europe and North America*, San Diego: San Diego University Press.

Bigo, D. (1998), 'Frontiers and Security in the European Union', in M. Anderson and E. Bort, *The Frontiers of Europe*, London: Pinter, pp. 148–64.

Faist, T. (1995), 'Boundaries of Welfare States; Immigrants and Social Rights on the National and Supranational Levels', in R. Miles and D Thränhardt (eds), *Migration and European Integration. The Dynamics of Inclusion and Exclusion*, London: Pinter, pp. 177–95.

Huysmans, J. (1998), 'Dire et écrire la sécurité: le dilemme normatif des études de sécurité', Paris: *Cultures et Conflits*, no. 31–2, pp. 177–202.

King, R. (1998), 'The Mediterranean: Europe's Rio Grande', in M. Anderson and E. Bort, *The Frontiers of Europe*, London: Pinter, pp. 109–34.

King, R. (1998), 'Towards a pattern of immigration into Southern Europe', in M. Anderson and E. Bort (eds), *Schengen and the Southern Frontier of the Europe Union*, Edinburgh: ISSI, pp. 115–40.

Leo, R. (1998), 'Schengen and its Daily Practice on the Borders. The Particular Situation in Friuli Venezia Giulia', in M. Anderson and E. Bort (eds), *Schengen and the Southern Frontier of the European Union*, Edinburgh: ISSI.

Spener, D. (2000), 'The Logic and Contradictions of Intensified Border Enforcement in Texas', in P. Andreas and T. Snyder (eds), *The Wall around the West*, Lanham: Rowman & Littlefield, pp. 115–38.

Torpey, J. (1999), *The Invention of the Passport: Surveillance, Citizenship and the State*, New York: Cambridge University Press.

Waever, O., B. Buzan, M. Kelstrup, and P. Lemaitre (1998), *Identity, Migration and the New Security Agenda in Europe*, London: Pinter.

Walker, N. (1998), 'The New Frontiers of European Policing', in M. Anderson and E. Bort (eds), *The Frontiers of Europe*, London: Pinter, pp. 165–86.

21. Ramifications of Enlargement for EU–Russia Relations and the Schengen Regime

Olga Potemkina

21.1 INTRODUCTION

Lithuania and Poland, both EU-candidate countries for the next round of enlargement, surround Kaliningrad, a part of Russia, as an enclave. This singular instance manifests the complexities of border management in the developing Union. As a unique phenomenon in the history of the European integration, it has raised never-before-seen issues relating to flexibilities in border crossing or the establishment of border agreements between the ex-Soviet countries.

From the EU side this puzzle of security concerns reaches beyond to further states. This chapter describes in particular the nexus between the Russian perspective and the Schengen regime.

21.2 SEEKING POLITICAL AND SECURITY BALANCE

Achieving balance between an open and secure Union, as well as between external and internal security, has become a task of top priority on the eve of the EU eastward expansion. Enlargement will no doubt cause significant changes in the European political landscape; the CEE countries will become new Member States and the countries of the 'near abroad' or 'direct neighbourhood' will be located along the whole perimeter of a new EU eastern border. The border will separate new Member States from equally new non-members: Russia, Ukraine, Belarus, and Moldova. Obviously, these countries will be obliquely involved in the enlargement process, as they are deeply connected with the future new Member States by common economic, social and cultural traditions. Besides, the policy of 'fuzzy borders' mainly presupposes expansion of the EU's influence on the adjacent countries. The example to be referred is the 'Northern Dimension' programme. Being beyond the purposes of Russia's accession to the European Union, it was intended for the closer engagement of Russian northern and western regions with the European integration. Thus, the EU has declared its desire to promote elimination of any barriers and dividing lines in Europe while at the same time to create an open Union, safe for its citizens. It is not casually that both processes – enlargement and building the European Area of Freedom, Security and Justice (AFSJ) – have been developing in parallel. As the enlargement is approaching its final stage, the collision between the internal and external policies of the EU becomes more and more visible (see Grabbe 2000). To a large extent, the challenges have emerged because of the dividing of the EU security policies (external and internal) between its three pillars, as well as the lack of a single mechanism for the coordination of security issues.

The aims that the EU is now attempting to achieve have a number of controversial aspects. From one side, the European AFSJ has been created to protect the EU citizens from 'dangers', which are expected to come from the East and abroad– illegal immigration, terrorism and drug trafficking. As it was stated by J.Zielonka, 'a hard-border regime may be difficult to maintain vis-à-vis the most advanced applicant states from central and Eastern Europe. However, if the EU's borders are with assertive and potentially unstable regional powers such as Russia, Iraq or Serbia, than an open, fuzzy type of border regime may well be questioned' (see Zielonka 2002). But at the same time, the EU external dimension is supposed to promote good relationships with the neighbouring countries by the means of building Euroregions, for example. The recent developments have proved it very problematic to combine both purposes in one project. While trying to balance between requirements of internal security and interests of external policies, the EU is gradually shifting towards maintaining the internal security at the expense of stability of the adjacent states and their border regions. But it should be mentioned that they are very soon to become buffer zones and to hold all the 'threats', from which the EU tries to protect its nationals. The absence of a political and legal mechanism for interaction with the countries of the 'direct neighbourhood' prevents a balance being reached between an open and secure Union.

The EU cooperation with Russia as well as with the other countries of 'near abroad' could obviously be placed in the context of the EU internal and external conflicting goals. The states could be considered in some cases as a source and transit of/for illegal migration and human trafficking and, at the same time, a buffer zone, which faces moral and financial challenges in dealing with a large inflow of migrants. The declared partners in the fight against organised crime and terrorism are, simultaneously, a peril that should be treated with proper caution and limited trust. According to how the

European Union reaches the balance between its internal and external policies, the EU cooperation with its 'near abroad' is to become a success or failure. Respectively, the ability of the EU future neighbours to combine protection of national interests with acceptance of the rules, which the 'civilised countries' have to implement, can provide for the achievements in the common struggle with organised crime.

As was outlined in the Political Declaration on Friendly Schengen Border Policy (FSBP) (see Emerson 2001),[1] several areas along the future European Union eastern border could be adversely affected, when the enlargement will move the present Schengen border eastwards. Among the regions in view there are:

- borders between Ukraine and the applicant countries (Poland, Hungary, Slovakia and Romania), which are crossed by many people depending on cross-border trade;
- the border between Moldova and Romania, with Moldavians acquiring dual Moldavian and Romanian citizenship to minimise their potential losses from Romania's joining the Schengen area;
- the Narva–Ivangorod border between Estonia and Russia; and
- borders of Russian Kaliningrad with Lithuania and Poland.

The recommendations of FSBP for the facilitated border crossings were elaborated, including provision of adequate consular services; upgrading of border facilities; special bilateral agreements for border regions, such as long-term multi-entry national visas at a low charge, short-term visas etc. Two Russian borderland regions were referred to in the Declaration.

The next chapter gives a more precise examination of Russian perspectives and views on the expected impact of the candidate countries accepting the package of Schengen rules.

21.3 NEW BORDERS OF THE EU: CHALLENGES FOR RUSSIA

In 1999 the list of the so-called 'Russian concerns' for the consequences of the EU enlargement was forwarded to the European Commission by the Russian government. The Schengen regime was mentioned in the list. The problem is that up to the present time there are few politicians in Russia, who

[1] The Declaration was adopted by the Conference on New European Borders and Security Cooperation: Promoting Trust in an Enlarged European Union, Brussels, 6–7 July 2001, organised by the Centre for European Policy studies (CEPS), Brussels, the SITRA Foundation, Helsinki, and the Stefan Batory Foundation, Warsaw.

know what the Schengen acquis is. References are usually made to the Schengen Agreement (1985), and sometimes to the Schengen Implementation Agreement (1990). Meanwhile, another document is worth focusing on – this is the Protocol,[2] integrating the Schengen acquis into the European Union. It provided for the system of 'inclusion–exclusion' of the Member States, the future Member States and the third countries into/from the European AFSJ (see Monar 2000, p. 15).

The desire to be included in the Schengen zone has served as a stimulus for the candidates to accept the JHA acquis. The prospects for their joining the Schengen group are not the same as those fixed in the Protocols for the UK, Ireland and Denmark, as well as for Norway and Iceland.[3] No manoeuvres in the relations with their eastern neighbours are supposed. According to Art. 8 of the Protocol,[4] the Schengen acquis is to be accepted in full. The impact of this provision became clear as early as in 1998. At the ministerial meeting of the Member States with the applicants it was explained that the strict implementation of the Protocol means the impossibility of maintaining the special agreements for the facilitated visa regime between the candidate countries and their neighbours (Den Boer 2002). Thus, on the eve of enlargement the European Union took care to protect its future borders, having provided the grounds for the exclusion of its future neighbours from the Schengen area. This decision is to be implemented along the whole long eastern border of the EU with Ukraine (1152 kilometres), Belarus (1248 kilometres), and Moldova (450 kilometres) and with Russia, since when its border with the EU will become longer and reach 2257 kilometres.

The border between the EU and Russia after the accession of Estonia, Lithuania, Latvia and Poland will run across Tchudskoe Lake (Peipsy Jarve), Pskovskoe Lake, as well as Pskov, Leningrad and Kaliningrad oblast. The acceptance of the Schengen acquis by the candidate countries has the direct negative impact on Russia of introducing the strict visa regime instead of a liberal one, which allowed the borderland population to cross borders rather easily, to travel, to trade and to run businesses. As was already mentioned, the Schengen borders were considered as one of the Russian 'concerns' about the enlargement. While preparing for the accession, the candidate countries began to introduce measures that have gradually tightened the visa regimes:

1. After becoming independent, the Baltic States started elaborating the visa and migration policies according to the Euro-Atlantic orientation. It was always emphasised that the countries of the Baltic are expected to take 'responsibility for the security of one third of the whole EU

[2] Protocol is mentioned in the Amsterdam Treaty, Art.K.12 (5), further on, Protocol integrating the Schengen Acquis into the Framework of the European Union (hereinafter: Protocol).
[3] It is mentioned in the Amsterdam Treaty, Art.73q.
[4] Protocol integrating the Schengen Acquis into the framework of the European Union.

border after the enlargement.' As early as 1993 a visa regime had been introduced between Russia, Latvia, Lithuania and Estonia, but special exemptions were preserved for several categories of the population in Russia and Belarus. The provisions were made for the facilitated procedure of the issuing of visas for the border area population. However, even this facilitated procedure was not enough for maintaining the existing volume of border crossings, which fell by approximately 13% in 2000, as a result of an abolition of the simplified cross-border regime (see Cholewinski 2002, p. 107). To obtain a visa, even if it is long-term and multi-entry, Narva residents had to go to Pskov or Saint Petersburg. Besides, the factor of residence in a border region was not itself a reason to claim privilege for getting a visa. Only residents who wished to meet relatives in the border area belonging to Estonia, to visit graves of the relatives as well as those possessing property on the other side of the border, received a right to such privileges. The Russian authorities have expressed their dissatisfaction with the whole procedure that brought the Ivan-gorod residents a lot of inconvenience. The concerns were partly taken into account: the visa regime has been preserved, but the adjacent countries – Russia and Estonia – have agreed on issuing free multiple-entry visas for about 4000 borderland residents with a need to cross the border frequently. However, the existing plans to create a new Euroregion, including Estonian border regions and the Russian Pskov oblast, demand more thought to be devoted to developing the small border traffic model.

2. The visa regime on Russia's borders with Latvia and Estonia has been discussed in the format of bilateral relations. The main problem is still the 'absence of border agreements' among the states. It will have to be solved in the course of enlargement and creation of a 'friendly cross-border regime'. Actually, the expansion of the Schengen rules to the Russian–Estonian and Russian–Latvian borders is not able to change the environment, as the borders had been already closed.
3. As for the Central and East European countries, they did not undertake any steps to tighten the visa regime until the end of the 1990s. The citizens of Russia, as well as those of Ukraine, Belarus and Moldova used 'vouchers and other privileges in obtaining visas' for their trips to Poland, Czech Republic, Slovakia and Hungary. The statistics show that cross-border trade and intensive human contacts between these countries flourished in this period (see Cichocki 2001, p. 170). In 1997, Poland, meeting the EU requirements, adopted the Aliens Law, according to which the requirements for entries became stricter, and the price of vouchers increased. In a year Russia took measures in response to this. The volume of cross-border trade, which fell sharply

after 'the border crisis' in 1998, has never been restored. Nevertheless, Lithuania and Poland, having both initiated visas for Russians, preserved exemptions for the visa-free transit between Russia and Kaliningrad. But even then it was already clear that before the enlargement these privileges would be cancelled.

4. In October 2001 the Lithuanian government came forward with a 'draft Plan for the implementation of the Schengen acquis'. According to the plan, residents of Kaliningrad oblast were to lose their right to visa-free entry to Lithuania from 1 January 2003. In summer 2002 the EU negotiations with the candidate countries on JHA were finalised, and the respective chapters were closed. The countries took responsibility for strengthening their border regimes with their eastern neighbours in the near future. For example, Poland is to realise the costly programme of modernisation of its whole border infrastructure with Russia, Belarus and Ukraine. Modernisation does not mean only the equipping of the cross-border points, but strengthening control over the whole border environment. Thus, the border control for all Russian citizens was introduced as a measure for the preparation for joining the Schengen regime. In September 2002 Lithuania announced that the special facilitated visa regime for transit to Kaliningrad would be abolished from 1 January 2003.

21.4 THE KALININGRAD PUZZLE

The future of the Kaliningrad oblast has become an issue of Russian deep concern and the top priority question in the agenda of negotiations with the European Union, Poland and Lithuania. As a result of the enlargement, Kaliningrad will become a Russian exclave surrounded by the EU territory. Its border with Poland is 206 kilometres long, and with Lithuania – 227 kilometres long. It has been argued recently that Russia should have given its attention to Kaliningrad earlier, lack of time made it more difficult to find a solution for a special transit regime. This argument seems to lack credibility.

First, Kaliningrad, together with the Schengen regime, was included in the above mentioned list of Russia's concerns about the consequences of enlargement. Besides, as early as in 1999 the problem of Kaliningrad oblast was mentioned in the Medium-term strategy for the development of relations between the Russian Federation (RF) and the EU (2000 to 2010). The oblast was called 'a pilot project' for RF–EU cooperation in the 21st century.[5]

[5] The Medium-term strategy for the development of relations between the RF and the EU (2000 to 2010), Diplomaticheskii vestnik, 11: Nov. 1999, p.36.

Second, if the consultations had started earlier, would it have drastically changed the positions of the sides? The whole process of talks and the results themselves show that the factor of time has not played a great role. What are the major pieces of the puzzle?

a) In January 2001, in keeping with the Commission's Enlargement Strategy Paper of November 2000, the Communication from the Commission to the Council was issued to outline some ideas and options for discussions with Russia, Poland and Lithuania. It stressed that the adoption of the acquis by Poland and Lithuania would have an impact on third countries in terms of visa requirements and border controls. It was admitted that though the requirements of the acquis for Kaliningrad will be no different than for the rest of Russia, the effects of the new rules might be greater for the Kaliningrad residents, taking into account the geographic situation of the oblast. It meant that the visa-free transit that was at that time available to Kaliningrad residents and several categories of Russian citizens would not be possible any more. Besides, people living in Kaliningrad would have to use a valid passport, and not an internal Russian one. The main idea of the Communication was stressed several times: it is neither necessary that the new requirements will impede the movement of people and the communication between the oblast and the rest of Russia, nor that the social, economic and humanitarian links will be decreased. The flexible visa regime could be established: 'The acquis provides for the issuance of transit visas, short-term visas, and long-term national visas allowing for smooth border crossing and the possibility of multiple entries'.[6] It should be noted that this position of the EU, first expressed in the Communication, has later changed, but only in its form, not the context. The Commission suggested that the responsibility for smooth border crossing should be shared by Russia (the cost of passports) and current/future Member States (cost of visas, presence of consular offices in Kaliningrad). The Communication enumerated several measures to provide for the more efficient operation of border crossing, and noted that the EU 'is already contributing to the development of infrastructure at border crossing points, modernisation of procedures and training to facilitate the movement of persons and goods across the future external border'. Special attention in the Communication was drawn to the EU–Russia cooperation in the fight against illegal border crossing and migration, as well as organised crime; a quick signing of the readmission agreement was regarded as one of the necessary measures for the development of cooperation.

[6] Ibid., p.5.

The Communication formulated the principal EU position in regard to the future visa regime between the new Member States – Lithuania and Poland – and Russia as well as the other countries of the 'direct neighbourhood'. All the future consultations and talks have demonstrated that the EU was not going to fall back from it, i.e. it was ready to discuss facilitating the visa procedure, not the visa regime itself. The flexibility offered in this field differed significantly from the flexibility that the other countries – Norway and Iceland – favoured, according to the Protocol:[7] the discussion of the possible visa-free travel/transit was not pre-supposed. The Commission's plan – 'a sweetener' – dealt exclusively with the technical solution of a problem.

b) The projects for modernisation and development of the border crossing points, as well as those for JHA cooperation were appreciated by the Russian authorities. They were admitted as very valuable for the development of good relations between Russia and the European Union. Several provisions regarding small-border traffic were also considered necessary for the maintenance and future development of regional cross-border cooperation between Russia, Belarus, Poland and Lithuania, in particular for the functioning of the Euroregions. Kaliningrad oblast forms a part of three Euroregions: 'Baltic' including Latvia, Lithuania, Poland, Denmark and Sweden; 'Saule' established between 18 regional and local authorities from Sweden, Lithuania and Latvia; 'Neman' that is supposed to link communities in Lithuania, Kaliningrad and Belarus. The Commission's proposals contained many details, but to now no serious expertise has existed to estimate whether the proposed scheme could really be applied to the concrete situation in the oblast. Several calculations made by Russian experts and based on the number of railway passengers and those travelling by car, showed that the Lithuanian consulate should have to issue from one to two thousand visas daily to maintain the former volume of communications between the oblast and mainland Russia. Lithuanian expertise differed significantly: assuming that the trains to Kaliningrad come half empty, it stated that only 50 visas a day would be enough to meet the necessary requirements. In any case, no official compatible expertise has been produced, which could satisfy all the partners involved.

c) The position of the Russian Government regarding the Commission Communication was expressed in the evaluation document sent to Brussels.[8] The document stated 'For that [Community policies on visas

[7] Art.6 of the Protocol Integrating the Schengen Acquis into the Framework of the European Union.

[8] Evaluation document, *Uniting Europe*, 138, 2 Apr.2001, p.6.

and on external borders] we rather need the principal political decision, while technicalities may be settled later on'. In the same month the Russian Government passed a decision 'On the measures providing for the social and economic development of Kaliningrad oblast'. The future of the region was planned in great detail. Main hopes were rested upon the establishment of the export-oriented industries, fishery and agrarian sector. At that time attention was focused on the economic problems of the oblast rather than visa rules. The Russian authorities expected that the visa-free regime for the oblast could be discussed and a positive result obtained. The RF Government's decision was not regarded officially as a direct answer to the Commission, but taken together with the 'Evaluation document' they were believed to become a cornerstone for further dialogue, which was expected to bring some definite results. The EU and Russia aimed to maximize their benefit from enlargement. However, each of them had different priorities. The main task of the EU was to place the Kaliningrad in an environment that would not impede the functioning of the EU single internal market and the European area of freedom, security and justice. Russia at that time highlighted the social and economic development of the oblast. Later on, as the consultations advanced, the accent shifted towards the visa regime, which had become a stumbling block in the dialogue.

d) The EU and Russia returned several times to the Kaliningrad problem in 2001. They made an attempt to solve it in the framework of the Northern Dimension Programme. The EU–Russia summit devoted three points to Kaliningrad in its Joint statement.[9] However, no progress was apparent. In Russian domestic plans for the recovery of the oblast no provision was made for the impact of the visa regime on economic development. The EU continued to speak about the solution that could be mutually acceptable to the EU and Russia as well as to Poland and Lithuania. In their numerous presentations the EU leaders and officials repeated the same ideas that had been laid by the Communication: 'transit visas, short-term visas, and long-term visas allowing for smooth border crossing and the possibility of multiple entries'. From their side, Russian authorities had been insisting on visa-free transit through Lithuania not only for the Kaliningrad residents, but also for the mainland Russian citizens. The idea of a possible facilitated cross-border regime for the oblast, so that people could maintain their economic and social contacts, was pronounced at the very beginning of consultations, but soon abandoned, as Russia decided to urge for the single visa regime for all Russian citizens.

[9] Joint Statement, EU–Russia Summit, 17 May 2001, http://europa.eu.int/comm/external.

Thus, the potentiality of small-border traffic has hardly been touched. The experts were discussing some 'innovative solution' of the Kaliningrad puzzle, which could satisfy all the partners involved. Poland and Lithuania found themselves in a rather inconvenient situation: they wanted neither to neglect the interests of their eastern neighbours nor to destroy their position in negotiations over accession. Faced with this jeopardy they actually supported the EU position, while stating their wish to maintain a good and fruitful relationship with Russia.

e) In 2002 the consultations were intensified. Being aware of its renewed role in the 'international cooperation against terrorism', Russia tried to put forward its demands for visa-free transit to and from Kaliningrad. A series of meetings followed in spring 2002 involving all interested partners – the EU, Russia, Lithuania and Poland. At the Ministerial Meeting of the Council of the Baltic Sea States (CBSS) in March Commissioner Chris Patten addressed the Russian Prime Minister Mikhail Kasyanov and Foreign Minister Igor Ivanov and made it clear that the EU was not going to override its basic rules here, including Schengen, nor undermine the enlargement negotiations themselves. At the same time Commissioner Patten made the assurance that the EU was ready to continue making a major effort to find solutions to outstanding issues.

f) Among the meetings where Kaliningrad was discussed, the EU–Russia Ministerial in the framework of the JHA Council in April 2002 is worth mentioning. The event could be called a real breakthrough in EU–Russia relations. The Action Plan on the fight against organised crime (1999) was reviewed, and some practicalities were defined including the cooperation between Russia and Europol. As for the visa issue, the sides proved not to be able to overcome a deadlock, which had by then became quite obvious. Subsequently, the achievements in EU–Russia cooperation in JHA matters shifted from the agenda of the dialogue, and it concentrated mainly on visa-free transit to Kaliningrad. Thus, the promise given by the Danish Presidency in July 2002 to work on the agreement between Russia and Europe was sidestepped.

g) Still with a view to bring the consultations to a final result the Russian side stated that it was ready to examine the feasibility of the readmission agreement with the EU. This agreement had been among unresolved issues in EU–Russia relations for some time. The reason was that Russia did not feel able to take responsibility for the illegal migrants using Russian territory as a transit route to European countries. Aware of the fact that fortifying the eastern border with Kazakhstan demanded tremendous efforts, Russia had tried to postpone the decision. Now given the chance to maintain visa-free transit, it was considered worth concluding a readmission agreement, first with Lithuania and then, in time, with the EU. Having declared its intention, Russia stepped into the dangerous road of, perhaps, losing more than it was likely to gain.

h) On 13 May, 2002 the EU General Affairs Council approved the Common Line which set out the 'basic positions of the Schengen acquis', including multiple-entry visas for certain professionals like lorry drivers issued on an ad hoc basis; flexibility with visa fees; and visa exemptions for certain categories of persons. In the process of dialogue the European Union suggested active cooperation to provide for the economic development of Kaliningrad. Additional sources were allocated to improve the cross-border infrastructure, to facilitate border crossings and the movement of goods. In addition, the EU committed itself to support the fight against criminality, pollution and disease in the oblast – everything that was regarded as a 'danger' coming from the future EU enclave.

21.5 A TEST FOR TENSILE STRENGTH OF RUSSIA–EU CONNECTIONS

Nevertheless, the dialogue on Kaliningrad came to its most dramatic stage, threatening to spoil EU–Russia relations. The visa regime was among the most urgent items at the EU–Russia Summit in May 2002. No agreement was achieved. Making his comments on the results of the Summit, the RF President Vladimir Putin noted the thorny discussion on the matter and stressed that solving the question of Kaliningrad's future economic development would serve as a test for the quality of Russia's cooperation with the European Union. Actually, since then all the other issues of EU–Russia relations were put aside until the transit problem was solved. The question was raised concerning the violation of the Russian citizens' constitutional right to free movement from one part of the country to another. But it clashed with the interests of a sovereign state (Lithuania) to control the movement of people across its territory. It should be mentioned, however, that the question of an extraterritorial corridor through Lithuania or Poland has never been raised in official Russian discourse.

Lithuania re-stated its intention to find a flexible solution for the transit issue in cooperation with the EU and Russia, but asked for certain political and legal guarantees and burden sharing in the event of some proceedings going further than the options that the Common line comprised. The EU Summit in Seville invited the Commission to submit a new additional study on the possibilities for the transit of people and goods to and from Kaliningrad. In July 2002 the consultations reached a new phase.

21.6 TOWARDS A COMPROMISE

In July 2002 the idea of Russia's joining the list of countries in possession of a right for visa-free entry to the European Union appeared. The proposal was made in the course of a tense discussion between the representatives of the Russian Ministry of Foreign Affairs and the EU Commission during their meeting in Brussels. The EU re-affirmed its intention to find an effective and flexible solution to the problem according to Schengen acquis. The same measures were suggested (short-term and long-term visas, increasing the amount of consulates in Kaliningrad, etc.). Continuing to insist upon visa-free transit, Russia raised the question of joining the visa-free list. The EU raised the still outstanding issue of the readmission agreement between the EU and Russia. The deadline was fixed – the Kaliningrad visa problem should have been resolved by the EU Summit in Brussels on 24–25 October, so that to pass the decision to the EU-Russia Summit on 11 November.

a) To speed up the process a personal representative of the RF President was put in charge of Kaliningrad. Dmitry Rogozin, the Head of the RF State Duma Committee for international affairs, passed to the EU Commission a draft 'memo of intent', which contained Russia's plan for free transit to Kaliningrad as an interim phase towards establishing a visa-free regime between the European Union and Russia. The plan was based on the assumption that no special acquis existed on transit of people and goods from one part of a third country to another through the EU territory. So the plan included a non-stop high-speed train, which could move through Lithuania, and, in addition, a non-stop bus moving in accordance with approved schedules and routes. The Russian authorities suggested that both the railway and bus tickets should be sold to Russian citizens upon producing internal or international valid passports. Russia expressed its readiness to provide the passenger lists to the Lithuanian authorities. Issuing transit visas at the border for the passenger travelling by car was offered as well. Russia's readiness to sign a readmission agreement with Lithuania was confirmed. During August 2002 Dmitry Rogozin carried out a series of meetings with the senior officials in the Member States.
b) The whole set of EU–Russia relations was put at risk, and in the event of a negative result on the Kaliningrad consultations the probability of a boycott of the EU–Russia Summit in November was announced. To avoid this undesirable development the way out needed to be found,

and this happened on 18 September 2002. The Commission came forward with a Communication to the EU Council.[10] Actually, the Commission found 'pre-solution' to the problem. The scope for delivery of a special travel document was set as follows:

- The common rules on visas contain the list of third states whose nationals must possess visas to cross the external borders; the conditions and procedures for issuing visas; a uniform format for visas and rules on a uniform visa (Article 62 of EC Treaty);
- Procedures and conditions for issuing visas are introduced by secondary legislation; and
- Technical modifications of secondary legislation is almost an endless exercise, particularly since the new circumstances appear.

It was suggested that a new 'Facilitated Transit Document' (FTD) equal to a multiple-entry transit visa be issued by the Lithuanian consulates after examining the list of passengers who travel to Kaliningrad frequently and directly from the Russian mainland. The EU agreed to deliver the FTD on the basis of an internal Russian passport until the end of 2004, but on the basis of a valid international passport from 2005. The Communication noted that Poland would establish a visa regime for all Russian citizens from 1 July 2003, while Lithuania postponed it only for the Kaliningrad residents; all the other Russian citizens were due to have visas from 1 January 2003. At this stage of consultations Poland actually moved away from the scene, because no reasons were found to use Polish territory for transit from different parts of Russia. As for the small-border traffic issue, it has been postponed until the transit issue is decided. The idea of the 'list of frequently travelling Russian citizens' seemed very unclear. At first the list was supposed to be examined by Russian authorities and then submitted to Lithuania. The bureaucratic procedure in two neighbouring countries could just complicate the whole matter rather than facilitate it. The Commission said that it did not exclude the possibility of visa substitution by electronic cards, but qualified this plan as technically difficult, expensive and thus imaginable only in the long term.

c) The Commission accepted Russia's proposal for a non-stop train, but it was stated in the Communication that the study of the legal and technical feasibility of 'visa-free non-stop train' could be started only

[10] Communication from the Commission to the Council. *Kaliningrad: Transit*, 2002.

after Lithuania's accession to the EU. In this way the EU answered Lithuania's concerns about being refused permission to join the Schengen group in the event of visa-free transit by train being permitted for Russia. Making reference to the EU Common positions, the Commission did not support the idea of issuing visas for car passengers at the border, except in some special circumstances. The first reaction of the Russian authorities to the proposed innovative solution was rather negative. The Kaliningrad authorities declared that they would not be able to provide all the Kaliningrad residents with international valid passports by 2005. In addition, Russia was not satisfied by the terms of the feasibility study for the non-stop train. The attitude to the FTD was more cautious, though several politicians and experts called it 'a visa surrogate'. Nevertheless, the Commission initiative itself was appreciated in Russia, being regarded as a step out of the deadlock. Thus the talks about boycotting the Summit in November faded. Though it might seem surprising, the European Union did not reject the idea of the eventual establishment of a visa-free regime for Russia. On the contrary, the Communication mentioned the Commission's interest in the proposal as well as some its 'useful elements', which were already under discussion in the Partnership and Cooperation Agreement (PCA) bodies. It is obvious that the useful elements meant the intensification of the cooperation against organised crime, but mainly related to the readmission agreement. On 30 September 2002 the Commission's Communication was approved by the EU General Affairs and External Relations Council, though certain differences in the Member States opinions were demonstrated, mainly regarding the terms of the study of the feasibility of visa-exemption for passengers on non-stop trains. The RF Ministry of Foreign Affairs (RFA) studied the Council decisions and declared that 'addressing the issue of the transit of persons and goods between the Kaliningrad oblast and the rest of Russia demonstrates that the EU is aware of the problems arising from the enlargement and the accession of Lithuania and Poland'. But at the same time Russia has not discovered any changes in the EU position on the key issues that were vital for Kaliningrad's future development – maintaining the visa-free regime for the railway and bus passengers. The discussions were expected to continue until the final decision was to be taken at the EU–Russia summit in November.

d) The Russian position brought another small shift from the side of the European Union. On 22 October 2002 the EU General Affairs and External Relations Council, further to its decisions of 30 September and discussions with Lithuania and Russia, produced conclusions which were seen to be a compromise by all sides involved. The proposals were modified to the greater advantage of Russia, though the visa regime was re-confirmed with the application of a facilitated procedure for the issuing of visas. The Council Conclusions stated that from 1 January 2003 Lithuania would implement national regulations for border control, in a flexible manner so as not to disrupt the flow of railway passengers. At the same time Lithuania would be authorised with a right to refuse entries to its territory. From 1 July 2003 the FTD is due to be issued for all forms of transit between Kaliningrad and mainland Russia. Both the EU and Lithuania promised that the procedure for delivering the FTD would be as flexible as possible, especially for the passengers of trains.

e) Lithuania was assured that the special arrangements for transit would not delay or postpone its full membership of the Schengen group. The binding guarantees will be included into the Accession Treaty that 'the EU would provide assistance for Lithuania for additional costs for the implementation of the whole Kaliningrad "package" and a decision on the non-stop train will be taken only after Lithuania's accession to the EU membership in the Schengen group'. Having received the guarantees, Lithuania expressed the desire to start discussing the terms of reference for the feasibility study of the non-stop train soon after the Copenhagen Summit in December 2002, where the final decision on enlargement was to be taken. So the compromise in fact was reached on the terms of launching the feasibility study: meeting Russia's demands the EU agreed to bring the date forward.[11] Another passage made Russian politicians prematurely optimistic – the hope appeared that Lithuania would preserve a visa-free regime for the train transit from 1 January till 1 July 2003, though it was not clearly stated in the text of Conclusions.

f) The Summit in Brussels in October 2002 approved the Council Conclusions without any changes. Meanwhile, it was not the last word in the long debate on Kaliningrad. The final decision was taken at the EU–Russia Summit on 11 November 2002. The sides managed to come to a more appreciable compromise on the arrangements for the transit of persons and goods. The sides re-confirmed that a FTD scheme would be established on the basis of legislation that the EU would introduce. The FTD will be valid for direct transit to Kaliningrad within a limited period of time. The document will be issued free of charge or at a very low cost. The innovative proposal arose of two types of FTD for Russian citizens. The first one is for multiple-entry transit via all forms of transport by land. It would be

[11] 2459th General Affairs and External Relations Council meeting, Luxembourg, 21–2 October 2002, Council Conclusions, p. 2.

obtainable on the basis of an application to a Lithuanian consulate. In addition, Russian citizens will be able to get a Facilitated Rail Travel Document (FRTD) for single trips on train through Lithuania. Actually, the scheme that had been suggested by Dmitry Rogozin and rejected by the EU a few months earlier was agreed this time. A person hoping to obtain a FRTD will have to submit his/her personal data at the time of ticket purchase. This information is then forwarded to the competent Lithuania authorities, who decide whether the railway ticket can be sold to the passenger. Later on, a FRTD would be received at or before the Lithuanian border upon the appropriate checking procedure. The sides stated their readiness to discuss the technicalities of the FTD scheme in cooperation with Lithuania. It is worth mentioning that Russia took note of the EU's intention to review the operation of the FTD scheme no later than 2005.[12] It means that the agreed regime is temporary and might be abolished when Lithuania joins the Schengen area. Russia seems to hope that by that time a high-speed non-stop train is link Kaliningrad with mainland Russia, the visa-free regime will be maintained. On 1 January new rules were established regulating transit through Lithuania to Kaliningrad; Russian citizens reserved their right to travel to Kaliningrad visa-free until 1 July, while non-citizens of the RF, travelling to Kaliningrad from Russia, are obliged to possess visas. That was the result of the intensive Russian–Lithuanian consultations, which took place in December 2002.

21.7 IN LIEU OF CONCLUSION

The detailed analysis of the debates over the Kaliningrad transit seems necessary to demonstrate that a small and unclear trade-off was achieved by Russia after two years of intensive consultations and talks that have sometimes threatened EU–Russia relations. In fact, the consultations have become concentrated almost exclusively on the Kaliningrad transit, while putting aside other highly urgent questions. In addition, the issue of transit of goods was not solved at the Summit in November 2002. No matter what is being declared, the compromise is obviously technical, not political. The visa-free regime is preserved only for the following half year, because the FTD scheme is based upon Lithuania's authorisation of entries to its territory. Beyond any remarks on the Belarus President's personality and his political course, Lukashenko's comment of the EU–Russia summit in November was

[12] See the Joint statement on Kaliningrad, 10th EU Russia Summit, 11 Nov 2002, http://www.europa.eu.int/comm/external-relations/russia/summit-11-02/js-Kalin.htm..

very precise: 'A visa was pink, and now it will be blue and a bit cheaper – what success is Russia speaking about?'.[13] Therefore, the constitutional right of Russian citizens has not been defended for free movement from one part of their country to another. Surely, the FTD scheme could provide for facilitation of travelling, in the event of it working properly. The proposed scheme is too obscure, and this fact casts doubts on its normal functioning. Actually, the railway booking offices are charged with primary control over the flow of passengers. The case of booking flights is always referred to, but this procedure needs notification only, but not authorisation, so it is not so complicated. The whole plan has been drawn up within the original framework of the EU Communication on Kaliningrad issued in January 2001: the visa regime and the facilitated procedure of the issuing of visas. Therefore the compromise may be considered as rather formal.

The proposed technical solution could be acceptable, if Russia does not have to pay a considerable price for it. At the summit the RF confirmed its intention for a readmission agreement with Lithuania covering people of all nationalities. Though it has not been declared directly, issuing of the FTD was dependent on the results of the talks on readmission: the proper agreement should be concluded no later than 30 June 2003. Besides, from 2002, the EU and Russia will launch negotiations for a bilateral readmission agreement. As a rule, a country signs a readmission agreement in exchange for a visa-free regime; at least, that was the case for the candidate countries. Russia is going to sign the agreement with Lithuania, once it obtains some assurance on the possibility of visa-free transit to Kaliningrad: a FTD scheme and a non-stop train in the future. Besides, while accepting the idea of visa-free entry for all Russian citizens as a remote possibility, the EU is urging Russia to sign the same agreement as quickly as possible.

In fact, the EU used the whole situation around Kaliningrad to speed up the process of talks about readmission. The inequality and asymmetry of relations between the European Union and Russia has thus been re-established. It is quite clear that with its intentions of becoming a civilised country, Russia will have to sign the required agreements, but it can do so only after having obtained the same action from its southern and eastern neighbours. This process will undoubtedly take many years; in any case, it would bring results later than 30 June 2003. It means that Russia will carry the burden of illegal migrant deportation alone, possessing neither financial, nor political resources for this initiative at the moment. The expected readmission agreement with Lithuania is senseless without Belarus, as the border does not separate the countries, and the flow of illegal migrants comes to Lithuania from Russia through Belarus. President Lukashenko's possible participation in negotiations will complicate the matter. Russia's intention for

[13] Izvestia, 19.11.2002.

readmission has been clearly re-stated, but it does not mean that the agreement is realisable.

The EU's firm position on Kaliningrad is surely not based on its concerns that the flows of illegal immigrants would rush immediately into a 'Kaliningrad breach.' Even now the illegal route passes through Ukraine, Belarus and Moldova. It is obvious that the EU was not eager to create a precedent for granting Russia visa privileges for Kaliningrad. The demands for a facilitated visa regime at the other parts of its new eastern border could follow. Having created the Schengen defensive system, the EU has no intention to leave it ajar even in one place. The complexity of border disputes strains the relations between Russia and the European Union, as well as between the candidate states and the countries of the 'direct neighbourhood.' Several positive points should be mentioned while speaking about the consequences of enlargement and of the Schengen rules spreading eastwards. The candidates' preparations to join the Schengen group have influenced their 'near abroad'. Whether they wanted to or not, Russia, Belarus, Ukraine and Moldova have been involved in the common process of improving borders management and cooperation against illegal border crossings. The new eastern EU neighbours will have to settle their disputes concerning delimitation and demarcation of borders, as well as signing border agreements. However, at the moment every adjacent state is trying to tighten its eastern border while relaxing the western border regime. There is no systematic approach to the border management. Thus, the urgency of readmission agreements could only aggravate the situation, each country trying to gain benefits at the expense of the others.

The FTD scheme for Kaliningrad with its expected inclusion in the Accession Treaty, though being a rather modest achievement, has become the first mechanism to face the consequences of the Schengen acquis expansion to the east. The additional efforts of the European Union, as well as of all the interested sides, should be concentrated on the creation of a new border regime model, including small-border traffic. In fact it should be based upon principle rules, which could be common for all borderlands, while taking into consideration the national specific demands. The model could be created in the frames of the new EU 'Eastern Dimension' policy, which would regulate the economic, political and cultural relations between the EU and the adjacent non-members, stressing the need for cross-border cooperation. The imperative for its emergence is obvious on the eve on enlargement. The Eastern Dimension could provide for combining the currently conflicting EU goals of internal security and stability in the borderland of a wider Europe.

REFERENCES

Cholewinski, R. and E. Slavenas (2002), 'Foreign Policy Implications of the EU Justice and Home Affairs Acquis: The Case of Baltic States', in M. Anderson and J. Apap (eds), *New European Borders and Security Cooperation: Promoting Trust in an Enlarged European Union*, The Hague: Kluwer International Law.

Cichocki, J. (2001), 'Direct Neighbourhood: Border Issues and Visa Regulations – an Eastern Perspective', in I. Kempe (ed.), *Beyond EU Enlargement. The Agenda of Direct Neighbourhood for Eastern Europe*, Gutersloh: Bertelsmann Foundation Publishers.

Communication from the Commission to the Council, *The EU and Kaliningrad*, Brussels, 17.1.2001, COM(2001) 26 final.

Communication from the Commission to the Council, *Kaliningrad: Transit*, Brussels, 18.09.2002, COM(2002) 510 final.

Den Boer, M. (2002), 'To what Extent Can There Be Flexibility on the Application of Schengen in the New Member States?', in M. Anderson and J. Apap (eds), *New European Borders and Security Cooperation: Promoting Trust in an Enlarged European Union*, The Hague: Kluwer International Law.

Emerson, M. (2001), *The Elephant and the Bear. The European Union, Russia and their Near Abroad*, Brussels: Centre for European Policy Studies, CEPS.

Grabbe, H. (2000), *The sharp edges of Europe: security implications of extending EU border policies eastwards*, The Institute for Security Studies, Western European Union, Occasional papers, 13.

Monar, J. (2000), *Justice and Home Affairs in a Wider Europe: The Dynamics of Inclusion and Exclusion; One Europe or Several*, Working paper 07/00, Brighton: University of Sussex.

Zielonka, J. (2001), 'How New Enlarged Borders will Reshape the European Union', *Journal of Common Market Studies*, **39** (3), pp. 507–36.

22. Conclusion: A Practical Set of Recommendations

Joanna Apap

This last chapter is thematically structured according to the issues discussed in the previous chapters to offer the reader a practical set of recommendations in each of the following five areas:

1. Consequences of enlargement on Justice and Home Affairs
2. Fundamentals of EU Justice and Home Affairs (JHA) policy post-enlargement
3. Scenarios of crime, law and justice in an enlarged European Union
4. Towards an immigration and asylum policy for Europe
5. Future of Justice and Home Affairs policies and processes

22.1 Consequences of enlargement on Justice and Home Affairs

It is imperative that the EU and the candidate states should agree upon clear benchmarks and a transparent priority order in which JHA measures need to be accomplished both before and after enlargement. The candidate countries need to accept and understand that they are being monitored; however, they should be involved in a closer dialogue with the EU to ensure that regional sensitivities are taken into account and that practical measures are not overlooked. On the other hand, the candidate states must also fully accept that high standards are entailed, and thus embrace the challenges ahead with positive enthusiasm that can appear to be lacking in times of uncertainty. The candidate states and the EU are partners, not competitors. They both have equally high stakes in a successful accession, as well as fully efficient, effective and operational JHA measures. For these to occur, it is recommended that a balanced approach consisting of open and accepting dialogue (instead of continual dictation and counter-reactive statements) and practical implementation in the technical aspects to take place. Criticisms from both sides need to be clear, precise and appropriate.

22.2 Fundamentals of EU JHA policy post-enlargement

The fundamentals of the JHA policy post-enlargement should incorporate the following: trust and confidence between the candidate countries and EU, democratic method of policy-making through the elimination of the unanimity procedure, and also a clear division of EU and national competencies. It can be implied that different legal cultures often clash when forced to come to a compromise, thus the basic element of trust is of utmost importance. If the last two factors are applied, it will become clear who has the mandate to act within a distinct capacity, and thus the responsibility that comes with the post can then become accountable.

22.3 Scenarios of crime, law and justice in an enlarged European Union

The authors emphasize that there needs to be a clear distinction between what is an imaginary risk and a real one. Migratory policies have often suffered at the hands of imaginary insecurity, which proclaims that migrants are the derivatives of insecurity. These myths further complicate the situation of the candidate states and their possible destabilising potentials towards the EU's Immigration Policy. Thus, for the EU's Immigration Policy to strike a balance between security and migration, it should include the following factors:

- a clear understanding of the subjects in discussion; and
- a highly distinguishable separation between myths and realities.

Chapters 5 to 11 are presented in the 'problem and solution' format, explaining the new criminal challenges and the type of new institutional responses. The emerging theme is that traditional aspects of crimes will remain as accession states join the EU. However, due to new technologies which facilitate communication and transport, other areas of crime of a more trans-border character will bring new façades to the ever-growing challenges to the area of Justice and Home Affairs. In order for the EU to be effective and efficient in combating crimes, it needs to have first an expansion in operational powers for EU organizations such as Europol, and second, increase or maintain close cooperation with non-EU organizations such as the Stability Pact and Council of Europe. Questions that are left opened-ended in this session are evaluative: have these organizations/agencies been efficient and effective? And most important of all, how efficient and effective will these organizations be when other agencies are created alongside and have to operate within the remit of 25–27 Member States?

22.4 Towards an immigration and asylum policy for Europe

The overall feeling is that the EU's move towards a Common Immigration Policy has not been done with an openness that it required. In fact, it has become increasingly restrictive; negotiations in the Council have embraced the Lowest Common Denominator. Although the role of the state has been diminishing in immigration policies, the EU is the exception. It still retained much of the power that states exerted in past years. Border Guards are necessary, but the tightening of the borders does not necessarily provide security. The difference between immigration and asylum needs to be strongly highlighted and maintained. Hence, the EU can and should maintain the element of openness in establishing a Common Immigration Policy via (1) adopting basic integration measures – the adoption of the directive on family reunification was a first step in this direction, (2) avoiding the acceptance of the Lowest Common Denominator, and (3) maintaining a strict separation between asylum and immigration issues and measures. Some of the questions that are left open remain on the practical side: (1) how can we distinguish between migrants and asylum seekers? And (2) how can the EU maintain a secure border while providing openness for those who seek it?

22.5 Future of Justice and Home Affairs policies and processes

Normative aspects need to be included in the adopted policies, bringing intelligence services closer to the decision-making process. A first step is strengthening Europol's operational powers while bringing Europol and other third pillar agencies under the scrutiny of the European Parliament and European Court of Justice. Access to the European Court of Justice should be improved, and an annual report needs to be submitted by the European Parliament summarizing activities and priorities in the area of criminal law. Adding to these suggestions the dimension of flexibility, it is recommended that all approaches taken to adopt, revise and implement future JHA policies should incorporate some element of flexibility so as to incorporate differences in existing EU Member States and the CEECs. Nonetheless, it should be noted that flexibility contains both risks and opportunities, and a desired policy would explore the opportunities while successfully avoiding the risks.

Consolidated References and Additional Recommended Readings

Anderson, M. (1996), *Frontiers: Territory and State Formation in the Modern World*, Cambridge: Polity.

Anderson, M. (1998), 'Transfrontier Cooperation – History and Theory', in G. Brunn and P. Schmitt-Egner (eds), *Grenzüberschreitende Zusammenarbeit in Europa; Theorie–Empirie–Praxis*, Baden Baden: Nomos.

Anderson, M. (2000), 'Counterterrorism as an Objective of European Police Cooperation', in F. Reinares (ed.) (2000), *European Democracies Against Terrorism: Governmental policies and intergovernmental cooperation*, The Oñati International Institute of the Sociology of Law, London: Ashgate, pp. 227–44.

Anderson, M. (2000), 'Transfrontier Cooperation and Assessment', in L. Hedegaard and B. Lindström (eds), *North European and Baltic Integration Yearbook*, Berlin: Springer-Verlag.

Anderson, M. and J. Apap (2002), *Striking a Balance between Freedom, Security and Justice in an Enlarged European Union*, Brussels: Centre for European Policy Studies, CEPS.

Anderson, M. and J. Apap (2002), *Police and Justice Cooperation and the New European Borders*, The Hague: Kluwer Law International.

Anderson M. and M. den Boer (1996), *Policing the European Union: Theory, Law and Practice*, Oxford: Clarendon Press.

Anderson, M. et al. (1996), *Policing the European Union: Theory Law and Practice*, Oxford: Clarendon Press.

Apap, J. (2001), *Freedom of Movement of Persons in the EU: A Practitioner's Guide*, The Hague: Kluwer Law International.

Apap, J. (2002), *The Migrant Worker and EU Public Policy: An Evaluation of the emerging EU Public Policy Process towards Migration of Labour from outside the Union*, The Hague: Kluwer Law International.

Arendt, H. (1963), *On Revolution*, USA: Viking Press.

Bade, K. (2000), *Europa in Bewegung*, Munich: Beck Verlag.

Baldwin-Edwards, M. (2002), *Immigration and the Welfare State: a European Challenge to American Mythology*, Universita Pompeu Fabra, Conference on Europe-Mediterranean Immigration Policy, Barcelona.

Barbe, E. (2002), 'Le mandat d'arrêt européen: en tirera-t-on toutes les conséquences?', in G. de Kerchove and A. Weyembergh (eds), *L'espace pénal européen: enjeux et perspectives*, Brussels: Editions de l'Université de Bruxelles, pp. 113–17.

Battjes, H. (2002), 'A Balance between Fairness and Efficiency? The Directive on International Protection and the Dublin Regulation', *European Journal of Migration and Law*, **4**, The Hague: Kluwer Law International, pp. 159–92.

Beccaria, C. (1995), 'On Crimes and Punishments', trans. by R. Davies, in R. Bellamy and C. Beccaria (eds), *On Crime and Punishments and Other Writings*, Cambridge: Cambridge University Press, Ch. 1.

Best, E. (2001), 'The Treaty of Nice: Not Beautiful but it'll do', *Eipascope*, No. 1, Maastricht: European Institute of Public Administration, EIPA, pp. 1–8.

Bieber, R. and J. Monar (eds) (1997), *Justice and Home Affairs in the European Union: The development of the third pillar*, Brussels: European University Press.

Bigo, D. (1994), 'The European Internal Security Field: Stakes and Rivalries in a Newly Developing Area of Police intervention', in M. Anderson and M. den Boer (eds), *Policing Across National Boundaries*, London: Pinter, pp. 161–73.

Bigo, D. (1996), *Polices en Réseaux: l'Expérience Européenne,* Paris: Presses de Sciences Po.

Bigo, D. (1997), 'Security, Borders and the State', in P. Ganster, A. Sweedler, J. Scott and W. D. Eberwein (eds), *Borders and Border Regions in Europe and North America*, San Diego: San Diego University Press, pp. 81–104.

Bigo, D. (1998), 'Frontiers and Security in the European Union', in M. Anderson and E. Bort (eds), *The Frontiers of Europe*, London: Pinter, pp. 148–64.

Bigo, D. (2002), 'Security and Immigration: Towards a Governmentality of Unease Alternatives', *Cultures et Conflits*, No. 31–32.

Blangiardo G. (ed.) (2002), *Report on Migrations in Lombardy*, Milan: Fondazione Ismu.

Bleeker, K.A.M. (1993), *Verantwoorde communautaire sanctionering van het gemeenschapsrecht*, Nederlands Juristenblad, pp. 1009–13.

Boeles, P. (2001), 'Directive on Family Reunification: Are the Dilemmas Resolved?', *European Journal of Migration and Law*, **3**, pp. 61–71.

Boeles, P. and A. Kuijer (1993), 'Harmonization of Family Reunification', in H. Meijers et al. (eds), *A New Immigration Law for Europe? The 1992 London and 1993 Copenhagen Rules on Immigration*, Utrecht: Dutch Centre for Immigrants, pp. 25–34.

Bonnefoi, S. (1998), *Europe et sécurité intérieure: Trevi, Union Européenne, Schengen*, Paris: Delmas.

Bontempi, R. (2001), 'Hacia una Política Europea de Inmigración y un Régimen Común en Materia de Asilo', *Revista Cidob d'affers Internacionals*, no. 53, 123.

Bouteillet-Paquet, D. (2001) 'La Mise en Place d'un Système dissuasif de Répartition des Réfugiés sur le Territoire Communautaire', *L'Europe et le droit d'asile*, Paris: L'Harmattan, no. 396, pp. 201–32.

Brochmann, G. and T. Hammar (1999), *Mechanisms of Immigration Control*, Oxford: Berg.

Brücker, H., G. Epstein, B. McCormick, G. Saint-Paul, A. Venturini, and K. Zimmerman (2001), 'Managing Migration in the European Welfare State', in T. Boeri, G.H. Hanson and B. McCormick (eds), *Immigration Policy and the Welfare State*, Oxford: A Report for the Fondazione Rodolfo Debenedetti.

Bruggeman, W. (2000), 'Europol – A European FBI in the making?', lecture in the Cicero Foundation Great Debate as part of the seminar on Justice and Home Affairs: How to implement the Amsterdam Treaty, Paris, 13–14 April.

Bruggeman, W. (2001), 'International Law Enforcement Cooperation: a critical assessment', *European Journal on Criminal Policy and Research*, **9** (3), pp. 283–90.

Bruggeman, W. (2001) 'Europol's Contribution to Police Accountability: What is the Appropriate Model? Paper presented to the conference on Policing and Public Accountability in Europe: Designing European Police Networks (September), Maastricht: European Institute of Public Administration, EIPA.

Buruma, Y. (1995), 'De repressieve Kant van de Europese Unie', *Justitiële verkenningen*, no. 1, pp. 41–4.

Caritas-Migrantes (2002), *Immigrazione*. Dossier statistico 2002, Roma: Nuova Anterem.

Cha, V.D. (2000), 'Globalization and the Study of International Security', *Journal of Peace Research*, **37** (3), pp. 391–403.

Cholewinski, R. (1996), *The Protection of Migrant Workers in International Law*, Oxford: Oxford University Press.

Cholewinski, R. (1997), *Migrant Workers in International Human Rights Law: Their Protection in Countries of Employment*, Oxford: Clarendon Press.

Cholewinski, R. (2002), 'Family Reunification and Conditions Placed on family Members: Dismantling a Fundamental Human Right', *European Journal of Migration and Law*, The Hague: Kluwer Law International, 4, pp. 271–90.

Cholewinski, R. (2002), *The Legal Status of Migrants Admitted for Employment: A Comparative Study of Law and Practice in Selected European States*, Strasbourg: Council of Europe.

Cholewinski, R. (2002), 'Borders and Discrimination in the European Union', in M. Anderson and J. Apap (eds), *New European Borders & Security Cooperation. Promoting Trust in an European Union*, Brussels: Centre for European Policy Studies, CEPS, pp. 83–100.

Cholewinski, R. and E. Slavenas (2002), 'Foreign Policy Implications of the EU Justice and Home Affairs Acquis: The Case of Baltic States', in M. Anderson and J. Apap (eds), *New European Borders and Security Cooperation: Promoting Trust in an Enlarged European Union*, The Hague: Kluwer International Law.

Christodoulidis, E. and T. Scott Veitch (1994), 'Terrorism and Systems Terror', *Economy and Society*, Routledge, **23** (2).

Cichocki, J. (2001), 'Direct Neighbourhood: Border Issues and Visa Regulation–an Eastern Perspective', in I. Kempe, *Beyond EU Enlargement. The Agenda of Direct Neighbourhood for Eastern Europe*, Gutersloh, Bertelsmann Foundation Publishers, pp. 165–79.

Cloos, J., G. Reinesch, D. Vignes and J. Weyland (1993), *Le Traité de Maastricht. Genèse, analyse, commentaires*, Brussels: Bruylant.

Cornelius W., P.L. Martin and J.F. Hollifield (eds) (1994), *Controlling Immigration. A Global Perspective*, Stanford: Stanford University Press.

Craig, P. (2002), 'The Evolution of the Single Market', in J. Scott and C. Barnard (eds), *The Law of the Single European Market*, Oxford: Hart, pp 1–41.

Crepau, F. (ed.) (1995), *Droit d'asile – de l'Hospitalité aux Controles Migratoires*, Brussels: Bruylant.

Curtin, D. and S. Peers (eds) (2002), *Joint Submissions by the Standing Committee of Experts on International Immigration, Refugee and Criminal Law, the Immigration Law Practitioners Association, Statewatch, and The European Council of Refugees and Exiles to Working Group X*, Utrecht and London.

Dal Lago, A. (1999), *Non-persone. L'esclusione dei migranti in una società globale*, Milan: Feltrinelli.

Davis, P. and L. Finch (1993), *Defence Planning in the Post-Cold War Era: Going to Flexibility, Adaptiveness and Robustness of Capability*, Santa Monica: CA: Rand Corporation.

De Búrca, G. and B. de Witte (2002), *The Delimitation of Powers between the EU and its Member States*, CR 2002/03, Policy Papers (Series on Constitutional Reform of the EU), European University Institute, Robert Schuman Institute of Advanced Studies.

De Hert, P. (1995), 'La Commission Européenne sur la Voie d'une Police Supranationale', *Revue de Droit de Police*, **1**(2), pp. 21–9.

De Lobkowicz W. (2002), 'L'Europe et la Securité Intérieure', Paris: *La Documentation Française*, Paris, pp. 91–3.

De Ruyver, B., G. Vermeulen and T. Vander Beken (2002), *Strategies of the EU and the US in Combating Transnational Organized Crime*, Institute for International Research on Criminal Policy (IRCP), Ghent University, Maklu (Antwerp/Apeldoorn).

De Schutter, B., K. Caronez and P. De Hert (2000), *Bestrijding van het Voetbalvandalisme in het Licht van het Vrij Verkeer van Personen*, Brussels: VUB-onderzoeksrapport.

De Tocqueville, A. (1835), *Democracy in America*, Vol. I, Part II, Ch. 5, p. 191–234.

Dehaene, J. (2002), 'Nieuw EU-Verdrag of zware crisis', *Europa van Morgen*, no. 9, 12 June 2002.

Demanet, G. (1985), 'De l'utilisation Frauduleuse des Cartes Bancaires. Une Nouvelle Incrimination est-elle necessaire?', *Revue de Droit Pénal et de Criminologie* , **65** (2), pp. 915–32.

Den Boer, M. (1996), 'Police Cooperation', in J. Monar, N. Neuwahl, D. O'Keefe and W. Robinson (eds) (1996), *Guide to the EU*, London: Butterworths, pp. 247–49.

Den Boer, M. (ed.) (1997), *Undercover Policing and Accountability from an International Perspective*, European Institute of Public Administration, EIPA, Maastricht.

Den Boer, M. (1997), 'Justitie en Binnenlandse Zaken in het nieuwe Verdrag van Amsterdam', *Nederlands Juristenblad*, **72** (35), pp. 1625–30.

Den Boer, M. (1998), *Taming the Third Pillar: Improving the Management of Justice and Home Affairs Cooperation in the EU*, Maastricht: European Institute of Public Administration, EIPA.

Den Boer, M. (2000), 'The Incorporation of Schengen into the TEU: A Bridge too Far?', in J. Monar and W. Wessels (eds), *The Treaty of Amsterdam: Challenges and Opportunities for the European Union*, London: Continuum, pp. 297–319.

Den Boer, M. (2002), 'To what Extent Can There Be Flexibility on the Application of Schengen in the New Member States?', in M. Anderson and J. Apap (eds), *New European Borders and Security Cooperation: Promoting Trust in an Enlarged European Union,* Brussels: Centre for European Policy Studies, CEPS.

Den Boer, M. (ed.) (2002), *Organised Crime: A Catalyst in the Europeanisation of National Police and Prosecution Agencies?*, Maastricht: European Institute of Public Administration, EIPA.

Denayer, W. (2001), 'Urban Governance, Workfare, and the Conservative Revolution against the Welfare State', *Ethiek & Maatschappij*, **3** (2), pp. 59–79.

DiMaggio, P. (1997), 'Culture and Cognition', *Annual Review of Sociology*, **23**, pp. 263–87.

Duverger, M. (1994), *Europa de los hombres: una metamorfosis inacabada*, Madrid: Alianza.

Emerson, M. (2001), *The Elephant and the Bear. The European Union, Russia and their Near Abroad*, Brussels: Centre for European Policy Studies, CEPS.

Faist, T. (1995), 'Boundaries of Welfare States; Immigrants and Social Rights on the National and Supranational Levels', in R. Miles and D Thränhardt (eds), *Migration and European Integration. The Dynamics of Inclusion and Exclusion* London: Pinter, pp. 177–95.

Faria, C. (2001), 'Post-Laeken Assessment Justice and Home Affairs', Eipascope, n. 1, Maastricht: European Institute of Public Administration, EIPA, pp. 7–9.

Flore, D. (1999), 'Une Justice Pénale Européenne après Amsterdam', *Journal des Tribunaux. Droit Européen*, **7** (60), pp. 121–8.

Freeman, G. P. (1994), 'Can Liberal States Control Unwanted Immigration?', *Annals of the American Academy of Political and Social Sciences,* No. 534, pp. 17–30.

Geddes, A. (2001), 'International Migration and State Sovereignty in an Integrating Europe', *International Migration*, **39** (6), pp. 21–41.

Glover S., C. Gott, A. Loizillon, J. Portes, R. Price, S. Spencer, V. Srinivasan and C. Willis (2001), *Migration: an Economic and Social Analysis*,. London: Research, Development and Statistics Directorate (RDS), Home Office.

Golding, M. (1999), 'My Philosophy of Law', in L. Wintgens (ed.), *The Law in Philosophical Perspectives*, Dordrecht: Kluwer Academic Publishers, pp. 55–79.

Grabbe, H. (2000), *The Sharp Edges of Europe: Security Implications of Extending EU Border Policies Eastwards*, The Institute for Security Studies, Western European Union, Occasional papers, no. 13.

Groenhuijsen, M.S. (2001), 'Hervorming van het strafprocesrecht met het oog op de belangen van het slachtoffer: *We ain't seen nothing yet*', Delikt & Delinkwent, pp. 645–53.

Guild, E. (ed.) (1999), *The Legal Framework and Social Consequences of Free Movement of Persons in the European Union*, The Hague: Kluwer Law International.

Guild, E. (2001), *Immigration Law in the European Community*, The Hague: Kluwer Law International.

Guild, E. (2001), 'Primary Immigration: The Great Myths', in E. Guild and C. Harlow (eds), *Implementing Amsterdam: Immigration and Asylum Rights in EC Law*, Oxford: Hart Publishing, pp 65–94.

Guild, E. (2003), 'Intersecting Worlds? Understanding the Legal Framework of European Labour Migration in Susan Strange's Modern World', in D. Bigo and E. Guild (eds), *Controlling Frontiers: Free Movement into and within Europe*, Aldershot: Ashgate.

Guild, E. and D. Bigo (2002), 'The Legal Mechanisms – Collectively Specifying the Individual: The Schengen Border System and

Enlargement', in M. Anderson and J. Apap (eds), *Police and Justice Cooperation and the New European Borders*, The Hague: Kluwer Law International, pp. 121–38.

Guild, E. and C. Harlow (eds) (2001), *Implementing Amsterdam: Immigration and Asylum Rights in EC Law,* Oxford: Hart Publishing.

Guild, E. and J. Niessen (1996), *The Developing Immigration and Asylum Policies of the European Union, Adopted Conventions, Resolutions, Recommendations, Decisions and Conclusions*, The Hague: Kluwer Law International, pp. 251–73.

Hailbronner, K. (1998), 'European Immigration and Asylum Law under the Amsterdam Treaty', *Common Market Law Review*, **35**, 1047–67.

Hermant, D. and D. Bigo (2000), 'Les politiques de Lutte contre le Terrorisme: Enjeux français', in F. Reinares (ed.) (2000), *European Democracies against Terrorism: Governmental Policies and Intergovernmental Cooperation*, The Oñati International Institute of the Sociology of Law, London: Ashgate.

Huysmans, J. (1998), 'Dire et écrire la sécurité: le dilemme normatif des études de sécurité', Paris: *Cultures et Conflits*, no. 31–2, pp. 177–202.

Huysmans, J. (2000), 'The European Union and the securitization of Migration', *Journal of Common Market Studies*, **38** (5), pp. 751–78.

Jurgens, E. (2002), 'National Parliamentary Control on Justice and Home Affairs Policy Making', in *Integraded Security in Europe. A Democratic Perspective*, Special Edition of Collegium, News of the College of Europe, no. 22, pp. 84–9.

Kaptein, P.J.G. and Verloren Van Themaat, P. (1995), *Inleiding tot het recht van de Europese Gemeenschappen na Maastricht*, Deventer, Kluwer.

King, R. (1998), 'The Mediterranean: Europe's Rio Grande', in M. Anderson and E. Bort (eds), *The Frontiers of Europe*, London: Pinter, pp. 109–34.

King, R. (1998) 'Towards a Pattern of Immigration into Southern Europe', in M. Anderson and E. Bort (eds), *Schengen and the Southern Frontier of the Europe Union*, Edinburgh: ISSI, pp. 115–40.

Klages, R. (2002), 'Final Report on Constitutional and Ethical Principles of Democratic Control on National and European Institutions', in *Integraded Security in Europe. A Democratic Perspective*, Special Edition of Collegium, News of the College of Europe, no. 22, pp. 128–30.

Klip, A. (1997), 'Uniestrafrecht is op hol geslagen', *Nederlands Juristenblad*, no. 15, pp. 663–71.

Lahav, G. and V. Guiraudon (2000), 'Comparative Perspective on Border Control: Away From the Border and Outside of the State', in P. Andreas and T. Snyder (eds), *The Wall Around the West*, Lanham: Rowman & Little, pp. 55–80

Leo, R. (1998), 'Schengen and its Daily Practice on the Borders. The Particular Situation in Friuli Venezia Giulia', in M. Anderson and E.

Bort (eds), *Schengen and the Southern Frontier of the European Union*, Edinburgh: ISSI.

Lluch, Toni, (2001), 'Hacia una política común de asilo para la Unión Europea', *Revista Cidob d'affers Internacionals*, no. 53, 144.

Loader I. and R. Sparks (2002), 'Contemporary Landscapes of Crime, Order and Control: Governance, Risk and Globalization', in M. Maguire, R. Morgan and R. Reiner (eds), *The Oxford Handbook of Criminology* (3rd Edn), Oxford University Press, pp. 83–111.

Ludlow, P. (2001), 'A Commentary on the EU', *A View from Brussels*, Brussels: Centre for European Policy Studies, CEPS Commentary.

Macleod, I., I. Hendry and S. Hyett (1996), *The External Relations of the European Communities*, Oxford: Clarendon Press.

Massey, D. S., J. Arango, G. Hugo, A. Kouaouci, A. Pellegrino and J. E. Taylor (1999), *Worlds in Motion; Understanding International Migration at the End of the Millennium*, Oxford: Clarendon Press, pp. 254–74.

Modood, T., R. Berthoud, J. Lakey, J. Nazroo, S. Virdee and S. Beishon (1994), *Ethnic Minorities in Britain: Diversity and Disadvantage*, London: Policy Studies Institute.

Monar, J. (2000), *Justice and Home Affairs in a Wider Europe: The Dynamics of Inclusion and Exclusion*, ESRC 'One Europe or Several', Working paper 07/00, Brighton, iversity of Sussex.

Monar, J. (2001), 'Justice and Home Affairs', in: G. Edwards and G. Wiessala (eds), *The European Union. Annual Review of the EU 2000/2001*, Blackwell, Published in association with *Journal of Common Market Studies*, pp. 131–2.

Monar, J. (2002), 'The Problems of Balance in EU Justice and Home Affairs and the Impact of 11 September', in Anderson, M. and J. Apap (eds), *New European Borders & Security Cooperation. Promoting Trust in a European Union*, Centre for European Policy Studies, CEPS, Brussels, pp. 163–5.

Monar, J. and W. Wessels (eds) (2001), *The Treaty of Amsterdam: Challenges and Opportunities for the European Union*, London: Pinter.

Mueller, G. and D. J. Besharov, (1999), 'Evolution and Enforcement of International Criminal Law', *International Criminal Law*, vol. I., pp. 257–67.

Muus P. (1998), *A Study on the Expected Effects of Free Movement for Legally Residing Workers From Third Countries Within the European Community, Migrants, Minorities and New Forms of Citizenship in the European Union*, Florence: EUI.

Nash, K. (2001), 'The "Cultural Turn" in Social Theory: Towards a Theory of Cultural Politics', *Sociology*, **35** (1), pp. 77–92.

Nevzat, S. (1999), *States and Strangers: Refugees and Displacements of Statecraft*, Minneapolis: University of Minnesota Press.

Notaro, N. (2001), 'The EC and WTO Trade and Environment Case |Law: Procedural Aspects, Legal Principles and Institutional Matters', in A. Dashwood, J. Spencer, A. Ward and C. Hillion (eds), *The Cambridge Yearbook of European Legal Studies*, vol. 3, Oxford: Hart, pp. 327–50.

Palidda, S. (1999), 'La Criminalisation des Migrants', *Actes de la Recherche en Sciences Sociales*, no. 129, pp. 39–49.

Palidda, S. (2000), *Polizia postmoderna; Etnografia del nuovo controllo sociale*, Milan: Feltrinelli.

Pastore, F. (2000), 'Justice and Home Affairs: Decision-Making after Amsterdam', *European Law Review,* **25** (2), pp. 190–191.

Pastore, F. (2001), 'La Rotta Di Enea. Relazioni Euromediterranee e Migrazioni', *EuropaEurope*, no. 1, pp. 165–79.

Pastore, F. (2001), *Reconciling the Prince's two 'Arms'. Internal–External Security Policy Coordination in the EU*, Occasional Papers no. 30, Paris: Institute for Security Studies, Western European Union (ISS/WEU).

Pastore, F. (2002), 'Reconciling the Prince's Two Arms. Internal-External Security Policy Coordination in the European Union', in M. Anderson and J. Apap (eds), *New European Borders & Security Cooperation. Promoting Trust in a European Union*, Brussels: Centre for European Policy Studies (CEPS), pp. 57–82.

Pastore, F., P. Romani and G. Sciortino (1999), *L'Italia Nel Sistema Internazionale Del Traffico Di Persone*, Roma: Commissione per le politiche d'integrazione degli immigrati, working paper 5.

Peck, J. and A. Tickell (1994), 'Searching for a new Institutional Fix: the after-Fordist Crisis and Global–Local Disorder', in A. Amin (ed.), *Post-Fordism*, London: Blackwell, pp. 280–315.

Peers, S. (1998), 'Building Fortress Europe: The Development of EU Migration Law', *Common Market Law Review*, **35**, pp. 1235–72.

Peers, S. (2000), *EU Law in Justice and Home Affairs*, Harlow: Longman.

Pisuisse, C.S. and M.M. Teubner (1999), *Elementair Europees Gemeenschapsrecht*, Groningen, Wolters-Noordhoff.

Rath, J. (1993), 'The Ideological Representation of Migrant Workers in Europe: a Matter of Racialization?', in J. Wrenchs and J. Solomos (eds), *Racism and Migration in Western Europe*, Providence: Berg, pp. 212–38.

Recasens, A. (2000), 'The control of police powers', *European Journal of Criminal Policy and Research*, **8** (3), pp. 247–69.

Reinares, F. (ed.) (2000), *European Democracies against Terrorism: Governmental policies and intergovernmental cooperation*, The Oñati International Institute of the Sociology of Law, London: Ashgate.

Robin, S. and L. Barros (1999), *Measures Undertaken to Prevent and Combat the Employment of Foreigners in an Irregular Situation in Certain OECD Member Countries*, DEELSA/ELSA/MI(99)4, Paris: OECD.

Rousseau, J.J. (1762), *Du Contrat Social*, Book 2, Chapter I.

Salt, J. (2000), *Current Trends in International Migration in Europe*, Council of Europe, Strasbourg.

Schain, M. (1999), 'Minorities and Immigrant Incorporation in France. The State and the Dynamics of Multiculturalism', in C. Joppke and S. Lukes (eds), *Multicultural Questions*, Oxford: Oxford University Press, pp. 199–223.

Schneider, F. and D. Enste (2000), *Shadow Economies Around the World: Size, Causes and Consequences*, Washington, DC: International Monetary Fund, working paper WP/00/26.

Schutte, J. (1995), 'Aard en werking van de Europese instellingen. Een overzicht', *Justitiële verkenningen*, no. 1, 94–9.

Schutte, J. (2000), 'Unification and Harmonisation of Criminal Procedures in the European Union', in J. Nijboer and W. Sprangers (eds), *Harmonisation in Forensic Expertise. An Inquiry into the Desirability of and Opportunities for International Standards*, Amsterdam: Thela Thesis, pp. 43–55.

Schutte, J. (2002), 'De rechtsinstrumenten van de Europese Unie voor de ontwikkeling van gezamelijk optreden van de Lidstaten op het gebied van politiële en justitiële samenwerking in strafzaken', *Delikt en Delinkwent*, no. 5, pp. 84–115.

Sciortino, G. (2000), *L'Ambizione Della Frontiera. Le Politiche Di Controllo Migratorio in Europa*, Roma: FrancoAngeli.

Silverman, M. (1992), *Deconstructing the Nation: Immigration, Racism and Citizenship in Modern France*, London: Routledge.

Smith, S. (1999), 'The increasing Insecurity of Security Studies: Conceptualizing Security and Change', special issue of *Contemporary Security Policy*, **20** (3), 72.

Spener, D. (2000), 'The Logic and Contradictions of Intensifies Border Enforcement in Texas', in P. Andreas and T. Snyder (eds), *The Wall around the West*, Lanham: Rowman & Littlefield.

Stessens, G. (1994), *De bevoegdheid van de Europese Gemeenschap tot het vaststellen van sancties: op weg naar een communautair strafrecht?*, Rechtskundig Weekblad.

Storbeck, J. (1997), 'Coordinating the flow of European Intelligence: Europol's Accountability Mechanisms', in M. Den Boer (ed.), *Undercover Policing and Accountability from an International Perspective,* Maastricht: European Institute of Public Administration, EIPA.

Swyngedouw, E. (1997), 'Excluding the other: the Production of Scale and Scaled Politics', in R. Lee and J. Wills (eds), *Geographies of Economics*, London: Arnold, pp. 167–77.

Swyngedouw, E. (1997), 'Neither Global nor Local: Globalization and the Politics of Scale', in K. Cox (ed.), *Spaces of Globalization. Reasserting the Power of the Local*, New York: Guilford Press, pp. 137–66.

Terrif, T., S. Croft, L. James and P.M. Morgan (1999), *Security Studies Today*, Cambridge: Polity Press.

Thalhammer, E., V. Zucha, E. Enzenhofer, B. Salfinger and G. Ogris (2000), *Attitudes Towards Minority Groups in the European Union. A Special Analysis of the Eurobarometer Year 2000 Survey*. Vienna: European Monitoring Centre on Racism and Xenophobia.

Thomas, F. (1993), De Europese Rechtshulpverdragen in Strafzaken, Story-Scientia, 1980.

Thwaites, N. (2002), 'Final Report on Police and Judicial Cooperation in the European Union', in *Integrated Security in Europe. A Democratic Perspective*, Special Edition of *Collegium*, *News of the College of Europe*, no. 22.

Tilly, C. (ed.) (1975), *The Formation of National States in Europe*, Princeton: University Press.

Torpey, J. (1999), *The Invention of the Passport: Surveillance, Citizenship and the State*, New York: Cambridge University Press.

Tribalat, M. (1996), *De L'Immigration à L'Assimilation: Une Enquete Sur Les Immigrés Et Leur Enfants*, Paris: La Découverte.

Valkeneer, D. De (1991), *Le Droit de la Police*, Brussels: De Boeck.

Van der Klaauw, J. (2001), 'Building Partnerships with Countries of Origin and Transit', in Clotilde Marinho (ed.), *Asylum, Immigration and Schengen Post-Amsterdam, a First Assessment*, Maastricht: European Institute of Public Administration, EIPA, pp. 21–46.

Van der Klaauw, J. (2002), 'The Trafficking of Human Beings in the European Union: Specific Problems of Victims and Asylum-Seekers', in C. Faria (ed.), *Managing Migration Flows and preventing Illegal Immigration*, Maastricht: European Institute of Public Administration, EIPA, pp. 29–47.

Van Der Net, C. (2000), *Grenzen stellen op het Internet*, Deventer: Gouda Quint.

Van Het Loo M., S. De Spiegelaire, G. Lindstrom, J. Kahan and G. Vernez (2001), *A Comparison of American and Dutch Immigration and Integration Experiences: What lessons can be learned?*, The Hague: WRR working document 120.

Van Krieken, P.J. (2000), (ed.), *The Asylum Acquis Handbook*, The Hague, T.M.C. Asser Press, pp. 104–14.

Veld Foglia, M. (2002), '(Nog) geen strafrecht in de Eerste Pijler?', *SEW*, **5** (5), pp. 162–69.

Vercher, A. (1992), *Terrorism in Europe. An International Comparative Legal Analysis*, Oxford: Clarendon Press.

Waever, O., B. Buzan, M. Kelstrup and P. Lemaitre (1998), *Identity, Migration and the New Security Agenda in Europe*, London: Pinter.

Walker, N. (1997), 'Deficient Weaponry, Reluctant Marksmen and Obscure Targets', in M. Den Boer (ed.), *Undercover Policing and Accountability from an International Perspective*, Maastricht: European Institute of Public Administration, EIPA.

Walker, N. (1998), 'The New Frontiers of European Policing', in M. Anderson and E. Bort (eds), *The Frontiers of Europe*, London: Pinter, pp. 165–86.

Wright, V. (1998), 'Intergovernmental Relations and Regional Government: A Skeptical View', in P. Le Gales and C. Lequesne (eds), *Regions in Europe*, London: Routledge, pp. 39–49.

Wyngaert, C. Van den (1997), 'Organised crime, proactive policing and international police cooperation in criminal matters: Who controls the police as an international context?', in M. Den Boer (ed.), *Undercover Policing and Accountability from an International Perspective*, Maastricht: European Institute of Public Administration, EIPA.

Wyngaert, C. Van den (2000), *International Criminal Law*, The Hague: Kluwer Law International.

Yepes-Enriquez, R. (2001), 'Enforcement of the prohibition of chemical weapons in its wider perspective', in R. Yepes-Enriquez and L. Tabassi (eds), *Treaty Enforcement and International Cooperation in Criminal Matters, with Special Reference to the Chemical Weapons Convention*, The Hague: T.M.C. Asser Press.

Zielonka, J. (2000), 'How New Enlarged Borders will Reshape the European Union', *Journal of Common Market Studies*, **39** (3), pp. 507–36.

Index